KB169223

독학사 2단계

영어영문학과

영문법

시대에듀

머리말

학위를 얻는 데 시간과 장소는 더 이상 제약이 되지 않습니다. 대입 전형을 거치지 않아도 '학점은행제'를 통해 학사학위를 취득할 수 있기 때문입니다. 그중 독학학위제도는 고등학교 졸업자이거나 이와 동등 이상의 학력을 가지고 있는 사람들에게 효율적인 학점 인정 및 학사학위 취득의 기회를 줍니다.

학습을 통한 개인의 자아실현 도구이자 자신의 실력을 인정받을 수 있는 스펙으로서의 독학사는 짧은 기간 안에 학사학위를 취득할 수 있는 지름길로 많은 수험생들의 선택을 받고 있습니다.

이 책은 독학사 시험에 응시하는 수험생들이 단기간에 효과적인 학습을 할 수 있도록 다음과 같이 구성하였습니다.

01 단원 개요
핵심이론을 학습하기에 앞서 각 단원에서 파악해야 할 중점과 학습목표를 정리하여 수록하였습니다.

02 핵심이론
시험에 출제될 수 있는 내용을 '핵심이론'으로 수록하였으며, 이론 안의 '더 알아두기' 등을 통해 내용 이해에 부족함이 없도록 하였습니다.
※ 본문 291~308쪽의 내용(제8편 화법)은 2025년부터 평가영역에서 제외되었으므로, 학습 시 참고하시기 바랍니다.

03 실전예상문제
해당 출제영역에 맞는 핵심포인트를 분석하여 구성한 '실전예상문제'를 수록하였습니다.

04 추록
2025년 시험부터 적용되는 개정 평가영역에 따라 시험을 대비할 수 있도록 관련 내용을 '추록'으로 수록하였습니다.

05 최종모의고사
최신 출제유형을 반영한 '최종모의고사(2회분)'를 통해 자신의 실력을 점검해 볼 수 있으며, 실제 시험에 임하듯이 시간을 재고 풀어 본다면 시험장에서의 실수를 줄일 수 있을 것입니다.

영문법은 영어라는 자연언어 현상에 내재해 있는 질서, 즉 형식(form) · 의미(meaning) · 사용(use)과 관련한 규칙들을 연구하는 학문입니다. 음성과 음운 · 단어 형태 · 문장의 통사 규칙과 같이 정확성(accuracy) · 구조(structure)와 관련한 형식을 살펴보고, 단어 · 구 · 절 · 문장의 문법적인 의미성(meaningfulness)을 살펴봅니다. 또한, 단어 · 문장 · 단락 간의 언어적 맥락과 화자와 청자 간의 사회적 맥락의 적절성(appropriateness)에 따른 기능(function)을 살펴봅니다. 이렇게 형식 · 의미 · 사용에 관한 규칙인 영문법을 학습하면 영어 자체에 대한 이해를 깊게 할 수 있을 뿐만 아니라 영어 의사소통능력(communicative competence)도 향상시킬 수 있을 것입니다.

편저자 드림

BDES

독학학위제 소개

독학학위제란?

「독학에 의한 학위취득에 관한 법률」에 의거하여 국가에서 시행하는 시험에 합격한 사람에게 학사학위를 수여하는 제도

- ✓ 고등학교 졸업 이상의 학력을 가진 사람이면 누구나 응시 가능
- ✓ 대학교를 다니지 않아도 스스로 공부해서 학위취득 가능
- ✓ 일과 학습의 병행이 가능하여 시간과 비용 최소화
- ✓ 언제, 어디서나 학습이 가능한 평생학습시대의 자아실현을 위한 제도
- ✓ 학위취득시험은 4개의 과정(교양, 전공기초, 전공심화, 학위취득 종합시험)으로 이루어져 있으며, 각 과정별 시험을 모두 거쳐 학위취득 종합시험에 합격하면 학사학위 취득

독학학위제 전공 분야 (11개 전공)

국어 국문학 / 영어 영문학 / 심리학 / 경영학 / 컴퓨터 공학 / 간호학

법학 / 행정학 / 가정학 / 유아 교육학 / 정보 통신학

※ 유아교육학 및 정보통신학 전공 : 3, 4과정만 개설
   (정보통신학의 경우 3과정은 2025년까지, 4과정은 2026년까지만 응시 가능하며, 이후 폐지)
※ 간호학 전공 : 4과정만 개설
※ 중어중문학, 수학, 농학 전공 : 폐지 전공으로 기존에 해당 전공 학적 보유자에 한하여 2025년까지 응시 가능

※ 시대에듀는 현재 4개 학과(심리학과, 경영학과, 컴퓨터공학과, 간호학과) 개설 완료
※ 2개 학과(국어국문학과, 영어영문학과) 개설 진행 중

독학학위제 시험안내

과정별 응시자격

단계	과정	응시자격	과정(과목) 시험 면제 요건
1	교양	고등학교 졸업 이상 학력 소지자	• 대학(교)에서 각 학년 수료 및 일정 학점 취득 • 학점은행제 일정 학점 인정 • 국가기술자격법에 따른 자격 취득 • 교육부령에 따른 각종 시험 합격 • 면제지정기관 이수 등
2	전공기초		
3	전공심화		
4	학위취득	• 1~3과정 합격 및 면제 • 대학에서 동일 전공으로 3년 이상 수료 (3년제의 경우 졸업) 또는 105학점 이상 취득 • 학점은행제 동일 전공 105학점 이상 인정 (전공 28학점 포함) ➜ 22.1.1. 시행 • 외국에서 15년 이상의 학교교육과정 수료	없음(반드시 응시)

응시방법 및 응시료

- 접수방법 : 온라인으로만 가능
- 제출서류 : 응시자격 증빙서류 등 자세한 내용은 홈페이지 참조
- 응시료 : 20,700원

독학학위제 시험 범위

- 시험 과목별 평가영역 범위에서 대학 전공자에게 요구되는 수준으로 출제
- 시험 범위 및 예시문항은 독학학위제 홈페이지(bdes.nile.or.kr) ➜ 학습정보 ➜ 과목별 평가영역에서 확인

문항 수 및 배점

과정	일반 과목			예외 과목		
	객관식	주관식	합계	객관식	주관식	합계
교양, 전공기초 (1~2과정)	40문항×2.5점 =100점	–	40문항 100점	25문항×4점 =100점	–	25문항 100점
전공심화, 학위취득 (3~4과정)	24문항×2.5점 =60점	4문항×10점 =40점	28문항 100점	15문항×4점 =60점	5문항×8점 =40점	20문항 100점

※ 2017년도부터 교양과정 인정시험 및 전공기초과정 인정시험은 객관식 문항으로만 출제

합격 기준

■ 1~3과정(교양, 전공기초, 전공심화) 시험

단계	과정	합격 기준	유의 사항
1	교양	매 과목 60점 이상 득점을 합격으로 하고, 과목 합격 인정(합격 여부만 결정)	5과목 합격
2	전공기초		6과목 이상 합격
3	전공심화		

■ 4과정(학위취득) 시험 : 총점 합격제 또는 과목별 합격제 선택

구분	합격 기준	유의 사항
총점 합격제	• 총점(600점)의 60% 이상 득점(360점) • 과목 낙제 없음	• 6과목 모두 신규 응시 • 기존 합격 과목 불인정
과목별 합격제	• 매 과목 100점 만점으로 하여 전 과목(교양 2, 전공 4) 60점 이상 득점	• 기존 합격 과목 재응시 불가 • 1과목이라도 60점 미만 득점하면 불합격

시험 일정

1단계 2월 중 → 2단계 5월 중 → 3단계 8월 중 → 4단계 10월 중

■ 영어영문학과 2단계 시험 과목 및 시간표

구분(교시별)	시간	시험 과목명
1교시	09:00~10:40(100분)	영어학개론, 영국문학개관
2교시	11:10~12:50(100분)	중급영어, 19세기 영미소설
중식 12:50~13:40(50분)		
3교시	14:00~15:40(100분)	영미희곡Ⅰ, 영어음성학
4교시	16:10~17:50(100분)	영문법, 19세기 영미시

※ 시험 일정 및 세부사항은 반드시 독학학위제 홈페이지(bdes.nile.or.kr)를 통해 확인하시기 바랍니다.

※ 시대에듀에서 개설되었거나 개설 예정인 과목은 빨간색으로 표시하였습니다.

독학학위제 단계별 학습법

1단계 평가영역에 기반을 둔 이론 공부!

독학학위제에서 발표한 평가영역에 기반을 두어 효율적으로 이론을 공부해야 합니다. 각 장별로 정리된 '핵심이론'을 통해 핵심적인 개념을 파악합니다. 모든 내용을 다 암기하는 것이 아니라, 포괄적으로 이해한 후 핵심내용을 파악하여 이 부분을 확실히 알고 넘어가야 합니다.

2단계 시험 경향 및 문제 유형 파악!

독학사 시험 문제는 지금까지 출제된 유형에서 크게 벗어나지 않는 범위에서 비슷한 유형으로 줄곧 출제되고 있습니다. 본서에 수록된 이론을 충실히 학습한 후 '실전예상문제'를 풀어 보면서 문제의 유형과 출제의도를 파악하는 데 집중하도록 합니다. 교재에 수록된 문제는 시험 유형의 가장 핵심적인 부분이 반영된 문항들이므로 실제 시험에서 어떠한 유형이 출제되는지에 대한 감을 잡을 수 있을 것입니다.

3단계 '실전예상문제'를 통한 효과적인 대비!

독학사 시험 문제는 비슷한 유형들이 반복되어 출제되므로, 다양한 문제를 풀어 보는 것이 필수적입니다. 각 단원의 끝에 수록된 '실전예상문제'를 통해 단원별 내용을 제대로 학습하였는지 꼼꼼하게 확인하고, 실력을 점검합니다. 이때 부족한 부분은 따로 체크해 두고, 복습할 때 중점적으로 공부하는 것도 좋은 학습 전략입니다.

4단계 복습을 통한 학습 마무리!

이론 공부를 하면서, 혹은 문제를 풀어 보면서 헷갈리고 이해하기 어려운 부분은 따로 체크해 두는 것이 좋습니다. 중요 개념은 반복학습을 통해 놓치지 않고 확실하게 익히고 넘어가야 합니다. 마무리 단계에서는 '최종모의고사'를 통해 실전연습을 할 수 있도록 합니다.

COMMENT
합격수기

> 저는 학사편입 제도를 이용하기 위해 2~4단계를 순차로 응시했고 한 번에 합격했습니다.
> 아슬아슬한 점수라서 부끄럽지만 독학사는 자료가 부족해서 부족하나마 후기를 쓰는 것이 도움이 될까 하여
> 제 합격전략을 정리하여 알려드립니다.

#1. 교재와 전공서적을 가까이에!

학사학위 취득은 본래 4년을 기본으로 합니다. 독학사는 이를 1년으로 단축하는 것을 목표로 하는 시험이라 실제 시험도 변별력을 높이는 몇 문제를 제외한다면 기본이 되는 중요한 이론 위주로 출제됩니다. 시대에듀의 독학사 시리즈 역시 이에 맞추어 중요한 내용이 일목요연하게 압축·정리되어 있습니다. 빠르게 훑어보기 좋지만 내가 목표로 한 전공에 대해 자세히 알고 싶다면 전공서적과 함께 공부하는 것이 좋습니다. 교재와 전공서적을 함께 보면서 교재에 전공서적 내용을 정리하여 단권화하면 시험이 임박했을 때 교재 한 권으로도 자신 있게 시험을 치를 수 있습니다.

#2. 시간확인은 필수!

쉬운 문제는 금방 넘어가지만 지문이 길거나 어렵고 헷갈리는 문제도 있고, OMR 카드에 마킹까지 해야 하니 실제로 주어진 시간은 더 짧습니다. 1번에 어려운 문제가 있다고 해서 시간을 많이 허비하면 쉽게 풀 수 있는 마지막 문제들을 놓칠 수 있습니다. 문제 푸는 속도도 느려지니 집중력도 떨어집니다. 그래서 어차피 배점은 같으니 아는 문제를 최대한 많이 맞히는 것을 목표로 했습니다.
① 어려운 문제는 빠르게 넘기면서 문제를 끝까지 다 풀고 ② 확실한 답부터 우선 마킹한 후 ③ 다시 시험지로 돌아가 건너뛴 문제들을 다시 풀었습니다. 확실히 시간을 재고 문제를 많이 풀어 봐야 실전에 도움이 되는 것 같습니다.

#3. 문제풀이의 반복!

여느 시험과 마찬가지로 문제는 많이 풀어 볼수록 좋습니다. 이론을 공부한 후 실전예상문제를 풀다 보니 부족한 부분이 어딘지 확인할 수 있었고, 공부한 이론이 시험에 어떤 식으로 출제될지 예상할 수 있었습니다. 그렇게 부족한 부분을 보충해가며 문제 유형을 파악하면 이론을 복습할 때도 어떤 부분을 중점적으로 암기해야 할지 알 수 있습니다. 이론 공부가 어느 정도 마무리되었을 때 시계를 준비하고 최종모의고사를 풀었습니다. 실제 시험시간을 생각하면서 예행연습을 하니 시험 당일에는 덜 긴장할 수 있었습니다.

학위취득을 위해 오늘도 열심히 학습하시는 동지 여러분에게도 합격의 영광이 있으시길 기원하면서 이만 줄입니다.

이 책의 구성과 특징

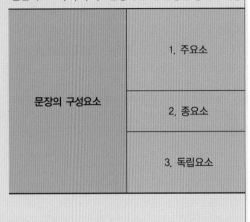

01 단원 개요

핵심이론을 학습하기에 앞서 각 단원에 서 파악해야 할 중점과 학습목표를 확인 해 보세요.

02 핵심이론

평가영역을 바탕으로 꼼꼼하게 정리된 '핵심이론'을 통해 꼭 알아야 하는 내용을 명확히 파악해 보세요.

※ 본문 291~308쪽의 내용(제8편 화법)은 2025년부터 평가영역에서 제외되었으므로, 학습 시 참고하시기 바랍니다.

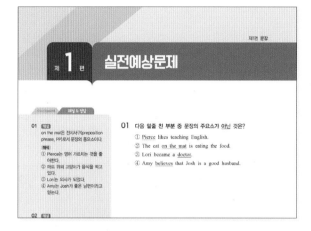

03 실전예상문제

'핵심이론'에서 공부한 내용을 바탕으로
'실전예상문제'를 풀어 보면서 문제를
해결하는 능력을 길러 보세요.

04 추록

개정 평가영역을 분석하여 반영한 '추록'
을 통해 추가된 내용을 학습해 보세요.

05 최종모의고사

'최종모의고사'를 실제 시험처럼 시간을
정해 놓고 풀어 보면서 최종점검을 해
보세요.

목차

핵심이론 + 실전예상문제

CONTENTS

목차

추록(2025년 시험부터 추가되는 내용)

최종모의고사

제 **1** 편

문장

영어 문장은 주요소, 종요소, 독립요소로 구성된다. **주요소**는 주어, 동사, 목적어, 보어, **종요소**는 수식어(형용사, 부사), 연결어(전치사, 접속사), **독립요소**는 감탄사, 삽입구, 동격어구가 있다. 또한 영어의 문장은 주요소 성분의 결합에 따라 일반적으로 1, 2, 3, 4, 5문형이 있다. 문장은 형태와 사용에 따라 서술문(평서문), 의문문, 감탄문, 기원문, 명령문이 있다.

문장의 구성요소	1. 주요소	(1) 주어
		(2) 동사
		(3) 목적어
		(4) 보어
	2. 종요소	(1) 수식어
		(2) 연결어
	3. 독립요소	(1) 감탄사
		(2) 삽입구
		(3) 동격어구

출제 경향 및 수험 대책

1. 문장의 요소 : 주요소, 종요소, 독립요소 및 각 요소의 세부 요소 구분
2. 문장 5형식
   (1) 문장의 주요소인 주어, 동사, 목적어, 보어의 형태와 사용에 따른 제1~5문형 구분
   (2) 제2문형에서 보어의 사용과 의미
   (3) 제3문형에서 자동사로 착각하기 쉬운 타동사
   (4) 제4문형의 제3문형 변화 및 사용 전치사
   (5) 제3형식과 제4형식 동사의 구분
   (6) 제5문형의 대표적 동사 표현 및 목적격 보어의 사용과 의미
3. 문장 종류
   (1) 평서문과 (Yes/No, Wh-) 의문문의 전환 관계
   (2) 부가의문문 형태 및 사용
   (3) (Yes/No, Wh-) 간접의문문

합격의 공식 SD에듀

잠깐!

자격증 · 공무원 · 금융/보험 · 면허증 · 언어/외국어 · 검정고시/독학사 · 기업체/취업
이 시대의 모든 합격! SD에듀에서 합격하세요!
www.youtube.com → SD에듀 → 구독

제 1 장 문장의 요소

주요소

영어 문장의 주요소는 **주어, 동사, 목적어, 보어**가 있다. 영어의 문장은 구조상 주어를 포함하고 있는 어구, 즉 주부(주어부, subject)와 동사를 포함하고 있는 어구, 즉 술부(서술부, predicate)로 나눈다.

1 주어(subject)

주어는 문장에서 동작과 상태의 주체가 되는 명사, 대명사, 명사 상당어구와 같이 주부의 중심이고, 우리말의 '~은/~는, ~이/~가'에 해당한다.

2 동사(verb)

동사는 문장에서 주어의 동작이나 상태를 설명하는 술부의 중심이고, 우리말의 '~이다/~하다'에 해당한다.

예

• Josh studies linguistics.

  [주부 [주어 Josh]] [술부 [동사 studies [목적어 linguistics]]].

• The book on the desk is an English dictionary.

  [주부 [주어 The book] [전치사구 on the desk]] [술부 [동사 is [보어 an English dictionary]]].

3 목적어(object)

목적어는 동사가 표현하는 동작의 대상(물)을 의미하고 영어에서는 2개, 3개의 목적어를 취하는 경우도 있다.

- Josh teaches linguistics.

  [주어 Josh] [동사 teaches [목적어 linguistics]].

- Josh gave Amy books.

  [주어 Josh] [동사 gave] [간접목적어 Amy] [직접목적어 books].

4 보어(complement)

보어는 주어나 목적어의 의미나 상태를 보충 설명하는데, 주어를 설명하는 주격보어(subject complement, SC)와 목적어를 설명하는 목적격보어(object complement, OC)가 있고 명사(구)나 형용사(구)가 쓰인다.

- Josh became a professor.

  [[주어 Josh] [동사 became [주격보어(명사) a professor]]].

- Josh is kind.

  [[주어 Josh] [동사 is [주격보어(형용사) kind]]].

- Josh believes Nathan a genius.

  [[주어 Josh] [동사 believes [목적격보어(명사) a genius]]].

- Josh believes Amy kind.

  [[주어 Josh] [동사 believes [목적격보어(형용사) kind]]].

제 2 절 종요소

영어 문장의 종요소는 수식어(형용사, 부사)와 연결어(전치사, 접속사)가 있다.

1 수식어(modifier)

수식어는 문장의 주어, 동사, 목적어, 보어를 한정하거나 설명하는 데 쓰이며 형용사와 부사가 있다.

(1) 형용사(adjective)

형용사는 명사나 대명사를 수식하며 특성과 상태를 표현한다.

- A smart professor teaches linguistics.

  [A [형용사 smart] [명사(주어) professor] [teaches linguistics]].

(2) 부사(adverb)

부사는 동사, 형용사, 다른 부사, 문장을 수식하며 장소, 방법, 시간, 정도, 빈도, 이유 등을 표현한다.

- A smart professor teaches linguistics well.

  [[A smart professor] [동사구 teaches linguistics] [부사 well]].

2 연결어(linking words)

영어의 문장 내에 연결어는 전치사, 접속사가 있다.

(1) 전치사(preposition)

전치사는 명사(구)와 결합하여 문장의 내용을 연결한다.

- A professor is teaching linguistics in the classroom.

  [A professor is teaching linguistics] [전치사(구) in [명사구 the classroom]].

(2) 접속사(conjunction)

접속사는 문장과 결합하여 문장의 내용을 연결한다.

- A professor is teaching linguistics and the students are taking notes.

  [문장1 A professor is teaching linguistics] [접속사 and [문장2 the students are taking notes]].

영어의 접속사는 등위접속사(coordinate conjunction)와 종속접속사(subordinate conjunction)가 있는데 이 내용은 제6편 연결어에서 자세히 다룬다.

제 3 절   독립요소

영어 문장의 독립요소는 감탄사, 삽입구, 동격어구가 있다.

1   감탄사(interjection)

감탄사는 문장에서 기쁨, 슬픔, 아픔, 놀람, 긍정, 부정 등을 나타낸다.

- Wow, I just won the lottery!
  [[감탄사 Wow,] I just won the lottery!]

2   삽입구(parenthesis)

삽입어구는 문장에 추가적인 정보를 제공한다.

- A professor is, so to speak, a living dictionary. ([어휘] so to speak : 말하자면, 즉)
  [A professor is, [삽입어구 so to speak], a living dictionary].

- A professor, I think, is a genius.
  [A professor, [삽입어구 I think], is a genius].

3   동격어구(appositive)

선행하는 명사(구)에 대한 추가 정보를 제공하며 명사 또는 명사 상당어구로 표현한다.

- Mr. Jensen, who is my professor, teaches linguistics.
  [Mr. Jensen, [동격어구 who is my professor], teaches linguistics].

- Josh knows the fact that Nathan has another cookie.
  [Josh knows [명사구 the fact [동격어구 that Nathan has another cookie]]].

제 2 장 문장 5형식

영어의 문장은 주요소인 주어, 동사, 목적어, 보어의 결합에 따라 크게 5개의 문형이 있고, 5개 문형의 구조와 동사 유형은 다음과 같다.

문형	구조	동사유형
		보어 / 목적어
제1문형	주어(S) + 동사(V)	[완전자동사]
제2문형	주어(S) + 동사(V) + 보어(C)	[불완전자동사]
제3문형	주어(S) + 동사(V) + 목적어(O)	[완전타동사]
제4문형	주어(S) + 동사(V) + 간접목적어(I·O) + 직접목적어(D·O)	[이중타동사]
제5문형	주어(S) + 동사(V) + 목적어(O) + 목적격보어(O·C)	[불완전타동사]

※ 제2편 품사 – 제4장 동사(65쪽) 참조

제 1 절 제1문형

1형식 문형은 목적어나 보어 없이 주어, **완전자동사**, 또는 부사(구)로 이루어진 문형이다.

> 주어(S) + 동사(V) (+ 부사구(AdvP)···) [완전자동사]

• Josh is going to school.

  [[주어 Josh] [완전자동사 is going] [부사구 to school]].

• Josh goes (to school)(by bus)(with his friend)(every day)

  [[주어 Josh] [완전자동사 goes] ([부사구 to school])([부사구 by bus])([부사구 with his friend])([부사구 every day])].

제 2 절 제2문형

2형식 문형은 목적어 없이 주어, 불완전자동사, (주격)보어로 이루어진 문형이고, 보어는 주어의 상태나 성질을 서술하는 명사나 형용사가 사용된다.

주어(S) + 동사(V) + 보어(C) [불완전자동사]

---

1 명사 보어

• Josh is a professor.

[[주어 Josh] [동사 is] [(주격)보어(명사) a professor]].

2 형용사 보어

• Nathan is intelligent.

[[주어 Nathan] [동사 is] [(주격)보어(형용사) intelligent]].

3 동사 종류

(1) 상태(~이다)

---

be, remain, stand, keep, stay, lie, hold, seem, appear, prove, turn out, ··· + 보어

예
• He stayed healthy.
• He kept silent.
• He seems happy.
• This ticket holds good for a week.

(2) 상태 변화(~이 되다)

---

go, come, become, run, grow, fall, turn, ··· + 보어

예

- He went hungry.
- His dreams come true.
- He became a scholar.
- The spring has run dry.

(3) 감각

> smell, taste, sound, look, feel, … + 보어

예

- This spaghetti smells good.
- This cookie tastes enjoyable.
- This sounds funny.
- He looked pale.

제 3 절 제3문형

3형식 문형은 보어 없이 주어, 완전타동사, 목적어로 이루어진 문형이고 목적어는 우리말의 '~을/~를'로 해석되며 명사, 대명사, 명사 상당어구가 사용된다.

> 주어(S) + 동사(V) + 목적어(O) [완전타동사]

예

- Josh likes linguistics.

  [[주어 Josh] [동사 likes] [목적어(명사) linguistics]].

- Nathan entered the classroom.

  [[주어 Nathan] [동사 entered] [목적어(명사구) the classroom]].

1 (자동사로 착각하기 쉬운) 타동사 중요 ★★

announce	answer	attack	attract
attend	approach	await	consider
confront	describe	discuss	face
enter	emphasize	influence	inhabit
greet	leave	marry	mention
oppose	reach	resemble	survive

예

- He announced a wedding in the newspapers.
- He answered the questions.
- The bees attacked the penguins.
- Honey attracts bears.
- He attends classes.
- He should approach the problem.
- We await his reply.
- They considered his suggestion.
- He is suddenly confronting many difficulties.
- He is describing the accident.
- He discussed his plans with his wife.
- The flower faces the light.
- He is entering the building.
- He emphasized the necessity for change.
- His adviser influenced him.
- People inhabit the city with work on all the ground floors. ([어휘] inhabit : 거주하다)
- They greeted each other with "Good morning!"
- He is leaving the office.
- Josh married Amy in 2012.
- He mentioned Korean cultures in his class.
- He opposed the sudden change.
- He is reaching London. ([어휘] reach : 도착하다)
- He reached his goal. ([어휘] survive : 도달하다)
- He resembles his mother.
- She survived her children. ([어휘] survive : 오래 살다)
- He survived the operation. ([어휘] survive : 살아남다, 극복하다)

※ 비교 참조 : (타동사로) 착각하기 쉬운 자동사(73쪽)

2 타동사 + 목적어 + 전치사구 중요★

> advise, assure, convince, inform, notify, remind, warn, … + A of B/A that ~

(1) 통지, 확인

[예]

- He informed her of the new regulation.
- We will notify you of our decision soon.
- She reminded him of his mother.

(2) 제거, 박탈

> cure, divest, ease, deprive, plunder, rid, relieve, rob, strip, … + A of B

[예]

- They robbed a genius of his invention.
- They deprived him of his liberty.
- We are going to rid ourselves of our plastic bag dependence.

(3) 공급

> endow, furnish, provide, present, supply, trust, … + A with B

[예]

- This class provides students with a basic understanding of English grammar.
- They supply senior citizens with medical aid.
- They presented him with a book as a prize.

(4) 방해, 금지

> dissuade, discourage, keep, prevent, prohibit, stop, … + A from B

[예]

- He can't stop her from saying what she thinks.
- The government tried to prevent the bird flu from spreading nationwide.
  ([어휘] : prevent a from b : A가 B하는 것을 막다)

• The new traffic law keeps drivers from running a yellow light.

　([어휘] : keep A from -ing : A가 하지 못하게 하다, 막다)

(5) 감사, 칭찬, 비난

> blame, excuse, forgive, praise, punish, reproach, thank, ⋯ + A for B

예

• Thank you for having me in this conference.

• He didn't blame her for criticizing him.

• Please forgive me for keeping you waiting.

제 **4** 절　제4문형

4형식 문형은 보어 없이 주어, 이중타동사(ditransitive verb) + 간접목적어(indirect object) + 직접목적어(direct object)로 이루어진 문형으로, 우리말에 '~에게(I·O) ~를(D·O) 준다'의 의미로 사용되는 타동사이므로 여격동사 혹은 수여동사(dative verb)라고도 한다.

> 주어(S) + 동사(V) + 간접목적어(I·O) + 직접목적어(D·O) [이중타동사]

4형식
Josh gave Nathan a book.
[[주어 Josh] [동사 gave] [간접목적어 Nathan] [직접목적어 a book]].

3형식
Josh gave a book to Nathan.
[[주어 Josh] [동사 gave] [(직접)목적어 a book] [전치사구 to Nathan]].

※ 직접목적어가 대명사인 경우는 4형식은 안 되고, 3형식만 가능하다.

　*The professor handed him it. (4형식)

　The professor handed it to him. (3형식)

　(* = ungrammatical, 비문법적)

1 4형식 → 3형식 : 전치사 to

bring, feed, grant, give, hand, lend, offer, owe, pass, pay, promise, read, recommend, sell, send, show, take, teach, tell, write

예

- He recommended her this dictionary. → He recommend this dictionary to her.
- The professor the winner a prize. → The professor gave a prize to the winner.

2 4형식 → 3형식 : 전치사 for

bake, build, buy, choose, cook, design, do, find, get, hire, leave, make, order, prescribe, rent

예

- He bought her a new dress. → He bought a new dress for her.
- He made her a cake. → He made a cake for her.

3 4형식 → 3형식 : 전치사 of

ask, beg, demand, favor, inquire, request, require

예

- May I ask you a favor? → May I ask a favor of you?
- He demanded her an apology. → He demanded an apology of her.

4 4형식 → 3형식 : 전치사 on

| play | He played her a trick. → He played a trick on her. |

5 4형식 → 3형식 : 전치사 against

| bear(악의를 품다) | They bear her no spite. → They bear no spite against her. |

6 4형식 → 3형식 : 전치사 + 간접목적어를 취할 수 없는 동사

> cost, envy, forgive, save, pardon, spare(목숨을 살려주다, 수고를 덜어주다)

예

- It cost him five dollars to buy it back.
- They envy us our new house.
- God will forgive him his sins.
- Her support saved him much time and trouble.

7 4형식 동사로 착각하기 쉬운 3형식 동사 중요 ★

> acknowledge, announce, believe, confess, describe, donate, explain, introduce, propose, say, suggest

예

* 표시는 비문법적 문장에 표시하였습니다.

- *He announced us his engagement.
  He announced his engagement to us.

- *He explained her a new rule.
  He explained a new rule to her.

- *He introduced us his sister.
  He introduced his sister to us.

제 5 절   제5문형

5형식 문형은 목적어와 함께 그 목적어에 대한 상태나 성질의 정보를 보충해주는 보어가 사용되어 주어, 불완전타동사, 목적어, 목적격보어로 이루어진 문형이고 목적격보어는 명사, 형용사, (원형, to)부정사, (현재, 과거)분사 등이 사용된다.

> 주어(S) + 동사(V) + 목적어(O) + 목적격 보어(O·C) [불완전타동사]

1 목적격보어 : 명사

예

• Josh believes Nathan a genius.

　[[주어 Josh] [동사 believes] [목적어 Nathan] [목적격보어(명사) a genius]].

2 목적격보어 : 형용사

예

• Josh made Amy happy.

　[[주어 Josh] [동사 made] [목적어 Amy] [목적격보어(형용사) happy]].

3 목적격보어 : 원형부정사

예

• The professor let the students take notes.

　[[주어 The professor] [동사 let] [목적어 the students] [목적격보어(원형부정사) take notes]].

4 목적격보어 : to부정사

예

• The professor helped the students (to) do their homework.

　[[주어 The professor] [동사 helped] [목적어 the students] [목적격 보어(to부정사) (to) do their homework]].

5 목적격보어 : 현재분사

예

• Josh saw Nathan entering the classroom.

[[주어 Josh] [동사 saw] [목적어 Nathan] [목적격보어(현재분사) entering the classroom]].

6 목적격보어 : 과거분사

예

• Nathan had his laptop stolen.

[[주어 Nathan] [동사 had] [목적어 his laptop] [목적격보어(과거분사) stolen]].

7 대표적 동사

(1) 지각동사(perception verbs)

see, look at, watch, hear, listen to, feel, observe, notice, witness

목적어 + 목적격보어 관계	
① 능동 : 동사원형	He saw her cross the crosswalk.
② 진행 : 현재분사	He saw her crossing the crosswalk.
③ 수동 : 과거분사	He looked at the goods displayed for sale.

(2) 사역동사(causative verbs) 중요 ★

make(강제), have(요청), let(허가, 허락)

목적어 + 목적격보어 관계	
① 능동 : 동사원형	② 수동 : 과거분사
She made her son clean the room.	He made his car repaired by the mechanic.
He had the server bring the new cup.	He had his wallet stolen in a subway.
The professor let the students play the piano.	Please let the window be opened.

(3) get(준사역동사)

목적어 + 목적격보어 관계	
① 능동 : to부정사	② 수동 : 과거분사
She got her son to eat spinach.	She got spinach eaten by her son.

(4) help(준사역동사)

목적어 + 목적격보어 관계	
① 능동 : 동사원형	② 능동 : to부정사
He helped her pack her suitcase.	He helped her to pack her suitcase.
The professor helped the students do their homework.	The professor helped the students to do their homework.

※ 동사 help는 목적보어 과거분사 표현에 잘 사용하지 않는다.

(5) 목적어 + 목적격보어 to부정사

필요, 바람	want, need
요청, 부탁	ask, request, require
허용, 허락	allow, enable, cause, forbid, lead, permit, promise
설득, 강요	advise, compel, drive, encourage, force, get, oblige, order, persuade, tell, urge

예

- She wanted her to read another book.
- He requested her to join the international meeting.
- The icy road caused the car to slip.
- The professor encouraged the students to participate in the workshop.

(6) 그 외 5형식 동사 표현

> catch, find, imagine, keep, leave, remember

예

- He kept her napping for three hours in the afternoon. (능동)
- Please keep the door shut. (수동, be closed)

제 **3** 장 문장의 종류

영어의 문장은 서술문(평서문), 의문문, 감탄문, 기원문, 명령문 5개의 종류가 있다.

제 **1** 절 서술문(평서문, declarative sentence)

서술문 혹은 평서문은 어떠한 사실, 생각, 행동, 상태 등을 서술하는 문장인데 긍정문과 부정문이 있고 영어의 기본 어순(word order)은 주어(S) + 동사(O) + 목적어(O)/보어(C)이다.

1 긍정문

예

- Josh is a smart professor.
- Nathan can speak many languages.
- Josh and Amy have three children. (do have)

2 부정문

예

- Josh is not a graduate student. (isn't)
- Nathan cannot speak German. (can't)
- Josh and Amy do not have three children. (don't)

제 2 절 의문문(interrogative sentence)

영어의 의문문은 일반 의문문(Yes/No)과 Wh- 의문문, 선택 의문문, 부가 의문문, 간접 의문문, 수사 의문문이 있다.

1 일반 의문문(questions) 중요 ★★

(1) Yes/No 의문문(yes/no question, 의문사가 없는 의문문)

문장의 어순상 be동사, 조동사, 일반동사로 시작하며 긍정(Yes) 혹은 부정(No)으로 대답한다. 의문문 자체에 부정어가 들어가면 부정 의문문(negative question)이라 한다.

서술문	의문문
S + V + O/C. (V → be, 조동사, 일반동사)	V + S + Ø + O/C ?

형태		Yes/No 의문문		대답
be동사	긍정	Is Josh a smart professor?	긍정	Yes, he is.
	부정	Isn't Josh a smart professor?	부정	No, he is not(isn't).
조동사	긍정	Can Nathan speak German?	긍정	Yes, he can.
	부정	Can't Nathan speak German?	부정	No, he cannot(can't).
일반동사	긍정	Do they have three children?	긍정	Yes, they have.
	부정	Don't they have three children?	부정	No, they have not(haven't).

영어의 일반 의문문과 그 대답에서는 의문문 자체의 긍정·부정 형식에 상관없이 대답하는 내용, 사실, 혹은 명제가 사실이면 긍정 대답, 거짓이면 부정으로 대답을 한다. 예를 들어, 우리말의 경우 "Josh는 똑똑한 교수가 아니지?"라는 부정의문문 형식에 "네"라고 대답하면 "네, Josh는 똑똑한 교수가 아니다"라는 부정의 대답, "아니오"라고 대답하면 "아니오, Josh는 똑똑한 교수다"라는 긍정의 답변이 되는데 이는 의문문 자체에 대한 긍정과 부정 답변이다.

반면에 영어의 경우 "Isn't Josh a smart professor?"라는 부정의문문 형식에 "Yes"라고 대답하면 "Yes, Josh is a smart professor(Josh는 똑똑한 교수다)." 긍정의 답변, "No"라고 대답하면 "No, Josh isn't a smart professor(Josh는 똑똑한 교수가 아니다)."라는 부정의 답변을 의미하는데 이는 사실과 내용에 대한 긍정과 부정 답변이다.

(2) Wh- 의문문(information question, 의문사가 있는 의문문)

어순상 의문사(who(m), what, which, when, where, why, how)로 시작하며 의문사와 관련된 정보(평서문의 주어, 목적어, 보어, 부사구 등)를 묻는 의문문이고, Yes/No가 아닌 구체적 정보로 대답한다.

서술문	Wh-의문문
S + V + O/C. (V → be, 조동사, 일반동사)	V + S + Ø + O/C ?

형태	Wh- 의문문	대답
be 동사	Who* is a smart professor?	Josh is a smart professor.
조동사	Who* can speak German?	Nathan can speak German.
	Which language can Nathan speak?	Nathan can speak German.
일반동사	Who* have three children?	Josh and Amy have three children.

※ 의문사이면서 동시에 문장의 주어인 Who는 어순 도치(inversion) 없이 그대로 사용한다.

2 선택 의문문(alternative question)

2개 이상의 대상을 선택하는 경우 사용하는 의문문이고 접속사 or를 사용한다.

예

• Is Josh living in Texas or in California?
• Can Nathan speak French or German?
• What do you want to have, apple, orange, or banana? (Banana, please.)

3 부가 의문문(tag question) 중요 ★★

서술문(평서문) 다음으로 상대방에게 동의나 의견을 확인하는 경우에 사용하고, 서술문이 긍정이면 부정 부가 의문문, 서술문이 부정이면 긍정 부가 의문문을 사용하고 Yes/No로 대답한다.

형태	(서술문 +) 부가 의문문	대답※	
be 동사	Josh is a smart professor, isn't he?	긍정	Yes, he is.
	Josh isn't a smart professor, is he?	부정	No, he is not(isn't).
조동사	Nathan can speak German, can't he?	긍정	Yes, he can.
	Nathan cannot speak German, can he?	부정	No, he cannot(can't).
일반동사	They have three children, don't they?	긍정	Yes, they do.
	They don't have three children, do they?	부정	No, they do not(don't).

※ 부가 의문문의 대답도 부가 의문문의 긍정·부정 여부에 상관없이 사실 혹은 명제 자체가 사실이면 긍정으로 대답, 거짓이면 부정으로 대답을 한다.

4 간접 의문문(indirect/embedded question) 중요 ★★

의문문이 다른 문장(주절)의 일부(종속절)로 사용되는 경우이고 어순은 일반 의문문 어순 [(Wh- +) 동사(V) + 주어(S)~?]과는 달리 [(Wh- +) 주어(S) + 동사(V)]로 사용된다.

(1) Yes/No 의문문의 경우 : if/whether + 주어(S) + 동사(V)

예

- Josh asked if/whether Nathan is a smart professor.

  [주절 Josh asked [종속절-간접의문문 if/whether Nathan is a smart professor]].

- Josh doesn't know if/whether Nathan speaks German.

  [주절 Josh doesn't know [종속절-간접의문문 if/whether Nathan speaks German]].

(2) Wh- 의문문의 경우 : Wh- + 주어(S) + 동사(V)

예

- Josh asked who is a smart professor.

  [주절 Josh asked [종속절-간접의문문 who is a smart professor]].

- Josh asked where Nathan lives in Texas.

  [주절 Josh asked [종속절-간접의문문 where Nathan lives in Texas]].

(3) Wh- 의문사가 문장에 나오는 간접의문문 : believe, think, guess, imagine, suppose 등과 같은 생각동사(사유동사)가 오는 경우

의문문	간접의문문	사유동사 의문문
Do you <u>believe</u>? + Who is Josh?	Do you <u>believe</u>? + Who Josh is.	Who do you <u>believe</u> Ø Josh is Ø ?
Do you <u>think</u>? + Where does Nathan live?	Do you <u>think</u>? + Where Nathan lives.	Where do you <u>think</u> Ø Nathan lives Ø ?

5 수사 의문문(rhetorical question)

상대방에게 정보를 얻기 위한 일반적인 의문문과는 달리 정확한 대답을 요구하기보다는 '강조'(assertion)를 나타내기 위해 사용하는데 긍정 형태의 경우 부정 강조를, 부정 형태의 경우 긍정 강조를 의미한다.

(1) 부정 강조 : 긍정 형태이지만 부정의 의미 강조

예

- Who knows? → Nobody knows.
- Why me? → It's unfair (to me).

(2) 긍정 강조 : 부정 형태이지만 긍정의 의미 강조

예

- Isn't Josh smart? → Josh is smart.
- Didn't Nathan tell you? → Nathan already told you.

제 3 절 감탄문(exclamatory sentence)

기쁨, 희망, 놀람, 슬픔, 등 감정을 표현하는 문장이며 의문사 what 또는 how로 시작하고 [주어(S) + 동사(V)]는 생략 가능하다.

	어순		예문
what	What (+ a/an) + 형용사 + 명사 (+ 주어 + 동사)!	단수	What a surprising news (it is)!
		복수	What beautiful people (they are)!
how	How + 형용사/부사 (+ 주어 + 동사)!	단수	How beautiful (this fall is)!
		복수	How fast (Josh walks)!

제 4 절 기원문(optative sentence)

기원, 소망, 저주 등을 표현하는 문장이며 조동사 may로 시작하거나 생략 가능하다.

서술문(평서문)	기원문
주어 + may + 동사(원형)	(May +) 주어 + 동사!
God may bless you.	May God bless you!
You may succeed.	May you succeed!

제 5 절 명령문(imperative sentence)

요청, 제안, 조언, 명령, 충고, 금지 등을 표현하는 문장이며 2인칭 You에게 직접 발화하는 직접 명령문과 1인칭 혹은 3인칭에게 발화하는 간접 명령문이 있다. 명령문은 주어 You는 생략 가능하고, be동사, 일반동사로 시작하는 긍정문 형식의 긍정 명령문, Do not 혹은 Never와 같은 부정 표현으로 시작하는 부정 명령문이 있다.

명령문	긍정	부정
직접	Be humble. Please write you name.	Don't be serious. Please never give up.
간접	Let us go fishing. Let him have a delicious meal.	Don't let me misunderstood. Don't let him down.

실전예상문제

01 해설

on the mat은 전치사구(preposition phrase, PP)로서 문장의 중요소이다.

해석

① Pierce는 영어 가르치는 것을 좋아한다.
② 매트 위의 고양이가 음식을 먹고 있다.
③ Lori는 의사가 되었다.
④ Amy는 Josh가 좋은 남편이라고 믿는다.

02 해설

Wow는 감탄사, and는 접속사, fast는 부사이다. teacher는 (목적격)보어로 문장의 주요소이다.

해석

① 와, Elizabeth가 온다!
② 교수와 학생들이 비디오를 시청하고 있다.
③ Nathan은 매우 빨리 달렸다.
④ Mike는 Mark가 좋은 선생님이라고 믿는다.

03 해설

③은 '주어+동사+목적어+목적격보어' 형식의 5형식 문장이고, 나머지는 모두 2형식이다.

해석

① Lynnelle은 과학자가 되었다.
② 이 음식은 맛있다.
③ Josh는 Lori가 숙련된 기술자라고 믿는다.
④ 너희 둘은 너무 재미있다.

어휘

• hilarious : 유쾌한, 즐거운

정답   01 ②   02 ④   03 ③

---

01 다음 밑줄 친 부분 중 문장의 주요소가 <u>아닌</u> 것은?

① <u>Pierce</u> likes teaching English.
② The cat <u>on the mat</u> is eating the food.
③ Lori became a <u>doctor</u>.
④ Amy <u>believes</u> that Josh is a good husband.

02 다음 밑줄 친 부분 중 문장의 주요소는?

① <u>Wow</u>, Elizabeth is coming!
② The professor <u>and</u> the students are watching the video.
③ Nathan ran very <u>fast</u>.
④ Mike believes Mark a good <u>teacher</u>.

03 다음 중 문장의 형식이 <u>다른</u> 것은?

① Lynnelle became a scientist.
② This food tastes delicious.
③ Josh believes Lori a skillful technician.
④ You two are hilarious.

04 다음 중 문장의 형식이 <u>다른</u> 것은?

① Babies cry.

② The dog is running to the playground.

③ Witzel walks very fast.

④ The professor is teaching English.

05 다음 중 문장의 종류가 <u>다른</u> 것은?

① They don't like to go fishing.

② He went to the bank yesterday.

③ She asked him if Josh is a good professor.

④ Don't let me down.

06 다음 중 의문문의 형태가 <u>잘못된</u> 것은?

① Isn't Matt a diligent student?

② Who can speak Korean fluently?

③ John asked where does Joey live.

④ Do you want to go skiing or go skating?

---

04 **해설**
④는 '주어 + 동사 + 목적어' 형식의 3형식 문장이고, 나머지는 모두 1형식이다.

해석
① 아기들은 운다.
② 개가 놀이터로 달려가고 있다.
③ Witzel은 매우 빨리 걷는다.
④ 그 교수는 영어를 가르친다.

05 **해설**
④는 부정 명령문이고 나머지는 모두 서술문(① 부정문, ② 긍정문, ③ 간접 의문문이 포함된 긍정문)이다.

해석
① 그들은 낚시하러 가는 것을 좋아하지 않는다.
② 그는 어제 은행에 갔다.
③ 그녀는 그에게 Josh가 좋은 교수인지 물었다.
④ 날 실망시키지 마.

어휘
• let down : 실망시키다

06 **해설**
③은 간접의문문으로 의문사 + 동사 + 주어(정확히 의문사 + 조동사 + 주어 + 동사) 어순이 아니라 의문사 + 주어 + 동사 어순인 John asked where Joey lived가 되어야 한다.
①은 Yes/No 부정 의문문, ②는 의문사 Who가 주어인 Wh-의문문, ④는 선택 의문문이다.

해석
① Matt은 부지런한 학생 아닌가요?
② 누가 한국어를 유창하게 말할 수 있나요?
③ John은 Joey가 어디에 살았는지 물었다.
④ 스키 타러 갈래요, 스케이트 타러 갈래요?

정답 04 ④   05 ④   06 ③

07 해설

사유동사 think가 있으면 의문사는 문두에 위치하므로 'Where do you think Cindy lives?'가 맞다.

해석
① Joey는 훌륭한 교수예요, 그렇죠?
② Daniel은 Cindy가 오늘 학교에 가는지 물었다.
③ Cindy가 어디 사는지 알아요?
④ Ivy가 너의 친한 친구니?

08 해설

조동사 can의 긍정 표현이므로 부가 의문문에서는 '~can't she?'가 맞다.

해석
① Cindy는 좋은 교수예요, 그렇죠?
② 그들은 차가 없죠, 그렇죠?
③ Ashley는 한국어를 말할 수 있어요, 그렇죠?
④ 그녀가 화가 났었죠, 그렇죠?

09 해설

'들어가다' 의미의 enter는 타동사이므로 전치사 into 없이 사용된다. enter into는 '시작하다', '관여하다' 라는 의미이다.

해석
① Nathan은 핸드폰을 도난당했다.
② Laurel이 Joey에게 책을 줬다.
③ Jeff는 그의 교실로 들어갔다.
④ Joey가 누구라고 생각하세요?

정답 07 ③　08 ③　09 ③

---

07 다음 중 의문문의 형태가 <u>잘못된</u> 것은?

① Joey is a wonderful professor, isn't he?
② Daniel asked whether Cindy goes to school today.
③ Do you think where Cindy lives?
④ Is Ivy your close friend?

08 다음 중 부가의문문의 형태가 <u>잘못된</u> 것은?

① Cindy is a good professor, isn't she?
② They don't have a car, do they?
③ Ashley can speak Korea, does he?
④ She was upset, wasn't she?

09 다음 중 어법상 <u>잘못된</u> 표현은?

① Nathan had his cell phone stolen.
② Laurel gave a book to Joey.
③ Jeff entered into his classroom.
④ Who do you believe Joey is?

10 다음 중 어법상 <u>잘못된</u> 표현은?

① The movie made Ivy a movie star.

② Online class let the students review class notes.

③ Laurel saw Naoko entering the building.

④ The teacher helped his student conducted research.

10 **해설**
④는 5형식 문장으로 불완전타동사인 help 동사는 목적어 다음에 원형부정사 혹은 to부정사가 와야 하므로 즉 (to) conduct가 적절하다.

해석
① 그 영화는 Ivy를 영화배우로 만들었다.
② 온라인 수업은 학생들이 수업 노트를 복습할 수 있도록 한다.
③ Laurel은 Naoko가 건물로 들어가는 것을 보았다.
④ 선생님은 그의 학생이 연구할 수 있도록 도와주었다.

어휘
• conduct research : 연구하다

정답 10 ④

여기서 멈출 거예요? 근거가 바로 눈앞에 있어요.
마지막 한 걸음까지 SD에듀가 함께할게요!

제 **2** 편

—

품사

(의미, 구조, 형태상 특성)

단원 개요

영어에는 명사, 관사, 대명사, 동사, 형용사, 부사, 전치사, 접속사의 8개 품사(Part of Speech, POS)가 있다(감탄사를 더해서 9개 품사로 보는 경우도 있다).

출제 경향 및 수험 대책

1. 명사
   - (1) 가산 명사 vs 불가산명사
   - (2) 일반명사 vs 집합명사
   - (3) 물질명사 vs 추상명사 vs 고유명사
   - (4) 명사의 수, 격, 성

2. 관사 : 정관사, 부정관사, 무관사의 사용과 의미

3. 대명사
   - (1) 대명사 및 부정대명사의 종류와 사용, 주어와 동사의 수 일치
   - (2) 의문대명사 및 관계대명사 구분 및 사용

4. 동사
   - (1) 규칙 vs 불규칙 동사형태
   - (2) 완전 vs 불완전 동사
   - (3) 자동사 vs 타동사
   - (4) 자동사로 착각하기 쉬운 타동사 vs 타동사로 착각하기 쉬운 자동사
   - (5) 동적동사 vs 상태 동사

5. 조동사 : had better, would rather ~ than, cannot but, cannot ~ too, used to

6. 형용사
   - (1) 수량 형용사 표현
   - (2) 한정 vs 서술 용법
   - (3) 주의해야 할 형용사 표현 및 구문

7. 부사
   - (1) 형용사, 부사가 같은 형태
   - (2) 동일형태, 다른 의미의 부사 표현
   - (3) 원급 비교 표현
   - (4) 비교급(강조) 및 최상급(강조)

8. 전치사 : 종류 및 사용

9. 접속사
   - (1) 등위접속사(FANBOYS), 종속접속사 구분, 종류, 의미
   - (2) 상관접속사 및 동사와의 수 일치
   - (3) 접속부사 의미와 사용

합격의 공식
SD에듀

잠깐!

자격증·공무원·금융/보험·면허증·언어/외국어·검정고시/독학사·기업체/취업
이 시대의 모든 합격! SD에듀에서 합격하세요!
www.youtube.com → SD에듀 → 구독

제 1 장 명사

제 1 절 명사의 기능

명사(noun)는 '이름이 있는 말(단어)'이다. 영어의 명사는 문장에서 주어, 목적어, 보어, 즉 문장의 주요소로서 기능한다.

예

- Birds fly. (1형식)

  [[명사–주어 Birds] [동사 fly]]

- Jeff became a linguist. (2형식)

  [[명사–주어 Jeff] [동사 became] [명사–보어 a linguist]]

- Josh loves Amy. (3형식)

  [[명사–주어 Josh] [동사 loves] [명사–목적어 Amy]]

- Laurel gave Joey a book. (4형식)

  [[명사–주어 Laurel] [동사 gave] [명사–간접목적어 Joey][명사–직접목적어 a book]]

- Josh calls Amy a queen. (5형식)

  [[명사–주어 Josh] [동사 calls] [명사–목적어 Amy][명사–목적(격)보어 a queen]]

제 2 절 명사의 분류

명사는 일반(보통)명사, 집합명사, 물질명사, 추상명사, 고유명사가 있고, 일반(보통), 집합명사는 셀 수 있는 **가산명사**(countable noun), 물질, 추상, 고유명사는 셀 수 없는 **불가산명사**(noncountable noun)로 구분한다.

1 가산명사(countable noun)

가산명사는 셀 수 있는 명사로서 단수(singular)와 복수(plural)가 있다. 단수명사 앞에는 부정관사(indefinite article a(n))를 붙일 수 있는데 자음(발음)으로 시작하는 명사 앞에는 a, 모음(발음)으로 시작하는 명사 앞에는 an을 사용한다. 복수명사 앞에는 수를 나타내는 수사(numeral) one, two, three 등과 수량형용사 (a) few, some, (a) lot(s) of, many 등을 사용하고 명사의 끝에는 복수를 나타내는 접미사(suffix) -(e)s를 붙인다.

> [예]
> • a pen(=one pen), two pens, three pens, …, some pens, …, many pens, …
> • an apple(=one apple), two apples, three apples, …, some apples, …, many apples, …

(1) 일반(보통)명사(common noun)

일반적으로 같은 종류의 사람, 사물에 공통적으로 사용하는 명사이다. 일반명사의 경우 전체를 언급하는 총칭표현과 추상명사를 의미하는 경우 주의할 필요가 있다.

[예]
• a cat, a pen, a book, a chair, a desk, …
• an apple, an orange, an egg, an umbrella, an office, …

① 총칭 표현(generic expression)
　　㉠ 대표 단수 : a(n)/the + 단수 일반명사
　　　　[예] A dog barks. / The dog barks.
　　㉡ 대표 복수
　　　　[예] Dogs bark.
② the + 단수 일반명사(추상명사를 의미)
　　[예]
　　• The pen is mightier than the sword.
　　　([해석] 펜은 칼보다 더 강하다, 문(文)은 무(武)보다 더 강하다.)
　　• The poet stirred in my mind when I saw the beautiful scenery.
　　　([해석] 내가 그 아름다운 경치를 보았을 때 내 마음에 시심(詩心)이 돋았다.)
　　• The elders found the child in themselves by that movie.
　　　([해석] 어른들은 그 영화를 보고 자신들의 동심을 발견했다.)

(2) 집합명사(collective noun)

사람, 사물의 집합체를 나타내는 명사이고 다음의 경우에 사용이 가능하다.

① 단수, 복수 취급 모두 가능한 경우
　　[예]
　　• class, committee, nation, public, family, audience, staff …

- Josh's family is large.
- Two families will live in this new house.

② **단수 형태이지만 복수 취급하는 경우**

    ㉠ 구성원 전체

      예

- Amy's family are all safe now.

      (All the family members of Amy's family)

    ㉡ 항상 복수 취급

      예

- All the cattle are in the prairie.
- The police are investigating this accident.
- People says that Josh is smart.

③ **물질명사로 취급하는 경우**

    예 clothing, furniture, machinery, mail, baggage, scenery

④ **참고**

    ㉠ people

    집합명사 people은 '사람'의 의미일 때는 복수 의미의 집합명사로 취급하지만, '국민, 민족'의 의미일 때는 보통명사 취급

      예

- Many people prefer to walk after meal.
- All the peoples from Asia are good-natured.

    ㉡ nation

    집합명사 nation은 '국민(전체)'의 의미일 때는 복수 의미의 집합명사로 취급하지만, '국가', '민족'의 의미일 때는 보통명사 취급

      예

- What can we do for the nation?
- This country is a country of contrast, but it is a nation of nations.

    ㉢ hair

    집합명사 hair는 '머리털(전체)'의 의미로 사용할 때는 복수 의미의 집합명사로 취급하지만, '머리카락'의 의미로 사용할 때는 보통명사 취급

      예

- Amy has dark brown hair.
- Josh pulled out two white hairs.

2 **불가산명사**(noncountable noun)

(1) 물질명사(material noun)

상황에 따라 다양한 모양으로 변하는 것을 지시하는 명사인데, 기체, 액체, 재료, 식품, 자연물 등이 있다.

[예]

- 기체 : air, gas
- 재료 : wood, glass, silk, paper
- 액체 : water, milk, wine, oil
- 식품 : coffee, bread, cheese, sugar, butter
- 자연물 : stone, rain, snow
- 기타 : money, fire, chalk

[예]

- People cannot live without air and water.
- Milk is good for children's health.

① 셀 수 없는 명사인 물질명사는 양을 표시하는 no, little, any, some, much 등과 함께 사용된다.

[예]

- We had much rain this summer.
- Nathan bought some furniture for his new office.

② 수를 나타내야 하는 경우는 '수사+단위명사+of'의 형태로 표시한다.

[예]

- a glass of water/milk/wine
- a cup of coffee/tea
- a cake of soap
- a bottle of wine
- a loaf of bread
- a sheet of paper
- a piece of furniture
- a pound of beef/bread/pork sausages
- a spoonful of salt/sugar/syrup/rice
- an ear of corn([어휘] ear : 이삭, 열매)

③ 물질명사는 불가산명사이기 때문에 원칙적으로 부정관사 단수형 a/an, 복수형이 없다. 하지만 그 물질로 만든 개체, 종류, 제품, 개별적 사건을 나타내는 경우 일반명사로 취급하여 단수, 복수형을 취할 수 있다.

[예]

- Laurel is tasting a good wine.
- Josh picked up a stone.

- Amy's father wearing glasses.
- There was a big fire in downtown New York last night.

(2) 추상명사(abstract noun)

눈으로 보거나 만질 수 없는 형체가 없는 추상적인 개념을 지시하는 명사이고, 원칙적으로 부정관사 a/an을 사용하거나 복수형을 사용하지 않고 단수 취급한다.

> [예]
>
> life, peace, time, advice, knowledge, beauty, confidence, luck, kindness, education, experience, news, …

① of (+ a) + 추상명사 = 형용사 의미

[예]

- It is of use to me. = It is very useful to me.
- of great consequence(significant), of no consequence(insignificant)
- of talent = talented
- of experience = experienced
- of wisdom = wise
- of ability = able
- of sense = sensible
- of importance = important
- of learning = learned

② all + 추상명사 / 추상명사 + itself = very + 형용사

[예]

- Jeff is all attention. (very attentive)
- Amy is all beauty. (very beautiful)
- Josh is discretion itself. (very discreet)

③ 전치사 + 추상명사 = 부사 의미

[예]

- Josh stepped on Nathan's foot on purpose. ([어휘] on purpose : 고의로, 일부러)
- Lori solved the math problem with difficulty. ([어휘] with difficulty : 힘겹게, 간신히)

with/without	in	by	on, to
with ease (쉽게)	in haste (급히)	by accident (우연히)	on purpose (고의로)
with care (주의 깊게)	in despair (절망하여)	by degrees (점점)	on occasion (가끔)
with safety (안전하게)	in reality (사실상)		to perfection (완벽히)
with patience (끈기있게)	in succession (연속해서)		
with kindness (친절히)			
without doubt (확실히)			
without hesitation (주저 없이)			

④ the + 형용사 = 추상명사 의미

예

- "The weak will die out and the strong will survive, will live on forever." - Anne Frank-

  ([해석] "약자는 죽고 강자는 살아남아 영원히 살 것이다." - 안네 프랑크 -)

- Immigration was a leap into the unknown several centuries ago.

  ([해석] 이민은 수 세기 전에는 미지의 세계로 도약하는 것이었다.)

- This movie is full of the horrible. ([해석] 이 영화는 공포로 가득 차 있다.)

- the good

- the beautiful

- the true

- the rich

(3) 고유명사(proper noun)

세상에 유일한 사람, 사물을 지시하는 명사인데 인명, 국가, 지명 등이 이에 해당한다. 단어의 첫 번째 글자는 대문자로 시작하고 부정관사(a/an), 정관사(the)를 사용하지 않고, 복수형도 사용하지 않는 것이 원칙이다.

예

Korea, Gyeongbokgung, England, Big Ben, America, Brooklyn Bridge, Empire State Building 등

고유명사에 부정관사, 정관사를 사용하게 되면 다음과 같이 다른 의미를 나타낸다.

① '~와 같은 사람', '~와 같은 곳'

예 a Newton, a Shakespeare, a Nelson, the Edison, the Naples

② '~라는 사람'

예 A Mr. Miller, three Johns

③ '~씨 가족', '~씨 부부'

　　예 the Lees, the Kims, the Rosses

④ '~의 작품', '~사 상품/제품'

　　예 a Picasso, a Millet, a Ford, two Hyundais

제 3 절　수, 격, 성

1 　수(number) 중요 ★

명사는 셀 수 있는 가산명사(countable noun)와 셀 수 없는 불가산명사(noncountable noun)가 있다. 가산명사는 일반(보통명사), 집합명사가 있고, 불가산명사는 물질명사, 추상명사, 고유명사가 있다. 가산명사는 셀 수 있는 명사로서 단수(singular), 복수(plural)가 있다. 단수명사 앞에는 부정관사(indefinite article a, an)를 붙일 수 있는데 자음(발음)으로 시작하는 명사 앞에는 부정관사 a, 모음(발음)으로 시작하는 명사 앞에는 부정관사 an을 사용하고 복수명사 앞에는 수를 나타내는 형용사 some, many 등을 사용하고 명사의 끝에는 복수를 나타내는 접미사(suffix) -(e)s를 붙인다.

	단수(singular)	복수(plural)
가산명사 (countable noun)	a pen(= one pen)	• two pens, three pens … • a few pens • some pens • a lot of pens • many pens • ∅ pens (∅ = bare : 무관사)
불가산명사 (noncountable noun)	• some money • a lot of money • much money • ∅ money	-

2 　격(case)

영어 문장에서 명사, 대명사가 하는 역할 및 위치에 따라 다른 단어에 대해 가지는 문법적인 관계를 표현하는 것으로서 형태는 동작과 상태의 주체를 나타내는 주격, 소유를 나타내는 소유격, 동작의 대상을 나타내는 목적격이 있다.

(1) 명사의 경우

명사는 사용되는 역할에 따라 주격, 소유격, 목적격으로 사용된다.

주격 (~은/~는, ~이/~가)	Josh is a smart professor.
	Nathan is a linguist.
소유격 (~의)	Josh's wife is Amy. (단수 's)
	Parents' day is the fourth Sunday of July. (복수 ')
목적격 (~을/~를)	Josh loves Amy.
	Lori ate an apple.

① 소유격은 명사 + 's (apostrophe)를 사용한다. 고유명사가 -s로 끝나는 경우도 's를 사용한다.

예

- Josh's wife
- The dog's food
- Johns's book
- Charles's car

> **! 더 알아두기**
>
> Jesus, Moses, Socrates, Columbus는 -s로 끝나더라도 '만 붙인다.
>
> 예
> - Jesus' disciples
> - Mores' authority
> - Socrates' death
> - Columbus' discovery of the New World

② -s로 끝나는 명사와 복수명사의 소유격은 '(apostrophe)만 붙인다.

예

- parents'
- the ladies'

③ 무생물의 소유격은 of + 명사로 표시한다.

예

- the windows of the car
- the legs of the desk

④ 복합 명사는 마지막에 's를 붙인다.

예

- father-in-law - father-in-law's car
- mothers-in-law - mothers-in-law's cars

⑤ 동격 명사는 마지막에 's를 붙인다.

예

- my friend Josh's wife
- my friend Nathan's car

⑥ **개별 소유와 공동 소유**

　ㄱ 개별 소유 : Josh's and Amy's pianos

　ㄴ 공동 소유 : Josh and Amy's piano

⑦ **독립 소유격**

　ㄱ 소유격 다음에 오는 palace, office, house, shop, store와 같은 공공건물, 집, 상점 등은 생략한다.

예

- palace : St. James's
- house : my cousin's
- shop : the bookseller's

　ㄴ 같은 명사가 반복되는 경우 소유격 다음 명사는 생략

예 car : This car is my brother's

⑧ **이중 소유격**

a, an, the, this, these, that, those, some, any, no, which, what, such, each, every 등은 소유격과 함께 사용할 수 없고, 'a, an, the, this, … + 명사 + of + 소유대명사'로 사용하고 이를 이중 소유격이라 한다.

예

- *my father's friend → a friend of my father's
- *my father's car → the car of my father's
- *Josh's this book → this book of Josh's

　(* = ungrammatical : 비문법적)

⑨ **시간, 거리, 가격, 무게를 나타내는 명사**

예

- one minute's walk
- today's newspaper
- five miles' distance
- a boat's length ([해석] 근소한 차이)
- three dollars' worth
- two pounds' of weight

⑩ **무생물을 의인화하는 경우**

예

- Heaven's will
- Nature's works
- Fortune's smile
- Truth's triumph

⑪ **관용적 표현**

for convenience's sake(형편상, 편의상)	at one's wit's end(어찌할 바를 몰라)
for mercy's sake(제발)	at one's finger's ends(~에 정통하여)
for conscience's sake(양심상)	at one's heart's content(마음껏)
for form's sake(형식상)	at a journey's end(여행 막바지에)
for pity's sake(제발)	

(2) 대명사의 경우

대명사는 주격, 소유격, 목적격, 소유대명사 형태가 고정되어 있다.

			주격	소유격	목적격	소유대명사[※]
1인칭	단수		I	my	me	mine
	복수		we	our	us	ours
2인칭	단수		you	your	you	yours
	복수		you	your	you	yours
3인칭	단수	남성	he	his	him	his
		여성	she	her	her	hers
		중성	it	its	it	-
	복수		they	their	them	theirs
			~은/~는, ~이/~가	~의	~을/~를	

※ 소유대명사는 명사 없이 독립적으로 사용하고 '(apostrophe) 없이 사용한다.
   This book is <u>his</u>. <u>Yours</u> is on the table(his = his book; yours = your book).

3 성(gender)

문법적으로 영어의 성 구별은 남성명사(masculine), 여성명사(feminine), 보통명사(common), 중성명사(neutral)가 있다.

- 남성명사 : he, boy, man, tiger, god
- 여성명사 : she, girl, woman, tigress, goddess
- 보통명사 : infant, child, baby, teacher, person
- 중성명사 : book, table, gold, childhood, intelligence, independence

(1) 남성명사와 여성명사를 구별하는 경우

> 예
> - husband - wife
> - nephew - niece
> - bridegroom - bride
> - bachelor - spinster
> - widower - widow
> - hero - heroine
>
> - monk - nun
> - wizard - witch
> - man-servant - maid-servant
> - ox, bull - cow
> - cock - hen
> - he-goat - she-goat

(2) 남성명사에 접미사 '-ess'를 붙이는 여성명사

> 예
> - God - Goddess
> - prince - princess
> - author - authoress
> - master - mistress
> - host - hostess
> - actor - actress
>
> - heir - heiress
> - waiter - waitress
> - emperor - empress
> - lion - lioness
> - tiger - tigress

(3) 보통명사(통성명사)

> 예
> - parent
> - spouse
> - monarch
> - friend
> - baby, chil, 동물을 나타내는 명사는 대명사 it 사용

(4) 중성명사 중요 ★

성의 구별 없이 무생물로 표현하지만 의인화되는 경우 남성명사, 여성명사로 사용한다.

> - 남성명사 : war, sun, winter, fear, …
> - 여성명사 : peace, moon, nature, mercy, liberty, ship, …
> - 국가명 : 경제, 사회, 문화 측면, 여성형 대명사 she 사용
> - 국토, 지리 측면, 중성명사 취급 it 사용

예
- England is proud of her dramatist Shakespeare.
- England is a part of the United Kingdom. It shares border with Wales and Scotland.

제 2 장 관사

영어의 관사(article)는 명사의 속성을 정의하는 **한정사**(determiner) 표현이고, 특정한 대상을 가리키는 **정관사**(the), 특정한 대상을 가리키지 않는 **부정관사**(a, an), 관사를 사용하지 않는 **무관사**가 있다.

제 1 절 정관사(definite article the) 중요 ★★

1 선행하는 명사를 가리킬 경우

예 My neighbor has a dog. <u>The</u> dog kept me awake last night.

2 고유명사 앞

(1) 국가의 공식 이름과 지역 이름

예
- the Republic of Korea
- the United States of America
- the United Kingdom

(2) 공공건물, 관공서 이름

예
- the Ministry of Education
- the Lincoln Memorial
- the City Hall of Seoul

> **더 알아두기**
>
> 역, 항구, 호수, 다리, 공항, 공원, 거리, 대학에는 일반적으로 the를 붙이지 않는다.
>
> 예
> - Seoul Station
> - Boston Harbor
> - Lake Superior
> - Brooklyn Bridge
> - DFW Airport
> - Central Park
> - Fifth Avenue

(3) 반도, 군도, 산맥 이름

예
- the Korean Peninsula
- the Hawaiian Islands
- the Philippines
- the Rocky Mountains

(4) 강, 바다, 선박, 해협 등의 이름

예
- the Han River
- the Thames
- the Pacific
- the Atlantic

(5) 철도, 열차, 항공기, 배, 신문, 잡지, 학회 이름

예
- the Pullman
- the Titanic
- the New York Times
- the Royal Academy

(6) 고유명사가 한정되는 경우

예
- Seoul is the capital of Korea.
- the Seoul of the 21 century

3 유일무이한 경우

예
- The sun is much larger than the earth.
- Young people around the world share the contemporary culture.

4 문맥상 전후관계로 누구나 알 수 있는 경우

예
- The library is next to the Student Union Building.
- Would you close the windows?

5 수식어구(형용사구, 형용사절)에 의해 한정되는 경우

예
- The gentleman with a red hat is holding a cane.
- The boy who lives next to my house is polite.

6 총칭표현(종족 대표)

예
- The dog barks.
- The dog is a faithful animal.
- The fox is a cunning animal.

7 시간, 수량의 단위를 나타내는 경우 : by the + 단위

예
- Pork is sold by the pound.
- Nathan rented the apartment by the month.
- The company hire a worker by the day.

8 신체의 일부를 표현하는 경우

(1) by : catch/seize/hold/pull/take + 사람 + by the 신체 일부

예
- Amy caught him by the hand.
- Josh seized me by the hand.

(2) on : pat/strike/tap/hit/beat/kiss + 사람 + on the 신체 일부

예
- Nathan patted him on the shoulder.
- Lori struck me on the head.

(3) in : look/stare + 사람 + in the 신체 일부

예
- Cindy looked me in the face.
- Jeff stared her in the eye.

9 기계, 발명품, 악기를 표현하는 경우

예
- The car was invented by Karl Benz.
- Amy plays the piano well.

10 서수(first, second, third, …), 최상급, only, last, same 앞에서 사용

예
- January is the first month of the year.
- Alaska is the largest state in the USA.
- Josh has the same belief as Amy.

11 관용표현

예

- in the morning
- in the afternoon
- in the evening
- in the daytime
- in the sun
- in the dark
- in the country

제 2 절 부정관사(indefinite article a/an)

1 발음상 자음 앞 a, 모음 앞 an

(1) 부정관사 a/an은 셀 수 있는 가산명사의 단수형 앞에 사용한다.

(2) 발음상 자음, 반모음(j, w)으로 발음하면 a, 모음(a, e, i, o, u)로 발음하면 an을 사용한다.

예

- a car, a house
- a university, a used car
- an hour, an herb tea

2 부정관사 a/an의 의미

(1) 대화에 처음 표현하는 불특정한 대상

예

- Nathan is a linguist.
- Nathan wants a new house in Seattle.

(2) one(하나)

[예]

- Rome wasn't built in a day. ([해석] 로마는 하루아침에 이루어지지 않았다.)
- Josh will stay in Dallas a week.

(3) 총칭표현(대표단수)

[예]

- A dog barks.
- A fox is a cunning animal.

(4) the same(같은)

[예]

- Josh and Amy are of an age.
- Birds of a feather flock together. ([해석] 유유상종)

(5) some(약간, 어느 정도)

[예]

- 일시적으로, 한동안 : Amy stayed in Dallas for a time.
- 다소, 약간 : He is to a degree difficult to get along with. ([어휘] to a degree : 다소, 약간)

(6) certain(어떤)

[예]

- A Mr. Kim stopped by the office to see you.
- Do you know a Mr. Jensen?

(7) per(마다)

[예]

- Josh visits his mother once in a week.
- Jeff writes journal papers twice a year.

제 3 절 무관사(zero article)

1 공공건물의 본래 목적으로 표현하는 경우

예

- Josh is going to school at 9 o'clock.
- Josh is going to the school to see Nathan.

at/in	go
at table	go to church
at school	go to hospital
at(in) church	go to bed
in class	go to sea

2 통신, 교통수단

예

- You can contact him by email/phone.
- Nathan came here by car/bus/train.

3 짝을 이루는 2개의 명사가 전치사 혹은 접속사로 연결되는 경우

예

- mother and daughter
- father and son
- husband and wife
- body and soul
- side by side
- arm in arm

4 식사, 질병, 운동, 계절, 학과 이름 중요 ★

[예]

- Josh and Amy are having breakfast in the hotel.
- Cindy is suffering from cancer.
- In spring, many flowers bloom.
- Josh and Amy are playing tennis.
- Josh majors in literature/linguistics/economics/statistics/management …

> **더 알아두기**
>
> **형용사 혹은 형용사구의 수식을 받는 경우는 관사 사용**
>
> [예]
> - Amy has no appetite because she had a heavy breakfast.
> - The breakfast Amy had in the morning was too heavy.
>
> **상대적으로 가벼운 질병은 부정관사 a/an 사용**
> [예] a stomachache, a toothache, a headache

5 관직, 신분, 혈통을 나타내는 표현이 주격보어(SC), 목적격보어(OC)로 사용되는 경우

[예]

- Mr. Kim was promoted to director of his college(SC).
- Employees elected Mr. Lee vice-president(OC).

6 호격, 가족관계를 나타내는 경우

[예]

- Server, two coffees, please.
- Mother, may I go out and play with Josh?

7 a kind of, a sort of 다음에 오는 경우

예 Jeff is a kind of gentleman.

8 생략과 반복

예
- A poet and statesman is dead. (동일인)
- A poet and a statesman are dead. (2인)

- the King and Queen
- a doctor and nurse
- a needle and thread
- a cup and saucer
- a knife and fork
- a watch and chain

9 man이 '남성', woman이 '여성', man이 '인간'을 표현하는 경우

예
- Man is mortal.
- Woman tend to live longer than man.

10 관용표현

(1) 전치사 + 명사

예
- in town
- at dawn
- at daybreak
- at noon
- at night
- at midnight
- at hand

(2) 동사 + 명사

> [예]
> - take part
> - take place
> - make room
> - make haste

11 관사의 위치 중요 ★

(1) all/both/double + the + 명사

[예]

- All the students were present.
- Josh paid double the price for that.

(2) such/rather/many/half/quite/what/whatever + a(n) + 형용사 + 명사

[예]

- Josh is such an excellent professor.
- Nathan is quite a gifted linguist.

(3) so/as/too/how/however + 형용사 + a(n) + 명사

[예]

- This difficult work cannot be done in so short a time.
- Josh is as kind a gentleman as Nathan is.

제 **3** 장 **대명사**

제 1 절 인칭대명사(personal pronoun)

인칭대명사는 사람을 가리키는 대명사이고, 인칭과 단·복수에 따라 주격, 소유격, 목적격, 소유대명사, 재귀대명사 형태가 있다.

			주격	소유격	목적격	소유대명사	재귀대명사
1인칭	단수		I	my	me	mine	myself
	복수		we	our	us	ours	ourselves
2인칭	단수		you	your	you	yours	yourself
	복수		you	your	you	yours	yourselves
3인칭	단수	남성	he	his	him	his	himself
		여성	she	her	her	hers	herself
		중성	it	its	it	-	itself
	복수		they	their	them	theirs	themselves

1 소유대명사(possessive pronoun)

(1) 소유대명사

소유대명사는 소유격 + 명사의 의미이므로 명사 없이 독립적으로 사용하고 '(apostrophe) 없이 사용한다.

예

- This book is his. Yours is on the table.
  (his = his book, yours = your book)

(2) 이중 소유격

a, an, this, these, that, those, some, any, no, which, what, such, each, every 등은 소유격과 함께 사용할 수 없고, 'a, an, this, … + 명사 + of + 소유대명사'로 사용하고 이를 이중 소유격이라 한다.

예

- *my father's friend → a friend of my father's
- *my father's car → the car of my father's

2 재귀대명사(reflexive pronoun)

인칭대명사 뒤에 단수의 경우 -self, 복수의 경우 -selves를 붙이면 된다.

(1) 재귀 용법

동작의 결과가 다시 주어 자신에게 돌아가는 경우이고 동사와 전치사의 목적어 자리에 사용된다.

예

- 동사의 목적어 : That child dresses herself.
- 동사의 목적어 : Seat yourself in this chair.
- 전치사의 목적어 : She sometimes talks to herself.
- 전치사의 목적어 : You have to believe in yourself.

(2) 강조 용법

강조하고 싶은 표현 뒤에 사용하며, 그 표현을 강조한다.

① 주어

예

- Jeff himself did it.
  (Jeff did it himself.)
- Amy herself painted the house.
  (Amy painted the house herself.)

② 목적어

예

- Josh wants to see Amy herself.
- Nathan talked to the president himself.

③ 추상명사 itself

예

- Joey is kindness itself.
  (Joey is very kind.)
- It is simplicity itself.
  (It is very simple.)

(3) 관용 표현 중요 ★

① 전치사 + 재귀대명사

예

- by oneself (자기 혼자서, 스스로)
- for oneself = for one's sake (자기 자신을 위하여), without other's help (혼자 힘으로)
- in itself (본래, 본질적으로)
- of itself (저절로)
- to oneself (독점하여, 자기 혼자에게만)
- beside oneself (제정신이 아닌)
- between ourselves (우리끼리 이야긴데)
- in spite of oneself (자기도 모르게)

② 동사 + 재귀대명사

예

- come to oneself (제정신이 들다, 의식을 찾다)
- pride oneself on (자랑스러워하다)
- present oneself at (출석하다)
- absent oneself from (결석하다)
- accustom oneself to (익숙해지다)
- avail oneself of (이용하다)
- overwork oneself (과로하다)
- overdrink oneself (과음하다)
- oversleep oneself (늦잠 자다)

제 2 절　지시대명사(demonstrative pronoun)

공간적, 시간적, 심리적으로 가까운 것(proximal)은 this/these, 먼 것(distal)은 that/those로 나타낸다.

1　this/these

(1) 가까운 것(proximal)

예 This is a good pen.

※ This pen is good의 this는 지시대명사가 아닌 지시형용사(this) + 명사(pen)

(2) 대용 : 단어 혹은 구

예 Josh bought a book and this is hard to read.

(3) 대용 : 문장(선행 또는 후행 문장)

예

- 선행 문장, 전방조응 : Amy has studied hard for 3 years. This made her pass the bar exam.
- 후행 문장, 후방조응 : Please remember this: Love conquers all.

(4) 후자(the latter) 중요 ★

예 Work and play are both necessary to health; this(= play) gives us rest, and that(= work) gives us energy.

(5) 현재 또는 현재와 가까운 시간

예

- Jeff got up late in this morning.
- Thing are too complicated these days.

2 that/those

(1) 멀리 있는 것(distal)

예 That is a good pen.

※ That pen is good의 'that'는 지시대명사가 아닌 지시형용사(that) + 명사(pen)

(2) 대용 : 단어 혹은 구

예 Josh bought a book and that is hard to read.

(3) 대용 : 문장(선행 문장)

예 To be, or not to be, that is the question. - Hamlet -

(4) 전자(the former) 중요 ★

예 Work and play are both necessary to health; this(= play) gives us rest, and that(= work) gives us energy.

(5) 명사 반복 대용

예

- The climate of California is milder than that(= climate) of New York in winter.
- The students in Korea are different from those(= students) in the USA.

(6) 막연한 사람

예 Heaven helps those who help themselves. ([해석] 하늘은 스스로 돕는 자를 돕는다.)

제 3 절 　부정대명사(indefinite pronoun)

1 one

(1) 일반적 의미 : '사람', '세상 사람', '누구나'

예 One should keep one's promise.

(2) 명사 대용(동일 종류)

예

- Josh lost his watch last week, so he should buy new <u>one</u>. (동종물)
- Josh lost his watch last week, but he found <u>it</u> in the living room. (동일물)

(3) (성질, 지시) 형용사 + one

예 Your idea is a good one in our new project.

2 one, another, other

(1) 둘 중에서 순서 없이 열거할 경우

예 Josh has two sisters; One lives in San Francisco, and the other lives in Chicago.

(2) 둘 중에서 전자와 후자(순서 중요)

예 Amy has a cat and a dog; the one is more active than the other.

(3) 셋 중에서 순서 없이 열거할 경우

> 예 Nathan has three brothers. One is a professor, another(= a second) (is) a doctor, and the other(= the third) (is) a school teacher.

(4) 넷 중에서 순서 없이 열거할 경우

> 예 Lori has four trees in her garden; one is pine, another (is) cherry tree, a third (is) persimmon tree, and a fourth (is) white birch.

3 another

(1) one more(하나 더)

> 예
> • Would you give me another cup of coffee?
> • Josh is staying in Hawaii another week.

(2) different(다른)

> 예 Amy doesn't like this one; give her another.

(3) A is one thing and B is another(A와 B는 별개이다)

> 예 Speaking is one thing and doing is (quite) another.
> ([해석] 말하는 것과 행동하는 것은 (전혀) 별개의 것이다.)

(4) 그 외 상호대명사

each other는 둘 사이, one another는 셋 이상에서 '서로'의 의미로 사용하나 명확히 구별하여 사용하지는 않는다.

> 예
> • They stared at each other.
> • They helped one another in this project.

4 some ～, others ～

> • some ～, others ～ : 일부는, 또 다른 일부는(집합의 구분이 명확하지 않은 일부)
> • some ～, the others ～ : 일부는, 다른 나머지 일부는(집합의 구분이 명확한 일부)

예

• Some went by subway; and others went by bus.
• There are thirty students in Josh's class; some are taught online, and the others are taught face-to-face.

5 some, any 중요 ★★

(1) some

> 약(about), 어떤(a certain)

예

• Jeff waited some one hour(about).
• Naoko went to some place in Hawaii(a certain).

(2) some, any

> • some : 긍정문
> • any : 부정문, 의문문, 조건문

① **긍정문 some + 가산명사** : Some of Nathan's questions were difficult to understand.
② **긍정문 some + 불가산명사** : Some of the milk was spilled.
③ **부정문 any** : Lori didn't seem to have any questions about the issue.
④ **의문문 any** : Is there anything interesting in today's news?
⑤ **조건문 any** : Nathan has a lot of good pencils: if you want any, he will give you some.

(3) some

> 권유, 의뢰를 표현하는 의문문, 긍정의 대답을 기대하는 의문문

예 Would you have some more coffee?

(4) any

> 긍정문, 어떤 ~일지라도, 무엇이나

[예] Any plan will do.

(5) ―thing, ―body

> some과 any 용법과 동일(―thing, ―body 대명사를 수식하는 형용사는 뒤에 위치한다)

[예]
- Josh saw something white on the highway.
- Is there anybody out there?

6 both

두 사람, 두 개, 양쪽(복수취급)

[예]
- both of the students
- Both Josh and Amy are professors.
- Both of them are university students.

7 either/neither(단수취급) 중요 ★

① either : 둘 중 하나
[예]
- Either plan A or plan B is excellent.
- Either of the two plans is excellent.

② neither : 둘 다 아님
[예]
- Neither plan A nor plan B is good.
- Neither of the two plans is good.

8 most/almost 중요 ★★

① most : 형용사/대명사(대부분)

　　㉠ 형용사

　　　　(○) most + 명사 : 대부분의 ~

　　　　예 Most students like a smart professor.

　　㉡ 대명사

　　　　(○) most of the (형용사) + 명사 : ~의 대부분

　　　　(×) most all (of) the + 명사

　　　　예 Most of the students like a smart professor.

② almost : 부사(거의 모든)

　　예

　　• Almost all (of) the students like a smart professor.

　　• (○) almost all (of) the + 명사

　　• (○) almost every + 명사

　　• (×) almost every of + 명사

9 all/every/each 중요 ★★

① all (of) (the) + 명사(가산명사 − 복수취급, 불가산명사 − 단수취급)

　　예

　　• All (of) (the) questions were difficult to understand.

　　• All (of) the students in Josh's class are good.

> **더 알아두기**
>
> 복수 명사 앞에서는 of가 생략 가능하나 복수 인칭대명사 앞에서 of는 생략 불가
>
> (○) All (of) the students like reading books.
> (×) All them like reading books.
> (○) All of them like reading books.

② every

　　형용사 every + 단수명사(단수취급)

　　부정대명사는 everyone, everybody, everything 형태

　　예

　　• Every dog has its day.

　　• Everyone has a chance in one's life.

③ each

each + 단수명사(단수취급)

[예]

- Each student has one's note.
- Each student of Josh's class was present.
- Each of us has one's own car.
- They each have one's own car(부사).

10 no/none

(1) no + 명사

[예]

- No reasons were accepted.
- No man is infallible here on earth. ([해석] 이 세상에서 과오를 절대로 범하지 않는 사람은 없다.)
- He has no car.

(2) none(대명사)

[예]

- None were reported.
- None of us are infallible.
- He has none of those qualities.

제 4 절 의문대명사, 관계대명사

1 의문대명사(interrogative pronoun)

의문대명사는 의문형용사, 의문부사와 구별되는데 의문대명사는 명사절 내에서 주어, 목적어, 보어의 명사 역할을 한다.

구분	의문대명사	의문형용사	의문부사
표현	who(whom) what which	whose what which	when where why how
문장 내 역할	명사 (주어, 목적어, 보어)	형용사	부사

(1) 명사절 내 주어

예

- Josh didn't know who was in the office.
- Amy knew what was on Josh's mind.

(2) 명사절 내 목적어

예

- Could you tell me who(m) Amy sent it to?
- You can choose which you prefer.

(3) 명사절 내 보어

예

- Do you know who Jeff is?
- She doesn't know what the time is.

2 관계대명사(relative pronoun) 중요 ★★

관계대명사는 그 선행사가 사람, 사물, 동물인지와 문법상 주격, 목적격, 소유격인지에 따라 다음과 같이 구분된다.

선행사	주격	목적격	소유격
사람	who	who(m) ∅	whose
사물, 동물	which	which ∅	whose of which
사람, 사물, 동물	that	that ∅	-

(1) 주격 관계대명사

① **사람** : who, that

예

- She thanked the man. (→ 주절)
  He helped her. (→ 관계사절 주어)
  She thanked the man who helped her.
  She thanked the man that helped her.

② **사물/동물** : which, that

예

- The pen is hers. (→ 주절)

  It is on the desk. (→ 관계사절 주어)

  The pen which is on the desk is hers.

  The pen that is on the desk is hers.

(2) 목적격 관계대명사 : 동사의 목적어

① **사람** : who, whom, that, ∅

예

- The man was Mr. Jensen. (→ 주절)
- Joey saw him last night. (→ 관계사절 목적어)
- The man who(m)   Joey saw last night was Mr. Jensen.

  The man that   Joey saw last night was Mr. Jensen.

  The man ∅   Joey saw last night was Mr. Jensen. (생략 가능)

② **사물/동물** : which, that, ∅

예

- The drama was very good. (→ 주절)
- Amy saw it last night. (→ 관계사절 목적어)
- The drama which   Amy saw last night was very good.

  The drama that   Amy saw last night was very good.

  The drama ∅   Amy saw last night was very good. (생략 가능)

(3) 목적격 관계대명사 : 전치사의 목적어

① **사람**

예

- Laurel is the professor. (→ 주절)
- I told you about her. (→ 관계사절 목적어)
- Laurel is the professor about whom I told you.

  Laurel is the professor   whom I told you about.

  Laurel is the professor   that I told you about.

  Laurel is the professor   ∅ I told you about. (생략 가능)

② **사물/동물**

[예]

- The music was wonderful. (→ 주절)
- Amy listened to it last night. (→ 관계사절 목적어)

  The music to which Amy listened last night was wonderful.

  The music   which Amy listened to last night was wonderful.

  The music   that Amy listened to last night was wonderful.

  The music   ∅ Amy listened to last night was wonderful. (생략 가능)

(4) 소유격 관계대명사

① **사람** : whose

[예]

- Josh knows the woman. (→ 주절)
- Her book was published lately. (→ 관계사절 소유격)
- Josh knows the woman whose book was published lately.

② **사물/동물** : whose, of which

　㉠ whose

　　[예]

- Josh has a cat. (→ 주절)
- Cat's (Its) color is black and white. (→ 관계사절 소유격)
- Josh has a cat whose color is black and white.

　㉡ of which

　　[예]

- Josh bought a chair. (→ 주절)
- The top of the chair was made of wood. (→ 관계사절 소유격)
- Josh bought a chair the top of which was made of wood.

  Josh bought a chair of which the top was made of wood.

제 4 장 동사

제 1 절 규칙동사, 불규칙동사

동사(verb)는 기본형(원형)-단순과거형-과거분사형의 변화에 따라 **규칙동사, 불규칙동사**로 구분된다.

1 규칙동사

규칙동사는 다음의 네 가지 방식이 있고, 단순과거형-과거분사형은 동일 형태이다.

(1) e로 끝나는 단어는 −d만 붙인다.

기본형	단순과거형	과거분사형	기본형	단순과거형	과거분사형
agree	agreed	agreed	live	lived	lived
change	changed	changed	use	used	used
hope	hoped	hoped	prepare	prepared	prepared

(2) 자음 + y로 끝나는 단어는 y → i로 고친 후 −ed를 붙인다.

기본형	단순과거형	과거분사형	기본형	단순과거형	과거분사형
dry	dried	dried	marry	married	married
try	tried	tried	carry	carried	carried

(3) 1음절(syllabus) 단모음 + 단자음으로 끝나는 단어는 자음을 하나 더 쓰고 −ed를 붙인다.

기본형	단순과거형	과거분사형	기본형	단순과거형	과거분사형
plan	planned	planned	beg	begged	begged
stop	stopped	stopped	rob	robbed	robbed

(4) 2음절이고 강세가 끝에 오는 경우 자음을 하나 더 쓰고 -ed를 붙인다.

기본형	단순과거형	과거분사형	기본형	단순과거형	과거분사형
admit	admitted	admitted	occur	occurred	occurred
control	controlled	controlled	prefer	preferred	preferred

2 불규칙동사

불규칙동사는 기본형-과거형-과거분사형의 형태에 따라 여덟 가지 유형이 있다.

(1) 모두 동일 형태

기본형	단순과거형	과거분사형	기본형	단순과거형	과거분사형
bet	bet	bet	put	put	put
burst	burst	burst	quit	quit	quit
cost	cost	cost	set	set	set
cut	cut	cut	shut	shut	shut
fit	fit/fitted	fit/fitted	split	split	split
hit	hit	hit	spread	spread	spread
hurt	hurt	hurt	upset	upset	upset
let	let	let			

(2) 기본형-과거분사형이 동일 형태

기본형	단순과거형	과거분사형
become	became	become
come	came	come
run	ran	run

(3) 단순과거형-과거분사형이 동일 형태

기본형	단순과거형	과거분사형	기본형	단순과거형	과거분사형
bend	bent	bent	mislay	mislaid	mislaid
bleed	bled	bled	pay	paid	paid
bring	brought	brought	read[ri:d]	read[red]	read[red]
build	built	built	say	said	said
burn	burnt	burnt	seek	sought	sought

buy	bought	bought	sell	sold	sold
catch	caught	caught	send	sent	sent
dig	dug	dug	shoot	shot	shot
feed	fed	fed	sit	sat	sat
feel	felt	felt	sleep	slept	slept
fight	fought	fought	slide	slid	slid
find	found	found	sneak	snuck/ sneaked	snuck/ sneaked
flee	fled	fled	speed	sped/ speeded	sped/ speeded
grind	ground	ground	spend	spent	spent
hang	hung	hung	spin	spun	spun
have	had	had	stand	stood	stood
hear	heard	heard	stick	stuck	stuck
hold	held	held	sting	stung	stung
keep	kept	kept	strike	struck	struck
lay	laid	laid	sweep	swept	swept
lead	led	led	swing	swung	swung
leave	left	left	teach	taught	taught
lend	lent	lent	tell	told	told
light	lit/lighted	lit/lighted	think	thought	thought
lose	lost	lost	understand	understood	understood
make	made	made	weep	wept	wept
mean	meant	meant	win	won	won
meet	met	met			

(4) 모두 다른 형태

기본형	단순과거형	과거분사형
be	was, were	been
go	went	gone

(5) 과거분사 -en형태

기본형	단순과거형	과거분사형	기본형	단순과거형	과거분사형
awake	awoke	awoken	hide	hid	hidden
bite	bit	bitten	prove	proved	proven/proved
break	broke	broken	ride	rode	ridden
choose	chose	chosen	rise	rose	risen
drive	drove	driven	shake	shook	shaken
eat	ate	eaten	speak	spoke	spoken
fall	fell	fallen	steal	stole	stolen
forget	forgot	forgotten	swell	swelled	swollen/swelled
forgive	forgave	forgiven	take	took	taken
freeze	froze	frozen	wake	woke/waked	woken
get	got	gotten/got	write	wrote	written
give	gave	given			

(6) 과거분사 -n형태

기본형	단순과거형	과거분사형	기본형	단순과거형	과거분사형
blow	blew	blown	see	saw	seen
do	did	done	swear	swore	sworn
draw	drew	drawn	tear	tore	torn
fly	flew	flown	throw	threw	thrown
grow	grew	grown	wear	wore	worn
know	knew	known	withdraw	withdrew	withdrawn
lie	lay	lain			

(7) 단순과거형 모음 a → 과거분사형 모음 u변화형태

기본형	단순과거형	과거분사형	기본형	단순과거형	과거분사형
begin	began	begun	shrink	shrank	shrunk
drink	drank	drunk	sing	sang	sung
ring	rang	rung	sink	sank	sunk
run	ran	run	swim	swam	swum

(8) 규칙형-불규칙형 모두 사용

기본형	단순과거형	과거분사형	기본형	단순과거형	과거분사형
burn	burned/ burnt	burned/ burnt	learn	learned/ learnt	learned/ learnt
dream	dreamed/ dreamt	dreamed/ dreamt	smell	smelled/ smelt	smelled/ smelt
kneel	kneeled/ knelt	kneeled/ knelt	spill	spilled/ spilt	spilled/ spilt
lean	leaned/ leant	leaned/ leant	spoil	spoiled/ spoilt	spoiled/ spoilt

제 2 절 완전동사, 불완전동사

동사는 보어의 유무에 따라서 불완전동사, 완전동사로 구분된다.

보어는 주어와 동사만으로는 문장의 의미가 완전하지 못한 불완전한 의미를 보충하는 역할을 하는 표현으로서 보어가 없어도 의미가 완성되는 동사가 완전동사(complete verb), 보어가 있어야만 문장의 의미가 완성되는 동사가 불완전동사(incomplete verb)이다.

				목적어 (object)		
				無		有
				자동사 (intransitive verb)		타동사 (transitive verb)
보어 (complement)	無	완전 (complete verb)			1형식			3형식
			완전	자동사	완전	타동사
	有	불완전 (incomplete verb)			2형식			5형식
			불완전	자동사	불완전	타동사

1 완전동사

(1) 1형식

예

- Josh is going to school.

  [[주어 Josh] [완전자동사 is going] [부사구 to school]].

- Josh goes (to school)(by bus)(with his friend)(every day)

  [[주어 Josh] [완전자동사 goes] ([부사구 to school])([부사구 by bus])([부사구 with his friend])([부사구 every day])].

(2) 3형식

예

- Josh likes linguistics.

  [[주어 Josh] [완전타동사 likes] [목적어(명사) linguistics]].

- Nathan entered the classroom.

  [[주어 Nathan] [완전타동사 entered] [목적어(명사구) the classroom]].

2 불완전동사

(1) 2형식

예

- Josh is a professor.

  [[주어 Josh] [불완전자동사 is] [주격보어(명사) a professor]].

- Nathan is intelligent.

  [[주어 Nathan] [불완전자동사 is] [주격보어(형용사) intelligent]].

(2) 5형식

예

- Josh believes Nathan a genius.

  [[주어 Josh] [불완전타동사 believes] [목적어 Nathan] [목적격보어(명사) a genius]].

- Josh made Amy happy.

  [[주어 Josh] [불안전타동사 made] [목적어 Amy] [목적격보어(형용사) happy]].

- The professor let the students take notes.

  [[주어 The professor] [불완전타동사 let] [목적어 the students] [목적격보어(원형부정사) take notes]].

- The professor helped the students (to) do their homework.

  [[주어 The professor] [불완전타동사 helped] [목적어 the students] [목적격보어(to부정사) (to) do their homework]].

- Josh saw Nathan entering the classroom.

  [[주어 Josh] [불완전타동사 saw] [목적어 Nathan] [목적격보어(현재분사) entering the classroom]].

- Nathan had his laptop stolen.

  [[주어 Nathan] [불완전타동사 had] [목적어 his laptop] [목적격보어(과거분사) stolen]].

제 3 절 타동사, 자동사

동사는 **목적어**의 유무에 따라서 타동사, 자동사로 구분된다. 목적어는 주어가 특정 대상에 대해 행위를 하는 객체인데 그러한 목적어가 필요한 동사가 **타동사**(transitive verb, vt), 목적어가 필요 없는 동사가 **자동사**(intransitive verb, vi)이다.

				목적어 (object)		
			無		有	
			자동사 (intransitive verb)		타동사 (transitive verb)	
보어 (complement)	無	완전 (complete verb)		1형식		3형식
			완전	자동사	완전	타동사
	有	불완전 (incomplete verb)		2형식		5형식
			불완전	자동사	불완전	타동사

1 타동사

(1) 3형식

예

- Josh likes linguistics.

  [[주어 Josh] [완전타동사 likes] [목적어(명사) linguistics]].

- Nathan entered the classroom.

  [[주어 Nathan] [완전타동사 entered] [목적어(명사구) the classroom]].

(2) 5형식 중요 ★

예

- Josh believes Nathan a genius.

  [[주어 Josh] [불완전타동사 believes] [목적어 Nathan] [목적격보어(명사) a genius]].

- Josh made Amy happy.

  [[주어 Josh] [불완전타동사 made] [목적어 Amy] [목적격보어(형용사) happy]].

- The professor let the students take notes.

  [[주어 The professor] [불완전타동사 let] [목적어 the students] [목적격보어(원형부정사) take notes]].

- The professor helped the students (to) do their homework.

  [[주어 The professor] [불완전타동사 helped] [목적어 the students] [목적격보어(to부정사) (to) do their homework]].

- Josh saw Nathan entering the classroom.

  [[주어 Josh] [불완전타동사 saw] [목적어 Nathan] [목적격보어(현재분사) entering the classroom]].

- Nathan had his laptop stolen.

  [[주어 Nathan] [불완전타동사 had] [목적어 his laptop] [목적격보어(과거분사) stolen]].

2 자동사

(1) 1형식

예

- Josh is going to school.

  [[주어 Josh] [완전자동사 is going] [부사구 to school]].

- Josh goes (to school)(by bus)(with his friend)(every day)

  [[주어 Josh] [완전자동사 goes] ([부사구 to school])([부사구 by bus])([부사구 with his friend])([부사구 every day])].

(2) 2형식

예

- Josh is a professor.

  [[주어 Josh] [불완전자동사 is] [주격보어(명사) a professor]].

- Nathan is intelligent.

  [[주어 Nathan] [불완전자동사 is] [주격보어(형용사) intelligent]].

> **더 알아두기**
>
> **타동사로 착각하기 쉬운 자동사** 중요 ★★
>
> | | |
> |---|---|
> | add to | His soothing vocals add to the lyrical atmosphere of the song. |
> | account for | This can account for the mysterious phenomenon. (설명하다) |
> | apologize to | He has to apologize to his colleague. |
> | arrive at | He arrived at the South Pole after 70 desperate days. |
> | assent to | They assent to his proposal. (동의하다) |
> | consent to | They gladly consent to his request. (동의하다) |
> | complain of | He complained of a stomachache. (호소하다)
He complained of the service. (불평하다) |
> | dissent from | He dissents from the established view. (의견을 달리하다) |
> | graduate from | He graduated from university last month. |
> | infringe on | They infringe on his property and rights. (침해하다) |
> | interfere with | Viennese audiences usually don't interfere with the music. (방해하다) |
> | listen to | He is listening to music. |
> | meddle in | She doesn't want to meddle in his private affairs. (간섭, 개입, 관여하다) |
> | object to | They object to genetically engineered food. (반대하다) |

participate in	Students actively participated in the essay contest.
refer to	This expression refers to various meanings. (언급하다, 표현하다)
rely on	She relies on her mother. (의지하다)
	He can rely on her word. (믿다)
reply to	He replied to her question.
speak of	He is going to speak of happiness.
subscribe to	He subscribes to that magazine. (구독하다)
	He subscribes to a statement. (서명, 기입하다)
sympathize with	She sympathized with the man in his grief. (공감, 동정하다)
talk about	He talked about going on a picnic.
tamper with	It might tamper with human brain system. (간섭하다)
wait for (on)	Time waits for no man./He will wait on the line.

제 4 절 동적동사, 정적동사

동사는 어떤 행위를 표현하는 **동적동사** 또는 **행동동사**(dynamic verb, action verbs)와 상태나 상황을 표현하는 **정적동사** 또는 **상태동사**(stative verb, non-action verbs)로 구분된다.

1 동적동사(행동동사)

동작, 행위, 활동, 성취, 업적 등을 나타내는 대부분의 동사이고, 진행형과 수동태가 가능하다.

예

- Josh plays tennis every day; Josh is playing tennis right now.
- Josh was sleeping when a guest came into his house.
- Josh can't talk right now because he is eating lunch.
- The cheese was eaten by Josh.

2 정적동사(상태동사) 중요 ★★

지각, 감각, 인지, 소유, 선호, 감정, 상태 등을 나타내는 동사이고, 진행형과 수동태가 불가능하다.

지각 및 감각	feel, see, sound, hear, taste, smell, seem, appear 등
인지	think, believe, know, understand, forget, remember 등
소유	own, have, possess, belong 등
선호	hope, need, want, prefer 등
감정	like, love, hate 등
상태	be, exist, live, belong, own, have, contain, resemble 등

예

- Did Josh see any problems with that?
- This soup tastes great.
- Josh thinks that coffee is great.
- The students like Josh's class.
- Josh has a sports car.

- *Josh is knowing Dr. Sabbagh.
- *Josh is wanting a sandwich for his lunch.
- *This pen is belonging to Josh.

더 알아두기

정적동사는 항상 고정된 것이 아니라 그 쓰임에 따라 동적동사로도 사용가능하다.

I see what you mean. (정적동사)
I am seeing Mr. Witzel tomorrow. (동적동사, meet의 의미)

He thinks that English grammar is easy. (정적동사, believe의 의미)
He is thinking about English grammar right now. (동적동사, 지금 현재 생각하고 있는 과정 혹은 행위, thought is going through a person's mind)

He has a car. (정적동사, own의 의미)
He is having a good time. (동적동사, enjoy의 의미)

This soup tastes great. (정적동사)
The chef is tasting the soup. (동적동사, 맛을 보는 행위)

제 5 절 구동사(phrasal verb)

동사에 전치사 혹은 부사와 같은 소사(particle)가 더해져 원래의 의미와는 다른 새로운 의미를 나타낸다.

예

- Josh will put off his trip to Korea. (put off = postpone, 연기하다)
- Josh, put on your jacket before you go out. (put on = wear, 입다)
- Josh put the newspapers away. (put away = arrange, 정리하다)
- Josh put the spoon back in the kitchen. (put back = return, 원래 자리에 돌려놓다)

1 분리 가능한 구동사(separable) 중요 ★★

전치사 혹은 부사가 동사와 분리 가능한 형태가 있다.

예

- Josh will put off his trip. (동사 + 소사 + 명사)
- Josh will put his trip off. (동사 + 명사 + 소사)
- Josh will put it off. (동사 + 대명사 + 소사)

ask out = ask somebody to make a date	pick apart = find fault with
back up = support, aid	pick up = take or lift upward
back off = move backward from a certain position	pick off = shoot one by one
blow out = put out fires, flames, or lights	pin down = define clearly
bring back = return	point out = make a comment on, call attention to
bring up = raise children, mention	print out = create a paper copy
call back = return a phone call	pull off = be successful, achieve a goal
call off = cancel, postpone	put away = put in its usual, original place
call up = make a phone call	put back = return to its original place
cheer up = cause to feel more happier	put down = stop holding
clean up = make neat and clean	put off = postpone
come across = find unexpectedly	put on = put clothes
cross out = remove from a list, draw a line	put out = stop a fire, cigarette
figure out = find the solution, understand	shut off = turn off
fill in = supply with information in a blank	take back = return
fill out = write information on a form	take out = invite out and pay
fill up = fill with gas, water, coffee etc.	talk over = have a discussion
give away = get rid of by giving	tear down = destroy a building
give back = return	tear up = tear into small pieces
hand in = give homework to a teacher	think over = consider

hand out = give something to a person	throw away/out = discard
have on = wear	try on = put clothes on to see whether they fit
help out = be of help	turn around/back = change to the opposite direction
keep on = continue	turn down = decrease the volume
lay off = stop employment	turn off = stop a light, machine
leave on = not turn off (a light), not take off (clothing)	turn on = start a light, machine
look over = examine carefully	turn over = turn the top side to the bottom
look up = look for information in a dictionary	turn up = increase the volume
make up = invent	wake up = stop sleeping
pay back = return borrowed money	work out = solve
pass away = die, decease	write down = write a note on a piece of paper

2 분리 불가능한 구동사(nonseparable) 중요 ★★

전치사 혹은 부사가 동사와 분리가 가능하지 않은 형태가 있다.

예

• Josh will look into the problem. (동사 + 소사 + 명사)
• Josh will look into it. (동사 + 소사 + 대명사)

call on = ask	look into = investigate
come from = originate	run into = meet by chance
get over = recover	get off = leave (a bus/airplane/train/subway)
get in = enter (a car/taxi)	get on = enter (a bus/airplane/train/subway)
get out of = leave (a car/taxi)	

3 자동사 구동사

목적어 없이 자동사로 사용되는 구동사도 있다.

---

break down = stop operating

break out = happen suddenly

break up = separate, discontinue a relationship

come in = enter

dress up = put on special clothes

eat out = eat at a restaurant (outside of home)

fall down = lose an upright position

get up = rise to one's feet

give up = quit doing something

go on = continue

go out = leave the house to go somewhere

grow up = become an adult

hang up = end a telephone conversation

move in (to) = move into a new house

move out (of) = move out of old house

show up = appear, become visible

sit back = settle into a comfortable position

sit down = take a seat

speak up = speak louder, express opinion

stand up = rise to one's feet

start over = begin again

stay up = not go to bed

take off = leave, depart from the ground

---

4 세 단어로 된 구동사

동사 + 소사(전치사 혹은 부사) 형태 두 단어가 아닌 세 단어로 된 구동사도 있다.

---

come along (with) = accompany

come over (to) = visit

cut out (of) = remove with knife or scissors

drop in (on) = visit informally

drop out (of) = leave school

find out (about) = discover

fool around (with) = indulge in horseplay

get along (with) = return, recover

get back (from) = have smooth relationship

get through (with) = finish a task completely

get together (with) = join, meet

go back (to) = return

go over (to) = approach, visit

grow up (in) = become an adult

hang around (with) = spend a lot of time

hang out (with) idle time = spend time idly

keep away (from) = prevent from coming close

look out (for) = be careful

run out (of) = become used up

set out (for) = begin a trip

sign up (for) = engage by written agreement

sit around (about) = sit and do nothing

tear out (of) = remove paper by tearing

watch out (for) = be careful

제 5 장 조동사

영어 문장의 술부에서 주요 의미를 담당하고 있는 본동사(main verb) 앞에 위치하여 보조하는 역할을 하는 부분이 조동사이다. 영어의 조동사는 be, do, have와 같은 **일반 조동사**(primary auxiliary verb), will, shall, can, may, must, should, ought to와 같은 **법**(mood), 서법, 또는 **양상 조동사**(modal auxiliary verb), have to, had better, would rather, used to, be going to와 같은 **준조동사**(quasi auxiliary verb)가 있다.

이 중 조동사는 본동사 혹은 문장(명제)의 본래 의미에 필요성, 조언, 의무, 허락, 능력, 가능성, 개연성 등과 같이 본동사가 기술하는 사건에 대한 화자의 판단, 의견, 태도를 표현하는 특수한 동사이다. 또한 서법 조동사 또는 양상 조동사(modal auxiliary verbs)라고도 한다.

제 1 절 can/could, may/might

1 can/could

(1) 능력

예
- Josh can/can't speak French as well as Korean.
- Josh's son could/couldn't walk when he was fourteen months old.

(2) 허가, 허락

예
- If you are in a hurry, you can leave early.
- If you finish the test, you can go home now.

(3) 추측, 강한 의혹

예
- Can it be true?
- Josh cannot be hungry. He already ate two sandwiches.
- Josh is absent today. He could be sick today.

(4) 정중한 요청

정중한 요청의 경우, could는 can의 과거형태가 아니고, 좀 더 공손한 표현이다.

예

- Can I please borrow your note?
- Could I please borrow your note?
- Can you please close the door?
- Could you please close the door?

2 may/might

(1) 추측

can보다는 가능성이 낮은 추측

예

- It may/might not rain tomorrow.
- It may/might not rain tomorrow.
- Josh is absent today. He may/might be sick today.

> **더 알아두기**
>
> **가능성 정도** 중요 ★
> - 100% sure : Josh is sick today.
> - 99% sure : Josh can/could be sick today.
> - 95% sure : Josh must be sick today.
> - 50% sure or less : Josh may/might be sick today.

(2) 허가, 허락

can보다는 좀 더 formal한 허가, 허락

예

- If you finish the test, you may/might not go home now.
- You may/might not have some cookies after you finish your homework.

(3) 정중한 요청

예

- May I please borrow your note?
- May I ask your full name?

(4) 양보구문

예 Whatever others may say, Josh will not(won't) change his mind.

(5) 기원문

예 May you be very happy!

제 2 절 shall/should, will/would

1 shall/should

(1) 미래 표현

1인칭 평서문, will이 더 일반적

예
- I shall be forty in May.
- I shall arrive at 10 pm.

(2) 정중한 표현

제안을 위한 정중한 표현

예 Shall I close the door?

(3) 상대방의 의향, 의지 질문

예
- What time shall we make it?
- Shall we go skiing?

(4) 추측, 당연(90% certainty)

예
- Josh should not be at work at 11 pm.
- Josh should arrive soon.
- Josh should do well on the test tomorrow.

(5) 조언, 의무

예

- You should study hard for your final exam.
- The young should respect the old.

(6) 주장, 명령, 요구, 제안, 충고 등의 동사의 명사절 that절

주장(insist, urge, maintain), 명령(order, command), 요구(demand, require, request, ask), 제안 (propose, advise, recommend, suggest) 등의 동사가 that절을 목적어로 취하는 경우 that절 내의 동사는 (should) + 동사원형을 사용하고 should는 생략 가능하다.

예

- Josh insisted that Amy (should) study Ph.D. course.
- Nathan ordered that Lori (should) follow the company regulations.

(7) 요구, 권고, 소망을 나타내는 형용사 뒤의 that절

It is	important, necessary, essential, imperative, vital, urgent, advisable, desirable	that everybody (should) vote.

(8) 주관적 감정, 판단을 나타내는 어구 뒤의 that절

It is	natural, surprising, strange, curious, wonderful, regrettable, a pity	that Jeff (should) accept the offer.

2 will/would 중요 ★

(1) will

① 미래

예

- Josh will be forty next year.
- Nathan will be here at 7 pm.

② 주어의 의지

예

- The phone is ringing. I will get it.
- I will lose weight within 6 months.
- The door will not open.

③ 습관, 경향

예

- He will keep asking silly questions.
- Boys will be boys.

④ (정중한) 요청

예

- Will you please help me?
- Will you come with me this morning?

(2) would

① (will보다 정중한) 요청

예

- Would you please help me?
- Would you please pass me the salt?

② 과거의 습관, 반복적 동작

예

- After lunch, he would take a nap.
- My father would exercise every morning (if he had time).

③ 과거에 대한 확실한 추측

예 Amy would be about thirty when Josh met her. ([해석] Josh가 Amy를 만났을 때, 그녀는 대략 30살이었을 것이다.)

④ 현재나 미래에 대한 추측

예 Josh would be tired tomorrow if he worked hard today.

⑤ 소망(want, like)

예

- I would like a banana, please.
- I would like to find out more about Europe.

제 3 절 must, ought to

1 must

(1) (강한) 필요

예 You must go to class today.

(2) (강한) 금지

예 You must not open the window.

(3) (강한) 추측(95%)

예 Amy isn't in class today. She must be sick.

2 ought to

(1) 조언

예 You ought to study tonight.

(2) 추측(90%)

예 Amy ought to do well on the final exam tomorrow.

제 4 절　기타 조동사 중요 ★★

1 do

(1) 부정문

예
- We don't like to watch the movie.
- Josh doesn't change his clothing style.

(2) 강조

예
- We do love to go skiing.
- Josh does love his wife Amy.

(3) 대동사

예
- I think as you do[think].
- People who deceive us once are capable of doing so again.

(4) 의문문 - 대답

예

- Do you know her? - Yes, I do[know her].
- Does Josh love his wife? - Yes, he does[love his wife].
- Did you read the book? - Yes, I did[read the book].

(5) 부가의문문

예

- You don't want to be a poet, do you?
- He knows how to drive a car, doesn't he?

2 need/dare

need와 dare는 평서문에서 본동사로 사용되며 to부정사를 목적어로 취하고, 부정의문문에서는 조동사로 사용된다.

(1) need

① 본동사 (+ to부정사)	㉠ 긍정문	We need your help. We need to wax his car.
	㉡ 부정문	we don't need your help. We don't need to wax his car.
② 조동사	㉠ 부정문	We need not do it. (→ 본동사 : We do not need to do it.)
	㉡ 의문문	Need we do it? (→ 본동사 : Do we need to do it?)

(2) dare(감히 ~하다)

① 본동사 (+ to부정사)	㉠ 긍정문	Witzel dared to jump across the brook.
	㉡ 부정문	Joey does not dare to challenge the society's rules.
② 조동사	㉠ 부정문	Witzel dares not to tell you any more.
	㉡ 의문문	How dare you tell me such a thing?

3 had better + 동사원형 : 경고, ~하는 게 낫다

[예]

- I had better do the dishes before I go out.
- You'd better study now for your final.
- You'd better not study now for your final.

4 would rather A than B : B보다는 (차라리) A하다

[예]

- He would rather become a doctor than a bullfighter.
- He would rather live in the country than in the big city.

5 cannot(couldn't) but + 동사원형 : ~하지 않을 수 없다

= cannot help -ing(동명사)

= have no choice but to(부정사)

[예]

- He cannot but laugh.
  = He cannot help laughing.

6 cannot ~ too : 아무리 ~해도 지나치지 않다

[예]

- One cannot use too much attention.
- Holidays cannot be too many.

7 may/might as well : ~하는 게 낫다

may/might as well A as B : B하느니 A하는 게 낫다

[예]

- I may as well go to the store now.
- You may as well read some book as look at the ceiling.

8 may well + 동사원형 : ~하는 것이 당연하다

예

- You may well believe it.
- You may well not believe it.

9 used to + 동사원형 vs be used to + 동사원형 vs be/get used to + 명사/동명사

(1) used to + 동사원형 : ~하곤 했다

예

- There used to be an old persimmon tree in the garden.
- He used to skip his classes.
- They used to live in Chicago. Now they live in Seoul.

(2) be used to + 동사원형 (+ by 명사) : 타동사 use의 수동태 구문, ~하는 데 사용되다

예

- The fund will be used to help the underprivileged by the government.
  ([어휘] the underprivileged : 소외계층, 저소득층)
- This educational application is used to teach college students.
- The goldfish were used to check the purity of the water.

(3) be/get used to + 명사/동명사 : ~에 익숙해지다

예

- The company is used to much stronger growth.
- Life is not fair, get used to it. - Bill Gates -

- Josh is used to living in Seoul.
- You will soon get used to living in a big city.

제 6 장 형용사

제 1 절 형용사의 종류

형용사(adjective)는 사람이나 사물의 모양, 성질, 성격, 상태 등을 나타내고, 성상·수량·지시 형용사가 있다.

1 성상형용사 : 사람이나 사물의 특성, 모습, 상태 표현

(1) 원래 형용사 표현

> 예 a beautiful mountain, an old man

(2) 분사 형태

> 예
> - a good-looking jacket, an existing problem
> - a printed journal, excited audience

(3) 고유명사

> 예 an Italian food, a Korean dynasty

(4) 물질명사

> 예 a gold ring, a silver spoon

2 수량형용사 : 수나 양을 표현 중요 ★★

(1) 수

① **기수** : one, two, three, …
② **서수** : first, second, third, …
③ **배수** : half, two times, three times, …
④ **부정** : (a) few, any, some, many, …

(2) 양 : (a) little, any, some, much, …

(3) 가산·불가산 명사 앞에 오는 수량 표현

명사		표현	
가산	단수	a/an	another
		one	every
		each	a single
	복수	a few(조금 있는)	few(거의 없는)
		one of	each of
		both	fewer
		many	several
		a number of	a majority of
		numerous, various, a variety of	a couple of
불가산		a little(조금 있는)	little(거의 없는)
		a great deal of	a large amount of
		much	less
모두		no	any
		all	several
		more	a lot of, lots of
		most	plenty of
		some	other

① many (+ 가산명사 복수) vs much (+ 불가산명사)

예

- Many people prefer to walk around barefoot.
- He has won many awards.

※ many a/an + 단수명사 - 단수동사

예

- Many a man comes and goes. ([해석] 많은 사람이 왕래한다)
- Many a pickle makes a mickle ([해석] 티끌 모아 태산) ([어휘] pickle : 미량 / mickle : 많음, 다량).

- Much more information was provided at a time.
- We spend much time going to and from schools, work, or home.

② a few : 수, 조금 있는, 긍정 vs few : 수, 거의 없는, 부정

[예]

- A few graduate students participated in the conference.
- Few graduate students participated in the conference.

③ not a few(= quite a few = a good many = many : 수, 상당히 많은)

[예]

- Not a few foreign investors have offered to join hands with Korea.
- He corrected quite a few errors.

④ only a few(= but few) : 수, 약간, 아주 조금

[예]

- Only a few countries around the world have space programs.
- But few people were interested in jazz.

⑤ a little(양, 조금 있는, 긍정) vs little(양, 거의 없는, 부정)

[예]

- He has a little money left.
- He has little money left.

⑥ not a little = quite a little = much : 양, 많은

[예]

- He lost not a little gambling.
- It gives us quite a little pleasure.

⑦ little better than = as good as : ~과 거의 같은

[예]

- He is little better than an eccentric.
- He is little better than a begger.

⑧ little short of = almost : 거의 ~한, ~에 가까운

[예]

- His success is little short of a miracle.
- He is little short of broke.

3 지시형용사(대명형용사) : 대명사 역할을 하면서 명사 수식

(1) 지시형용사 : this book, that school

(2) 의문형용사 : what book, which school

(3) 소유형용사 : his book, my school

💡 더 알아두기 🔍

수사 표현

1. 특정 수 표현

four hundred, four thousand, four million, four billion, four trillion

123,	456,	789,	198,	765
trillion	billion	million	thousand	
조	십억	백만	천	
one hundred and twenty-three trillion	four hundred and fifty-six billion	seven hundred and eighty-nine million	one hundred and ninety-eight thousand	seven hundred and sixty-five

※ 막연한 수 표현은 복수형 가능

hundreds of people(수백 명의 사람들)
thousands of people(수천 명의 사람들)
millions of people(수백만 명의 사람들)
billions of people(수십억 명의 사람들)
trillions of books(무수한 책)

2. 시각, 날짜, 연도 표현

• (at) 7:35 (a.m.) = (at) seven thirty-five (a.m.)
• (at) 11:25 (p.m.) = (at) eleven twenty-five (p.m.)

• AmE : 월-일-년, 2.22.2022, February twenty second twenty twenty-two
• BrE : 일-월-년, 22.2.2022, twenty second (of) February twenty twenty-two

• AmE : Tuesday, February 22, 2022
• BrE : Tuesday, 22 February 2022

• 1987 = nineteen eighty-seven
• 1990's = the nineteen nineties
• 2022 = two thousand (and) twenty-two / twenty twenty-two
• 2000's = the two thousands
• the 21st century = the twenty-first century

• He was born in February.
• He was born in 2002.
• He was born on Tuesday, February 22, 2002, in Boston, Massachusetts.

3. 화폐, 지폐 표현

예
- £7.05 = seven pounds (and) five pence
- $35.73 = thirty-five (dollars and) seventy-three (cents)
- $1,500 = one thousand five hundred dollars (fifteen hundred dollars)
- $35,223 = thirty-five thousand two hundred twenty-three dollars

- AmE, bill, a $10 bill(10달러 지폐)
- BrE, note, a £5 note(5파운드 지폐)

4. 명사에 숫자가 포함된 경우

예
- Queen Elizabeth II = Queen Elizabeth the Second
- Henry VII = Henry the Seventh
- World War II = World War Two 또는 The Second World War

5. 분수(분자 기수 - 분모 서수로 읽음)

예
- 1/4 = one quarter, a quarter
- 1/3 = one third
- 1/2 = one half, a half
- 2/3 = two thirds
- 3 2/5 = three and two fifth

6. 소수

예
- 3.14 = three point one four
- 23.45 = twenty-three point four five

7. 배수사 중요 ★

(1) 배수사 + as 원급 as

예
- She makes money twice as much as he does.

- This room is three times as large as that room.
  = This room is three times larger than that room.
  = This room is three times the size of that room.

(2) 배수사 + 비교급 than

예
- This house is three times bigger than that house.
- There were four times more books delivered than he placed an order.
※ half와 twice 다음에는 비교급 than을 쓸 수 없다.

(3) 배수사 + the 명사 (of)

[예]

- He demanded double the (usual) price.
- He sold for the treble the price([어휘] treble : 3배).
- The company paid him half the amount he had requested.
- The African continent is four times the size of the European continent.

제 2 절 형용사의 용법 중요 ★

1 한정용법(attributive use)

형용사가 명사 앞 또는 뒤에서 수식하는 용법

(1) 전치수식(pre-modification)

형용사가 명사 앞에서 수식하는 용법

[예]

- Josh is a [wonderful] professor.
- This is a [beautiful] flower.
- He found an [empty] space.

(2) 후치수식(post-modification)

형용사가 명사 뒤에서 수식하는 용법

① -thing, -body, -one으로 끝나는 대명사를 수식하는 경우

[예]

- He heard something [funny].
- Please give me something [cold].

② -able, -ible로 끝나는 형용사가 최상급, all, every 다음에 오는 명사를 수식하는 경우

[예]

- This is the best way [feasible].
  He tried every method [possible].

③ '전치사 + 명사'의 수식어 표현

[예]

- a glass full [of water]
- He has a book useful [for university students].

④ **형용사절(관계사절)이 명사를 수식하는 경우**

예

- Josh met a friend [who lives in Chicago].
- Lori sent a package to her friend [who came from England].

⑤ **서술용법**

예 She is the greatest novelist [alive].

⑥ **관용어구**

God almighty(전능하신 신)	attorney general(법무장관)
president-elect(대통령 당선자)	sectary general(사무총장)
heir apparent(법정추정 상속인)	proof positive(확증)
notary public(공증인)	the sum total(총합계)
poet laureate(계관 시인)	the authorities connected(관계당국)
England proper(영국 본토)	the body politic(국가, 국민)
literature proper(순수문학)	from time immemorial(태고부터)

---

2 **서술용법(predicative use)**

형용사가 주격보어나 목적격보어로 사용되는 경우

(1) 주격보어

예

- The tiger is still [alive].
- This sunflower is [beautiful].

(2) 목적격보어

예

- He found this story [interesting].
- The heat turned the milk [sour].

🔔 더 알아두기 ﾞ

주의해야 할 형용사 표현 및 구문 중요 ★★

1. 'It is + 형용사 + for 목적격 + to부정사' 구문
   easy, difficult, (un)important, (un)necessary, (im)possible, (in)convenient, proper, natural, strange, pleasant, comfortable, dangerous 등과 같이 난이도, 중요도, 당위성 등을 의미하는 형용사 표현은 사람을 주어로 하지 않고, to부정사 구문의 타동사 목적어나 전치사의 목적어가 문두로 위치하여 'It is + 형용사 (+ for 목적격) + to부정사' 구문으로 표현된다.

   예
   - *Kim is very difficult to master English in a few years.
   - English is very difficult for Kim to master in a few years.
   - It is very difficult for Kim to master English in a few years.

   - *Kim is impossible to work with Lori.
     Lori is impossible for Kim to work with.
   - *Lori is impossible for Kim to work.
     It is impossible for Kim to work with Lori.

   - *He is very dangerous to swim in this river.
   - This river is very dangerous for him to swim in.
   - It is very dangerous for him to swim in this river.

   - It is easy (for us) to please him.
     He is easy (for us) to please.

   - It is difficult (for us) to please him.
     He is difficult (for us) to please.

   - It is pleasant (for us) to be with Lori.
     Lori is pleasant (for us) to be with.

2. 목적어를 취하는 형용사 : worth, like, opposite, near + 명사/~ing
   예
   - This paper is worth reading.
   - Josh and Amy are very like each other. (닮은)
   - Nathan and Lori are opposite each other. (마주 보고 있는)
   - His house is near the highway.

3. the + 형용사 용법
   (1) 복수 보통명사(~하는 사람들)
   예
   - The young are the hope of the country.
   - The rich are not always happy.

(2) 추상명사(~한 것)

[예]
- The true always wins.
- The impossible is sometimes possible.

(3) 단수 보통명사

[예]
- The accused is his student. (피고인)
- The deceased is a young actor. (고인)

4. 혼동하기 쉬운 형용사

(1)	amiable(상냥한, 호감을 주는)	He is an amiable person.
	amicable(관계가 우호적인)	He has an amicable relationship with her.
(2)	classic(일류의, 우수한, 전형적인)	Air pollution in the classic example.
	classical(고전의, 클래식의)	He is listening to classical music.
(3)	considerable(중요한, 상당한)	He overcame considerable hardship.
	considerate(신중한, 이해심이 있는)	He is considerate of the underprivileged.
(4)	contemptible(경멸한 만한, 비열한)	Backbiting is a contemptible thing.
	contemptuous(멸시하는)	A contemptuous smile started up on his face.
(5)	continual(거듭 되풀이 되는)	She was annoyed by his continual intervention.
	continuous(계속되는)	The company needs a continuous feedback from customers.
(6)	comparable(비교할 수 있는)	He believes that his income is comparable with the average.
	comparative(비교의)	He is studying comparative linguistics.
(7)	credible(믿을 만한)	Democracy needs a credible media.
	creditable(칭찬할 만한, 훌륭한)	His achievement of straight A's is very creditable to him.
	credulous(쉽게 잘 속는)	The swindler preys upon the credulous.
(8)	economic(경제의)	Korea showed rapid growth and economic expansion.
	economical(경제적인, 절약하는)	An economical way to read more is to borrow books from a library.
(9)	beneficial(유익한)	Drinking green tea can be beneficial to our skin.
	beneficent(인정 많은)	He is very beneficent to the underprivileged.
(10)	healthy(건강한)	The young think they permanently stay healthy.
	healthful(건강에 좋은)	Kimchi is a healthful diet.
(11)	historic(역사상 중요한)	Martin Luther King delivered a historic speech in 1963.
	historical(역사적인)	The story of this movie is based on a historical event.
(12)	imaginable(상상할 수 있는)	He has tried every means imaginable. (형용사 최상급, all, every, no와 함께 강조어로 사용됨)
	imaginative(상상력이 풍부한)	He is an imaginative writer.
	imaginary(공상의)	Dragons are imaginary animals.

(13)	industrial(산업의)	Mutual cooperation enhances their industrial synergy.
	industrious(근면한)	He is an industrious graduate student.
(14)	ingenuous(순진한, 솔직한)	He is an innocent and ingenuous person.
	ingenious(재능 있는)	She is an ingenious playwright.
(15)	respectable(존경할 만한)	He is a respectable young man.
	respectful(정중한, 경의를 표하는)	It was an adequately respectful ceremony to the veterans.
	respective(각자의)	Most people have their own respective goals as New Year's resolutions.
	respected(존경받는, 평판 있는)	Dr. Lee is respected as a scholar.

제 7 장 부사

제 1 절 부사(adverb)의 종류

1 양태부사(manner) : how에 대한 답변

> well, carefully, gladly, loudly, quietly, heartily, quickly 등

예
- Josh speaks Korean very well.
- This letter was carefully written.

2 시간부사(time)

> ago, before, already, then, just, now, still, yet, soon, later, late, early, ever, once, yesterday, today, tomorrow, last year, next year 등

예
- He came here yesterday.
- Josh already studied the subjects.

3 장소부사(place)

> here, there, up, down, above, inside, back, away, far, everywhere 등

예
- Please bring it here at once.
- He looked everywhere for his car key.

4 정도부사(degree)

> very, much, enough, fully, completely, nearly, too, almost 등

예

- This bluebonnet is very beautiful.
- He completely forgot to send Nathan an email.

5 빈도부사(frequency) 중요 ★

(1) 종류

> - always, all the time, usually, often, frequently, sometimes, once
> - hardly/rarely/scarcely/seldom/barely(거의~않다), never 등

예

- Josh always gets up at 6 am.
- Dr. Kim is usually punctual.
- He hardly ever speaks.

(2) 위치

빈도부사는 보통 일반동사 앞, be동사나 조동사의 뒤에 위치한다.

예

- Josh always comes to class early.
- Josh is always punctual.
- Josh has always been punctual.

6 초점부사(focusing)

> just, only, also, primarily, notably, mostly, exclusively 등

예

- They only ate the gimbap at the top of that mountain.
- This room is for employees only(exclusively).

제 2 절 부사의 기능

1 동사 수식

예

- Josh works fast.
- Josh politely asked Amy for an opinion.
- The manager wanted to increase income significantly.

2 형용사 수식

예

- Amy felt really happy.
- Amy had a totally different view.
- This book is absolutely free.

3 부사(구) 수식

예

- Dr. Jensen, thank you very much.
- Josh finished his work extremely quickly.
- This book is available only in North America.
- He did quite well on his final.

4 명사, 대명사 수식

예

- Even the youngest children enjoyed the classical music concert.
- Even a fool can solve this math problem.

5 문장 전체 수식

예

- Surprisingly, no one was seriously injured.
- Maybe he got stuck in the traffic jam.

더 알아두기 Q

1. 형용사와 부사 형태가 같은 표현 중요 ★★

early(이른, 일찍)	low(낮은, 낮게)
fast(빠른, 빨리)	near(가까운, 가까이에)
hard(부지런한/어려운, 열심히/강하게)	pretty(예쁜, 매우/상당히)
high(높은, 높게)	tight(꽉 죄는, 단단히)
late(늦은, 늦게)	well(건강한, 잘/제대로)
last(최후의, 마지막으로)	wide(넓은, 넓게)

예

- The early bird catches the worm. (형용사, 일찍 일어나는)
- He gets up early in the morning. (부사, 일찍)

- He is a very fast speaker. (빠른)
- He answered even faster than the computer. (빠르게)

- He is a very hard worker. (부지런한)
- It is raining hard. (강하게)

- This room has a high ceiling. (높은)
- The bird is flying high. (높게)

- There are many pretty cafes in Seoul. (예쁜)
- The rule of the game is pretty simple. (상당히)

2. 다른 뜻으로 사용되는 두 형태의 부사 표현

(1)	hard(열심히)	He studied very hard last week.
	hardly(거의 ~않다)	There is hardly any time left.
(2)	high(높게)	He jumped very high.
	highly(매우)	His statements were highly logical.
(3)	near(가까이)	She sat near to the window.
	nearly(거의)	Nearly 60 percent of students use laptops.
(4)	late(늦게)	He arrived late for class.
	lately(최근에)	He bought a used car lately.
(5)	pretty(매우, 상당히)	The rule of the game is pretty simple.
	prettily(예쁘게, 적절히)	The rooms are simply but prettily furnished.

제 3 절 형용사 및 부사의 비교변화

1 원급(형용사, 부사) 중요 ★★★

(1) as + 원급 + as

> as + 원급 + as~ : ~만큼 −한(하게)
> not + as(so) + 원급 + as~ : ~만큼 −하지 않은

[예]
- Josh is as tall as Nathan.
- Josh is not so tall as Nathan.

(2) 부정주어 ~ + as(so) + 원급(형용사, 부사) + as~ : ~만큼 −한 것은 없다(최상급 의미)

[예]
- Nothing is so important as love.
- No one in this school is as tall as Nathan.

(3) as A as (A) can be, as A as anything : 더할 나위 없이

[예]
- I am as tired as (tired) can be.
- They are as rich as (rich) can be.

(4) as ~ as possible, as ~ as one can : 가능한 한 ~한/하게

[예]
- Nathan ran as fast as possible. (Nathan ran as fast as he can.)
- Come as early as possible. (Come as early as you can.)

(5) as ~ as any + 명사 : 무엇에도(누구에게도) 못지않게 ~하여(최상급 의미)

> as ~ as ever + 과거동사 : 누구에게도 못지않게 ~ 하여, 더없이 ~하여(최상급 의미)

[예]
- This film is as good as any movie Bong has ever directed.
- He is as great a film director as ever lived in Korea.
- He can communicate as well as he ever could.

(6) as(so) long as ∼ : (조건) ∼하는 한, ∼한다면

예

- As long as the earth remains, day and night will never cease.
- Amy can stay as long as she wants to.
- You can play the piano as long as you like.

(7) 배수/분수 + as ∼ as − : −만큼 ∼한

예

- Nathan ate twice as much as Josh did.
- This building is three times as tall as that one.

(8) not so much A as B : A라기 보다는 차라리 B인

not A so much as B
less A than B
B rather than A
more B than A

예

- It is not so much a phone as a camera.

- Dr. Lee is not so much a professor as a scholar.
  = Dr. Lee is not a professor so much as a scholar.
  = Dr. Lee is less a professor than a scholar.
  = Dr. Lee is a scholar rather than a professor.
  = Dr. Lee is more a scholar than a professor.

(9) the same (+ 명사) as

예

- Nathan has the same laptop computer as Josh does.
- Nathan's laptop computer is the same as Josh's.

2 비교급(the comparative) 중요 ★★★

(1) 비교급 than

① 비교급 강조

> much, (by) far, a lot, a little (bit), even, still 등이 비교급 앞에 쓰여 강조

[예]
- This car is much faster than that one.
- This story is much more interesting than that story.
- Nathan is much taller than Josh.
- He is far older than she is.
- He drives a lot more carefully than he used to.

> **더 알아두기** 🔍
>
> **very는 원급(형용사, 부사) 강조**
> *Nathan is very taller than Josh.
> *This car runs very faster than that one.
> Nathan is very tall.
> Nathan drives very carefully.

② the + 원급 + than : 동일인, 동일물의 서로 다른 성질을 비교하는 경우

[예]
- Josh himself is more intelligent than smart.
- Diamond is more symbolic than beautiful.

(2) the + 비교급

> the를 잘 사용하지 않는 비교급에서 예외적으로 the를 사용하는 경우

① the + 비교급 (+ 주어 + 동사) ~, the + 비교급 (+ 주어 + 동사) ~ : ~할수록, …하다

[예]
- The more we have, the more we want.
- The sooner, the better.

② the + 비교급 of A and B(= of the two)

[예] Nathan is the teller of Nathan and Josh(= of the two).

③ 원인, 이유를 나타내는 부사구, 부사절이 있는 경우

예 Josh studied the harder because his advisor praised him all the time.

(3) 비교 대상 없는 비교급(than이 없는 비교급)

예

- the higher education
- the higher class, the upper class
- the younger generation
- the greater part of
- the lower animal

(4) 열등 비교

예

- Josh is less tall than Nathan.
- Josh is not so tall as Nathan.

3 최상급(the superlative) 중요 ★★★

(1) the + 최상급

① 최상급의 비교 범위 표현은 in + 명사(장소, 단체 단수명사) 또는 of + 명사(장소, 단체 복수 명사)를 사용한다.

예

- City hall is the oldest building in the city.
- City hall is the most beautiful building of all the structures.

② one of the + 최상급 복수 명사

예

- Seoul is one of the largest cities in the world.
- It is one of the most interesting TV shows I have ever seen.

③ 최상급 강조

much, far, by far, far and away, quite, even, the very를 사용한다.

예

- Dr. Lee is by far the university's most valuable scholar.
- His daughter is the very most important being to him.

(2) the가 없는 경우

① **명사 또는 소유격이 사용되는 경우**

예 Reading novels is her greatest pleasure to her.

② **동일인, 동일물의 성질, 상태를 서술하는 경우**

예 She is most comfortable when she is alone.

③ **부사의 최상급 표현**

예 He arrived fastest of all.

(3) 최상급을 이용한 표현

> at (the) best : 아무리 잘 해도
> at (the) least : 적어도, 최소한
> at (the) most : 기껏해야, 고작해야
> at (long) last : 마침내, 드디어
> at one's best : 가장 좋은 상태에서

제 4 절 부사수식어구

1 very/much 중요 ★★

very	원급(형용사, 부사)	the + very + 최상급	현재분사
much	비교급(형용사, 부사)	much + the + 최상급	과거분사

(1) 수식 대상

예

- This is a very interesting story.
- This story is much more interesting than that story.

(2) the + very + 최상급

> much + the + 최상급

[예]
- This is the very interesting story I have ever read.
- This is much the most interesting story I have ever read.

(3) 과거분사가 명사를 수식하는 한정용법으로 사용되는 경우 또는 동사로서의 성격을 잃고 형용사적인 용법으로 사용되는 표현인 tired, pleased, surprised, satisfied, delighted 등은 much 대신 very로 수식

[예]
- She was very tired with a long journey.
- A very distinguished professor presided at the conference.

(4) alike, afraid, fond 등과 같은 서술 형용사는 much로 수식

[예] They are much alike in character.

2 배열순서

(1) 왕래발착 동사와 사용되는 경우 : 장소 + 방법 + 시간부사

> 그 외 동사와 사용되는 경우 : 방법 + 장소 + 시간부사
> (왕래발착 동사 : go, come, leave, arrive, start, depart, meet, return, begin, stop 등)

[예]
- She came to Korea by airplane last week.
- She played the violin beautifully at the concert last night.

(2) 장소, 시간을 나타내는 경우 어순 : 작은 단위 → 큰 단위

[예] Josh met Amy at a coffee shop on Elm street at 2 pm yesterday.

제 8 장 전치사

제1절 전치사구의 기능

전치사(preposition)는 명사, 대명사, 동명사, 명사절 등의 명사 상당어구(nominal) 앞에서 시간, 이유, 장소, 방법을 나타내는 표현을 목적어로 취한다.

1 전치사의 목적어

(1) 명사

[예] Josh came from South Carolina.

(2) 대명사

[예] Don't count on him too much.

(3) 동명사

[예] He answered the question without thinking.

(4) 명사절

[예] She felt regret for what she has done to him.

(5) 동사

[예] He is jogging along the Han river.

(6) 형용사

[예] Will you stay for long?

(7) 부사

[예] It is about five minutes' walk from here.

(8) 전치사구

[예] He appeared from behind the door.

2 전치사구의 기능

전치사구는 문장에서 명사 수식, 2형식 주격 보어, 5형식 목적격 보어와 같은 형용사 기능을 하는 반면에 동사, 형용사, 부사, 문장을 수식하는 부사 기능을 한다.

(1) 형용사 기능

예

- The flowers along the Han river are beautiful.
- Every student except Jeff passed the exam.

(2) 부사 기능

예

- He is jogging along the Han River.
- Every student passed the exam except Jeff.
- Except Jeff, every student passed the exam.

제 2 절 전치사의 종류

1 장소 및 시간 중요 ★

(1) at/on/in

장소 관련 at은 특정한 지점, on은 접촉, in은 장소의 내부를 의미하고, at < on < in으로 갈수록 확장되는 범위의 개념을 나타낸다. 시간 관련 at은 특정한 시점, on은 특정 날짜, in은 월, 연도 등을 의미하고, at < on < in으로 갈수록 확장되는 범위의 개념을 나타낸다.

표현	전치사		예
장소	at	지점 번지	at the station, at the bust stop at Elm Street, at Fifth Avenue
	on	표면 위 일직선 상 지점	on the table, on the 2nd floor on the Han river, on the wall
	in	큰 공간 내 장소	in the room in the town, in the city in the country, in the world

시간	at	시각 시점	at 7 am, at noon/(mid)night at the beginning/end of the month
	on	날짜 요일 특정일	On December 31 On Friday On New Year's Eve
	in	월 연도 계절 세기 ~시간 후에 아침/오후/저녁	in December in 2022 in winter in the 21st century in two days/months in the morning/afternoon/evening
숙어	at		at any rate, at best, at ease, at first, at hand, at home, at all times, at times, at least, at once, at the latest, at high speed, at a good pace, at regular intervals, at the age of, at a charge of, at one's expense, at one's fingertips, at random, at stake
	on		on time, on/upon request, on/upon arrival, on a regular basis, on the recommendation of
	in		in place, in time, in effect, in advance, in particular, in a timely manner

(2) 시점 및 시간

전치사		예
since	~이래로	It has been raining since last night.
from (~to)	~부터	from now on, from 2019 to 2021
until	상황, 상태가 계속될 때까지	The library will be open until 10 pm.
by	행동이 발생할 때까지	You should submit the homework by 10 pm.
before	~전에	Let's leave at 10 am, not before.
prior to		The new product will be out prior to Christmas Day.
after	~후에	He will leave New York the day after tomorrow.
between	~사이에	He will call you between 3:30 and 4:00.
past	~지나서	They met at half past six.
while	~중에(접속사)	While sleeping, he had a strange dream.

(3) 기간

전치사		예
for	~동안(+ 시간 표현)	He stayed in New York for three weeks.
during	~동안(+ 명사)	He called on me during my stay in New York.
over	~동안	Weather has steadily increased over the past five years.
through	~동안, 내내	He worked from Monday through Friday.
throughout		Bears do not sleep all throughout the winter.
within	~이내에	He is planning to mail the letter within three days.

2 위치

전치사		예
above	~위에(수직)	The champion raised the a trophy above his head.
over	~위에	The autumn sky over his head was beautiful.
below	~아래	The country is sinking below sea level.
under	~아래(수직)	There is something under your chair.
beside	~옆에	There is an old town beside the sea.
next to	~옆에(나란히)	Please have a seat next to me.
behind	~뒤쪽에	There is a garden behind the house.
between	~사이에	There is a tea table between the sofa and the desk.
among	~사이에	There is an old house among the trees.
near	~근처에	There is a small village near the capital.
around	~근처에	Let's sit around the fire.
past	~지나서	There is a famous store past the city park.

3 방향

전치사		예
from	~에서, ~로부터	Josh came from South Carolina.
to	~로, ~쪽으로(목적지)	He went from east to west.
across	~을 가로질러	He swam across the channel.
through	~을 통과하여	He passed through a village.
along	~을 따라서	He went along the river.
for	~을 향해	The airplane departed for California.
toward(s)	~쪽으로(방향)	The captain sailed toward the west.
into	~안으로	He walked into the classroom.
out of	~밖으로	He walked out of the subway.

4 이유, 양보, 목적 중요 ★

전치사		예
because of		The train was delayed because of bad weather.
due to	~때문에	The train was delayed due to the fog.
owing to		He failed the exam owing to his lack of study.
on account of		The airport was closed on account of the fog.
despite		Despite the inconvenience, customers visit the new mall.
in spite of	~에도 불구하고	In spite of the changed schedule, he followed his regular schedule.
with all		With all the difficulties, he managed to get his work done.
notwithstanding		Notwithstanding the danger, he finally climbed the mountain.
for	~을 위해서	He takes vitamins for skin problems.

5 제외, 부가

전치사		예
except(for)	~을 제외하고는	Everyone except Josh went to the concert.
apart from		Apart from the cost, the plan was a good one.
aside from		Aside from his salary, he receives his pension every month.
barring	~이 없이	Nobody knows, barring him.
without	~이 없다면	He went out without a coat.
but for	~제외하고는	He would have failed without her help.
instead of	~ 대신에	He takes tea instead of coffee every morning.
in addition to		In addition to the cars, the motor show offered other attractions.
besides	~에 더해서	He can speak German besides English.
apart from		Who else went there apart from you?

6 기타

전치사		예
by	~에 의해, ~함으로써	This game was created by John. Make the sauce by boiling the cream.
through	~에 의해서	They talked each other through interpreters.
throughout	~ 전역에, 전반에	Christmas cheer spreads throughout the country.
with	~와 함께, ~을 가지고	He had a dinner with a friend.
without	~없이	A guest entered the house without knocking.
as	~로서	English is spoken as an official language.
like	~처럼	He drank like a fish last night.
unlike	~와 달리	Unlike Gauguin, Van Gogh's legacy lives on.
against	~에 반대하여	The lawyer showed an evidence against the police.
beyond	~이상으로	The painting was beyond his expectations.
following	~에 이어	Refreshments will be served following the lecture.
plus	~에 더하여	He has wealth plus ability.
amid	~한 가운데	He was standing amid a holiday crowd.

제 **9** 장 접속사

접속사(conjunction)는 단어와 단어, 구와 구, 절과 절, 문장과 문장을 대등한 관계로 연결시키는 **등위 접속사**(coordinating conjunction)와 문장과 문장을 주종 관계로 연결시키는 **종속 접속사**(subordinating conjunction)가 있다.

제 1 절 등위 접속사(coordinating conjunction)

영어에서 등위 접속사는 For, And, Nor, But, Or, Yet, So (FANBOYS), 7개가 있다.

1 for : 왜냐하면, 그 까닭은

예

- It is morning, for the birds are singing.
- He did it for they asked him to do it.

2 and

(1) 단어, 구, 절, 단일 개념을 연결

예

- Amy loves her daughter and son.
- This culture is incorporated with European tradition and American tradition.
- My mother stopped at the mall and my father went to the baseball stadium.

(2) 행동, 상태 동시성

예 I cannot think and talk at the same time.

(3) 시간적 전후 관계

> 예 Josh went to his house and (then) cleaned up his room.

(4) 명령문 + and : ∼해라, 그러면 ∼

> 예
> - Hurry, and you will be in time.
> - Work hard, you will pass the exam.

(5) go, come, try, send 다음 and는 to부정사로 대용 가능

> 예
> - Come and play baseball with me next week.
> - Come to play baseball with me next week.

3 nor : −도 또한 −아니다

예

- Neither you nor anyone else has the right over me.
- He was not present in class, nor was she.
- The day was bright, nor were there clouds above.
- Amy didn't come to work yesterday, nor did she call.

4 but : 대조

예

- We are poor but happy.
- He did not come on Saturday, but on Sunday.
- He is rich, but he is not happy.
- They tried to help us, but they made things worse.

5 or

(1) 양자택일 : 또는, 혹은, 이든지

[예]

- You or I am to blame.
- Will you have tea or coffee?
- You may have a blue one or a green one or a yellow one.

(2) 동격어구 : 즉, 곧

[예]

- That country was called Siam, or Thailand
- The distance is ten miles, or about sixteen kilometers.

(3) 명령문 + or : ~해라, 그렇지 않으면 ~

[예]

- Take a vacation, or you will get sick.
- Make haste, or you will be late for the concert.

6 yet : 그렇지만

[예]

- He was very tired, yet he couldn't sleep.
- The news was spread fast. Yet no one responded to it.

7 so

(1) (그) 결과, 따라서

[예]

- He was excited, so he couldn't get to sleep.
- He passed the exam, so he can attend the university next year.

(2) 목적 so (that) : ~하기 위하여

[예]

- Please check that carefully so (that) you won't miss any mistakes.
- Switch the light off so (that) we can sleep well.

제 2 절 종속 접속사(subordinating conjunction)

종속 접속사는 시간, 이유, 양보, 조건, 결과, 정도, 목적 등을 나타내고 그 관계는 종속절로 표현하여 종속절을 만든다.

1 시간

시간의 부사절에서 현재동사가 미래를 나타내고, 현재완료가 미래를 나타낸다.

> when, while, after, before, since, as, as soon as, until, by the time

[예]

- When she was born, her parents were just twenty five.
- While he cooked dinner while she watched TV.
- He has known her since she was only five.
- You can stay here until he comes back.
- Dinner will be ready by the time you get home.

2 이유

> because, since, as, now that, on the ground that, seeing that, considering that

[예]

- As he had no money, he could not buy a new house.
- He passed the exam since he studied very hard.
- Now that everyone is here, we can start the ceremony.

3 양보

> though, although, even though, even if, as, no matter how

예

- Although he was a man of the world, he was simple and direct.
- Even if everybody knows it, we need to be strategic.
- No matter how hard I study, I feel like I am spinning my wheels.
- Child as he was, he was brave.

4 조건

조건의 부사절에는 현재동사가 미래 의미를, 현재완료 동사가 미래완료를 나타낸다.

> if, unless, as long as, in case

예

- If it is necessary, he can cook dinner tonight.
- Please don't come unless she tells you to.
- As long as the earth remains, day and night will never cease.
- The verb is plural in case the subject is plural.

5 결과, 정도, 목적

> so ~ that, such ~ that, so that ~

예

- It was so dark that he couldn't find the book.
- There was such a crowd that we could hardly move.
- He studied hard so that he could pass the exam(He studied hard in order to pass the exam).

6 명사절

(1) that

① **주어** : That he was in error was beyond doubt.

② **목적어** : He believes that you will get on in the world.

③ **보어** : The key point is that you are still responsible.

④ **동격** : There is no doubt that we were wrong from the start.

(2) whether/if

예

- Whether it rains or not doesn't matter.
- He doesn't know whether she will succeed or not.
- He asked if she knew Korean.

(3) 의문사

예

- When the man died is the beginning of the investigation.
- He wanted to know who correct the answer.
- The question is why this product is so popular.

제 3 절 상관접속사(correlative conjunction) 중요 ★★

두 단어가 짝을 이루어 접속사 역할을 한다.

(1) both A and B(A와 B 모두) : 복수 동사

예

- Both Josh and Amy have a wonderful memory of Australia.
- He likes both to read books and to watch movies.

(2) either A or B(둘 중에 하나) : B에 주어 동사 수일치

neither A nor B(둘 다 아님) : B에 주어 동사 수일치

〔예〕

- Either he or I am in charge of the task.
- Neither he nor I am able to do it right now.

(3) not only (not merely) A but also B(A뿐만 아니라 B도) : B에 주어 동사 수일치

= B̲ as well as A(A뿐만 아니라 B도) : B에 주어 동사 수일치

〔예〕

- Not only you but also Amy is a friend of mine.
  = Amy as well as you is a friend of mine.

- He not only teaches linguistics but also writes poets.
  He is not only diligent but also careful.

- They as well as she feel excited.
- She is intelligent as well as generous.

(4) not A but B̲(A가 아니라 B) : B에 주어 동사 수일치

〔예〕

- Josh is not timid, but careful.
- Not Lori but Amy likes the flower.

(5) such A̲ as B(B와 같은 A) : A에 주어 동사 수일치

〔예〕

- Such inventors as Edison are rare.
- He has never seen such a beautiful woman as you in his life.

(6) whether A or B

〔예〕

- Whether it rains or it snows is not certain.
- He couldn't decided whether to leave or not.

제 4 절 접속부사(conjunctive adverb) 종요 ★

내용상 앞 문장과의 관계를 보여주는 **접속사 역할**을 하지만 문법적으로 부사이다.

1 원인, 결과

therefore, accordingly, consequently, then, hence

예

• The weather was bad. Therefore, they postponed their journey.
• He said he would come; consequently, I waited for him.

2 양보, 대조

however, nonetheless, nevertheless, still

예

• It is raining hard. However, we decided to go out.
• People say about the issue. Nevertheless, it was the truth.

3 부가

moreover, likewise, besides

예

• He was very busy yesterday. Moreover, he couldn't sleep well.
• He doesn't like the idea at all; moreover, it seems illiegal.

4 조건

> otherwise

[예]

• Please do something. Otherwise, nothing is going to happen.
• Search something. Otherwise, it is hard to find a good job.

5 시간

> then

[예]

• He went to his house. Then he cleaned the rooms.
• Nobody was at home. Then suddenly, the telephone rang.

> ⚡ 더 알아두기 🔍
>
> 시간을 표현하는 접속부사 then이 문두에 나오는 경우 then 다음에 쉼표(comma)를 보통 쓰지 않는다. 그 외 시간을 나타내는 짧은 표현인 now, today, tomorrow, soon 등이 문두에 나오는 경우에도 쉼표 생략이 가능하다.

• Then the professor asked the students to close their books.
• Now we are going to have a pop quiz.
• Today the midterm exam begins fifteen minutes late.
• Tomorrow there will be a final exam.

더 알아두기

접속부사 구두점 : 쉼표(comma), 세미콜론(semicolon) 사용법

예

- It is a rainy day. However, she is happy.
- It is a rainy day; however, she is happy.
- It is a rainy day. She, however, is happy.
- It is a rainy day. She is happy, however.

- He couldn't persuade his parents however hard he tried. (접속부사, 양보)
- However hard he tried, he couldn't persuade his parents.
  (= He couldn't persuade his parents no matter how hard he tried.)

- It is a rainy day, but she is happy. (등위접속사)
- It is a rainy day. But she is happy.

제 **2** 편

실전예상문제

01 다음 중 어법상 맞는 표현은?

① His family are all healthy.

② They eat many beef.

③ The police is investigating the case.

④ Linguistics are his favorite subject.

---

02 다음 중 어법상 <u>잘못된</u> 표현은?

① Can you swim in the Han River?

② They are arriving at Boston Harbor.

③ You can contact her by the email.

④ A professor and poet was dead.

---

01 해설

① 의 family는 단수 형태이지만 구성원 전체를 의미하는 경우 복수 취급한다. ② 의 beef는 물질명사이므로 much를, ③ 의 the police는 단수 형태이지만 항상 복수 취급하기 때문에 are, ④ 의 linguistics는 단수 취급하는 학문명이기 때문에 is를 사용해야 한다.

해석

① 그의 가족은 모두 건강하다.
② 그들은 쇠고기를 많이 먹는다.
③ 경찰이 그 사건을 조사 중에 있다.
④ 언어학은 그가 가장 좋아하는 과목이다.

02 해설

통신수단은 관사를 사용하지 않고 by email로 표현한다.
① 강은 정관사 the를 사용한다.
② 항구는 정관사 the를 사용하지 않는다.
④ 동일인인 경우 부정관사를 맨 앞에만 사용한다.

해석

① 당신은 한강에서 수영할 수 있어요?
② 그들이 보스턴 항구에 도착하고 있다.
③ 당신은 그녀에게 이메일로 연락할 수 있습니다.
④ 교수이자 시인인 사람이 죽었다.

정답 01 ① 02 ③

03 다음 중 밑줄 친 부분을 생략할 수 <u>없는</u> 것은?

① The man <u>that</u> she saw last night was Joey.

② The movie <u>which</u> she watched last night was sad.

③ She is the teacher <u>whom</u> I told you about.

④ The book <u>which</u> is on the table is Amy's.

04 다음 중 밑줄 친 표현이 <u>잘못된</u> 것은?

① You have to believe in <u>yourself</u>.

② He wants to see Laurel <u>herself</u>.

③ He is kindness <u>himself</u>.

④ Heaven helps those who help <u>themselves</u>.

해설 & 정답   checkpoint

03 **해설**
④의 주격 관계대명사는 생략할 수 없다.
①·②·③과 같이 목적격 관계대명사의 경우만 생략 가능하다.

해석
① 그녀가 어젯밤에 본 남자는 Joey 였다.
② 그녀가 어젯밤에 본 영화는 슬펐다.
③ 그녀가 내가 너에게 말했던 선생님이다.
④ 테이블 위에 있는 책은 Amy의 것이다.

04 **해설**
추상명사에 대한 재귀대명사는 itself
① 주어 you에 대한 전치사의 목적어로 사용되는 재귀대명사는 yourself
② 목적어를 강조하는 재귀대명사 herself
④ 막연한 사람을 나타내는 표현인 those에 대한 재귀대명사 표현

해석
① 너 자신을 믿어야 해.
② 그는 Laurel을 직접 보고 싶어한다.
③ 그는 친절한 그 자체이다.
④ 하늘은 스스로 돕는 자를 돕는다.

정답   03 ④   04 ③

05 해설

confess는 4형식 동사가 아닌 3형식 동사로 She confessed the fact to him이 맞다(자백하다).

① reach는 타동사이므로 전치사 없이 목적어를 취할 수 있다(도착하다).

② object는 자동사로 to와 함께 사용된다(반대하다).

④ tamper는 자동사로 with와 함께 사용된다(간섭하다).

해석

① 그녀가 타고 있는 기차가 서울에 도착하고 있다.

② 그녀는 그의 제안에 반대했다.

③ 그녀는 그에게 그 사실을 고백했다.

④ 이것은 인간의 뇌를 손상시킬 수 있다.

06 해설

belong은 상태동사로서 진행형을 사용하지 않는다.

① play는 동작동사로서 진행형이 가능하다.

③ taste는 주로 상태동사 표현이지만 여기에서는 맛을 보는 행위를 표현하는 행동동사이다.

④ see는 주로 상태동사 표현이지만 여기에서는 meet의 의미가 있는 행동동사이다.

해석

① 그는 테니스를 치고 있다.

② 그 펜은 그의 것이다.

③ 요리사가 수프를 맛보고 있다.

④ 그는 오늘 오후에 그녀를 만날 예정이다.

정답 05 ③ 06 ②

05 다음 중 동사의 표현이 <u>잘못된</u> 것은?

① The train she is taking is reaching Seoul.

② She objected to his proposal.

③ She confessed him the fact.

④ This might tamper with human brain.

06 다음 중 어법상 <u>잘못된</u> 표현은?

① He is playing tennis.

② The pen is belonging to him.

③ The cook is tasting the soup.

④ He is seeing her this afternoon.

07 다음 중 동사의 표현이 잘못된 것은?

① She will put her trip off.

② They tore the old building down.

③ He ran into an old friend at the airport.

④ He looked the problem into.

07 해설

look into는 분리가 불가능한 구동사이다.

→ He looked into the problem.

① put off는 분리 가능한 구동사이다(연기하다).

② tear down은 분리 가능한 구동사이다(무너뜨리다).

③ run into는 분리가 불가능한 구동사이다(우연히 만난다).

해석

① 그녀는 여행을 연기할 것이다.

② 그들은 그 오래된 건물을 허물었다.

③ 그는 공항에서 옛 친구를 우연히 만났다.

④ 그는 그 문제를 조사했다.

08 다음 중 밑줄 친 부분에 공통으로 들어갈 표현은?

- _____ somebody please help me?
- She _____ take a nap after lunch.
- Amy _____ be tired tomorrow if she worked hard today.
- I _____ like an apple, please.

① will

② would

③ can

④ could

08 해설

첫 번째 would 정중한 요청, 두 번째 would 과거의 습관, 세 번째 would 현재나 미래에 대한 추측, 네 번째 would는 소망(like, want)의 사용이다.

해석

- 누가 좀 도와주시겠어요?
- 그녀는 점심식사 후에 낮잠을 자곤 했다.
- Amy가 오늘 열심히 일한다면 내일 피곤할 것이다.
- 사과 하나 주세요.

정답 07 ④ 08 ②

09 해설

정도의 차이는 있으나 추측을 표현하는 조동사 can, could, may, might, must로 표현한다. ①의 can은 허가, 허락을 표현한다.

해석

① 당신은 시험을 다 끝냈습니다. 이제 가도 됩니다.
② 그는 오늘 결석했다. 아마도 아픈 것 같다.
③ 그는 이미 샌드위치를 두 개 먹었다. 배고픈 것 같다.
④ 날씨가 매우 흐리고 어둡네요. 곧 비가 올 거예요.

10 해설

would rather A than B(B보다는 차라리 A하다)의 표현으로 동사원형이 사용된다.
① need가 본동사로 사용되는 경우 to부정사를 목적어로 취한다.
We don't need to do it now.
② had better + 동사원형 표현(~하는 게 낫다).
④ cannot help —ing(동명사) 표현으로 laughing이 맞다.

해석

① 우리는 지금 그것을 할 필요는 없다.
② 기말시험을 위해서 지금 공부하는 게 좋겠다.
③ 나는 마지막 순간을 불평하기보다는 즐기겠다.
④ 그는 웃지 않을 수 없다.

정답   09 ①   10 ③

---

09 다음 중 밑줄 친 표현의 쓰임이 <u>다른</u> 것은?

① You finished the exam. You <u>can</u> leave now.

② He was absent today. He <u>may</u> be sick today.

③ He already ate two sandwiches. He <u>could</u> be hungry.

④ It is very cloudy and dark. It <u>must</u> rain soon.

10 다음 중 어법상 맞는 표현은?

① We don't need do it now.

② You had better to study now for your final exam.

③ I would rather spend my last minutes playing than complaining.

④ He cannot help to laugh.

제 **3** 편

—

시제와 상

단원 개요

영어의 시제와 상은 일반적으로 12개로 분류된다. **시제**는 **현재, 과거, 미래**, **상**은 **단순, 진행, 완료, 완료진행형**이 있다. **시간**(time)은 현재, 과거, 미래가 있는 반면에 문법에서 동사를 통해 이 시간 개념을 표현하는 것이 반드시 일치하는 것은 아니다. **시제**(tense)는 동사의 어형 변화를 통해 시간을 나타내는 문법적인 수단으로서 (형태소적인 측면에서) 영어에는 현재(-(e)s)와 과거(-(e)d), 두 시제만 존재하고 미래어미는 존재하지 않아 will/be going to를 사용한다. **상**(aspect)은 동사의 행동이 이루어지는 방법이며 영어에서는 '진행(progressive)'과 '완료(perfective)'를 나타내며 시제와 결합하여 여러 복합동사구를 표현한다. 규칙과 불규칙 형태 동사에 따른 시제와 상의 형태소에 따른 결합과 사용을 구별할 필요가 있다.

시제 \ 상		단순 (simple)	진행 (progressive)	완료 (perfect)	완료진행 (perfect progressive)
표현 (형태소)	현재	V(∅)/V-(e)s	be + <u>V-ing</u>	have + *V*-en	have + <u>be</u>-en + <u>V-ing</u>
	과거	V-(e)d			
현재 (present)	규칙	walk/walks	am/are/is walking	have/has walked	have/has been walking
	불규칙	write/writes	am/are/is writing	have/has written	have/has been writing
과거 (past)	규칙	walked	was/were walking	had walked	had been walking
	불규칙	wrote	was/were writing	had written	had been writing
미래 (future)	규칙	will walk	will be walking	will have walked	will have been walking
	불규칙	will write	will be writing	will have written	will have been writing

또한 시제와 관련하여 가정법은 가정법 과거, 가정법 과거완료, 혼합 가정법, 가정법 미래, but for/without, I wish, as if 가정법 등이 있다.

출제 경향 및 수험 대책

1. 시제
   (1) 현재, 과거, 미래 시제 용법과 의미
   (2) 시제와 함께 쓰이는 (시간) 부사 표현
2. 상
   (1) 현재 진행, 완료, 완료진행 용법과 의미, 시제 표현
   (2) 과거 진행, 완료, 완료진행 용법과 의미, 시제 표현
   (3) 미래 진행, 완료 용법과 의미, 시제 표현
   (4) by the time 표현

3. 가정법
   (1) 가정법 과거, 과거완료, 혼합가정법 형태 및 의미
   (2) but for/without, I wish, as if 가정법 형태 및 의미

합격의 공식 SD에듀

잠깐!

자격증 · 공무원 · 금융/보험 · 면허증 · 언어/외국어 · 검정고시/독학사 · 기업체/취업
이 시대의 모든 합격! SD에듀에서 합격하세요!
www.youtube.com → SD에듀 → 구독
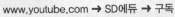

제 1 장 시제

제 1 절 현재시제

1 현재의 상태, 습관, 반복적 행위나 상태

예

- She lives in Burbank, California.
- She wakes up at 6 am everyday.
- She teaches English at a university.

2 불변의 사실, 진리, 속담

예

- The earth moves around the sun.
- Water consists of hydrogen and oxygen.
- Slow and steady wins the race.

3 미래시제 대용

(1) 왕래발착 동사, 시작·종료 동사 중요 ★

go, come, start, depart, leave, arrive, return 등의 왕래발착 동사와, open, begin, close, end, finish 등과 같이 시작과 종료를 나타내는 동사는 부사(구) 표현과 함께 미래를 의미한다.

예

- She comes to Seoul next month.
- The plane starts for Seattle tomorrow morning.
- Spring semester begins next week.

(2) 시간, 조건 부사절에서 미래시제 대용 [중요] ★★

when, before, after, until, as soon as, by the time, once, if, as long as 등과 같이 시간과 조건을 표현하는 (종속)접속사가 부사절을 만드는 경우 미래를 의미한다.

[예]

- When she finishes her work, she will learn Python.
- She will stay at home if it rains tomorrow.

> **더 알아두기**
>
> when과 if절이 형용사절 또는 명사절로 사용되면 미래시제 사용이 가능하다.
>
> - 형용사절 : The day will come when you will be most thankful for her support.
> - 명사절 : She doesn't know if it will rain tomorrow.

4 역사적 현재 : 역사적인 인물이나 문헌에 있는 말을 인용하는 경우

[예]

- Caesar crosses the Rubicon, and enters Italy.
  ([해석] 시저(카이사르)가 루비콘강을 건너 이탈리아로 들어간다.)
- Pascal says, "Man is a thinking reed." ([해석] 파스칼은 "인간은 생각하는 갈대이다."라고 말한다.)

제 2 절 과거시제

1 과거 특정 시점의 동작, 상태

[예]

- She lived in Seoul in 2002.
- It rained last night.
- She was a professor.

2 과거의 습관, 반복적 동작 중요 ★

〔예〕

- She sometimes went fishing.
- She often met her teacher during the vacation.

> **❗ 더 알아두기 ◯**
>
> 과거의 습관을 나타내는 표현으로 used to (+ 동사원형), would도 있다.
>
> - He used to live in Chicago. (Now he lives in Seoul.)
> - He would come here to his advisor during the vacation.

3 역사적 사실

〔예〕

- The World War II ended in 1945.
- The Korean War broke out in 1950.

4 과거 경험에 never, ever를 사용하는 경우

〔예〕

- Josh never visited Africa before.
- Did you ever hear anything like this?

5 과거완료(대과거, pluperfect) 대용 중요 ★

〔예〕

- Josh (had) finished his homework before Amy came in.
  (1st, finished → 2nd, came)
  (Amy가 도착하기 전에 Josh는 숙제를 끝냄)

• Josh and Amy went out to dinner after Josh (had) finished his homework.

(1st, finished → 2nd, went out)

(Josh가 숙제를 끝낸 후에 Josh와 Amy는 외식하러 나감)

더 알아두기 🔍

과거시제와 함께 쓰이는 표현 중요 ★

1. 명백한 과거시제 부사구 : 과거 연도, 월, 일

예

- He went to England in 2012.
- He was born on Tuesday, June 4, 2002.
- He studied English yesterday.

2. last, ago

예

- He came to Seoul last week.
- This picture was taken last month.
- The bridge was built three years ago.

3. 의문사 when, what time

예

- *When have you been to Africa?
  When did you go to Africa?

- *At what time have you arrived in Seoul?
  At what time did you arrive in Seoul?

제 3 절 미래시제

1 단순미래 : 미래에 대한 예측

예

- She will be thirty next year.
- He will come here on time.

2 의지미래

(1) 주어

예

- He will do it right now.
- She won't listen to my words.

(2) 화자

예

- I will do it.
- I will go there now.

(3) 청자

예

- Will you go there?
- Shall he go there? (Will you let him go there?)

3 will/be going to

will과 be going to 모두 미래를 표현하는 데 쓰이지만, will은 의지, 약속을 표현하는 반면에 be going to는 사전에 결정해 놓은 계획을 표현하는 데 쓰인다.

예

- Nathan will finish his work tomorrow.
  Nathan is going to finish his work tomorrow.

- The phone is ringing. I will get it.
- She won't tell him about her age.
- The engine won't start.

- Q : Why did he buy the paint?
  A : He is going to paint his house tomorrow.

- They will get married.
- They are going to get married next month.
  (= They are getting married next month.)

4 미래 의미 표현(~할 예정이다) 중요 ★★★

(1) be about to + 동사원형(막 ~하려고 하다)

예
- He is about to leave the office.
- He is about to face difficulties.

(2) be due to + 동사원형

예
- He is due to graduate in February.
- He is due to return home in two years.

(3) be expected to + 동사원형(~할 것으로 기대된다)

예
- He is expected to be here in an hour.
- The package is expected to arrive at 5 pm.

(4) be planned to + 동사원형

예
- The new building is planned to be constructed on March.
- The concert is planned to be held outdoor next month.

(5) be scheduled to + 동사원형

예
- He is scheduled to see a doctor next Monday.
- The new musical is scheduled to be released this Friday.

(6) be supposed to + 동사원형

예
- He is supposed to drop by the office today afternoon.
- He is supposed to take over her jobs.

(7) be to + 동사원형

예
- They are to go out for dinner.
- He is to visit Korea next month.

제 2 장 상

제 1 절 현재시제 + 진행상

현재 진행형은 am/are/is + V-ing 형태이다.

1 현재 진행 중인 동작

예

- It is raining now.
- The birds are singing beautifully.
- She is listening to the lectures.

2 현재의 반복적 동작, 습관, 버릇 중요 ★

always, continually, constantly 등의 부사와 함께 사용되어 반복적인 동작이나 습관을 나타낸다.

예

- She is always losing her car keys.
- He is always complaining about the service.

3 가까운 미래

예

- Josh is coming to Korea next week.
- Nathan is leaving Korea tomorrow morning.
- Josh is playing tennis with Nathan tomorrow.

❗ 더 알아두기 🔍

진행형을 사용할 수 없는 상태 동사 표현 중요 ★★

1. 감각(see, smell, hear, taste, feel)

   예
   - This spaghetti tastes delicious.
     *This spaghetti is tasting delicious.
   ※ The cook is tasting the spaghetti. ([어휘] taste : '맛을 보다'는 행동동사)

2. 감정(love, like, hate, dislike)

   예
   - He loves her.
   - *He is liking her.

3. 소유(have, own, possess, belong)

   예

He has a sports car.	This sports car belongs to him.
*He is having a sports car.	*This sports car is belonging to him.
※ He is having lunch. (eat)	
He is having a great time in California. (enjoy, undergo, experience, ⋯)	

4. 존재(be, exist), 상태(look, appear, seem, lack, resemble)

   예
   - She resembles her mother. (resemble, 3형식 타동사)
     *She resembles with her mother.
     *She is resembling her mother.
     *She is resembled by her mother.

5. 인식(know, believe, understand)

   예
   - He knows the secrets of her success in business.
     *He is knowing the secrets of her success in business.

제 2 절 현재시제 + 완료상 중요 ★★

현재완료형 형태는 have/has + 과거분사(-en, past participle p.p.)이고 과거의 불특정한 시점에 이미 끝난 동작이나 상태, 과거에 끝난 일이지만 현재와 관련된 동작이나 상태, 과거부터 현재까지 반복되는 일, 과거에 시작하여 현재까지 계속되는 동작이나 상태를 표현한다.

1 완료

> already, just, yet, by the time 등과 함께 쓰임

예

- The exam has just finished.
- He has already completed his duties.

2 경험

> ever, once, before, seldom, never 등과 함께 쓰임

예

- Have you ever been to Los Angeles?
- He has never been to America.

3 결과

예

- He has left his cell phone in the office. (So he doesn't have it now.)
- He has now returned to the USA.

> 🔔 더 알아두기 🔍
>
> - have been to (경험) vs have gone to (결과)
> - He has been to Africa. (Africa를 방문한 경험이 있다.)
> - He has gone to Africa. (Africa로 떠났다.)

4 계속

(1) 동작

현재완료진행형, *have/has* be-en V-ing

예

- He has been teaching linguistics for forty years.
- He has been learning computer science for ten years.

(2) 상태

상태 동사는 진행형을 사용하지 않기 때문에 현재완료형 사용, *have/has* + -en (p.p.)

예

- *He has been knowing her for thirty years since she was a freshman.

  He has known her for thirty years since she was a freshman.

⚠ 더 알아두기 🔍

완료형과 함께 쓰이는 표현 중요 ★★

1. so far, thus far, until now, up to now, up to present, by 시간, …

   예
   - He has not had any car accident so far.
   - Until now, only some parts of the book has been published.
   - They will have been married for twenty five years by the end of the next year.

2. since, for
   완료형과 함께 쓰이는 since는 '과거의 특정 시점'을 표현하는 반면에 for는 '기간'을 표현한다.

   예
   - He has lived in Seoul since 2000.
   - It has been twenty years since they met.

   - He has lived in Seoul for twenty years.
   - It has rained for five days.

3. lately, of late, in recent years, recently, …

   예
   - He has been to Africa lately.
   - His new book of poetry has recently been published.
   - He has not met her in recent years.

---

4. already, yet, just, now, at last, finally, …

예

- He has already completed his duties.
- He has just finished the test.
- He has now discovered why.

※ just now (at this moment)는 현재, 과거시제형과 사용

예

- He is just now starting to study it.
- He was here just now. (방금 전에)

5. always, often, occasionally, ever, never, before, twice, …

예

- Have you ever been to Africa?
- He has been to Africa twice.
- He has never been to Iceland before.

6. during, over, in

예

- What islands have you visited during this visit?
- The comedian has gained in popularity over recent years.
- He has not watched TV in years.

제 3 절 기타 시상

1 과거시제 + 진행상

과거진행형은 was/were + V-ing 형태이다.

(1) 과거 시점의 진행 중인 동작

예

- He was drinking coffee.
- Josh was studying linguistics when Amy came home.
- Josh and Amy were playing tennis together.

(2) 과거의 반복적 동작, 습관, 버릇

> 예
>
> • He was always speaking ill of others.
> • He was always forgetting other's names.

더 알아두기

과거진행형 vs 과거 시제의 사건(event) 순서 중요 ★

① 주절 과거진행형 vs 부사절 (단순)과거시제

> 예
>
> • Amy was standing under a tree when it began to rain.
> (1st event, standing → 2nd event, began to rain)
> (나무 아래에서 쉬고 있는데 비가 내리기 시작하는 경우)

② 주절 (단순)과거시제 vs 부사절 (단순)과거시제

> 예
>
> • Amy stood under a tree when it began to rain.
> (1st event, began to rain → 2nd event, stood)
> (비가 내리기 시작해서 나무 아래로 피한 경우)

---

2 과거시제 + 완료상 중요 ★★

과거완료형 형태는 had + 과거분사(-en, past participle p.p.)이고 과거(기준)보다 더 이전에 시작된 일이 과거 특정 시점까지 영향을 미치는 경우와 과거(기준)에 발생한 일과 그보다 먼저 발생한 일, 즉 대과거(pluperfect)를 구분할 때 과거완료로 표현한다.

(1) 완료

> 예
>
> • The exam had already finished when he arrived at the classroom.
> • He had already completed his duties before his manager came to work.

(2) 경험

> 예
>
> • No one had ever heard the plans before.
> • They had never thought about starting up a business.

(3) 결과

[예] When he came home, he realized that he had left his cell phone in the office.

(4) 계속

① 동작

과거완료진행형, *had* <u>be</u>-en <u>V-ing</u>

[예]

- He had been waiting for two hours when she came back.
- He had been living in Seoul for twenty years when he got married.

② 상태

상태 동사는 진행형을 사용하지 않기 때문에 과거완료형, *had* + *-en* (p.p.)

[예]

- He had known her for thirty years since he was a freshman at Berkeley.
- He had owned that laptop for ten years when he bought a new one.

3 미래 시제 + 진행형 : 미래진행형

미래진행형은 will/shall + be + V-ing 형태이고 미래시점의 진행 중인 동작을 표현한다.

[예]

- He will be drinking coffee when he goes to work.
- Josh will be studying linguistics when he goes to graduate school.
- It will be raining when you go out.

4 미래 시제 + 완료형 : 미래완료형 중요 ★★

미래완료형 형태는 will have + 과거분사(-en, past participle p.p.)이고 미래의 특정 시점까지의 동작이나 상태를 표현하는데 주로 until, before, by, by the time 등과 함께 쓰인다.

[예]

- Josh will have finished his homework by the time Amy come home.
- The subway will have left by noon.
- She will have been in hospital for one year by next Monday.
- Dinner will have been ready when she gets home.
- Dr. Lee will have known him for thirty years by next year.

⚡ 더 알아두기 🔍

주절 시제 표현 중요 ★

by the time : ~할 때까지, ~할 즈음에
by the time + 단순과거 (주어 + 동사), 주절 과거완료 (had p.p.)
by the time + 단순현재 (주어 + 동사), 주절 미래완료 (will have p.p.)

예
- By the time he was 7, he had written five symphonies.
- By the time he finishes writing this book, he will have written over 300 pages.

그러나 위의 공식처럼 반드시 주절의 시제가 고정되어 있는 것은 아니다.

(1) by the time + 단순과거, 주절 단순과거

　예
- By the time he died, he held over 700 patents.
- By the time the fire was brought under control, the entire warehouse was destroyed.

(2) by the time + 단순현재, 주절 단순현재

　예
- "In the business, by the time you realize you're in trouble, it's too late to save yourself. Unless you're running scared all the time, you're gone." - Bill Gates -
- "By the time we see that climate change is really bad, your ability to fix it is extremely limited ····. The carbon gets up there, but the heating effect is delayed." - Bill Gates -

(3) by the time + 단순현재, 주절 현재완료

　예 "By the time a man asks you for advice, he has general made up his mind what he wants to do, and it looking for a confirmation rather than counseling." - Sydney J. Harris -

(4) by the time + 단순현재, 주절 단순미래

　예 "You can't just ask customers what they want and then try to give that to them. By the time you get it built, they'll want something new." - Steve Jobs -

제 3 장 가정법

영어에서 말하는 법(mood)은 화자의 태도 및 마음의 상태에 따라서 3가지 표현방식이 있는데, 있는 사실을 그대로 말하는 직설법(indicative), 명령조로 말하는 명령법(imperative), 사실이 아니거나 존재하지 않는 것을 말하는 가정법(subjunctive)이 있다.

> • 직설법 : I am hungry.
> • 명령법 : Give me something to eat.
> • 가정법 : If I had enough money, I would go to a gourmet restaurant.

이 중 if와 관련하여 조건-결과를 나타내는 표현은 직설법 형태이다.

1. if 부사절 단순현재, 주절 단순현재 (~하면 ~이다) (zero conditional)

예

• If you touch the button, it sounds alarm.
• If it is necessary, I can cook dinner tonight.

2. if 부사절 단순현재, 주절 단순미래 (~하면 ~일 것이다) (first conditional)

예

• If it rains tomorrow, he will not(won't) go to the mountain.
• If you go out, will you buy her coffee?

※ 조건의 부사절에는 미래 의미는 현재시제, 미래완료 의미는 현재완료로 표현할 수 있다.

또한 if와 관련한 가정법은 실제 일어나지 않았던 또는 않은 일에 대한 가정, 소망을 표현하는데 그 가정의 시제에 따라 가정법, 과거, 과거완료, 혼합가정법, 미래 등이 있다.

제 1 절 가정법 과거(second conditional) 중요 ★★

'현재' 사실과 다른 일, 실현 가능성이 희박한 일, 미래에 대한 가정을 표현할 때 쓴다.

if절	주절
if + 주어 + 동사의 과거형 (be동사는 were)	주어 + would + 동사원형 should could might

예

- If she loved him, he would marry her.
- If he knew her phone number, he would call her.
- If he bought the sports car tomorrow, he would regret it.
- If he were a bird, he would fly to her.
- If he were rich, he could study abroad.

제 2 절 가정법 과거완료(third conditional) 중요 ★★

'과거' 사실과 다른 일, 실현 가능성이 희박한 일에 대한 가정을 표현할 때 쓴다.

if절	주절
if + 주어 + had -en(p.p.)	주어 + would + have + -en(p.p.) should could might

예

- If he had been her, he should have bought the used car.
- If he had studied harder, he would have passed the bar exam.
- If he had run all the way, he would have gotten there in time.
- If he had not helped her, she would have failed the test.
- If he had taken a taxi, he would not have missed the flight.

제 3 절 혼합가정법 중요 ★★★

if절과 주절에 가정법 과거와 가정법 과거완료 형태가 혼합되어 있는 가정법이다.

1. if절 : 가정법 과거(현재 가정)	주절 : 가정법 과거완료(과거 아쉬움)
if + 주어 + 동사의 과거형 (be동사는 were)	주어 + would + have + -en(p.p.) should could might

예

- If she knew him well, she would not have replied like that.
- If he were her, he would have bought a sports car.

2. if절 : 가정법 과거완료(과거 가정)	주절 : 가정법 과거(현재 아쉬움)
if + 주어 + had -en(p.p.)	주어 + would + 동사원형 should could might

예

- If he had taken her advice then, he would be happier now.
- If he had submitted the application form, he would be working there now.

제 4 절 가정법 미래

가능성이 희박한 '미래'를 가정한다.

if절	주절
if + 주어 + should + 동사의 과거형 were to would	주어 + will + 동사원형 can may would could should …

예

- If he were to be born again, he could marry her.
- If the sun were to move around the earth, he would marry her.

- If it should snow tomorrow, he will stay home all day long.

• If he should be a famous singer, she would be the most famous actor.

• If he would succeed, he would have to work hard.
• If he would cook well, he could be the main chef in the restaurant.

※ 미래에 실현 가능성의 희박한 정도는 were to > would > should의 경향이 있다.

제 5 절 if 생략 중요 ★★★

if를 생략하면서 be동사나 조동사를 도치시켜 표현한다.

1 가정법 과거

예

• If he were rich, he could study abroad.
  → Were he rich, he could study abroad.

• If she were as tall as him, she would be a volleyball player.
  → Were she as tall as him, she would be a volleyball player.

2 가정법 과거완료

예

• If he had been her, he should have bought the used car.
  → Had he been her, he should have bought the used car.

• If he had studied harder, he would have passed the bar exam.
  → Had he studied harder, he would have passed the bar exam.

제 6 절   그 외 가정법 표현

1 but for/without 가정법 중요 ★★★

but for, without이 가정법 과거(if it were not for, 만일 ~이 없다면), 가정법 과거완료(if it had not been for, 만일 ~이 없었더라면)를 대신해 사용되는데, 주절의 시제를 통해 가정법 과거, 가정법 과거완료를 판단한다.

예

- But for/Without cars, we would not travel a long distance.
  (= If it were not for cars, ~)
  (= Were it not for cars, ~)

- But for/Without the heat of the sun, nothing in the world could live.
  (= If it were not for the heat of the sun, ~)
  (= Were it not for the heat of the sun, ~)

- But for/Without his dedication, none of our goals would have been achieved.
  (= If it had not been for his dedication, ~)
  (= Had not been for his dedication, ~)

- But for/Without her timely advice, he would have failed.
  (= If it had not been for her timely advice, ~)
  (= Had not been for her timely advice, ~)

2 I wish 가정법

(1) I wish + 주어 + 과거동사

가정법 과거(현재 사실과 다른 소망)

예

- I wish I were a bird.
- I wish I lived in the country.

(2) I wish + 주어 + had + -en(p.p.)

> 가정법 과거완료(과거 사실과 다른 소망)

[예]
- I wish I had learned Spanish.
- I wish I had proposed her at that time.

(3) I wish + 주어 + 조동사 과거 + 동사원형

> 현재 사실과 다른 소망

[예]
- I wish I could see her everyday.
- I wish she could go to the party.

(4) I wish + 주어 + 조동사 과거 + have + -en(p.p.)

> 과거 사실과 다른 소망

[예]
- I wish I would have studied harder.
- I wish I would have helped the underprivileged.

3 as if 가정법 중요 ★★

(1) as if + 주어 + 과거동사 : 가정법 과거(현재 사실과 다른 가정)

as if절에 가정법 과거가 오면 주절의 시제가 현재이든 과거이든 주절의 시제와 같은 시제를 표현한다.

[예]
- She talks as if she knew everything. (= In fact, she doesn't know everything.)
- She talked as if she knew everything. (= In fact, she didn't knew everything.)

(2) as if + 주어 + had + −en(p.p.) : 가정법 과거완료(과거 사실과 다른 가정)

as if절에 가정법 과거완료가 오면 주절의 시제가 현재이든 과거이든 주절의 시제보다 한 시제 앞선 시제를 표현한다.

예

- She looks as if she had seen an angel. (= In fact, she didn't see an angel.)
- She looked as if she had seen an angel. (= In fact, she had not seen an angel.)

4 It is (hight) time (that) + 주어 + 과거동사

가정법 과거(~해야 할 시간이다)

예

- It is time you went to bed.
  (= It is time you should go to bed.)
  (vs It is time for you to go to bed. 'It is time 의미상의 주어 + to부정사')

- It is time we went home. It is almost midnight.
  (= It is time we should go home.)

제 3 편 실전예상문제

checkpoint 해설 & 정답

01 **해설**

(일반적인, 불변의) 사실이므로 → Water consists of hydrogen and oxygen.가 되어야 한다.
① 역사적인 인물이나 문헌의 말을 인용하는 경우(역사적 현재), ③ 현재의 상태, ④ 왕래발착 동사의 미래시제 대용으로 모두 현재시제로 표현한다.

해석

① 파스칼은 "인간은 생각하는 갈대"라고 말한다.
② 물은 수소와 산소로 이루어져 있다.
③ 그는 캘리포니아 버뱅크에 살고 있다.
④ 그는 다음 주에 샌프란시스코에 온다.

02 **해설**

조건의 부사절에서는 현재시제가 미래시제 대용, if it rains tomorrow.
① 왕래발착동사 현재시제는 미래시제 대용
③ 진행상을 통해 가까운 미래를 표현한다.
④ 타동사 know의 목적어 역할을 하는 if-명사절에서는 미래시제 will의 사용이 가능하다.

해석

① 비행기는 내일 아침 시애틀로 출발한다.
② 만약 내일 비가 온다면 그는 집에 있을 것이다.
③ 그는 다음 주에 한국을 떠난다.
④ 그는 내일 비가 올지 안 올지 모른다.

정답 01 ② 02 ②

---

01 다음 중 어법상 <u>잘못된</u> 표현은?

① Pascal says, "Man is a thinking reed."
② Water is consisting of hydrogen and oxygen.
③ He lives in Burbank, California.
④ He comes to San Francisco next week.

02 다음 중 어법상 <u>잘못된</u> 표현은?

① The plane departs for Seattle tomorrow morning.
② He will stay at home if it will rain tomorrow.
③ He is leaving Korea next week.
④ He doesn't know if it will rains tomorrow.

03 다음 중 어법상 잘못된 표현은?

① He left before she arrived here.

② Did you ever see an orca?

③ It rained a lot last night.

④ The World War II ended in 1945.

04 다음 중 밑줄 친 부분에 들어갈 수 없는 표현은?

> • The new skyscraper is _____ be constructed next year.
>
> • They are _____ perform in England over the next three days.
>
> • The movie is _____ be released next month.

① scheduled to

② expected to

③ planned to

④ destined to

해설 & 정답   checkpoint

03 해설

① 과거완료(대과거) had left 대신, ② ever, never와 과거경험 표현, ③ 과거시제표현 last night, ④ 역사적 사실은 과거시제를 사용한다.

해석

① 그는 그녀가 여기 도착하기 전에 떠났다.

② 범고래를 본 적이 있어?

③ 어젯밤에 비가 많이 왔다.

④ 제2차 세계대전은 1945년에 끝났다.

어휘

• orca, killer whale : 범고래

04 해설

① be scheduled to, ② be expected to, ③ be planned to는 be about to, be due to, be supposed to, be to 표현과 같이 미래(~할 예정이다) 의미 표현인 반면에 ④ be destined to는 '~할 운명/숙명이다'의 표현이다.

해석

• 새로운 고층 건물이 내년에 건설된 예정이다.

• 그들은 다음 3일 동안 영국에서 공연할 예정이다.

• 그 영화는 다음 달에 개봉될 예정이다.

정답   03 ②   04 ④

checkpoint **해설 & 정답**

05 해설
① belong, ③ resemble(3형식 타동사이기 때문에 with 불필요), ④ taste 상태 동사로서 진행형 불가, ② own, possess의 의미 have는 상태 동사여서 진행형이 불가하지만, eat, enjoy, go through, undergo, experience 의미의 have는 진행형이 가능하다.

해석
① 이 스포츠카는 Lori 것이다.
② 김씨 부부는 아이슬란드에서 여름휴가를 보내고 있다.
③ 그녀는 어머니를 닮았다.
④ 그 스파게티는 맛이 좋다.

06 해설
① over와 ② so far는 현재완료와 함께 쓰이는 표현 ③ since + 과거(시점)는 현재완료와 함께 쓰이는 표현이지만, 여기서는 접속사 이유(because) 의미로 사용되어 현재완료와 함께 쓰이지 않아도 된다. ④ just now 표현은 과거시제와 함께 사용(He was here just now), just, now가 현재완료와 함께 쓰임

해석
① 그 배우는 최근 몇 년 동안 인기를 얻었다.
② 정부는 지금까지 총 5건의 명단을 발표했다.
③ 지금은 별로 바쁘지 않아서 사무실을 빠져나갈 수 있다.
④ 그는 방금 여기에 왔다.

정답 05② 06④

05 다음 중 어법상 맞는 표현은?

① This sports car is belonging to Lori.
② The Kims are having a summer vacation in Iceland.
③ She is resembling with her mother.
④ The spaghetti is tasting delicious.

06 다음 중 어법상 잘못된 표현은?

① The actor has gained in popularity over recent years.
② The ministry has issued five lists in total so far.
③ I can get away from the office since we're not very busy now.
④ He has been here just now.

07 다음 중 동사의 시제가 <u>잘못된</u> 것은?

① He is playing tennis with her tomorrow afternoon.

② He was always complaining the service at the Mall.

③ He is knowing the secrets of her successful film making.

④ He will be driving when he goes to work.

08 다음 중 밑줄 친 부분에 공통으로 들어갈 표현은?

> • Online shopping _____ increasingly popular since the invention of the internet.
>
> • The economy _____ by more than 50% a year for six consecutive years.
>
> • The amount of information in the world _____ a lot in the past 20 years.

① grows

② had grown

③ is growing

④ has grown

07 해설

① 가까운 미래를 나타내는 현재진행형, ② 과거의 반복적인 동작, 습관, 버릇 등을 표현하는 과거진행형, ③ 인식을 나타내는 상태 동사 know는 진행형 불가, ④ 미래시점의 진행 중인 동작을 표현하는 미래진행형

해석

① 그는 내일 오후에 그녀와 테니스를 칠 것이다.
② 그는 항상 쇼핑몰에서 서비스를 불평했다.
③ 그는 그녀의 성공적인 영화 제작 비결을 알고 있다.
④ 그는 출근할 때 운전을 하고 있을 거예요.

08 해설

since (+ 과거 시점), for (+ 기간), in the past 20 years 표현은 완료형과 함께 쓰이는 표현이다. ③의 현재 진행형보다는 현재완료 진행형인 has been growing이 더 잘 어울린다.

해석

• 온라인 쇼핑은 인터넷의 발명 이후 점점 더 인기를 얻고 있다.
• 경제는 6년 연속 매년 50% 이상 성장했다.
• 지난 20년 동안 세계 정보의 양이 많이 증가했다.

정답　07 ③　08 ④

안심Touch

09 해설

when 부사절보다 선행하는 주절의 사건, 주절의 시간보다 선행하는 what 목적절의 사건, 'by the time + 과거시제, 주절 과거완료' 구문에서 선행사건을 표현하는 과거완료형이 적절하다.

해석

• 1791년 그가 죽었을 때, 모차르트는 600곡 이상의 작품을 썼다.
• 그는 자신이 쓴 글을 수정하고 개선하려고 온종일 애썼다.
• 그가 죽었을 때, 그는 거의 30권의 책과 250개의 잡지 기사를 집필했다.

09 다음 중 밑줄 친 부분에 공통으로 들어갈 표현은?

> • When he died in 1791, Mozart _____ more than 600 pieces.
> • He spent a whole day trying to revise and improve what he _____.
> • By the time of his death, he _____ nearly 30 books and 250 magazine articles.

① writes
② has written
③ had written
④ was writing

10 해설

미래 특정 시점을 표현하는 (by) next year은 미래완료형과 함께 쓰이고, 'by the time + 현재시제, 주절 미래완료' 구문에서 주절에 미래완료형이 쓰인다. 첫 번째 문장 be동사, 두·세 번째 문장은 수동태 be + p.p.의 형태로 spent, discovered와 함께 사용된 표현이다.

해석

• 다음 주 금요일이면 그는 여기에 10년 동안 있게 된다.
• 내년까지, 탄소 배출의 사용과 기후 변화 사이의 관계에 대한 연구에 5천만 달러가 사용될 것이다.
• 컴퓨터가 그러한 단계에 도달할 때쯤, 현재의 기술로는 실용적이지 않은 새로운 응용 프로그램들이 발견될 것이다.

10 다음 중 밑줄 친 부분에 공통으로 들어갈 표현은?

> • Next Friday he _____ here for ten years.
> • By next year, $50 million _____ spent on the research of the relationship between the use of carbon emission and climate change.
> • By the time computers reach such a stage, it is likely that new applications _____ discovered which are impractical with current technology.

① will be
② will have
③ will have been
④ has been

정답 09 ③ 10 ③

11 다음 중 밑줄 친 부분에 들어갈 표현은?

> _____ rich, I would travel around the world within three years.

① If I am
② If were I
③ Had Been I
④ Were I

11 해설
주절이 would + 동사원형의 형태로 보아 가정법 과거이고, if절의 be동사의 형태는 were를 쓰는데 이 문장에서는 if가 생략된 후 be동사가 도치된 형태이다.

해석
내가 부자라면 3년 안에 세계 여행을 할 텐데.

12 다음 중 밑줄 친 부분에 들어갈 표현은?

> _____ enough money, he could have bought a new car.

① Had he
② If had he saved
③ Had he saved
④ If he saved

12 해설
주절이 could + have + bought의 형태로 보아 가정법 과거완료이고, if절이 if he had saved enough money인데 이 문장에서는 if가 생략된 후 조동사 had가 도치된 형태이다.

해석
그가 돈을 충분히 모았더라면, 새 차를 살 수 있었을 것이다.

13 다음 중 밑줄 친 부분에 들어갈 표현은?

> If he had taken her timely advice then, he _____ happier now.

① be
② were to
③ would be
④ would have been

13 해설
if절은 'then' 표현으로 보아 과거사실과 반대되는 가정법 과거완료, 주절은 'now'의 표현으로 보아 현재사실과 반대되는 가정법 과거이다. 즉 if절 과거 과정과 주절 현재의 아쉬움이 있는 혼합 가정법구문이다. 주절은 would + 동사원형(be동사) 형태가 맞다.

해석
그때 그가 그녀의 충고를 적시에 받아들였더라면, 그는 지금 더 행복했을 것이다.

정답 11 ④ 12 ③ 13 ③

14 해설

but for 가정법 : 주절 could + 동사 원형의 형태로 보아 가정법 과거(if it were not for, 만일 ~이 없다면)를 타나내는데 이 문장에서는 if가 생략된 후 be동사가 도치된 형태이다.

해석

태양이 없었<u>다면</u>, 이 세상에 어떤 것도 살 수 없었을 거야.

14 다음 중 밑줄 친 부분을 잘 표현한 것은?

> <u>But for</u> the sun, nothing in the world could live.

① If had not been for
② If were not for
③ Had not been for
④ Were it not for

15 해설

I wish 가정법 : A의 대화에서 동사 'said'로 보아 과거 사실에 대한 소망이나 유감을 나타내므로 B의 대답은 I wish 가정법 과거완료가 적절하다.

해석

A : Lori와 나는 오랫동안 아무 말도 하지 않았어.
B : 당신이 그녀에게 사과 한마디만 <u>했더라면 좋았을 텐데요.</u>

15 다음 중 밑줄 친 부분에 들어갈 표현은?

> A : Lori and me said nothing each other for a long time.
> B : I wish you _____ just one word of apology to her.

① said
② could say
③ had said
④ had not said

정답 14 ④ 15 ③

제 **4** 편

—

구와 절

www.sdedu.co.kr

단원 개요

준동사(verbal)는 동사의 의미와 기능을 갖고 있으면서 형태가 바뀌어 문장 내에서 명사, 형용사, 부사와 같이 다른 품사의 기능을 하는 동사이고 영어에서는 (to, 원형)부정사, 동명사, (현재, 과거)분사가 있다.

준동사 (verbals)		문장 내 역할			
		동사	명사	형용사	부사
1. 부정사	to부정사	×	○	○	○
	원형부정사	5형식 문장에서 지각동사, 사역동사, 준사역동사의 목적격보어로 사용			
2. 동명사		×	○	○	×
3. 분사	현재분사	×	×	○	○
	과거분사	×	×	○	○

출제 경향 및 수험 대책

1. to부정사
   (1) 명사, 형용사, 부사적 용법과 의미
   (2) 원형부정사 종류, 의미, 관용표현
   (3) 독립부정사, 부정표현, 시제 및 수동태, 의미상의 주어, 관련 표현
2. 동명사
   (1) 동사, 명사적 용법과 의미
   (2) 시제 및 수동태, 의미상의 주어, 관용표현
3. to부정사 vs 동명사 사용 동사 표현
4. 분사 및 분사구문
   (1) 형용사(한정 vs 서술), 동사, 부사적 용법과 의미
   (2) 분사구문의 형태 및 의미
   (3) 독립분사, 비인칭 독립분사, 분사구문 생략 표현

 잠깐!

자격증 · 공무원 · 금융/보험 · 면허증 · 언어/외국어 · 검정고시/독학사 · 기업체/취업
이 시대의 모든 합격! SD에듀에서 합격하세요!
www.youtube.com → SD에듀 → 구독

제 1 장 부정사

부정사(infinitive, in-('not') + finite('end'))는 (주어의) 인칭, 수 등에 제한을 받지 않고 품사와 형태가 변하지 않는 동사이고 to부정사(to + 동사원형)와 **원형부정사**(to 생략)가 있다. to부정사는 문장 내에서 명사, 형용사, 부사의 역할을 한다.

제 1 절 명사적 용법

to부정사는 문장 내에서 주어, 목적어, 보어(주격, 목적격)가 되는 명사 역할을 한다.

1 주어

to부정사는 문장 내에서 주어 역할을 한다. 가주어(expletive, 허사) it을 사용하는 경우 진주어 역할을 하고, to + 동사원형을 동명사로 바꾸어 사용 가능하다.

예

- [To learn] a foreign language is interesting.
- It is interesting [to learn] a foreign language.
- [Learning] a foreign language is interesting.

2 목적어

to부정사는 문장 내에서 (동사의) 목적어 역할을 한다. '의문사 + to 부정사' 또는 '의문사 + 주어 + should + 동사원형'으로 사용 가능하다. 단, 의문사 why는 to부정사와 함께 사용되지 않는다.

예

- He wants [to learn] foreign language.
- He likes [to ride] a bike.
- He decided [to read] an English novel.

- He decided [what to do]. (= He decided what he should do.)
- He decided [when to leave]. (= He decided when he should leave.)
- He decided [where to meet] his friend. (= He decided where he should meet his friend.)
- He decided [whom to support]. (= He decided whom he should support.)
- He decided [how to adopt] the system. (= He decided how he should adopt the system.)

3 보어

to 부정사는 2형식 문장에서 주격보어, 5형식 문장에서 목적격 보어 역할을 한다.

(1) 주격보어(2형식, 주어 + 동사 + 보어)

예
- His hobby is [to play] the guitar.
- To see is [to believe].

(2) 목적격보어(5형식, 주어 + 동사 + 목적어 + 목적격보어)

예
- The professor encouraged her students [to apply for] the writing center.
- The president asked her employees [to study] market trends.

제 2 절　형용사적 용법

형용사(구/절)는 명사 앞에서 수식하는 **전치수식**(pre-modification)과 뒤에서 수식하는 **후치수식**(post-modification)이 있는데 to 부정사의 형용사적 사용은 후치수식의 한정용법이 있고, 문장 내 주격 보어 역할의 서술적 용법이 있다.

1 한정적 용법(attributive use) : 명사 수식

예
- He has some good news [to report].
- Who is the first person [to find out] the general theory of relativity.
- He has no house [to live in].
- They have four children [to take care of].

2 서술적 용법(predicative use) : 명사 서술(보어)

문장 내에서 (형용사) 주격보어 역할을 하며, 예정, 의무, 가능, 의도/조건, 운명 등을 나타내고 'be + to부정사' 형태로 사용된다.

(1) 예정(will/be going to)

예

- He [is to arrive] in Seoul tomorrow afternoon.
- The international conference [is to be held] next month.

(2) 가능(can/be able to)

예

- Love [is not to be bought] with money.
- Nobody [was to be seen] on the street.

(3) 의무(must/should/have to)

예

- He [is to submit] his assignment by 5 pm today.
- People [are to wear] masks in public places.

(4) 의도, 조건(intend to)

예

- If he [is to catch] a plane, he has to leave early for the airport.
- If he [is to live] in a foreign country, he has to learn the language and culture.

(5) 운명(be destined to)

예

- They [were never to see] each other again.
- He [was to become] a global superstar.

제 **3** 절 　 **부사적 용법** 중요 ★★

to부정사는 목적, 원인, 조건, 결과, 이유, 판단, 양보, 정도 등과 같이 문장 내에서 부사 역할을 한다.

1 　목적(in order to)

예

- He departed early [(in order) to avoid] traffic jams.
- He is on a diet [to lose] weight.

2 　원인

happy, pleased, delighted, glad, surprised, sorry 등 감정이나 태도를 나타내는 형용사와 함께 쓰인다.

예

- He is very happy [to see] her.
- The candidate was very pleased [to hear] the election results.

3 　조건

예

- [To hear] him speak English, you will think he is a native speaker.
- He should be happy [to go] with her. (감정 형용사와 함께 사용되는 경우)

4 　결과

grow up, live, wake up, awake 등과 같은 무의지 동사와 함께 쓰인다.

예

- He grew up [to become] a superstar.
- She lived [to be] one hundred years old.

5 이유, 판단

must be, cannot be, 감탄문과 함께 쓰인다.

[예]

• He must be upset [to say] such a thing.
• He cannot be smart [to believe] such a thing.
• How foolish he was to trust her!

6 양보

[예]

• [To do] his best, he could not pass the exam.
• He would not trust her [to explain] it.

7 정도

[예]

• Art is difficult [to understand]. (It is difficult to understand art.)
• This spring water is safe [to drink]. (It is safe to drink this spring water.)

제 4 절 원형부정사(bare/root infinitive) 중요 ★★★

원형부정사는 'to + 동사원형'으로 사용하는 to부정사와는 달리 'to'를 생략하고 사용하는 부정사이다. 원형부정사가 'to'를 생략했다고 하여 '동사원형'과 같은 것이 아니다. 원형부정사는 5형식 문장에서 목적격 보어 역할을 하는 준동사인 반면에 동사원형은 주어와 함께 쓰이는 본동사이다. 원형부정사를 목적격보어로 갖는 동사는 지각동사, 사역동사, 준사역동사가 있다.

1 지각동사

지각동사 (see, look at, watch, behold, hear, listen to, smell, taste, feel, notice, observe 등)	+ 목적어	+ 원형부정사(현재분사)

예

- He saw a woman [climb] the steep mountain.
- He heard her [laugh] happily. (He heard her [laughing] happily.)

2 사역동사

사역동사 (make, have, let)	+ 목적어	+ 원형부정사

예

- She had him [clean] the whole house.
- He made a horse [jump] a barrier.

3 준사역동사

준사역동사 (help, get, cause, order, allow, force, compel, oblige 등)	+ 목적어	+ 원형부정사/to부정사

예

- The professor helped the students [do](/to do) their homework.
- He helped his wife [clean](/to clean) the house.

4 원형부정사를 사용하는 관용표현 중요 ★★★

(1) all - have to do is ~ : ~하기만 하면 된다

    예 All you have to do is read what you see.

(2) cannot but ~ : ~하지 않을 수 없다

   예 He cannot but laugh.

   ※ 동편 제2장 동명사 – 제3절 기타용법 3. 관용 표현(173쪽) 참조

(3) can do no other than ~ : ~할 도리 외에는 없다

   예 He can do no other than study.

(4) do nothing but ~ : 단지 ~할 뿐이다

   예 He does nothing but laugh.

(5) do anything but ~ : ~이외에 뭐든지 한다

   예 It wouldn't do anything but press this bar.

(6) had better ~ : ~하는 것이 좋다

   예 He had better do the dishes before he goes out.

(7) make believe ~ : ~처럼 보이게 하다

   예 He made believe not to hear her.

(8) may well ~ : ~하는 것은 당연하다

   예 He may well believe it.

(9) may as well do ~ : ~하는 편이 낫다

   예 He may as well go to the store now.

(10) might as well ~ as – : –하느니 ~하는 게 더 좋다

   예 You might as well get eat it up as throw it away.

(11) why not ~ : ~하는 게 어때?

   예 Why not ask him to help you?

(12) would rather ~ (than –) : –보다는 차라리 ~하겠다

   예 Students often say they would rather play than study.

(13) would as soon ~ as - : -하느니 차라리 ~하겠다

> 예 He would as soon stay home as go out.

제 **5** 절 기타 부정사

1 독립부정사(absolute infinitive)

문장 전체를 수식하는 부사적 용법이다.

lucky to say : 운 좋게도	to do one justice : 공정하게 말해서	
needless to say : 말할 필요도 없이	to cut a long story short	간단히 말해서, 요약하자면
so to speak : 다시 말해서, 즉	to make a long story short	
strange to say : 말하기에 이상하지만	to make matters better : 금상첨화	
to be honest : 정직하게 말하면	to make matters worse : 설상가상으로	
to be sure : 확실히	to say nothing of~	
to begin with : 우선	not to speak of~	~은 말할 것도 없이
to be frank (with you) : 솔직히 말하면	not to mention~	
to conclude : 결론적으로	to be brief	요약하면
to tell the truth : 사실은	to sum up	

예

- Needless to say, human beings should be given equal opportunity.
- You are a fish out of water, so to speak.
- To tell the truth, Josh has never been to Korea.
- To do him justice, he is not an efficient man.
- To make matters worse, it began to snow.
- Josh can speak Tagalog, not to mention English.
- To sum up, he is against the plan A.

2 대부정사(pro-infinitive)

'to + 동사원형' 형태의 to부정사가 반복되어 사용되는 경우 'to'만 사용하는 것을 대부정사라고 한다.

例

- You may call me if you would like [to] (call me).
- You may go out if you want [to] (go out).
- A : Would you like to have a pizza?
  B : Yes, I love [to] (have a pizza).

3 분리 부정사(split infinitive)

'to + 동사원형' 형태의 to부정사는 원칙적으로 분리되지 않는데 (특히 구어체에서) 'to'와 '동사원형' 사이에 '부사'가 위치하는 경우를 분리 부정사라 한다.

例

- He began [to slowly get up] off the bed.
- He used [to secretly admire] his advisor.
- He would like [to fully understand] metaphysical philosophy.
- He wanted her [to thoroughly read] the journal article.
- It is difficult [to completely change] the plan at this time.

4 부정 표현

부정어를 to부정사(to + 동사원형) 앞에서 표현한다.

例

- He wants [not to disturb] students in the library.
- He told a lie to his mother [not to disappoint] her.
- He left home early [not to be] late for his flight.
- He decided [not to visit] Korea.
- His efforts [not to fail] the exam worked.

5 시제 및 수동태

to부정사 시제 및 수동태와 관련된 형태는 (1) to + 동사원형, (2) to + be + -en(p.p.), (3) to + have + -en(p.p.), (4) to + have + been + -en(p.p.), (5) to + be + -ing 다섯 개다. 이 중 (1)과 (2)는 문장의 본동사와 to부정사의 시제가 같은, 즉 일치하는 단순 부정사이고, (3)과 (4)는 문장의 본동사보다 to부정사의 시제가 앞선 완료 부정사, (5)는 진행형이다.

to부정사 시제 및 수동태	단순 부정사	(1) to + 동사원형
		(2) to + be + -en(p.p.) → 단순형 수동태
	완료 부정사	(3) to + have + -en(p.p.)
		(4) to + have + been + -en(p.p.) → 완료형 수동태
	진행형	(5) to + be + -ing

(1) 단순 부정사

① to + 동사원형

예

- He seems [to be] strange. (= It seems that he is strange.)
- He seemed [to be] strange. (= It seemed that he was strange.)
- She thinks him [to be] honest. (= She thinks that he is honest.)
- She thought him [to be] honest. (= She thought that he was honest.)

② 단순형 수동태 : to + be + -en(p.p.)

예

- She seems [to be loved]. (= It seems that she is loved.)
- She seemed [to be loved]. (= It seemed that she was loved.)

(2) 완료 부정사

① to + have + -en(p.p.)

예

- He seems [to have been] strange. (= It seems that he was strange.)
- He seemed [to have been] strange. (= It seemed that he had been strange.)
- She thinks him [to have been] honest. (= She thinks that he was honest.)
- She thought him [to have been] honest. (= She thought that he had been honest.)

② 완료형 수동태 : to + have + been + -en(p.p.)

예

- She seems [to have been loved]. (= It seems that she was loved.)
- She seemed [to have been loved]. (= It seemed that she had been loved.)

(3) 진행형 : to + be + -ing

예

- She seems [to be doing] her best. (= It seems that she is doing her best.)
- She seemed [to be doing] her best. (= It seemed that she was doing her best.)
- She seems [to have been doing] her best. (= It seems that she was doing her best.)
- She seemed [to have been doing] her best. (= It seemed that she had been doing her best.)

(4) 희망, 소원, 기대 표현 + 완료 부정사 : 이루지 못한 사실

소망동사 과거형(wanted, hoped, wished, expected, intended, desired 등)	+ 완료 부정사
be동사의 과거형(was, were)	

예

- He hoped [to have met] her yesterday. (= He had hoped to meet her yesterday.)
- He was [to have gone] to the movies with her last week. (= He had been to go to the movies with her last week.)

6 관련 표현

(1) too + 형용사/부사 + to부정사, so ~ that can't - : 너무 ~해서 ~할 수 없다

예

- The problem is too difficult to solve.
- *The problem is too difficult to solve it.
  (= The problem is so difficult that one can't solve.)
- The issue was too complicated to find a clue.

(2) 형용사/부사 + enough + to부정사, so ~ that can - : ~할 정도로 충분히 -하다

예

- He is qualified enough to apply for the job.
  (= He is so qualified that he can apply for the job.)
- He was smart enough to find a loophole in the new system.

(3) so ~ as to + 동사원형, enough to + 동사원형, so ~ that can − : −할 만큼 ~하여

예

- He was so smart as to answer the difficult question in a minute.
- He is so well known as to need no introduction to audiences.

(4) so as to + 동사원형, in order to + 동사원형, ~ so that may − : ~를 위해 ~하다

예

- She studied aborad to earn her doctorate degree.
- He turned on the TV so as to watch the drama.

제 6 절   부정사의 의미상의 주어 중요 ★★

to부정사의 의미상의 주어는 to부정사의 동작을 행동하는 주체를 의미하고, 일반적으로 for + 목적격 형태를 사용하고, 사람의 성격, 성질을 나타내는 경우 of + 목적격 형태로 표현하는 반면에 불특정 다수인 경우 의미상의 주어를 표현하지 않아도 된다.

일반적으로	for + 목적격 + to부정사
사람의 성격, 성질을 나타내는 형용사와 함께 사용 (good, kind, nice, wise, clever, polite, rude, careful, careless, foolish, stupid, silly, cruel, considerate, thoughtful 등)	of + 목적격 + to부정사
to부정사의 주체가 일반인(불특정 다수)	to부정사

예

- It is possible [for him to climb] Mount Everest.
- It takes a lot of money [for him to buy] a new house in downtown New York.

- It is considerate [of him to take care of] stray cats.
- It is wise [of him to accept] her offer.

- It is difficult [to master] English in a year or two.
- It is important [to learn] from experience.

제 2 장 동명사

동명사(gerund)는 동사원형 + -ing 형태로 원래 동사의 성질과 의미를 갖고 있으면서 문장에서는 **동사** 역할과 **명사** 역할, 즉, 주어, 목적어, 보어 역할을 한다. (※ to부정사가 문장 내에서 명사, 형용사, 부사 역할을 한 반면에 동명사는 명사 역할을 한다.)

제 1 절 동사적 동명사

동명사는 동사의 성질과 의미를 갖고 있으므로 그 자체로 목적어, 보어, 수식어를 취할 수 있고, being + 과거분사 형태의 수동형 동명사로도 쓰인다.

1 목적어

예

- His hobby is [collecting] postcards. (postcards는 동명사 collecting의 목적어)
- He likes [reading] mystery novels. (mystery novels는 동명사 reading의 목적어)

2 보어

예

- He is proud of [being] a volunteer. (a volunteer는 동명사 being의 보어)
- [Being] a teacher is very rewarding. (a teacher는 동명사 being의 보어)

3 수식어

예

- He objected to [being treated] like a beginner. (being treated는 수동형 동명사)
- [Walking] fast is the best way to lose weight. (부사 fast는 동명사 walking을 수식)

- The office will contact you after carefully [reviewing] your papers. (부사 carefully는 동명사 reviewing을 수식)

제 2 절 명사적 동명사

동명사는 문장 내에서 주어, (동사, 전치사) 목적어, 보어의 명사적 역할을 한다.

1 주어

[예]

- [Seeing] is believing. (seeing, 주어 / believing, 보어) (To see is to believe.)
- [Running] is one of the easiest ways to lose weight.
- [Speaking] English is not easy.

2 목적어

(1) 동사

[예]

- He enjoyed [studying] in the graduate school.
- He likes [fishing] and [hunting].
- He stopped [reading] a book and began [walking] around the park.

(2) 전치사

[예]

- He is very fond [of studying] in the library.
- He is very good [at singing].
- Thank you [for informing] me of his plan.

3 보어

예

- Seeing is [believing]. (seeing, 주어 / believing, 보어) (To see is to believe.)
- His dream is [studying abroad].
- What he likes best over the weekend is [listening to music].

제 3 절 기타 용법

1 시제 및 수동태 중요 ★★

동명사 시제와 관련된 형태는 (1) 동사원형 + -ing, (2) being + -en(p.p.), (3) having + -en(p.p.), (4) having + been + -en(p.p.)로 총 네 개이다. 이 중 (1)과 (2)는 문장의 본동사와 동명사의 시제가 같거나 그 이후의 사건일 때 사용하는 **단순 동명사**이고, (3)과 (4)는 문장의 본동사보다 동명사의 시제가 앞선 **완료 동명사**이다.

동명사 시제 및 수동태	단순 동명사	(1) 동사원형 + -ing
		(2) being + -en(p.p.) → 단순형 수동태
	완료 동명사	(3) having + -en(p.p.)
		(4) having + been + -en(p.p.) → 완료형 수동태

(1) 단순 동명사

① 동사원형 + -ing

예

- He is proud of [being] a volunteer. (= He is proud that he is a volunteer.)
- He was proud of [being] a volunteer. (= He was proud that he was a volunteer.)
- He doesn't mind her [passing] the exam. (= He doesn't mind that she will pass the exam.)

② 단순형 수동태 : being + -en(p.p.)

예

- Nobody likes [being ignored]. (= Nobody likes that she or he is ignored.)
- He doesn't like [being asked] to tell a white lie. (= He doesn't like that he is asked to tell a white lie.)

(2) 완료 동명사

① having + −en(p.p.)

예

- He is proud of [having been] a volunteer. (= He is proud that he was a volunteer.)
- He was proud of [having been] a volunteer. (= He was proud that he had been a volunteer.)
- He didn't mind her [having passed] the exam. (= He didn't mind that she had passed the exam.)

> 🔔 **더 알아두기** 🔍
>
> 미래 지향적 의미인 to부정사에 비해 동명사는 상대적으로 과거의 의미를 지니고 있어서 완료 동명사 대신에 단순 동명사를 사용하기도 한다.
>
> 예
> - He is proud of [having been] a volunteer.
>   → He is proud of [being] a volunteer.

② **완료형 수동태** : having + been + -en(p.p.)

예

- He is proud of [having been educated] in the graduate school. (= He is proud that he was educated in the graduate school.)
- He appreciated of [having been taken care of]. (= He appreciated that he had been taken care of.)

---

2 동명사의 의미상의 주어

동명사의 의미상의 주어는 문장(주절)의 주어 및 목적어와 일치하거나, 일반인(불특정 다수)인 경우, 문맥상 분명한 경우는 밝히지 않는데, 그렇지 않은 경우는 동명사 앞에 소유격(구어체에서는 목적격도 가능)을 사용하여 동명사의 의미상의 주어, 즉 행위의 주체를 표현한다.

(1) 의미상의 주어를 밝히지 않는 경우

① 문장의 주어와 일치하는 경우

예

- He enjoys [playing] the piano.
  (= He enjoys that he plays the piano.)

• He repented of [having] spent all his money.

(= He repented that he had spent all his money.)

② 문장의 목적어와 일치하는 경우

예

• Thank you very much for [inviting] us to this wonderful venue.

• He thanked her for [giving] him a ride to the airport.

③ 일반인(불특정 다수)

예

• [Walking] fast is one of the best exercises.

• [Mastering] English is not an easy task.

④ 문맥상 분명한 경우

예

• [Reading] to your students will help to develop their listening skills.

• The best way is [relaxing] your muscles.

(2) 의미상의 주어를 밝히는 경우 : 소유격 사용

① 사람

예

• His constant [complaining] is getting on her nerves.

• He doesn't like her [leaving] early.

• He suggested Josh's [attending] the conference next month.

② 사물 : of + 명사(소유격을 사용하지 않음)

예

• He complained of the hotel room [being] messy.

• The probability of this result [being] false is less than 1%.

3 관용표현 중요★★

(1) look forward to + 동명사 : 기대하다, 고대하다

(※ to 다음에는 명사, 동명사 가능)

예

• He is looking forward to [seeing] her again.

• Children are looking forward to [eating] pizzas tonight.

(2) have difficulty (in) + 동명사 : 어려움을 겪다

> • have trouble (in) + 동명사
> • have a hard time (in) + 동명사

[예]

• Many foreign students have difficulty (in) [learning] Korean.

• He had a great difficulty (in) [finding] his job in the USA.

(3) have fun + 동명사 : 즐거운 시간을 갖다

> have a good time + 동명사

[예]

• He has fun [talking] with her.

• He had a good time [learning] a foreign language.

(4) spend/waste + 시간/돈 (in/on) + 동명사 : ~하는 데 시간/돈을 쓰다

[예]

• He spends every Sunday afternoon (in) playing baseball with his children.

• He spent his daily life (in) writing books.

(5) cannot help + 동명사 : ~하지 않을 수 없다

> • cannot help but + 원형부정사
> • cannot but + 원형부정사
> • can do nothing but + 원형부정사
> • have no choice but + to부정사
> • have no alternative but + to부정사
> • there is nothing for it but + to부정사

[예]

• He cannot help smiling at her.

• He cannot help but smile at her.

• He cannot but smile at her.

(6) keep on + 동명사 : 계속해서 ～하다

> go on + 동명사

예

- He just kept on crying.
- He went on talking with her until late at last night.

(7) feel like + 동명사 : ～하고 싶어 하다

> - feel inclined to + 동사원형
> - would like to + 동사원형
> - have a mind to + 동사원형

예

- He doesn't feel like walking now.
- He felt like walking in the rain.

(8) prevent A from + 동명사 : ～하지 못하게 하다

> - keep A from + 동명사
> - stop A from + 동명사
> - prohibit A from + 동명사
> - forbid A from + 동명사

예

- Parents prevent children from going outside at night.
- This law prohibits people from damaging nature.

(9) come near (to) + 동명사 : 하마터면 ～할 뻔하다

> - go near (to) + 동명사
> - be near + 동명사
> - nearly escaped (from) + 동명사
> - narrowly escaped (from) + 동명사

예

- He came near (to) falling over a rock.
- His recklessness came near (to) causing a disaster.

(10) make a point of + 동명사 : 꼭 ~하다, ~하는 것을 원칙으로 삼다

> • make it a rule to + 동사원형
> • make it a point to + 동사원형
> • be in the habit of + 동명사

예

- He makes a point of jogging for an hour every morning.
- He makes a point of breathing deeply when he exercises.

(11) adjust to + 동명사 : ~에 적응하다

예

- Human body needs to adjust to rising early in the morning.
- He adjusted to eating lunch alone.

(12) confess to + 동명사 : 자백하다, 시인하다

예

- He confessed to having heard about the information.
- He confessed to being a trained spy.

(13) object to + 동명사 : ~하는 것을 반대하다

예

- Dean objected to reorganizing departments.
- She objected to her husband spending too much money on furniture.

(14) go + 동명사 : ~하러 가다

예

- He went fishing in the river.
- Let's go shopping at the department store this weekend.

go biking/go bike riding (자전거 타러 가다)	go sailing (항해하러 가다)
go boating (보트 타러 가다)	go scuba diving (스쿠버 다이빙하러 가다)
go bowling (볼링하러 가다)	go shopping (쇼핑하러 가다)
go camping (캠핑하러 가다)	go skateboarding (스케이트보드 타러 가다)
go canoeing (카누 타러 가다)	go skating (스케이트 타러 가다)
go dancing (춤추러 가다)	go skiing (스키 타러 가다)
go fishing (낚시 가다)	go sightseeing (관광하러 가다)

go hiking (하이킹 가다)	go sledding (썰매 타러 가다)
go hunting (사냥하러 가다)	go snowboarding (스노우보드 타러 가다)
go jogging (조깅하러 가다)	go surfing (파도타기하러 가다)
go mountain climbing (등산하러 가다)	go swimming (수영하러 가다)
go riding (승마하러 가다)	go walking (산책하러 가다)
go running (달리기하러 가다)	go window shopping (윈도우 쇼핑하러 가다)

(15) see to + 동명사 : 반드시 ~하다 / ~하도록 주의하다

[예]

- Please see to buying the tickets for the opera.
- Parents should see to taking care of children.

(16) above + 동명사 : 결코 ~하지 않을 / ~할 사람이 아니다.

[예]

- He is above telling a lie.
- This book is above my understanding.

(17) on + 동명사 : ~하자마자

> upon + 동명사, as soon as + 주어 + 동사

[예]

- On seeing the paint, tourists began to take a picture.
- Upon reaching the top, climbers faced a beautiful landscape.

(18) in + 동명사 : ~할 때에는(~하자마자)

> when/while + 주어 + 동사, as soon as + 주어 + 동사

[예]

- In speaking English, you don't need to be afraid of making mistakes.
- He was prudent in recommending his students to the company.

(19) for the + 동명사 : ~하기만 하면

> if only + 주어 + 동사

예

- He can get it for the asking.
- You can pass the exam easily for the studying.

(20) not(never) - without + 동명사 : -하면 반드시 ~ 하다

> whenever 주어 + 동사, 주어 + 동사

예

- He never speaks without smiling.
- He never does anything without thinking it through.

(21) of one's own + 동명사 : 자신이 스스로 ~한

예

- It is a profession of his own choosing.
- It is a profession (that was) chosen by himself.

(22) be addicted to + 동명사 : ~에 중독되어 있다

예

- He is addicted to watching sports games on TV over the weekend.
- He is addicted to playing computer games.

(23) be busy (in) + 동명사 : ~하느라 바쁘다

> be busy with + 명사

예

- The students are all busy (in) preparing for the final.
- Koreans tend to be busy creating and doing new things.

(24) be committed to + 동명사 : ~에 전념하다

[예]

- This foundation is committed to ending poverty worldwide.
- This nonprofit organization is committed to protecting natural resources.

(25) be dedicated to + 동명사 : ~에 전념하다 / ~에 헌신하다

> be devoted to + 동명사

[예]

- She is dedicated to making her daughters successful in their careers.
- He was devoted to helping the underprivileged throughout his life.

(26) be far from + 동명사 : 결코 ~않다

> - above + 동명사
> - never

[예]

- He is far from being interested in sports.
- Far from reading the letter, he didn't even open it.

(27) be on the point of + 동명사 : 막 ~하려고 하다

> be about to + 동사원형

[예]

- He was on the point of departing for the flight.
- He was about to depart for the flight.

(28) be opposed to + 동명사 : ~에 반대하다

[예]

- He was opposed to making a proposal for the agenda.
- He is opposed to eating out for dinner.

(29) be/get used to＋동명사 : ～에 익숙하다

be/get accustomed to＋동명사

[예]

- He is quite used to living in a metropolitan city.
- He got accustomed to driving his new car.

※ used to부정사 : 과거의 습관, 상태. ~하곤 했다
- He used to live in a big city, but now he lives in a small town.
- He used to like classical music, but now he likes jazz.
※ 제2편 품사 – 제5장 조동사 – 제4절 기타 조동사(84쪽) 참조

(30) be worth＋동명사 : ～할 가치가 있다

be worthy of＋동명사

[예]

- The local museum is worth visiting.
- This novel is worth reading.

(31) it is no use＋동명사 : ～해 봐야 소용없다

there's no use＋동명사
it is of no use to＋동사원형
it is useless to＋동사원형

[예]

- It is no use crying over spilt(spilled) milk.
- It is of no use to cry over spilt(spilled) milk.
- It is useless to cry over spilt(spilled) milk.

(32) it goes without saying that 주어＋동사 : ～는 말할 필요도 없다

> it is needless to say that 주어＋동사

예

- It goes without saying that health is above wealth.
- It is needless to say that health is above wealth.

(33) there's no point in＋동명사 : ～해도 소용없다, 아무런 의미가 없다

예

- There is no point in going out if she doesn't want to.
- There is no point in waiting any longer, so they left early.

(34) there is no＋동명사 : ～하는 것은 불가능하다

> - it is impossible to＋동사원형
> - we cannot＋동사원형

예

- There is no denying the truth.
- It is impossible to deny the truth.
- We cannot deny the truth.

- There is no escaping from her.
- It is impossible to escape from her.
- We cannot escape from her.

(35) what do you say to＋동명사 : ～하는 것이 어떻습니까? (권유)

> - what do you think about＋동명사 (제안)
> - how about＋동명사
> - what about＋동명사
> - let's＋동사원형

예

- What do you say to going out for dinner tonight?
- What about going out for dinner tonight?

(36) when it comes to + 동명사 : ~의 점에서는, ~에 관해서는

예

- When it comes to playing the guitar, Josh can't beat Amy.
- When it comes to travelling to Europe, you had better ask Josh.

(37) would you mind + 동명사? : ~해 주시겠습니까?

> do you mind + 동명사?

예

- Would you mind closing the window?
- Do you mind waiting for me there?

> **❗ 더 알아두기 🔍**
>
> 'Would mind you~?'에 대한 대답
>
> 'Would you mind + 동명사?' 혹은 'Do you mind + 동명사?'는 '~해 주는 것이 싫습니까? / 꺼림니까?'의 의미로 Yes로 대답하면 '싫다'는 의미이고, No로 대답하면 '괜찮다'는 의미로 부탁을 들어준다는 의미이다.
>
> Yes, I would. (네, 싫습니다. 안 되겠습니다.)
> Not at all / Of course not. (싫지 않습니다. 괜찮습니다.)

(38) with a view to + 동명사 : ~를 위하여, ~를 목적으로

예

- The state government built a dam with a view to preventing flood and drought.
- He saved a lot of money with a view to traveling to Europe.

(39) the point of + 동명사 : ~의 목적, 요점

> the use of

예

- What's the point of having a car if you never drive it?
- What's the use of having a car if you never drive it?
- What's the point of seeing her?

(40) by + 동명사 : 수단 ~로, ~함으로써

> 예

> - They showed us they are happy by smiling.
> - We can improve our vocabulary by reading novels written in English.

(41) with + 동명사 : ~(행동과) 함께

> 예

> - His mother welcomed him with giving him a big hug.
> - He washed the dishes with listening to radio.

4 동사의 목적어로 사용되는 동명사 및 to부정사 중요 ★★

(1) 동명사를 목적어로 취하는 동사

★표시 동사는 동명사뿐만 아니라 to부정사도 목적어로 취한다.

동사		예문
1.	admit	He admitted using an unreasonable source.
2.	★advise	He advised starting early today.
3.	anticipate	He anticipates having a good time during the winter break.
4.	appreciate	He appreciated her coming in on Christmas Eve.
5.	avoid	He avoided answering her question in a direct way.
6.	★can't bear	He can't bear waiting in long lines.
7.	★begin	It began snowing.
8.	complete	He finally completed writing his final paper.
9.	consider	He will consider visiting two national parks.
10.	★continue	He continued talking to her.
11.	delay	He delayed leaving for Korea.
12.	deny	He denied holding the world record.
13.	discuss	They discussed entering into a new business.
14.	dislike	He dislikes eating alone.
15.	enjoy	He enjoyed watching movies.
16.	finish	He finished studying at 11 pm.
17.	★forget	He never forgot visiting Giant's Causeway.
18.	★hate	He hates telling a white lie.
19.	can't help	He can't help smiling at her.
20.	keep	He keeps hoping she will come.

21.	★like	He likes watching sports games.
22.	★love	He loves watching baseball games.
23.	mention	He mentioned going on a picnic.
24.	mind	Would you mind opening the window?
25.	miss	He missed being with his family.
26.	postpone	He postponed leaving Korea until next month.
27.	practice	He practiced kicking balls.
28.	★prefer	He prefers drinking coffee to drinking tea in the morning.
29.	quit	He quit drinking last year.
30.	recall	He doesn't recall meeting her last year.
31.	recollect	He doesn't recollect meeting her last year.
32.	recommend	He recommended using the new product.
33.	★regret	He regretted telling her his secret.
34.	★remember	He remembered meeting her last year.
35.	resent	He resented having been misled.
36.	resist	He couldn't resist smiling at her.
37.	risk	He risked losing all his money.
38.	★can't stand	He can't stand waiting in long lines.
39.	★start	It started snowing.
40.	stop	He stopped drinking last year.
41.	suggest	He suggested going to the opera.
42.	tolerate	He doesn't tolerate making a mistake.
43.	★try	He tried closing the window, but he couldn't budge the window.
44.	understand	He didn't understand her leaving graduate school.

(2) to부정사를 목적어로 취하는 동사

① 동사 + to부정사

★표시 동사는 to부정사뿐만 아니라 동명사도 목적어로 취한다.

동사		예문
1.	afford	He can't afford to buy a new car.
2.	agree	He agreed to help them.
3.	appear	He appears to be tired.
4.	arrange	He arranged to meet her at the radio station.
5.	ask	He asked to help them.
6.	★can't bear	He can't bear to wait in long lines.
7.	beg	He begged to help them.
8.	★begin	It began to snow.

9.	care	He doesn't care to watch the opera.
10.	claim	He claimed to have found more evidence.
11.	consent	He consented to help them.
12.	★continue	He continued to talk to her.
13.	decide	He decided to leave early today.
14.	demand	He demanded to help the underprivileged.
15.	deserve	He deserves to be paid well.
16.	expect	He expects to return to graduate school next year.
17.	fail	He didn't fail to return the books to the city library on time.
18.	★forget	He forgot to lock the front door.
19.	★hate	He hates to tell a white lie.
20.	hesitate	Please don't hesitate to contact us.
21.	hope	He hopes to arrive on time.
22.	intend	He intends to be a novelist.
23.	learn	He learned to play the guitar.
24.	★like	He likes to watch sports games.
25.	★love	He loves to watch baseball games.
26.	manage	He managed to complete his task early.
27.	mean	He didn't mean to underestimate the situation.
28.	need	He needs to have her opinion about the issue.
29.	offer	He offered to help them.
30.	plan	He is planning to study abroad next year.
31.	★prefer	He prefers to drink coffee in the morning.
32.	prepare	He prepared to study abroad.
33.	pretend	He pretended to understand everything she said.
34.	promise	He promised to come early.
35.	refuse	He refused to leak confidential information.
36.	★regret	He regretted to tell her that he didn't pass the exam.
37.	★remember	He remembered to lock the front door.
38.	seem	New comers seem to be friendly.
39.	★can't stand	He can't stand to wait in long lines.
40.	★start	It started to snow.
41.	struggle	He struggled to survive.
42.	swear	He swore to tell the truth.
43.	tend	He tends to use slang.
44.	threaten	He threatened to quit the support.
45.	★try	He is trying to learn a foreign language.

46.	volunteer	He volunteered to help them.
47.	wait	He waited to see you.
48.	want	He wanted to participate in the conference.
49.	wish	He wishes to visit Korea next year.

② 동사 + (대)명사 + to부정사

★표시 동사는 to부정사뿐만 아니라 동명사도 목적어로 취한다.

동사		예문
50.	★advise	He advised her to start early today.
51.	allow	He allowed me to use his laptop.
52.	ask	He asked her to help them.
53.	beg	He begged us to help them.
54.	cause	His carelessness caused him to break the vase.
55.	challenge	He challenged her to break the world record.
56.	convince	He convinced her to accept their offer.
57.	dare	He dared her to swim across the river.
58.	encourage	He encourage the students to take part in the workshop.
59.	expect	He expected her to find a good job.
60.	forbid	He forbids her to install other programs in his laptop.
61.	force	He forced her to help them.
62.	hire	He hired a native English speaker to teach students.
63.	instruct	He instructed the students to study English.
64.	invite	He invited her to participate in the movie preview.
65.	need	He needed her to work with them.
66.	order	He ordered them to reconsider the plan.
67.	permit	He permitted the students to look the word up in the dictionary.
68.	persuade	He persuaded her to go to the conference.
69.	remind	He reminded her to write her sister.
70.	require	He required the students to finish the test on time.
71.	teach	He taught her to drive a car.
72.	tell	He told her to go to the party.
73.	urge	He urged the students to prepare for the final exams.
74.	want	He wanted her to participate in the international conference.
75.	warn	He warned her to drive safely.

(3) to 부정사와 동명사를 모두 목적어로 취하는 동사 중요 ★★★

① 의미 차이가 (거의) 없는 경우

begin	like	hate
start	love	can't stand
continue	prefer	can't bear

예

- It began snowing. (= It began to snow.)
- He likes swimming. (= He likes to swim.)
- He can't bear telling a white lie. (= He can't bear to tell a white lie.)

※ 동사의 시제가 진행형인 경우 동명사보다는 to부정사를 사용한다.

예 It was beginning to snow.

② 의미 차이가 있는 경우

㉠ remember + to부정사 : 책임, 의무, 업무 수행을 기억하는 경우

remember + 동명사 : 과거에 있었던 일을 기억하는 경우

예

- He always remembers to lock the front door.
- He remembers seeing the Giant's Causeway. That was impressive.

㉡ forget + to부정사 : 책임, 의무, 업무 수행을 잊은 경우

forget + 동명사 : 과거에 있었던 일을 잊은 경우

예

- He often forgets to lock the front door.
- He forgot seeing the Giant's Causeway last year.

㉢ regret + to부정사 : 좋지 않은 소식을 알리게 되어 유감인 경우

regret + 동명사 : 과거의 일에 대해 후회하는 경우

예

- He regrets to tell her that she failed the exam.
- He regrets leaving the USA early.

㉣ try + to부정사 : 노력하다

try + 동명사 : 시험 삼아 해 보다

예

- He tried to climb Mount Everest last year.
- He tried closing the window, but he couldn't budge the window.

㉤ stop + to부정사 : ~하기 위해 멈추다 (목적, in order to)

stop + 동명사 : ~하는 것을 멈추다 (동사 stop의 목적어)

예

- He stopped (in order) to talk to her.
- He stopped talking to her.

제 3 장 · 분사

분사(participle)는 동사의 성질과 의미를 갖고 있으면서 문장에서 **형용사, 동사, 부사**적 역할을 한다. 동사원형 + -ing' 형태의 현재분사와 '동사원형 + -(e)d' 형태의 과거분사가 있다. (※ to부정사는 문장 내에서 명사, 형용사, 부사 역할, 동명사는 명사 역할, 분사는 형용사 역할을 한다.)

종류		현재분사	과거분사
형태		동사원형 + -ing	동사원형 + -(e)d (규칙동사)
의미		능동, 진행	수동, 완료
예	규칙	interesting satisfying	interested satisfied
	불규칙	teaching writing	taught written

※ 제2편 품사 – 제4장 동사 – 제1절 규칙동사 – 불규칙동사(66쪽) 참조

제 1 절 형용사적 기능 중요 ★★★

분사의 형용사적 기능에는 명사를 수식하는 한정적 용법과 명사의 동작과 상태를 설명하는 서술적 용법이 있다.

1 한정적 용법

한정적 용법은 명사 앞에서 수식하는 전치수식, 명사 뒤에서 수식하는 후치수식이 있다.

(1) 전치수식

① 현재분사	② 과거분사
Who wrote this <u>interesting</u> story?	This painting portrays a <u>wounded</u> solider.
Who is the <u>sleeping</u> baby over there?	There is a <u>burnt</u> wood on the table.
The best thing about falls is watching the <u>falling</u> leaves change colors.	<u>Fallen</u> leaves lay on the ground.
On the other side there was a <u>rising</u> sun.	The <u>rejected</u> people should apply again.
The <u>boring</u> professor always makes students sleep.	He gave me a <u>broken</u> radio.

Half of <u>working</u> women do 70 percent of the housework.	A freshly <u>baked</u> bread is perfect for lunch.
A <u>rolling</u> stone gathers no moss.	He doesn't like <u>fried</u> eggs, but <u>boiled</u> ones.
<u>Melting</u> chocolate can be an excellent dessert.	Spread <u>melted</u> chocolate on the bread.

❗ 더 알아두기 🔍

복합 형용사(compound adjective) 형태 중요 ★

1. 명사 + 현재분사	An English-speaking country An English-speaking world a time-saving process a time-consuming process	a problem-solving competence a rice-exporting country a wheat-producing country
2. 명사 – 과거분사	a sun-dried fruit a tongue-tied man a man-made satellite	a man-eating tribe a citizen-initiated referendum communist-influenced countries
3. 형용사 – 현재분사(-ing)	a good-looking man a free-standing tower	a hard-working man
4. 형용사 – 과거분사/ 형용사 – 명사 + –ed	a good-natured man a short-sighted man a long-haired man an old-fashioned man a tight-fisted banker a two-faced politician an absent-minded scientist a broad-minded parent	a hot-tempered man a cold-blooded animal a warm-hearted man a red-colored rose a blue-eyed man a black-haired man a long-nosed man a long-legged man
5. 부사 – 과거분사/ 부사 – 명사 + –ed	a well-known poet a well-dressed man a well-mannered man	a long-tailed monkey a deeply-rooted traditions
6. 명사 – 형용사	duty-free goods a brand-new watch a word-famous singer	a health-conscious generation fashion-conscious youths a pig-headed man
7. 형용사 – 명사	a first-class seat an one-way ticket a second-hand car deep-sea diving last-minute shoppers a high-quality speaker	a left-wing party a right-wing party long-term investment light-weight champion a fourth-floor office a fifty-floor building
8. 명사 – 명사	a part-time job	

> ⚡ **더 알아두기** 🔍
>
> **동명사와 현재분사의 구별** 중요 ★★
>
> 동명사는 목적, 용도의 '~하기 위한' 의미로 사용되어 명사 역할을 하는 반면에 현재분사는 상태, 동작의 '~하고 있는' 의미로 사용되어 형용사의 역할을 한다. 동명사는 동명사에, 현재분사는 명사에 강세가 온다.
>
> | 동명사 | 현재분사 |
> | --- | --- |
> | a sléeping car : 침대차 | a sleeping chíld : 자고 있는 아이 |
> | a dáncing room : 무도실 | a dancing gírl : 춤추고 있는 소녀 |
> | bóxing gloves : 권투 장갑 | a boxing mán : 권투 하는 사람 |
> | a búrning glass : 화경(태양열/집광 렌즈) | a burning mountáin : 불타는 산 |
> | a wáiting room : 대기실 | a waiting lády : 기다리고 있는 부인 |
> | a knítting needle : 뜨개바늘 | knitting móther : 뜨개질하시는 어머니 |

(2) 후치수식

① 현재분사	② 과거분사
The woman delivering a speech is a famous scholar.	He received a paper written in English.
The birds singing on a tree are magpies.	The leaves fallen on the park were cleaned by sweepers.
The sun rising from the East gives hope.	He likes apple pies baked in the oven.
She is a professor teaching music at university.	Soldiers wounded at battle welcomed back home.
The girl singing a jazz song on the stage is his youngest daughter.	The cell phone found under the desk is hers.
The students studying in the classroom will ask questions.	The people invited to the ceremony can enter the hall.
The candles burning on the table looks lantern.	The mountain covered with snow in winter is beautiful.
There are lots of ducks swimming in the lake.	There are lots of leaves fallen on the ground.

2 서술적 용법

서술적 용법은 주격보어와 목적격보어로 사용된다.

(1) 주격 보어

주격 보어 용법은 주어와의 관계가 능동이면 현재분사, 수동이면 과거분사를 사용한다.

① 현재분사	② 과거분사
능동관계	수동관계
상태 : sit, stand, lie 등 상태지속 : keep, remain 등 동작 : go, come, run 등	look, seem, appear, become, get, remain, grow, come, go, stand, lie 등
sit reading lie reading stand talking keep waiting come running	look surprised seem disappointed become bored get tired remain unsettled come in unnoticed
He sat reading the novel. (= He sat and was reading the novel.) He kept waiting in the lobby.	He seemed satisfied with her work. He sat surrounded by his students.

(2) 목적격보어

목적격보어 용법은 목적어와의 관계에 따라 결정된다.

① 지각동사의 목적격보어

목적어와의 관계가 능동이면 동사원형, 현재분사를 사용하고, 수동이면 과거분사를 사용한다.

㉠ 현재분사	㉡ 과거분사
see, look at, watch, hear, listen to, feel, smell, notice, observe	
능동관계	수동관계
see her run/running hear her play/playing the guitar watch her cross/crossing the street	see her carried out hear his name called feel oneself watched
He saw her listen/listening to music. He heard her play/playing the cello.	He saw her carried out of the house. He heard his name called on the street.

② **(준)사역동사의 목적격보어**

목적어와의 관계가 능동이면 원형부정사를 사용하고, 수동이면 과거분사를 사용한다.

㉠ 현재분사	㉡ 과거분사
make, have, let, get(준사역동사)	
능동관계	수동관계
make him wash the dishes have him watch the video let the students play the music get the students play/to play soccer	make oneself understood have a book stolen let the door closed/shut get his watch repaired
She made him wash the dishes. He let the students play the music in the classroom.	He couldn't make himself understood in German. He had his watch repaired in the department store.

제 2 절 동사적 기능

분사의 동사적 용법으로 진행형, 수동태, 완료형으로 사용된다.

1 진행형

현재분사 앞에 be동사를 붙여 진행형으로 사용한다.

예

- He is reading a novel.
- He is watching the opera.

2 수동태

과거분사 앞에 be동사를 붙여 수동태로 사용한다.

예

- This car is made in Korea.
- *The Pickwick Paper* was written by Charles Dickens.

3 완료형

과거분사 앞에 have를 붙여 완료형으로 사용한다.

예

- He has known her since childhood. (현재완료)
- He had already departed when she arrived. (과거완료)

제 3 절 부사적 기능 중요★★

분사는 문장에서 시간, 이유, 조건, 양보, 동시동작 및 연속동작의 부대상황과 같은 부사적 역할을 한다.

1 시간(when, while, after, as, since, as soon as) : ~할 때

예

- Walking down the street, he met his old friend.
  = While he was walking down the street, he met his old friend.

2 이유(because, as, since) : ~이므로

예

- There being no one to help him, he had to do it by himself.
  = Because there was no one to help him, he had to do it by himself.

3 조건(if, unless) : ~한다면

예

- Turning to the left, you can find the post office.
  = If you turn to the left, you can find the post office.

4 양보(though, although, even though, even if, while) : 비록 ～한다 할지라도

예

• Admitting what he said, she still doesn't believe it.

 = Though she admit what he said, she still doesn't believe it.

5 부대상황

(1) 동시동작(while, as) : ～하면서

예

• Listening to the radio, he had lunch.

 = As he listened to the radio, he had lunch.

(2) 연속동작(and + 동사) : 그리고 ～하다

예

• Saying goodbye to him, she left her home.

 = She said goodbye to him and left her home.

제 4 장 분사구문

분사구문(participial phrase)은 '접속사 + 주어 + 동사'로 이루어진 부사절이 있는 복문을 현재분사와 과거분사가 이끄는 분사구, 즉 부사구가 있는 단문으로 간략하게 나타낸 구문이다.

제 1 절 분사구문 형태 중요 ★★★

분사구문의 형태는 부사절의 (의미상의) 주어와 주절의 주어가 같은 경우와 다른 경우가 있다.

1 주어가 같은 경우

방법	현재분사	과거분사
예문	Because he studied hard, he will get a good final grade.	Because he was disappointed with low motivation, he quit his job.
(1) 접속사를 지운다. (부사절 → 부사구)	He studied hard, he will get a good final grade.	He was disappointed with low motivation, he quit his job.
(2) 부사절과 주절의 주어가 같은 경우 주어를 지운다.	Studied hard, he will get a good final grade.	Was disappointed with low motivation, he quit his job.
(3) 부사절의 동사원형에 -ing를 붙여 현재분사 혹은 -(e)d를 붙여 과거분사로 바꾼다.	Studying hard, he will get a good final grade.	Disappointed with low motivation, he quit his job.

2 주어가 다른 경우

(1) 일반적으로 부사절과 주절의 주어가 다른 경우는 그대로 종속절의 주어를 사용한다.
(→ 독립분사구문)

예

• After the sun had set, he gave up looking for her.

→ The sun having set, he gave up looking for her.

- As the dog barked at him, he ran away.
  → The dog barking at him, he ran away.

(2) 주어가 it, there, 사람 이름일 경우 사용 가능

예

- As it was fine, they went out to play tennis.
  → It being fine, they went out to play tennis.

- As there was no bus service, they had to walk to work.
  → There being no bus service, they had to walk to work.

(3) 일반적 대상(불특정 다수) one, we, you, they, people은 생략 가능

예

- If we speak strictly, tomatoes are vegetables in culinary terms.
  → Strictly speaking, tomatoes are vegetables in culinary terms.

(4) 인칭대명사(I, you, she, he, we, they)인 경우는 분사구문으로 바꿀 수 없다.

예

- When he called her, she was eating dinner.
- *he calling her, she was eating dinner.

3 접속사 + 분사구문

부사절의 접속사를 생략하면 의미 구분이 힘든 경우에는 보다 명확한 의미를 전달하기 위해서 접속사를 생략하지 않고 분사구문에 사용한다.

예

- While he played tennis, he felt a severe pain in his shoulder.
  = While playing tennis, he felt a severe pain in his shoulder.

- Once they are merged, they will show great teamwork.
  = Once being merged, they will show great teamwork.
  = Once merged, they will show great teamwork.

4 완료형 분사구문

분사구문 부사절의 시제가 주절의 동사보다 이전에 일어난 일을 나타낼 때는 'having -(e)n (p.p.)'의
형태로 완료형 분사구문을 표현한다.

예

- As he had seen her before, he recognized her at once.
  = Having seen her before, he recognized her at once.

- After he had finished lunch, he went playing tennis.
  = Having finished lunch, he went playing tennis.

5 being vs having been의 생략

예

- As he was left alone, he began to weep.
  = Being left alone, he began to weep.
  = Left alone, he began to weep.

- As he was born and brought up in New York, he knows little about a city life.
  = Having been born and brought up in New York, he knows little about a city life.
  = Born and brought up in New York, he knows little about a city life.
  (※ 원인, 이유를 나타내는 분사구문의 경우에는 보통 생략하지 않는다.)

6 분사구문의 부정

분사구문의 분사 앞에 not 또는 never로 표현한다.

예

- As he didn't know her address, he couldn't find her house.
  = Not knowing her address, he couldn't find her house.

- As he didn't want to anger her, he pretended to agree.
  = Not wanting to anger her, he pretended to agree.

제 2 절 분사구문의 의미

분사구문은 문장 내에서 시간, 이유, 원인, 조건, 양보, 동시동작과 연속동작의 부대상황 등 부사역할을 한다.
※ 동편 제3장 분사 – 제3절 부사적 기능(197쪽 참조)

1 시간(when, while, after, as, since, as soon as) : ∼할 때

[예]

• Left alone, he began to weep.
  = When he left alone, he began to weep.

2 이유(because, as, since) : ∼이므로

[예]

• Overcome with surprise, he was completely numb.
  = As he was overcome with surprise, he was completely numb.

3 조건(if, unless) : ∼한다면

[예]

• Some books, read carelessly, will do more harm than good.
  = Some books, if they are read carelessly, will do more harm and good.

4 양보(though, although, even though, even if, while) : 비록 ∼한다 할지라도

[예]

• Being invited to the party, he didn't come.
  = Though he was invited to the party, he didn't come.

5 부대상황

(1) 동시동작(while, as) : ～하면서

예

- Talking and laughing, the people climbed the mountain.
  = While they talked and laughed, the people climbed the mountain.

(2) 연속동작(and + 동사) : 그리고 ～하다

예

- The train started New Haven at 7 am, arriving in Boston at 10 am.
  = The train started New Haven at 7 am and arrived in Boston at 10 am.

제 3 절 그 외 분사구문

1 독립분사구문

분사구문의 (의미상의) 주어와 주절의 주어가 일치하지 않을 때 분사구문의 주어를 생략하지 않고 분사 앞에 사용하는데 이를 독립분사구문이라 한다.

(1) 시간

예

- When their dinner was over, they went out for a walk.
  = Their dinner being over, they went out for a walk.

- When all things are considered, he thinks that it is the best.
  = All things considered, he thinks that it is the best.

(2) 조건

예

- If the weather permits, they will start tomorrow.
  = The weather permitting, they will start tomorrow.

- If the conditions are equal, this regulation holds good.
  = The conditions being equal, this regulation holds good.

(3) 이유

예

- As the weather was fine, he kept the window open.

  = The weather being fine, he kept the window open.

- As it had rained all night, the road was wet.

  = It having rained all night, the road was wet.

(4) 부대상황(동시동작)

예

- He was singing and his brother was playing the guitar.

  = He was singing, his brother playing the guitar.

※ 독립분사구문에서도 being, having been은 생략 가능하다.
- After school was over, they played tennis.

  = School (being) over, they played tennis.

- After his work had been done, he went playing tennis.

  = His work (having been) done, he went playing tennis.

2 비인칭(무인칭) 독립분사구문

분사구문의 의미상의 주어가 one, we, you, they, people과 같은 일반인, 즉 불특정 다수를 나타내는 경우 주절의 주어와 일치하지 않더라도 주어를 생략하고 관용표현처럼 사용하는데 이를 비인칭(무인칭) 독립분사구문이라고 한다.

예

- If we speak generally, cats don't like water.

  → Generally speaking, cats don't like water.

- When we consider his age, he looks very young.

  → Considering his age, he looks very young.

- Granting that the house is old, he still wants to buy it.

  Granted that the house is old, he still wants to buy it.

- Judging from his accent, he seems to be an English.

- Talking of bears, here is a story for you.

- Frankly speaking, he didn't finish his homework yet.

- Supposing it were true, what would happen?

- Given good weather, the party will be held.

- Providing (that) all his work is done, he may go home.
  Provided (that) all his work is done, he may go home.

- His English is not bad, seeing that he has learned it for three months.

3 형용사, 명사 분사구문 중요 ★★★

(1) 형용사 앞에서 being, having been 생략 가능

예

- As he was angry at her words, he made no reply.
  = Being angry at her words, he made no reply.
  = Angry at her words, he made no reply.

(2) 부사 over 앞에서 being, having been 생략 가능

예

- When dinner was over, they went out for a walk.
  = Dinner being over, they went out for a walk.
  = Dinner over, they went out for a walk.

(3) 명사 앞에서 being, having been 생략 가능

예

- As he is an expert, he knows how to do it.
  = Being an expert, he knows how to do it.
  = An expert, he knows how to do it.

- As he was a man of social instincts, he had many acquaintances.
  = Being a man of social instincts, he had many acquaintances.
  = A man of social instincts, he had many acquaintances.

4 with + 목적어 + 목적보어 : 부대상황 분사구문 **중요** ★★

(1) with + 목적어 + 현재분사(목적어와 분사가 능동관계) : ∼을 하며, ∼을 하면서

예

- He ran into the house with tears running down his cheeks.
- He listened to her with his eyes shining.

(2) with + 목적어 + 과거분사(목적어와 보어가 수동관계) : ∼이 된 채로

예

- He sat on the couch with his arms folded.
- He was lying with his eyes closed.

(3) with + 목적어 + 형용사

예

- He talked to her with his mouth full.
- He left home with the door open.

(4) with + 목적어 + 부사(구)

예

- He enter the house with his shoes on.
- He was looking at her with his arms on the table.

(5) with + 목적어 + 전치사구

예

- He was climbing the mountain with a stick in his hand.
- He was walking with a book under his arm.

제4편 실전예상문제

01 다음 중 밑줄 친 부분의 쓰임이 다른 것은?

① It is interesting to learn a foreign language.
② Many foreigners visit the museum to learn more about kimchi.
③ They don't have any skills, so they want to learn any skills.
④ Homework helps students to learn things more deeply.

02 다음 중 밑줄 친 부분의 쓰임이 다른 것은?

① The summit meeting is to be held next week.
② Grandparents do not have many people to take care of them.
③ People are to wear masks in public locations.
④ He left early to avoid the congested roads.

해설 & 정답   checkpoint

01 해설
to부정사의 부사적 용법(목적)
① to부정사의 명사적 용법(주어)
③ to부정사의 명사 용법(목적어)
④ to부정사의 명사적 용법(목적격 보어)

해석
① 외국어를 배우는 것은 재미있다.
② 많은 외국인들이 김치에 대해 더 많이 배우려고 그 박물관을 찾는다.
③ 그들은 기술이 없어서 어떤 기술이라도 배우고 싶어 한다.
④ 숙제는 학생들이 더 깊이 배울 수 있도록 도와준다.

02 해설
to부정사 부사적 용법(목적)
① to부정사 형용사 서술적 용법(be + to부정사, 예정)
② to부정사 형용사 한정적 용법
③ to부정사 형용사 서술적 용법(be + to부정사, 의무)

해석
① 정상회담은 다음 주에 열릴 예정이다.
② 조부모님들은 그들을 돌볼 사람이 많지 않다.
③ 공공장소에서는 마스크를 착용해야 한다.
④ 그는 혼잡한 도로를 피하기 위해 일찍 떠났다.

정답 01 ② 02 ④

checkpoint 해설 & 정답

03 해설

사역동사 make + 목적어 구문에서 목적어 her가 가방을 열어야 하는 능동관계이므로 'open'이 맞다. 'her bag'이 make의 목적어는 구문에서는 'The customs officer made her bag open(ed).'로 쓰인다.
② 준사역동사 get 목적어 원형부정사/to부정사, ③ 지각동사 feel의 원형부정사 형태이고 현재분사형태 shaking도 가능, ④ 준사역동사 help 목적어 원형부정사/to부정사

해석
① 세관원이 그녀에게 가방을 열게 했다.
② 그녀는 남편에게 자신의 사진을 찍게 했다.
③ 당신은 5분 전에 건물이 흔들리는 것을 느꼈나요?
④ 그 교수는 학생들이 숙제하는 것을 도와주었다.

04 해설

원형부정사를 사용하는 관용 표현 :
① all you have to do is 원형부정사(~하기만 하면 된다) ② do nothing but 원형부정사(단지 ~할 뿐이다) ③ had better 원형부정사(~하는 것이 좋다), had better review로 표현하는 것이 옳다. ④ would rather ~ than -(-보다는 차라리 ~하겠다)

해석
① 당신은 핸드폰을 켜기만 하면 된다.
② 그는 웃기만 한다.
③ 너는 다음 시험 전에 그 부분을 복습하는 게 좋겠어.
④ 그는 잘못된 사람을 선택하느니 차라리 투표를 하지 않을 것이다.

정답 03 ① 04 ③

03 다음 중 어법상 잘못된 표현은?

① The customs officer made her opened her bag.
② She got her husband to take the picture of her.
③ Did you feel the building shaking five minutes ago?
④ The professor helped students to do their homework.

04 다음 중 어법상 잘못된 표현은?

① All you have to do is turn your cell phone.
② He does nothing but to laugh.
③ You had better to review the section before the next exam.
④ He would rather not vote than choose the wrong people.

05 다음 중 의미가 <u>다른</u> 하나는?

① Nothing remains but to laugh.

② There is nothing for it but to laugh.

③ He had no choice but to laugh.

④ He cannot help but to laugh.

05 해설

'~하지 않을 수 없다, 어쩔 수 없이 ~하다'의 관용표현

cannot but 원형부정사, cannot help 동명사, cannot help but 원형부정사, have no choice/alternative but to부정사, there is nothing for it but to부정사, be forced/compelled/bound/obliged to부정사

해석

(그는) 웃지 않을 수 없다. (웃을 수밖에 없다.)

06 해설

to부정사의 시제는 주절의 본동사의 시제와 일치하는 단순부정사, 본동사보다 앞선 완료부정사, 진행형으로 표현된다. ① 단순부정사, ② 단순형 수동태, ③ 완료부정사 수동태 표현으로 It seemed that he had been loved가 맞다. ④ 완료 진행형 형태로서 to have been doing이므로 주절 본동사 현재시제 seems 보다 한 시제 앞선 he was doing을 쓴다.

해석

① 그는 이상해 보였다.

② 그는 사랑받는 것 같다.

③ 그는 사랑받는 것처럼 보였다.

④ 그는 최선을 다했던 것 같다.

06 다음 중 문장이 <u>잘못</u> 전환된 것은?

① He seemed to be strange. → It seemed that he was strange.

② He seems to be loved. → It seems that she is loved.

③ He seemed to have been loved. → It seemed that he was loved.

④ He seems to have been doing his best. → It seems that he was doing his best.

정답 05 ④ 06 ③

07 **해설**

to부정사의 의미상의 주어는 일반적으로 for + 목적격이나 kind, thoughtful, wise 등 사람의 성격, 성질을 나타내는 형용사 다음에는 of + 목적격, 불특정 다수인 경우 표현하지 않아도 되는데 예문의 경우 두 번째 of + 목적격 형태이다.

해석
• 그가 도움을 주다니 정말 친절하구나.
• 그녀가 너에게 알려준 것은 사려 깊었다.
• 그녀의 제안을 받아들이다니 그는 현명하다.

08 **해설**

동명사의 의미상의 주어 표현 :
① 문장의 주어(he)와 일치하는 경우
② 문장의 목적어(her)와 일치하는 경우 의미상의 주어를 밝히지 않아도 된다. ③ 동명사의 의미상의 주어가 사물인 경우 of + 명사로 표현한다. ④ 동명사 의미상의 주어를 밝히는 경우 소유격(his)으로 표현한다.

해석
① 그는 셀 수 없이 많은 돈을 낭비한 것을 후회했다.
② 그는 역까지 태워다 준 그녀에게 감사했다.
③ 그녀는 리조트 방이 지저분하다고 불평했다.
④ 그녀는 그에게 다음 달에 열리는 국제회의에 참석할 것을 제안했다.

정답 07 ② 08 ④

---

07 **다음 중 밑줄 친 부분에 공통으로 들어갈 표현은?**

> • It was very kind _____ him to offer help.
> • It was thoughtful _____ her to let you know.
> • It is wise _____ him to accept her offer.

① for
② of
③ to
④ with

08 **다음 중 어법상 잘못된 표현은?**

① He repented of having wasted all his countless dollars.
② He thanked her for giving him a ride to the station.
③ She complained of the resort room being messy.
④ She suggested him attending the international conference next month.

09 다음 중 어법상 잘못된 표현은?

① They discussed entering into a new business.
② They postpone leaving the United States until next month.
③ The opposite party demanded to lower the highest income tax bracket.
④ Korea offered sending food and medicine worth $10million.

10 다음 중 어법상 잘못된 표현은?

① The executive observed the engineer fixing the machine.
② She made her car washed.
③ He heard his name mention in the auditorium.
④ The customer had the server bring him a new spoon.

09 해설
offer는 to부정사를 필요로 하는 동사, to send
① discuss는 동명사를 필요로 하는 동사, enter into는 '시작하다'는 의미
② postpone은 동명사를 필요로 하는 동사
③ demand는 to부정사를 필요로 하는 동사

해석
① 그들은 새로운 사업을 시작하는 것에 대해 논의했다.
② 그들은 다음 달까지 미국을 떠나는 것을 연기한다.
③ 야당은 최고 소득세율 등급을 낮출 것을 요구했다.
④ 한국은 1천만 달러 상당의 식량과 의약품을 보내겠다고 제안했다.

어휘
• income tax bracket : 소득세율 등급

10 해설
현재분사(능동관계) vs 과거분사(수동관계)를 나타내는 표현으로 ① 지각동사 observe는 목적어 engineer가 fix를 하는 능동적 관계를 나타내므로 fix/fixing이 적절 ② 사역동사 make는 목적어 her car가 수동적 관계를 나타내므로 과거분사가 적절 ③ 지각동사 hear는 his name이 불리는 수동적 관계를 나타내는 과거분사 mentioned가 적절 ④ 사역동사 have는 목적어 the server가 spoon을 가지고 오는 능동적 관계를 나타내는 bring이 적절하다.

해석
① 그 임원은 그 엔지니어가 기계를 고치는 것을 관찰했다.
② 그녀는 세차했다.
③ 그는 강당에서 자기 이름이 거론되는 것을 들었다.
④ 손님은 종업원에게 새 숟가락을 가져오라고 했다.

정답 09④ 10③

여기서 멈출 거예요? 끝장이 바로 눈앞에 있어요.
마지막 한 걸음까지 SD에듀가 함께할게요!

합 격 으 로   가 는   가 장   똑 똑 한   선 택   S D 에 듀 !

제 **5** 편

복합명사구

www.sdedu.co.kr

단원 개요

복합명사구는 관계사, 동격, 명사 수식어구를 포함한다. **관계사는 제한적 vs 비제한적 용법**, **관계대명사**(주격, 목적격, 소유격), 유사관계대명사(as, but, than), 복합관계사(복합관계대명사, 복합관계부사, 복합관계형용사)가 있고, **동격**은 **제한적 vs 비제한적 용법**, **동격 that**절에 대한 내용이고, 명사 수식어구는 수식 위치에 따라 **전위치**(명사, 형용사(구), (현재/과거)분사)와 **후위치**(형용사(구, 절))에 대한 내용이다.

출제 경향 및 수험 대책

1. 관계사
   (1) 제한적, 비제한적 용법과 의미
   (2) 관계 대명사 형태, 용법, 의미, 생략 가능 vs 생략 불가능 용법
   (3) 복합관계사, 복합관계부사, 복합관계형용사 형태, 용법, 의미
2. 동격
   (1) 제한적, 비제한적 용법과 의미
   (2) 관계대명사 that vs 동격 that 사용
3. 명사 수식어구 : 전위치 vs 후위치 수식어구 사용

자격증 • 공무원 • 금융/보험 • 면허증 • 언어/외국어 • 검정고시/독학사 • 기업체/취업

이 시대의 모든 합격! SD에듀에서 합격하세요!

www.youtube.com ➡ SD에듀 ➡ 구독

제 1 장 관계사

제 1 절 제한적 용법(restrictive use)

관계대명사(relative pronoun)가 이끄는 **형용사절**(adjective clause)이 앞에 있는 선행사를 수식하는 경우를 제한적 혹은 한정적 용법이라고 하고, 청자가 선행사에 대해 모르는 정보일 경우에 사용한다.

예

- The man who lives next door is a university professor.

- The professor who teaches Linguistics 301 is an excellent scholar.

- The climbers who reached the top were tired. (정상에 오르지 않은 등산객이 있을 수 있음)

- He has two daughters who became university professors.
  예 그에게는 대학 교수가 된 두 딸이 있다.
  (대학교수가 아닌 딸(들)이 있을 수 있음)

제 2 절 비제한적 용법(nonrestrictive use)

관계 대명사 앞에 comma(,)를 사용하여 선행사와 분리하여 수식하는 경우를 비제한적 또는 계속적 용법이라고 하고, 청자가 이미 알고 있는 선행사에 대해 **추가적, 부수적 정보 및 설명**을 하는 경우에 사용한다. 이 경우 관계대명사는 접속사(and, but, for, though) + 대명사를 의미하는 데 접속사 that 은 비제한적 용법에서는 사용 불가하다.

예

- Mr. Jensen, who lives next door, is a university professor.

- The professor, who teaches Linguistics 301, is an excellent scholar.

• The climbers, who reached the top, were tired. (등산객은 모두 정상에 등반하고 지침)

• He has three daughters, who became university professors. (딸은 모두 셋이고 모두 대학 교수)
(who = and they)

• Everyone likes Josh, who is hilarious. (who = for he)

• The man, who is not rich, is honest. (who = though he)

❗ 더 알아두기 🔍

비제한적 용법(계속적 용법)의 which는 앞에 나온 구, 절, 문장 또는 그 일부를 나타낸다.

[예]
• The concert, which I heard last week, was excellent.
• His wife was very intelligent, which was a source of great pride to him.

제 **3** 절   관계대명사(relative pronoun) 중요 ★★★

관계사절(relative clause)은 관계대명사가 이끄는 (형용사)절을 말하고, 관계대명사는 그 선행사(antecedent)가 사람, 사물, 동물인지와 문법상 주격, 동사나 전치사의 **목적격**, 소유격인지에 따라 다음과 같이 구분된다.

선행사	주격	목적격	소유격
사람	who	who(m) ∅	whose
사물, 동물	which	which ∅	whose of which
사람, 사물, 동물	that	that ∅	-
선행사를 포함하는 관계대명사	what	what	-

1 주격 관계대명사

(1) 사람 : who, that

She thanked <u>the man</u>. (→ 주절)

<u>He</u> helped her. (→ 관계사절 주어)

↓

She thanked the man <u>who</u> helped her.

She thanked the man <u>that</u> helped her.

(2) 사물/동물 : which, that

<u>The pen</u> is hers. (→ 주절)

<u>It</u> is on the desk. (→ 관계사절 주어)

↓

The pen <u>which</u> is on the desk is hers.

The pen <u>that</u>　 is on the desk is hers.

2 목적격 관계대명사 : 동사의 목적어 중요 ★★★

(1) 사람 : who(m), that, ∅

<u>The man</u> was Mr. Jensen. (→ 주절)

Joey saw <u>him</u> last night. (→ 관계사절 목적어)

↓

The man <u>who(m)</u> Joey saw last night was Mr. Jensen.

The man <u>that</u>　 Joey saw last night was Mr. Jensen.

The man ∅　　 Joey saw last night was Mr. Jensen. (생략가능)

(2) 사물/동물 : which, that, ∅

> The drama was very good. (→ 주절)
>
> Amy saw it last night. (→ 관계사절 목적어)
>
> ↓
>
> The drama which Amy saw last night was very good.
>
> The drama that Amy saw last night was very good.
>
> The drama ∅ Amy saw last night was very good. (생략가능)

🔍 더 알아두기 🔍

관계대명사의 생략 중요 ★★

(1) 주격 관계대명사

일반적으로 주격 관계대명사는 생략하지 않지만 몇 가지 예외적인 경우가 있다.

① (주격 관계대명사 + be동사) + 전치사구/형용사구/현재분사/과거분사

예

- The pen (which is) on the desk is hers. (+ 전치사구)
- She has to do her new project (which is) too difficult to do. (+ 형용사)
- The gentleman (who is) delivering a speech is my adviser. (+ 현재분사)
- This is the hospital (which was) established in 1958. (+ 과거분사)

※ 다음은 생략이 불가능한 경우이다.

㉠ 주격 관계대명사 + be동사 + 명사

예
- She knows a gentleman who is a professor of music.
- *She knows a gentleman a professor of music.

㉡ 주격 관계대명사 + 일반동사

예
- She met a man who played the guitar well.
- *She met a man played the guitar well.

㉢ 주격 관계대명사 + 조동사

예
- She met a man who can speak Italian well.
- *She met a man can speak Italian well.

② 주격 보어

예 She is not the woman (that) she used to be.

③ 주절이 there is, here is로 시작하는 경우

예 There is someone (who) wants to see you right now.

---

④ 관계대명사 다음에 there is/are 표현

   예 She advised him the difference (that) there is between virtue and vice.

⑤ 분열구문 It is ~ that 강조구문

   예 It was he (that) met the professor yesterday.

(2) 목적격 관계대명사는 생략 가능하다.

   예

- The man who(m)/that/∅ Joey saw last night was Mr. Jensen.
- The drama which/that/∅ Amy saw last night was very good.

3 목적격 관계대명사 : 전치사의 목적어 중요 ★★

(1) 사람

Laurel is the professor. (→ 주절)

I told you about her. (→ 관계사절 목적어)

↓

Laurel is the professor about whom I told you.

Laurel is the professor whom   I told you about.

Laurel is the professor that   I told you about.

Laurel is the professor ∅   I told you about. (생략 가능)

(2) 사물/동물

The music was wonderful. (→ 주절)

Amy listened to it last night. (→ 관계사절 목적어)

↓

The music to which Amy listened last night was wonderful.

The music which   Amy listened to last night was wonderful.

The music that   Amy listened to last night was wonderful.

The music ∅   Amy listened to last night was wonderful. (생략 가능)

4 소유격 관계대명사 중요 ★★

(1) 사람 : whose

Josh knows <u>the woman</u>. (→ 주절)

<u>Her book</u> was published lately. (→ 관계사절 소유격)

↓

Josh knows the woman <u>whose book</u> was published lately.

(2) 사물/동물 : whose, of which

① whose

Josh has <u>a cat</u>. (→ 주절)

<u>Cat's (Its)</u> color is black and white. (→ 관계사절 소유격)

↓

Josh has a cat <u>whose</u> color is black and white.

(Josh has a cat <u>of which</u> color is black and white.)

(Josh has a cat the color <u>of which</u> is black and white.) (its color → the color of it)

② of which

Josh bought <u>a chair</u>. (→ 주절)

The top <u>of the chair</u> was made of wood. (→ 관계사절 소유격)

↓

Josh bought a chair the top <u>of which</u> was made of wood.

Josh bought a chair　　　　<u>of which</u> the top was made of wood.

(Josh bought a chair <u>whose</u> top was made of wood.)

5 관계대명사 that 중요 ★★

(1) 선행사가 사람, 사물/동물인 경우

예

- She thanked the man that(who) helped her.
- The pen that(which) is on the desk is hers.

(2) 선행사가 사람 + 사물을 모두 포함하는 경우

> 예 He made notes of the people and places that excited my interest.

(3) 선행사가 all, no, little, much, 부정대명사 -thing인 경우

> 예
> • Is there something that I can do for you?
> • He fixed almost anything that needed repairing.

(4) 선행사가 의문대명사인 경우

> 예 Who that has spoken with her does not know the tenderness of her heart?

(5) 선행사가 형용사의 최상급, 서수사, the very, the only, the same, the first, the last 등 한정적 수식어를 받는 경우

> 예
> • He is the first man (that) solved one of the big mathematical problems.
> • He is the only man (that) she loves.

(6) 선행사가 보어인 경우

> 예 Fool that I am!

(7) 관계대명사와 be동사만 있는 경우

> 예
> • the powers that be
> • She was away back in the life that had been.

(8) that을 사용할 수 없는 경우

① 제한적 용법 ○, 비제한적 용법(계속적용법) ×

> 예
> • The professor who/that teaches Linguistics 301 is an excellent scholar.
> • The pen which/that is on the desk is hers.
>
> • The professor, who/*that teaches Linguistics 301, is an excellent scholar.
> • The pen, which/*that is on the desk, is hers.

② 전치사 + that ✕

예

- Laurel is the professor <u>about whom</u> I told you.
- Laurel is the professor <u>whom</u>   I told you <u>about</u>.
- Laurel is the professor <u>that</u>   I told you <u>about</u>.
- Laurel is the professor ∅   I told you <u>about</u>. (생략 가능)
- *Laurel is the professor <u>about that</u> I told you.

- The music <u>to which</u> Amy listened last night was wonderful.
- The music <u>which</u>   Amy listened <u>to</u> last night was wonderful.
- The music <u>that</u>   Amy listened <u>to</u> last night was wonderful.
- The music ∅   Amy listened <u>to</u> last night was wonderful. (생략 가능)
- *The music <u>to that</u> Amy listened last night was wonderful.

6   관계대명사 what

(1) 선행사를 포함하는 관계대명사

① 주어

예

- What I really need is telephone.
- What she said is not true.

② 목적어

예

- I will send what was promised.
- He accepted what she offered.

③ 주격 보어

예

- This is what she wants to do.
- This is what he said.

더 알아두기

주어 역할 관계대명사 what의 수 일치

① 주어 역할의 what절이 주격 보어를 취하는 경우, 보어가 복수형이어도 be동사는 단수형

[예]
  • What I need most is computers.
  • What is needed most is computers.

② what절을 and로 연결하면 복수형

  [예] What he said and what she said are my own business.

(2) 관용적 용법 중요 ★★

① **what is + 비교급** : 더욱 ~한 것은

  [예] He is smart, and what is better, warm-hearted.

② **what + 주어(we, you, they) + call = what is called(as we call it)** : 이른바, 소위

  [예] He is, what we call, a musical genius.

③ **what one is, 인격 / what one has, 재산**

  [예] We should judge people by what they are, not by what they have.

④ **what with A and (what with) B** : 어느 정도는 A 때문에, 어느 정도는 B 때문에

  what by A and (what by) B : 어느 정도는 A에 의해서, 어느 정도는 B에 의해서

  [예]
  • What with the rain and what with the cold, we postponed our trip.
  • What by efforts and what by luck, he attained his aims.

⑤ **A is to B what C is to D**

  = What C is to D, A is to B

  = Just as C is to D, so is A to B

  A가 B에 대한 관계는 C가 D에 대한 관계와 같다. (A is to B 강조, C is to D는 비유)

  [예]
  • Air is to man what water is to fish.
  • Reading is to the mind what food is to the body.
  • The cup is to Dionysus what the shield is to Ares.

⑥ **What with one thing and another** : 이런저런 이유로

  [예] What with one thing and another, he postpone the conference next month.

제 4 절 유사관계대명사(pseudo-relative pronoun)

유사관계대명사는 선행사 앞의 특정 단어와 호응을 이루는데 as, but, than이 쓰인다.

1 as

(1) 선행사에 as, so, such, the same 등의 표현이 있는 경우

① 주격

예

- Choose such friends as will benefit you.

  (= Choose those friends who will benefit you.)

② 목적격

예 Such movies as they are watching are good for education.

(2) 선행 또는 후속하는 주절

예

- He is absent today, as is often the case (with him).
- As is often the case with teenagers, he is crazy about motorcycle,

2 but

선행사에 no, not 등 부정어를 수반하는 경우 : but에(도) not 뜻이 포함됨. ~이 아닌 것 (= that/who ~ not)

예

- There is no rule but has some exceptions.

  (= There is no rule that does not have some exceptions.)

3 than

선행사에 비교급이 있는 문장에서 주격 또는 목적격 관계대명사 역할

(1) 주격

> 예 There are more food than are needed.

(2) 목적격

> 예 People usually eat more food than they need.

⚡ 더 알아두기 🔍

유사관계대명사 than의 목적격 관계대명사 사용의 경우

예

- He loves you more than (he loves) me. ([해석] 그가 나를 사랑하는 것보다 더 그가 당신을 사랑한다.)
- He loves you more than I (love you). ([해석] 내가 당신을 사랑하는 것보다 더 그가 당신을 사랑한다.)
- ※ 비격식 표현에서는 than me가 than I의 의미로 사용되기도 함)

제 5 절 복합관계사

1 복합관계대명사 : 관계대명사 + −ever 중요 ★

관계대명사 + −ever	절	선행사 + 관계대명사
whoever	명사절 (누구든지)	anyone who
	양보부사절 (누가 ~이라도)	no matter who
whomever	명사절 (~이든지)	anyone whom
	양보부사절 (누구를 ~하든지)	no matter whom
whosever	명사절 (누구 것이든)	anyone whose
	양보부사절 (누구의 ~뭐든지)	no matter whose
whatever	명사절 (무엇이든지)	anything that
	양보부사절 (아무리 ~일지라도)	no matter what
whichever	명사절 (어느 것이든)	anything which/that
	양보부사절 (어느 것이 ~하더라도)	no matter which

(1) 명사 용법

① 주어

예

- Whoever wants to succeed should work hard. (= Anyone who)
- Send it to whoever wants it. (= anyone who)
- Give this gift to anyone whosever writing is excellent. (= anyone whose)

② 목적어

예

- Show it to whomever you like. (= anyone whom)
- You may have whichever you want. (= anything that)

(2) 형용사 용법

예

- Read whatever book you want. (= any book that)
- You may take whichever laptop you want. (= any laptop that)

(3) 부사 용법(양보의 부사절 유도)

예

- Whoever may come, she will be satisfied with our food. (= No matter who)
- Whosever it may be, she wants to have it. (= No matter whose)
- Whatever you may do, I want you to do your all best. (= No matter what)

2 복합관계부사 : 관계부사 + -ever 중요 ★★

관계부사 + -ever	부사절	선행사 + 관계부사
whenever	시간 : 언제든지	at any time when
	양보 : 언제라도	no matter when
wherever	장소 : 어디든지	at any place where
	양보 : 어디서든지	no matter where
however	방법 : 어떻게 하든 양보 : 아무리 ~한다 해도	no matter how

(1) whenever

① 시간

예

- She will meet him whenever she wants. (= at any time when)
- Call me whenever you need help. (= at any time when)

② 양보

예

- Whenever you say to your junior, always be respectful.
- No matter when you say to your junior, always be respectful.

(2) wherever

① 장소

예

- He always sing a song wherever he goes. (= at any place where)
- He always carries some extra cash wherever he goes. (= at any place where)

② 양보

예

- The star is surrounded by teenagers wherever she may be.

  The star is surrounded by teenagers no matter where she may be.

(3) however

① 방법

예

- He always looks humble however he dresses up.

  He always looks humble no matter how he dresses up.

② 양보

예

- He couldn't persuade his parents however hard he tried.

  He couldn't persuade his parents no matter how hard he tried.

(4) 관계부사

① 관계부사 = 전치사 + 관계대명사

선행사		관계부사	전치사 + 관계대명사
시간	the time	when	at/on/in + which
장소	the place	where	at/on/in + which
이유	the reason	why	for + which
방법	the way	how	at/on/in(/by) + which ○ the way ~ ○ how ~ × the way how ~ (선행사와 관계부사 함께 사용 ×)

예

- This season is the time when it's ripe. (= in which)
- The stage is the place where the musical takes place. (= on which)
- This is the reason why no extraterrestrials have contacted us yet. (= for which)

- This is the way he solved the question. (= in which)
- This is how he solved the question. (= in which)
- *This is the way how he solved the question.

- This is the way he lives.
- This is how he lives.
- *This is the way how he lives.

② 관계부사의 비제한적 용법(계속적용법)

　㉠ ~, when : ~, and then (그때)

　　예 They visited England in May, when it did not rain too much.

　㉡ ~, where : ~, and there (거기에서)

　　예 Josh visited Burbank, CA, where my best friend lived. (= and there)

3 복합관계형용사 : 관계형용사 + -ever 중요 ★

관계형용사 + -ever	절	선행사 + 관계형용사
whatever	명사절 : 무엇이든(지)	anything that
	양보부사절 : 아무리 -일지라도	no matter what
whichever	명사절 : 어느 것이든	anything which/that
	양보부사절 : 어느 것을 하더라도	no matter which

(1) whatever

예

- His parents will support whatever decision he made. (= any decision that)
- You may have whatever books you want. (= any books that)
- Whatever difficulties you may face, have a confidence. (= No matter what)
- He is innocent, whatever you may think. (= no matter what)

(2) whichever

예

- You may wear whichever dress you want. (= any dress which)
- You may select whichever laptop you like. (= any laptop which)
- Whichever mountain you may choose, it is dangerous to climb. (= No matter which)
- Whichever you select, cost is not a factor; I will pay. (= No matter which)

제 2 장 동격

제 1 절 제한적 용법 vs 비제한적 용법 중요 ★

동격(apposition)은 문장 내에서 특정 어구와 동일한 구조와 성격(동일 품사)을 갖춘 다른 어구를 나타낸다. comma를 사용하지 않는 제한적 용법은 내용상 필요한 정보를, comma를 사용하는 비제한적 용법은 추가적인 정보를 나타낸다.

1 제한적 용법(한정적 용법)

예

- My friend Josh earned Ph.D. degree. (친구 중에 Josh가 여러 명 있는데 그중 Josh)
- My husband a former fireman is good at cooking. ((전)남편이 여러 명 있(었)는데 그중 전직 소방관)
- His daughter Amy is 25 years old. (그의 하나뿐인 딸 Amy, Amy is his one and only daughter.)

2 비제한적 용법(계속적 용법)

예

- My friend, Josh, earned Ph.D. degree. (내 친구 중에 Josh는 한 명이고)
- My husband, a former fireman, is good at cooking. (남편이 전직 소방관)
- His daughter, Amy, is 25 years old. (Amy는 여러 딸 중에 한 명, Amy is one of his daughters.)

- Josh, a friend of mine, joined our fraternity.
- George Washington, the first president of the United States, a general in the army.
- Seoul, the capital of Korea, is an exciting city.
- He read books by Ernest Hemingway, a famous American novelist.

제 2 절 관계대명사 that vs 동격 that 종요★★

관계대명사 that은 주절과 함께 쓰이는 **불완전한 문장**(incomplete sentence)의 형용사절로서 제한적 용법에 사용되며 선행사가 사람이면 who, 사물이면 which로 대용 가능하고 목적격인 경우 생략 가능하다. 반면에 **동격 that**은 접속사로서 **완전한 문장**(complete sentence)의 명사절을 표현하고 who, which로 대용이 불가능하고 생략도 불가능하다.

1 관계대명사 that

① **주격** : 사람, 사물

예

- She thanked the man <u>who/that</u> helped her.
- The pen <u>which/that</u> is on the desk is hers.

② **동사 목적격** : 사람, 사물

예

- The man <u>who(m)/that/∅</u> Joey saw last night was Mr. Jensen.
  The drama <u>which/that/∅</u> Amy saw last night was very good.

③ **전치사 목적격** : 사람, 사물

예

- Laurel is the professor <u>about whom</u> I told you.
  Laurel is the professor <u>whom/that/∅</u> I told you about.

- The music <u>to which</u> Amy listened last night was wonderful.
  The music <u>which/that/∅</u> Amy listened <u>to</u> last night was wonderful.

2 동격 that

(1) 동격 that절을 취하는 명사

announcement that ~	(re)assurance that ~	belief that ~
chance that ~	claim that ~	confirmation that ~
evidence that ~	fact that ~	feeling that ~
idea that ~	impression that ~	news that ~
no doubt that ~	notion that ~	opinion that ~
proof that ~	reason that ~	report that ~
rumor that ~	statement that ~	truth that ~

(2) 주어

예

- The fact that the boxers played a put-up game was very clear.
- The opinion that the death penalty should be abolished will get stronger and stronger.

(3) 목적어

예

- What do you think about the rumor that he is a fashionista?
- He has a feeling that his dream will come true.

제3장 기타 명사 수식어구

제1절 전위치 수식어구(prepositional modifiers)

1 명사

예

- Josh is a university professor.
- Amy is a college professor.

2 형용사(구)

예

- Some people have inherent gifts.
- She has naturally beautiful voices.

3 (현재/과거)분사

예

- A drowning man will catch at a straw.
- Passed youth never comes back.

제 2 절 후위치 수식어구(postpositional modifiers)

1 형용사(구)

① 형용사

　㉠ The board members present in the meeting were all in favor of his proposal.

② 형용사구

　㉠ Who is the lady playing the violin?

③ to부정사

　㉠ Would you recommend historic places to visit in Seoul?

2 형용사절

㉠

- She thanked the man who/that helped her.
- The man who/that lives next door is a university professor.
- The pen which/that is on the desk is hers.
- The car which/that she bought yesterday is a sports car.

제 **5** 편 실전예상문제

01 다음 중 밑줄 친 부분에 공통으로 들어갈 표현은 무엇인가?

> • Anyone _____ wants to come is welcome.
> • My brother, _____ lives in Chicago, has two sons.

① who
② whom
③ which
④ of which

01 해설

관계사절 동사의 주어인 주격 관계대명사이고 선행사가 사람인 경우 who를 사용하는데 첫 번째는 제한적(한정적) 용법, 두 번째 문장은 비제한적(계속적) 용법이다.

해석
• 오고자 하는 사람은 누구라도 환영이다.
• 시카고에 사는 남동생은 아들이 두 명 있다.

02 다음 중 밑줄 친 부분에 공통으로 들어갈 표현은 무엇인가?

> • The woman _____ car he hit was upset.
> • His son, _____ major was chemistry, is a high-school teacher.

① who
② whom
③ whose
④ of which

02 해설

선행사와 관계사절 명사와 소유관계이고, 선행사가 사람인 경우 whose를 사용한다. 첫 번째 문장은 제한적(한정적) 용법, 두 번째 문장은 비제한적(계속적) 용법이다.

해석
• 그가 충돌한(부딪친) 차의 여성은 화가 났다.
• 화학을 전공한 그의 아들은 고등학교 교사이다.

정답 01 ① 02 ③

checkpoint 해설 & 정답

03 해설

선행사와 관계사절 명사와 소유관계이고, 선행사가 사물인 경우 whose, of which를 사용한다. 첫 번째 문장은 제한적(한정적) 용법, 두 번째 문장은 비제한적(계속적) 용법이다.

해석
• 그녀는 흰색인 집을 좋아한다.
• 미국 의회도서관은 1,700만 권의 장서가 있으며, 그중 절반은 영어로 쓰여져 있다.

04 해설

전치사＋관계대명사 which는 생략이 불가능. 단, 전치사 about이 관계사절에 남아 있는 경우 which 생략 가능 → The topic (which/that) she talked about was carbon emission.
① 주격 관계대명사＋be동사＋형용사(구) 구문에서 '관계대명사＋be동사'는 생략 가능
② (전치사의) 목적격 관계대명사 that은 생략 가능. 단, 전치사 about은 관계사절에 위치해야 함
③ 주절이 there is, here is로 시작하는 경우 주격 관계대명사 생략 가능

해석
① 그는 너무 감당하기 어려운 책임을 져야 했다.
② 그녀는 내가 당신에게 말했던 음악 교수이다.
③ 지금 당신을 만나고 싶어하는 사람이 있어요.
④ 그녀가 말한 주제는 탄소 배출이었다.

정답 03 ④ 04 ④

03 다음 중 밑줄 친 부분에 공통으로 들어갈 표현은 무엇인가?

> • She likes the house _____ color is white.
> • Library of Congress, 17 million books, _____ half are written in English.

① that
② which
③ in which
④ of which

04 다음 밑줄 친 부분 중 생략할 수 <u>없는</u> 것은?

① He had to bear responsibility <u>which was</u> too difficult to do.
② She is the professor of music <u>that</u> I told you about.
③ There is some <u>who</u> wants to see you right now.
④ The topic about <u>which</u> she talked was carbon emission.

05 다음 중 밑줄 친 부분에 공통으로 들어갈 표현은?

> • This jewelry is more valuable _____ is supposed to be.
> • Some people spend more money _____ they actually earn.

① as
② but
③ than
④ what

06 다음 중 밑줄 친 부분에 들어갈 표현은?

> _____ you select between two dishes, cost is not a factor; he will pay.

① whoever
② whomever
③ whatever
④ whichever

07 다음 중 밑줄 친 부분과 같은 의미 표현은 무엇인가?

> No matter whom you may ask, this questions will never be answered correctly.

① Whoever
② Whomever
③ Whosever
④ Whatever

05 해설
유사관계대명사 'than'이 첫 번째 문장에서는 선행사에 비교급이 있는 문장에서 주격 관계 대명사 역할을 하고, 두 번째 문장에서는 목적격 관계대명사 역할을 한다.

해석
• 이 보석은 생각했던 <u>것보다</u> 더 귀중하다.
• 어떤 사람들은 실제로 버는 <u>것보다</u> 더 많은 돈을 쓴다.

06 해설
복합관계대명사(관계대명사＋ever) 형태 양보부사절(no matter which, 어느 쪽을 택하더라도)로 동사 select의 목적어에 해당하는 whichever가 필요하다.

해석
두 가지 요리 중 어느 것을 선택하든지 <u>간에</u>, 가격은 중요하지 않다; 그가 지불할 것이다.

07 해설
복합관계대명사 양보 부사절(no matter whom, '누구에게 물어보아도')을 이끌고 동사 ask의 목적어에 해당하는 whomever 표현이 적절하다.

해석
당신이 <u>누구에게</u> 물어도 이 질문은 결코 정확하게 대답할 수 없을 것이다.

정답 05 ③ 06 ② 07 ②

08 해설

복합관계대명사 whichever의 명사절 목적어 역할(어느 것이든→anything that)

① 복합관계대명사 whoever의 명사절 목적어 역할(누구든지)
② 복합관계부사 wherever의 장소 부사절(어디든지)
③ 복합관계부사 whenever의 양보 부사절(언제라도)

해석

① 그가 <u>누구</u>를 초대하든 그 파티는 성공할 것이다.
② 그는 가는 <u>곳마다</u> 항상 노래를 부른다.
③ 자녀에게 말을 할 <u>때</u>는 항상 자녀를 존중해야 한다.
④ 당신이 원하는 것은 <u>어느 것이든</u> 선택할 수 있다.

09 해설

관계부사 방법 표현은 the way how 는 비문법적 표현, the way ~ 또는 how ~

① 관계부사 시간 표현 the time when
② 관계부사 이유 표현 the reason why
④ 관계형용사 양보부사절 표현 no matter which

해석

① 아무도 스키를 타러 가지 않는 겨울에는 무슨 일이 일어날까?
② 지구 온난화는 열대야가 더 빈번한 이유(원인)이기도 하다.
③ 그것은 근본적으로 한국의 젊은 이들이 게임을 즐기는 방식을 변화시켰다.
④ 그는 어떤 식으로든 매우 곤란한 입장에 처해 있다.

정답 08 ④ 09 ③

---

08 다음 중 밑줄 친 부분을 잘못 표현한 것은?

① <u>Whoever</u> he invites, the party will be a success. → Anyone whom
② He always sing a song <u>wherever</u> he goes. → at any place where
③ <u>Whenever</u> you say to your children, always be respectful. → No matter when
④ You can choose <u>whichever</u> you want. → no matter which

09 다음 중 어법상 잘못된 표현은?

① What happens during the winter time when nobody goes skiing?
② Global warming is also the reason why we have more frequent tropical nights.
③ It essentially changed the way how young people enjoyed games in Korea.
④ He is in a very difficult position whichever way he turns.

10 다음 중 밑줄 친 that의 쓰임이 <u>다른</u> 것은?

① The evidence <u>that</u> has come out so far is not conclusive.

② He made notes of the people and restaurants <u>that</u> excited her interest.

③ There is no doubt <u>that</u> they were wrong from the start.

④ The existence of water significantly increases the chance <u>that</u> life may also be found on the planet.

10 해설

관계대명사 that과 동격의 that의 쓰임에 관한 문제로 관계대명사 that은 불완전한 문장의 형용사절로 주절과 함께 쓰이는 반면에 동격 that은 완전한 문장의 명사절로 쓰인다. 선행사가 사람과 사물을 포함하는 관계대명사 that절, that은 관계사절 내에서 주어 역할
① the evidence that 동격절
③ no doubt that 동격절
④ the chance that 동격절

해석
① 지금까지 나온 증거는 단정적이지 않다.
② 그는 그녀가 관심을 갖는 사람들과 식당들을 메모했다.
③ 그들이 처음부터 틀렸다는 것은 의심의 여지가 없다.
④ 물의 존재는 행성에서 생명체가 발견될 가능성을 상당히 증가시킨다.

정답 10 ②

여기서 멈출 거예요? 고지가 바로 눈앞에 있어요.
마지막 한 걸음까지 SD에듀가 함께할게요!

제 **6** 편

연결어

단원 개요

연결어는 등위관계 절, 명사절, 형용사절, 부사절에 대한 내용이다. **등위관계 절**은 등위 및 종속관계 구분, 등위관계의 병렬구조 및 등위접속사를 포함하고, **명사절**은 that, whether/if의 접속사절, 의문대명사, 의문형용사, 의문부사의 의문사절, 복합관계대명사 등의 관계사절을 포함하고, **형용사절**은 관계대명사가 이끄는 주격, 목적격, 소유격 관계사절을 포함하고, **부사절**은 시간, 장소, 조건, 양보, 이유, 목적, 결과, 양태 및 비교, 비례의 부사절을 포함한다.

출제 경향 및 수험 대책

1. 등위관계 절
    (1) 병렬구조(단어, 구, 절)
    (2) 등위접속사(FANBOYS) 용법
2. 명사절
    (1) 접속사절(완전한 절 – that, whether/if) 용법
    (2) 의문사절(불완전한 절 – 의문대명사, 의문형용사, 완전한 절 – 의문부사) 용법
    (3) 관계사절(불완전한 절 – 복합관계대명사) 용법
3. 형용사절 : 관계대명사 주격, 목적격(생략 가능), 소유격 용법
4. 부사절 : 부사절 용법 및 표현

잠깐!

자격증 · 공무원 · 금융/보험 · 면허증 · 언어/외국어 · 검정고시/독학사 · 기업체/취업

이 시대의 모든 합격! SD에듀에서 합격하세요!

www.youtube.com → SD에듀 → 구독

제 1 장 등위관계의 절

제 1 절 등위관계, 종속관계

등위관계는 **등위 접속사**(coordinating conjunction)를 통해 단어와 단어(word), 구와 구(phrase), 절과 절(clause), 문장과 문장(sentence) 같이 문법적으로 동일한 범주를 대등한 관계로서 연결하고, 추가, 결합 및 나열(and), 대조 및 역접(but, yet), 선택(or), 이유(for), 결과(so), 부정(nor) 등을 나타낸다.

반면에 종속관계는 **종속 접속사**(subordinating conjunction)를 통해 문장과 문장 관계에서 한쪽은 **주절** (main clause), 다른 한쪽은 **종속절**(subordinate clause)의 주종 관계로서 연결한다. 종속접속사는 크게 명사절, 형용사절, 부사절로 사용되는데, 명사절은 접속사, 의문사, 관계사로 표현하고, 형용사절은 관계대명사 주격, 동사 및 전치사의 목적격, 소유격으로 표현하고, 부사절은 시간, 장소, 조건, 양보, 이유, 목적, 결과, 양태 및 비교, 비례 등을 나타낸다.

제 2 절 등위관계 표시

1 병렬구조(parallelism, 평행구조)

(1) 단어 + 단어

명사	He is interested in human linguistics and psychology. He likes hip hop, jazz, and classical music.
형용사	He told her a quick and definite willingness about the plan.
부사	He thinks about the plan systematically and seriously.
전치사	Government of, by, and for the people, shall not perish from the earth. It snowed on and off over the past week.
동사	Pope loved and prayed for the human race.

(2) 구 + 구

[예]

- He is not ill with the body but with the mind.
- Doing yoga or walking as often as possible will help relieve your stress and anxiety.
- To get a ticket to the final and to see my favorite player in person, I started a part time job as a painter.

(3) 절 + 절

[예]

- The train stars from Seoul at 7 am, and it arrives at Yeosu at 10 am.
- He is a professor, and she is a musician.
- The mushroom looks great, but you can't eat it.

2 위치

(1) 등위접속사 : 연결어구의 중간

[예]

- He bought a book a week ago, and he has just finished reading it.
- *He bought a book a week ago. And he has just finished reading it.

(2) 종속접속사 : 절과 절 사이 또는 문장 맨 앞

- (종속접속사 + 종속절) + 주절
- 주절 + (종속접속사 + 종속절)

[예]

- He can't wait to go to bed because he is so tired.
- *He can't wait to go to bed, because he is so tired.
- *He can't wait to go to bed. Because he is so tired.

제 3 절 and, but, or, for- 절

영어에서 등위 접속사는 for, and, nor, but, or, yet, so 7개가 있고 두자어로 FANBOYS라 한다.

[영어 등위접속사 FANBOYS]

F	A	N	B	O	Y	S
o	n	o	u	r	e	o
r	d	r	t		t	

1 for : 왜냐하면, 그 까닭은

예

• It is morning, for the birds are singing.

• He did it for they asked him to do it.

2 and

(1) 단어, 구, 절, 단일개념을 연결

예

• Amy loves her daughter and son.

• This culture is incorporated with European tradition and American tradition.

• My mother stopped at the mall and my father went to the baseball stadium.

(2) 행동, 상태 동시성

예 I cannot think and talk at the same time.

(3) 시간적 전후 관계

예 Josh went to his house and (then) cleaned up his room.

(4) 명령문 + and : ～해라. 그러면 ～

예

- Hurry, and you will be in time.
- Work hard, you will pass the exam.

(5) go, come, try, send 다음 and는 to 부정사로 대용 가능

예

- Come and play baseball with me next week.
  Come to play baseball with me next week.

3 nor : -도 또한 - 아니다 중요★

예

- Neither you nor anyone else has the right over me.
- He was not present in class, nor was she.
- The day was bright, nor were there clouds above.
- Amy didn't come to work yesterday, nor did she call.
- The coffee wasn't hot, nor was it cold.

4 but : 대조

예

- We are poor but happy.
- He did not come on Saturday, but on Sunday.
- He is rich, but he is not happy.
- They tried to help us, but they made things worse.

5 or

(1) 양자택일 : 또는, 혹은, 이든지

예

- You or I am to blame.

- Will you have tea or coffee?
- You may have a blue one or a green one or a yellow one.

(2) 동격어구 : 즉, 곧

예

- That country was called Siam, or Thailand
- The distance is ten miles, or about sixteen kilometers.

(3) 명령문＋or : ～해라. 그렇지 않으면 ～

예

- Take a vacation, or you will get sick.
- Make haste, or you will be late for the concert.

(4) 양보 : ～하건 ～하건

예 Rain or shine, I will go.

6 yet : 그렇지만

예

- He was very tired, yet he couldn't sleep.
- The news was spread fast. Yet no one responded to it.

7 so

(1) (그) 결과, 따라서

예

- He was excited, so he couldn't get to sleep.
- He passed the exam, so he can attend the university next year.

(2) 목적 so (that) : ～ 하기 위하여

예

- Please check that carefully so (that) you won't miss any mistakes.
- Switch the light off so (that) we can sleep well.

제 2 장 명사절

명사절은 문장에서 주어, (동사, 전치사의) 목적어, 보어 역할을 한다.

주어		When the man died is the beginning of the investigation.
목적어	동사	He wanted to know who correct the answer.
	전치사	This documentary is about how pollution affects human life.
보어		The question is why this product is so popular.

제 1 절 + 접속사절(완전한 절, complete clause)

1 that 절

(1) 역할

주어	That he was in error was beyond doubt.
목적어	He believes that you will get on in the world.
보어	The key point is that you are still responsible.
동격	There is no doubt that we were wrong from the start.

(2) that 동격절을 취하는 명사표현 중요 ★

announcement that ~	(re)assurance that ~	belief that ~
chance that ~	claim that ~	confirmation that ~
evidence that ~	fact that ~	feeling that ~
idea that ~	impression that ~	news that ~
no doubt that ~	notion that ~	opinion that ~
proof that ~	reason that ~	report that ~
rumor that ~	statement that ~	truth that ~

예

- The government overlooked the fact that factory location is very important to company.
- Did you hear the news that there are a lot of fake news?

(3) that절을 취하는 형용사표현

be afraid that ~	be convinced that ~	be sorry that ~
be aware that ~	be glad/happy that ~	be sure that ~

예

- Please be aware that it may take up three weeks for your order to arrive.
- He was sure that he left his wallet in the office.

2 whether/if절

(1) 역할

주어		Whether he is rich or not is not important.
목적어	동사	He doesn't know whether she will succeed or not. He asked if she knew Korean.
	전치사	He doesn't know the answer to whether or not she is the right person for the job.
보어		The problem is whether the product is arrived on time.

(2) if절의 비문법성 중요 ★

① '주어' 사용 불가

예 *If he is rich or not is not important.

※ 가주어 it으로 시작하는 경우 if 사용 가능

It doesn't matter whether/if she comes or not.

② '전치사 목적어' 사용 불가

예 *He doesn't know the answer to if she is the right person for the job.

③ '보어' 사용 불가

예 *The problem is if the product is arrived on time.

④ 'or not' 사용 불가

예

- He doesn't care whether or not she's coming.

  He doesn't care whether she's coming or not.
- *He doesn't care if or not she's coming.

  He doesn't care if she's coming or not.

⑤ 'to부정사' 사용 불가

예

- He doesn't know whether to accept or decline.
  *He doesn't know if to accept or decline.

제 2 절 + 의문사절 중요 ★★★

who, whom, whose, which, what, when, where, why, how 등의 의문사가 명사절을 이끌고 명사절 내 의문사의 역할을 따라 **의문대명사, 의문형용사, 의문부사**가 있다.

구분	의문대명사	의문형용사	의문부사
표현	who(m) what which	whose what which	when where why how
문장 내 역할	명사 (주어, 목적어, 보어)	형용사	부사

1 의문대명사

의문대명사는 의문사 자체가 명사절의 주어, 목적어, 보어 역할을 하고 있기 때문에 주어, 목적어, 보어가 없는 불완전한 절이 온다.

의문대명사 + 불완전한 절(incomplete clause)		
who(m)	누가 ~하는지	Who will be elected as the next president is everyone's concern.
what	무엇이(을) ~하는지	The new air cleaner reflects what the customers need.
which	어느 것이(을) ~하는지	He can't decide which is optimal.

의문대명사 who절의 주절 내 명사(절) 역할	
주어	Who has done it is a big question to her.
동사의 목적어	Tell her who has done it.
전치사의 목적어	There is no doubt about who has done it.
보어	The big question is who has done it.

2 의문형용사

의문형용사는 '의문형용사＋명사'가 명사절의 주어, 목적어, 보어 역할을 하고 있기 때문에 주어, 목적어, 보어가 없는 불완전한 절이 온다.

의문형용사＋불완전한 절(incomplete clause)		
whose	~누구의	He wasn't told whose idea it was.
what	무슨, 어떤	Could you tell me what color she likes?
which	어느 것/쪽	Which book do you want to read?

> **더 알아두기**
>
> **의문형용사 what vs which**
>
> what은 한정되지 않은 불특정한 것 또는 수(부정수) 중에서 선택하는 '무슨, 무엇, 어떤'의 의미인 반면에 which는 한정된 특정된 것 또는 수(일정수) 중에서 선택하는 '어느 (것/쪽)'의 의미를 나타낸다.
>
> 예
> • What color would you like?
> • Which color would you like, blue or green?

3 의문부사

의문부사는 명사절 내에서 부사 역할을 하기 때문에 주어, 동사 등 완전한 절이 온다.

의문부사＋완전한 절(complete clause)		
when	언제 ~하는지	He doesn't know when she will come today.
where	어디서 ~하는지	Where he will open his new store hasn't been decided.
why	왜 ~하는지	The general manager didn't talk about why that program was chosen.
how	어떻게 ~하는지	He asked her how old she was.

더 알아두기

what vs that 중요 ★

what + 불완전한 절	명사절	He will send what was promised.
that + 완전한 절	명사절	He was told that cure-all did not exist.
	형용사절	He made a proposal that might help her.
	부사절	He was so busy that he could not help her.

제 3 절 + 관계사절

복합관계대명사는 그 자체가 명사절의 주어, 목적어 역할을 하고 있기 때문에, 주어, 목적어, 보어가 없는 불완전한 절이 온다.

복합관계대명사 + 불완전한 절(incomplete clause)		
who(m)ever	~하는 사람이 누구든지	They will welcome whoever comes.
whatever	~하는 것은 무엇이든지	Whatever she says will be considered.
whichever	어느 것을 하든지	They can offer whichever seat she prefers.

더 알아두기

what의 사용

what	
관계대명사	He gave her what he bought.
의문사	He asked her what he bought.
주어	What he said is true.
보어	That is what he desires most.

제 3 장 형용사절

형용사절은 관계대명사가 이끄는 관계사절을 말하는데, 관계대명사는 그 선행사가 사람, 사물, 동물이냐 문법상 주격, 동사나 전치사의 **목적격**, 소유격이냐에 따라 다음과 같이 구분된다.

선행사	주격	목적격	소유격
사람	who	who(m) ∅	whose
사물, 동물	which	which ∅	whose of which
사람, 사물, 동물	that	that ∅	–
선행사를 포함하는 관계대명사	what	what	–

※ 좀 더 자세한 내용은 제5편 복합명사구 – 제1장 관계사(215쪽) 참조

1 주격

(1) 사람 : who, that

> She thanked <u>the man</u>. (→ 주절)
>   <u>He</u> helped her. (→ 관계사절 주어)
> She thanked the man <u>who</u> helped her.
> She thanked the man <u>that</u> helped her.

(2) 사물/동물 : which, that

> <u>The pen</u> is hers. (→ 주절)
>   <u>It</u> is on the desk. (→ 관계사절 주어)
> The pen <u>which</u> is on the desk is hers.
> The pen <u>that</u>   is on the desk is hers.

2 목적격 중요 ★★

(1) 동사의 목적격

① **사람** : who, whom, that, ∅

> The man was Mr. Jensen. (→ 주절)
> Joey saw him last night. (→ 관계사절 목적어)
> The man who(m) Joey saw last night was Mr. Jensen.
> The man that   Joey saw last night was Mr. Jensen.
> The man ∅   Joey saw last night was Mr. Jensen. (생략 가능)

② **사물/동물** : which, that, ∅

> The drama was very good. (→ 주절)
> Amy saw it last night. (→ 관계사절 목적어)
> The drama which Amy saw last night was very good.
> The drama that   Amy saw last night was very good.
> The drama ∅   Amy saw last night was very good. (생략 가능)

(2) 전치사의 목적격

① **사람**

> Laurel is the professor. (→ 주절)
> I told you about her. (→ 관계사절 목적어)
> Laurel is the professor about whom I told you.
> Laurel is the professor whom   I told you about.
> Laurel is the professor that   I told you about.
> Laurel is the professor ∅   I told you about. (생략 가능)

② **사물/동물**

> The music was wonderful. (→ 주절)
> Amy listened to it last night. (→ 관계사절 목적어)
> The music to which Amy listened last night was wonderful.
> The music which   Amy listened to last night was wonderful.
> The music that   Amy listened to last night was wonderful.
> The music ∅   Amy listened to last night was wonderful. (생략 가능)

3 소유격 중요 ★★

(1) 사람 : whose

> Josh knows <u>the woman</u>. (→ 주절)
> <u>Her book</u> was published lately. (→ 관계사절 소유격)
> Josh knows the woman <u>whose book</u> was published lately.

(2) 사물/동물 : whose, of which

① whose

> Josh has <u>a cat</u>. (→ 주절)
> <u>Cat's (Its)</u> color is black and white. (→ 관계사절 소유격)
> Josh has a cat <u>whose</u> color is black and white.

② of which

> Josh bought <u>a chair</u>. (→ 주절)
> The top <u>of the chair</u> was made of wood. (→ 관계사절 소유격)
> Josh bought a chair the top <u>of which</u> was made of wood.
> Josh bought a chair <u>of which</u> the top was made of wood.

부사절

종속접속사와 함께 표현되는 부사절은 시간, 장소, 가정, 조건, 양보, 이유, 목적, 결과, 양태, 비교, 비례, 기호 등을 나타낸다.

제 1 절 시간의 부사절

after	~한 후에	every time	~할 때마다
before	~하기 전에	the first time	처음 ~했을 때
since	~한 이래로	the last time	마지막으로 ~했을 때
until	~할 때까지	the next time	다음에 ~할 때
when	~할 때	the moment	~하는 순간에, ~하자마자
whenever	~할 때마다	the instant	~하자마자, ~하자 곧
while	~하는 동안	as soon as	~하자마자
once	~하지마자, 일단~하면	no sooner A than B	A 하자마자 B인
as, just as	동시에 ~할 때	soon after	이어서, 곧
as, so long as	~하는 한	shortly after	직후, 하자마자
by the time	~(할) 때까지(는)	immediately after	BrE ~하자마자 곧 ([어휘] immediately after (BrE) : ~ 하자마자 곧, BrE : 영국식 영어)

예

- When she was born, her parents were just twenty five.
- While he cooked dinner while she watched TV.
- He has known her since she was only five.
- He will stay here until she comes back.
- Dinner will be ready by the time you get home.

※ 시간의 부사절의 미래 의미는 현재시제, 미래완료 의미는 현재완료로 표현할 수 있다.

제 2 절 장소의 부사절

where	(위치) ~하는 곳에(서) (방향) ~하는 곳으로 (상황) ~하는 경우에는 (대조, 범위) ~인 것에 비하여

[예]

- The car is not where he parted it.
- He will take you where your mother once lived.
- Where ignorance is bliss, it is('tis) folly to be wise.
- Where money is concerned, he is as hard as nails.

제 3 절 조건절 중요 ★

if	~라면	providing (that)	~라면
unless	~가 아니라면	provided (that)	~라면
only if	~인 경우에만	in case (that)	~인 경우에
even if	비록 ~라고 할지라도	in the event (that)	~인 경우에
as(so) long as	~하는 한	supposing (that)	~이라면
as far as	~하는 한	assuming (that)	~이라면
given that	감안하면, 가정하면	according as	~의 조건으로
whether or not	~인지 아닌지		

[예]

- If it is necessary, he can cook dinner tonight.
- Please don't come unless she tells you to.
- The verb is plural in case the subject is plural.
- Given that all are equal before the law, everyone has the right to vote.
- As long as the earth remains, day and night will never cease.
- According as she has money, she will go there.

※ 조건의 부사절에는 미래 의미는 현재시제, 미래완료 의미는 현재완료시제로 표현할 수 있다.

제 4 절 양보절 중요 ★

though	~임에도 불구하고	before	~하느니 차라리
although	~임에도 불구하고	no matter how	어떻게 하든
even though	비록 ~이지만, 불구하고	as	~하지만, 이지만
if	~이라 할지라도	whether A or B	~이든 아니든
even if	할지라도, 비록	no matter who	(= whoever)
while	~인데도	no matter what	(= whatever)
whereas	~임에 반하여	no matter where	(= wherever)
when	~에도 불구하고	no matter how	(= however)

예

- Although he was a man of the world, he was simple and direct.
- Even if everybody knows it, we need to be strategic.
- He delivered an informative if dull lecture.
- While he wanted to marry her, his parents were against it.
- He is reserved, whereas his wife is very sociable.
- How can he get high grades when he cuts classes so often?
- Child as he was, he was brave. (명사 + as + 주어 + 동사, as앞 명사는 관사 없음)
- Poor as he is, he always helps the underprivileged. (형용사/부사 + as + 주어 + 동사)
- I would starve before I would go begging.
- Whether it's sunny or not, we will go hiking.
- No matter how hard I study, I feel like I am spinning my wheels.

제 5 절 이유절

as	~때문에	now that	이제 ~하게 되었으니
because	~때문에	seeing that	~인 것으로 보아
since	~때문에	considering that	~을 고려하면
inasmuch as	~때문에	on the ground that	~이라는 근거로

예

- As he had no money, he could not buy a new house.
- He passed the exam since he studied very hard.

- Their father is also guilty inasmuch as he know what they were going to do.

  ([해석] 그들이 무엇을 하려는지 그들의 아버지가 알고 있었으므로 그들의 아버지 또한 유죄이다.)

- Now that everyone is here, we can start the ceremony.

제 6 절 목적절 중요 ★

so that	~하기 위해서	lest	~하지 않도록
in order that	~하기 위해서	for fear that	~하지 않도록
in case	~하지 않도록, 대비하여		

예

- He studied hard so that he could pass the exam.

  (= He studied hard in order to pass the exam.)

- He went early in order that he might find her at the conference.

- Make haste lest you (should) be late.

- He wrote down her phone number for fear that he (should) forget it.

- Take your umbrella in case it rains. (should rain).

제 7 절 결과의 부사절 중요 ★

so + 형용사/부사 + that	-너무 ~해서 -이다 (so 원인; that ~ 결과)
such a(n) + 명사 + that	-너무 ~해서 -이다 (such 원인; that ~ 결과)
such that	-너무 ~해서 -이다 (such 원인; that ~ 결과)
so much/many/little/few + that	-너무/덜 ~해서 -이다

예

- It was so dark that he couldn't find the book.

- There was such a crowd that we could hardly move.

- His concern was such that he could hardly sleep.

제 8 절   양태 및 비교의 부사절 중요 ★

양태		비교	
as	~처럼, ~만큼	as	~과 같이, 마찬가지로
like	~처럼, ~만큼	than	~보다
as if	마치 ~인 것처럼		
as though	마치 ~인 것처럼		

예

- Do as we do.
- Nobody loves you like he does.
- As it happened, we were travelling in the South.
- He talked as if he knew all about her.
- He behaved as though he were her brother. (가정법 were)

- He is tall as she is.
- She can walk as quickly as he can.
- He is not so young as she.
- She respected him more than I did.
  (vs She respected him more than me.)
- It is much colder this winter than it was this time last year.

제 9 절   비례의 부사절

as + 비교급	~할수록, ~함에 따라 ~하다
according as	~에 준하여, ~에 따라
in proportion as	~하는 데 비례하여

예

- As he grew older, he became more talkative. (become, get, grow 등의 동사와 함께)
- According as the demand increases, the prices go up.
- As you go farther East, the sun sets earlier.

해설 & 정답 checkpoint

제 **6** 편   실전예상문제

01 다음 중 밑줄 친 부분에 공통으로 들어갈 표현은 무엇인가?

> • My mother stopped at the store _____ bought some groceries.
> • The descendants of Latin are referred to as the Romance languages, _____ they include French, Spanish, Italian, Portuguese, Romanian, and Catalan.

① and
② but
③ or
④ so

02 다음 문장과 의미가 같은 표현은 무엇인가?

> Neither you nor anyone else has right over me.

① You have right over me, and anyone else has right over me.
② You have right over me, but anyone else doesn't have right over me.
③ You don't have right over me, but anyone else has right over me.
④ You don't have right over me, and anyone else doesn't have right over me.

---

01 해설
첫 번째, 두 동사구를 연결하는 병렬 구조의 and 및 사건의 전후 관계를 나타내는 and (then) ;
두 번째, 두 문장을 연결하는 중문 (compound sentence)의 등위접속사 and

해석
• 엄마가 가게에 들러서 식료품을 사오셨다.
• 라틴어의 후손들은 로맨스어(로망스어)라고 불려지고, 여기에는 프랑스어, 스페인어, 이탈리아어, 포르투갈어, 루마니아어, 카탈로니아어가 포함된다.

02 해설
neither A nor B는 A도 아니고 B도 아니다 (A도 B도 아니다) 라는 표현

해석
당신이나 다른 그 누구도 나를 지배할 권리가 없다.
① 당신은 나를 지배할 권리가 있고, 다른 사람도 나를 지배할 권리가 있다.
② 당신은 나를 지배할 권리가 있지만, 다른 사람은 나를 지배할 권리가 없다.
③ 당신은 나를 지배할 권리가 없지만, 다른 사람은 나를 지배할 권리가 있다.
④ 당신은 나를 지배할 권리가 없고, 다른 사람도 나를 지배할 권리가 없다.

정답 01 ① 02 ④

03 해설

첫 번째, 두 단어를 병렬구조의 or;
두 번째, 두 문장을 연결하는 중문
(compound sentence)의 등위접속
사 or

해석

- 어떤 사람들은 커피에 설탕, 우유,
  혹은 크림을 첨가한다.
- 모든 사람이 복권이 좋은 생각이
  라고 생각하거나 복권에 당첨되면
  행복해질 것이라고 생각하는 것은
  아니다.

03 다음 중 밑줄 친 부분에 공통으로 들어갈 표현은 무엇인가?

> - Some people add sugar, milk, _____ cream to their coffee.
> - Not everyone thinks that the lottery is a good idea, _____ that winning it will make you happy.

① and
② but
③ or
④ so

04 해설

첫 번째, 문장의 주어 역할을 하는
명사절을 이끄는 접속사 that;
두 번째, 동사 believe 목적어 역할
을 하는 명사절을 이끄는 접속사
that

해석

- 그가 아직 살아있다는 사실은 구
  조대에 희망을 준다.
- 과학자들은 그들이 "우주에 우리가
  혼자인가?"라는 질문에 답하는 것
  에 한 걸음 가까워졌다고 믿는다.

04 다음 중 밑줄 친 부분에 공통으로 들어갈 표현은 무엇인가?

> - _____ he is still alive gives hope to the rescue team.
> - Scientists believe _____ they are one step closer to answering the question, "Are we alone in the universe?"

① whether
② which
③ what
④ that

정답 03 ③ 04 ④

05 다음 중 어법상 맞는 표현은 무엇인가?

① If he succeeds or fails is not important to his family.
② The local industrial performances will depend on if domestic consumption will rebound.
③ Scientists do care if evidence is randomly sampled or not.
④ He has to determine if to donate his life savings to charity.

06 다음 중 밑줄 친 부분에 공통으로 들어갈 표현은 무엇인가?

- The music during the movie depends on _____ character the same actor is now performing.
- _____ novel do you prefer to read, detective or romance?

① whom
② whose
③ what
④ which

05 해설

or not이 바로 이어지는 명사절은 if가 아니라 whether로 표현하지만, or not이 문미에 오는 경우는 if 사용 가능
① 주어 역할을 하는 명사절은 if가 아니라 whether
② on 전치사와 함께 쓰이는 명사절은 if가 아니라 whether
④ to부정사로 이어지는 명사절의 경우 if가 아니라 whether

해석
① 그가 성공하느냐 실패하느냐는 그의 가족에게 중요하지 않다.
② 국내 소비가 반등하느냐에 따라 국내 산업 실적이 좌우될 것으로 보인다.
③ 과학자들은 증거가 무작위로 추출되는지 여부에 신경을 쓴다.
④ 그는 평생 모은 돈을 자선단체에 기부할지 결정해야 한다.

06 해설

의문형용사 which : 첫 번째 which는 명사 character와 함께 주절 동사 depend on의 목적어 역할을 하는 반면에 두 번째 which는 명사 novel과 함께 동사 read의 목적어 역할을 한다. 의문형용사 what도 동일 조건에서 사용되나 여기서는 한정된 것 중에서 선택을 하는 의미이므로 which가 적절하다.
what은 한정되지 않은 불특정한 것 또는 부정수 중에서 선택하는 '무슨, 무엇'의 의미인 반면에 which는 한정된 특정된 것 또는 일정수 중에서 선택하는 '어느 것/쪽'의 의미이다.

해석
- 영화 속 음악은 같은 배우가 어떤 캐릭터를 연기하느냐에 따라 달라진다.
- 당신은 탐정소설과 로맨스소설 중 어떤 소설을 읽는 것을 더 좋아하나요?

정답 05 ③ 06 ④

07 해설

타동사 understand의 목적어 역할을 하는 명사절이 필요하고 밑줄 친 부분 이후는 완전한 절이 쓰여 있기 때문에 의문대명사, 의문형용사는 되지 않고 의문부사가 필요한데 내용상 이유를 나타내는 의문부사 why가 적절하다.

해석

많은 경제학자들은 왜 정부가 새로운 경제 정책을 결정했는지 이해하지 못한다.

07 다음 중 밑줄 친 부분에 들어갈 표현은 무엇인가?

> Many economists do not understand _____ the government has determined the new economic policy.

① what
② which
③ why
④ where

08 해설

'the moment는 '~하는 순간에', '~하자마자'의 의미로 'as soon as', 'no sooner A than B', 'soon after', 'shortly after', 'the instant', 'immediately after'와 같은 의미다.

해석

재즈 노래를 듣는 순간, 그는 Nina Simone과 사랑에 빠졌다.

08 다음 중 밑줄 친 부분과 의미가 같은 표현은 무엇인가?

> The moment he listened to jazz song, he fell in love with Nina Simone.

① As long as
② By the time
③ Until
④ As soon as

정답 07 ③ 08 ④

09 다음 중 밑줄 친 부분에 공통으로 들어갈 표현은 무엇인가?

> • _____ ignorance is bliss, it is folly to be wise.
>
> • _____ money is concerned, he is as hard as nails.

① Unless
② While
③ Where
④ Although

09 해설

'~하는 경우에'와 같은 상황을 표현하는 (장소의) 부사절 표현 where가 적절하다. 첫 번째는 '모르는 것이 행복일 경우에는 안다는 것은 어리석은 일이다, 모르는 것이 약이다'의 의미이고, 두 번째는 '돈에 관한 한 그는 지독하기 그지없다'는 의미

해석

• 모르는 것이 행복일 경우에는 안다는 것은 어리석은 일이다. (모르는 것이 약이다.)
• 그는 돈에 관한 한 철두철미하다.

어휘

• ignorance is bliss : 모르는 게 약
• as hard as nails : 냉혹한, 철두철미한

10 다음 중 밑줄 친 부분에 들어갈 표현은 무엇인가?

> • There was _____ a crowd that they could hardly move an inch.
>
> • He gave _____ witty an answer that everyone burst out laughing.

① so – so
② so – such
③ such – so
④ such – such

10 해설

결과를 나타내는 부사절 표현으로서 첫 번째는 such a(n) 명사 that, 두 번째는 so 형용사/부사 that 표현, 둘 다 '–너무 ~해서 –하다' 의미로 such, so는 결과, that~ 결과를 나타낸다.

해석

• 사람들이 너무 많아서 그들은 한 치도 움직일 수가 없었다.
• 그가 너무 재치 있는 대답을 해서 모두가 웃음을 터뜨렸다.

정답   09 ③   10 ③

여기서 멈출 거예요? 고지가 바로 눈앞에 있어요.
마지막 한 걸음까지 SD에듀가 함께할게요!

제 **7** 편

비교

비교는 규칙 및 불규칙형의 형용사와 부사를 사용하는 원급비교, 비교급, 최상급에 대한 내용이다. **원급비교**는 형용사 및 부사의 기본 형태를 사용하여 as, 배수/분수, the same, such 등과 함께 표현하고, **비교급**은 형용사와 부사의 비교급 형태 뿐만 아니라 than, the 등의 표현과 함께 우등, 열등 관계를 표현하고, **최상급**은 형용사 및 부사의 최상급 형태뿐만 아니라 the, at, as 등과 함께 원급, 비교급의 형태로도 표현한다.

1. 원급비교 : as, 배수/분수, the same, such 표현 긍정, 부정 원급 비교 용법
2. 비교급
   (1) 원급, 비교급, 최상급 강조 표현
   (2) than 비교급, the + 비교급 용법
   (3) 비교급 중요 구문 표현, 용법, 의미
3. 최상급
   (1) the + 최상급 용법
   (2) the를 사용하지 않는 최상급 표현
4. 최상급의 표현
   (1) 최상급을 포함하는 as 포함 원급비교
   (2) 최상급을 포함하는 than 비교구문

 자격증 · 공무원 · 금융/보험 · 면허증 · 언어/외국어 · 검정고시/독학사 · 기업체/취업
이 시대의 모든 합격! SD에듀에서 합격하세요!
www.youtube.com → SD에듀 → 구독

제 1 장 원급비교

1 as + 원급(형용사, 부사) + as~

(1) 긍정 표현

> • as + 원급 + as~ : ~만큼 -한(하게)
> • just + as + 원급 + as~ : 정확히
> • almost/nearly + as + 원급 + as~ : 거의

예

- Josh is as tall as Nathan.
- Josh is just as tall as Nathan.
- Josh is almost/nearly as tall as Nathan.

(2) 부정 표현

> • not + as(so) + 원급 + as~ : ~만큼 -하지 않은
> • not + **quite** + as + 원급 + as~ : **근소한 차이**
> • not + **nearly** + as + 원급 + as~ : **큰 차이**

예

- Josh is not as tall as Nathan.
- Josh is not quite as tall as Nathan. (Josh < Nathan)
- Josh is not nearly as tall as Nathan. (Josh <<< Nathan)

2 부정주어 ~ + as(so) + 원급(형용사, 부사) + as~

> ~만큼 -한 것은 없다(최상급 의미)

예

- Nothing is so important as love.
- No one at this school is as tall as Nathan.

3 as A as (A) can be, as A as anything : 더할 나위 없이

예

- I am as tired as (tired) can be.
- They are as rich as (rich) can be.

4 as ~ as possible, as ~ as one can : 가능한 한 ~한/하게

예

- Nathan ran as fast as possible. (Nathan ran as fast as he can.)
- Come as early as possible. (Come as early as you can.)

5 as ~ as any + 명사 : 무엇에도(누구에게도) 못지않게 ~하여(최상급 의미)

> as ~ as ever + 과거동사 : 누구에게도 못지않게 ~하여, 더없이 ~하여(최상급 의미)

예

- This film is as good as any movie Bong has ever directed.
- He is as great a film director as ever lived in Korea.
- He can communicate as well as he ever could.

6 as(so) long as ～ : (조건) ～하는 한, ～한다면

[예]
- As long as the earth remains, day and night will never cease.
- Amy can stay as long as she wants to.
- You can play the piano as long as you like.

7 배수/분수 + as ～ as − : −만큼 ～한

[예]
- Nathan ate twice as much as Josh did.
- This building is three times as tall as that one.

8 not so much A as B : A라기보다는 차라리 B인

[예] Dr. Lee is not so much a professor as a scholar.

9 the same (+ 명사) as : ～와 똑같이(은)

[예]
- Nathan has the same laptop computer as Josh does.
- Nathan's laptop computer is the same as Josh's.

10 as + 형용사 + as ever : 여전히

[예]
- Josh's mother is as considerate as ever.
- Nathan runs as fast as ever.

11 as early as ～ : ～만큼이나 일찍

예

- The new product will be sold online as early as next month.
- The company runs an international branch in Hong Kong as early as December.

12 as many/few + 명사 + as ～ : ～만큼 많은/적은

---

as much/little + 명사 + as ～ : ～만큼 많은/적은

예

- Josh had as many as books as Nathan had.
- Josh spend as much as money as Nathan did.

13 such (a)n + 형용사 + 명사 + as ～ : ～만큼 ～한

예

- This is not such a simple question as you think.
- He has never seen such a great woman as she.

제 2 장 비교급

제 1 절 변화

1 규칙변화

음절	구분	원급	비교급	최상급
1음절	-e로 끝나는 단어 -r/-st	wise large	wiser larger	wisest largest
	단모음 + 단자음 자음 + -er/-est	hot big	hotter bigger	hottest biggest
	자음 + y → 자음 + i -er/-est	cozy busy	cozier busier	coziest busiest
	그 외 -er/-est	smart young	smarter younger	smartest youngest
2음절	-er/-est	simple happy	simpler happier	simplest happiest
	-ful, -ous, -less, -ish, -ive, -ly more/most	useful famous	more useful more famous	most useful most famous
3음절 이상	more/most	important comfortable	more important more comfortable	most important most comfortable

2 불규칙변화 중요 ★

원급		비교급	최상급
good/well		better	best
bad/badly		worse	worst
many/much		more	most
little		less	least
late	(시간) 늦은	later	latest
	(순서) 나중	latter	last
far	(거리) 먼	farther	farthest
	(거리/정도/시간) 먼	further	furthest

제 2 절 비교급 비교

1 비교급 + than 중요 ★

(1) 비교급 강조

much, (by) far, a lot, a little (bit), even, still 등이 비교급 앞에 쓰여 강조를 표현

> **더 알아두기**
>
> **very는 원급(형용사, 부사) 강조**
>
> | | |
> |---|---|
> | Nathan is very tall. | This car runs very fast. |
> | *Nathan is very taller than Josh. | *This car runs very faster than that one. |
> | Nathan is much taller than Josh. | This car runs much faster than that one. |

> **더 알아두기**
>
> **강조표현**
>
> | 구분 | 표현 |
> |---|---|
> | 원급 | very, just, quite, too, almost, nearly, … |
> | 비교급 | much, far, by far, a lot, a bit, a little, a little bit, even, rather, somewhat, … |
> | 최상급 | much, far, by far, far and away, even, quite, the very, … |

(2) 'the + 원급 + than' : 동일인, 동일물의 서로 다른 성질을 비교하는 경우

[예]

- Josh himself is more intelligent than smart.
- Diamond is more symbolic than beautiful.

2 than이 없는 비교급 : 비교 대상이 없는 비교급(절대비교)

[예]

- the higher education
- the higher class
- the upper class
- the younger generation

- the greater part of
- the latter part of
- the lower animal

3 열등비교

예

- Josh is less tall than Nathan.
- Josh is not so tall as Nathan.

4 the + 비교급 중요 ★★

the를 잘 사용하지 않는 비교급에서 예외적으로 the를 사용하는 경우

(1) the + 비교급 (+ 주어 + 동사) ~, the + 비교급 (+ 주어 + 동사) ~

~하면 할수록 더 ~하다

예

- The harder he studies, the more he will learn.
- The more we have, the more we want.
- The sooner, the better.

(2) the + 비교급 of A and B (= of the two)

둘/두 개 중에 더 ~한

예 Nathan is the teller of Nathan and Josh. (= of the two).

(3) 원인, 이유를 나타내는 부사구, 부사절이 있는 경우

예 Josh studied the harder because his advisor praised him all the time.

(4) all the + 비교급 + for/because of : -하기 때문에 더욱 ~하다

= so much the + 비교급 + for/because

예

- She loves him all the more for his honesty.
- She likes him all the better because of his honesty.

5 그 외 중요 비교급 구문들 중요 ★★★

(1) no more than

> only, -에 지나지 않다, 불과, 같은 수/양/액수(수의 적음을 강조)

예

- They are no more than puppets.
- The rate is usually no more than 2 percent.
- He paid no more than she asked. (= only as much as)

(2) not more than

> at most, 많아야

예 He has not more than twenty dollars.

(3) no less than

> as many/much as, ~만큼(수의 많음을 강조)

예

- No less than 20,000 people came to the concert.

  (= As many as 20,000 people came to the concert.)

- He has no less than twenty dollars.

  (= He has as much as twenty dollars.)

(4) not less than

> at least, 적어도, 최소한

예

- He has not less than twenty dollars.

  (= He has at least twenty dollars.)

(5) no more A than B

> B와 같은 수/양/액수의 A밖에 없다

예 Josh has no more books than (only as many as books as) Nathan does.

(6) no less ~ than −(= just as ~ as)

> ~ 만큼, 같은 정도로, ~ 에 못지않게 −하여

예

- He is no less handsome than his brother.

  (= He is just as handsome as his brother.)

(7) A is not more ~ than B

> A는 B만큼 ~하지 않다

예

- Her question is not more difficult than his question.

  (= Her question is as easy as his question.)

(8) A is not less ~ than B

> A는 B 못지않게 ~하다

예

- He is not less handsome than his brother.

  (= He is as handsome as his brother.)

  (= He is probably more handsome than his brother.)

(9) A is no more B than C is D(= A is not B any more than C is D)

> C가 D가 아닌 것은 A가 B가 아닌 것과 같다. (A가 B가 아님을 강조)

예

- A whale is no more a fish than a horse is.

  (= A whale is not a fish any more than a horse is.)

- He is not a god any more than we are.

(10) not so much A as B

> A라기보다는 B
> = less A than B
> = more B than A

예

- He is not so much professor as a scholar.

- He is not so much smart than intelligent.
  = He is less smart than intelligent.
  = He is more intelligent than smart.

(11) know better than to + 동사원형

> ~할 만큼 어리석지 않다

예

- He knows better than to quarrel.
- He should have known better than to call her.

(12) 비교급 + and + 비교급

> 점점 더, 더욱 더

예

- The winter is getting darker and darker.
- The modern society is becoming more and more complicated.

(13) no longer = not ~ any longer

> 더 이상 ~ 아니다

예

- He is no longer a child.
- He is not a child any longer.

(14) more than + 수사

> ~ 이상의

예

- More than 300 students attended the conference.
- More than 95% of people in this town felt satisfied.

6 라틴어 비교급

라틴어 비교급은 than 대신에 전치사 + to(+ 목적격) 형태로 사용된다.

superior to	inferior to
major to	minor to
senior to	junior to
anterior to	posterior to
exterior to	interior to
A is preferable to B (prefer A to B) : B보다 A를 선호하는(한다)	

예

- Her car is superior to his car.
- Rural life is preferable to urban life.

제 3 장 최상급

제 1 절 the + 최상급

1 in + 명사(장소, 단체 단수명사)

> of + 명사(장소, 단체 복수명사)

예
- City hall is the oldest building in the city.
- City hall is the most beautiful building of all the structures.

2 one of the + 최상급 복수 명사 중요 ★

예
- Seoul has one of the most historic museums in the world.
- Seoul is one of the largest cities in the world.
- It is one of the most interesting TV shows I have ever seen.

3 최상급 강조 중요 ★

much, far, by far, far and away, quite, even, the very를 사용한다.

예
- Dr. Lee is by far the university's most valuable scholar.
- His daughter is the very most important being to him.

제 2 절 the를 붙이지 않는 경우

1 명사 또는 소유격이 사용되는 경우

[예]

- Reading novels is her greatest pleasure to her.
- He gave his most precious treasure to her.

2 동사 수식 부사의 최상급 표현

[예]

- She runs fastest in her team.
- She likes strawberry ice cream (the) best.
- he knows who was listening (the) most carefully.

3 동일인, 동일물의 성질, 상태를 서술하는 경우

[예]

- She is most comfortable when she is alone.
- She feels easiest with lots of books around her.

4 보어 역할을 하는 최상급 표현 중요★

다른 상대와의 비교가 아닌 경우에 사용

[예]

- This restaurant is busiest on the weekend.
  (*This restaurant is busiest in this area.)
  (*This restaurant is busiest one.)

5 (a) most가 'very'의 의미로 사용되는 경우

예

• Dr. Choi recommended a most unusual treatment.
• The new guideline sounds most reasonable.

6 most가 '대부분'의 의미로 사용되는 경우

예

• Most people know that news.
• She will spend most of time reading the reports next week.

제 **3** 절 **at + 최상급**

• at (the) best : 아무리 잘 해도
• at (the) least : 적어도, 최소한
• at (the) most : 기껏해야, 고작해야
• at (the) worst : 최악의 경우에
• at (long) last : 마침내, 드디어
• at the earliest : 아무리 빨라도
• at the latest : 아무리 늦어도
• at one's best : 가장 좋은 상태에서

제 4 장 최상급의 표현

제 1 절 최상급을 포함하는 원급 비교 중요 ★★★

(1) as + 원급 + as can/could be : 할 수 있는 한 최고로 ~하다

예
- She is as strong as can be.
- Her performance was as good as can be.

(2) as ~ as any + 명사 : 무엇에도(누구에게도) 못지않게 ~하여

as ~ as ever + 과거동사 : 누구에게도 못지않게 ~ 하여, 더없이 ~하여

예
- This film is as good as any movie Bong has ever directed.
- He is as great a film director as ever lived in Korea.
- He can communicate as well as he ever could.

(3) 부정주어 ~ + as(so) + 원급(형용사, 부사) + as~ : ~만큼 −한 것은 없다

(= 최상급 + of all + 복수명사)

예
- No (other) river in the world is so long as the Nile River.
  (= The Nile River is the longest of all the rivers in the world.)

제 2 절 최상급을 포함하는 비교 구문 중요 ★★★

(1) 부정주어 + 비교급 + than

(= 최상급 + of all + 복수명사)

예

- No (other) river in the world is longer than the Nile River.

  (= The Nile River is the longest of all the rivers in the world.)

(2) 주어 + 비교급 + than any other + 단수명사

(= 최상급 + of all + 복수명사)

예

- The Nile River is longer than any other river in the world.

  (= The Nile River is the longest of all the rivers in the world.)

(3) 주어 + 비교급 + than all the (other) + 복수명사

(= 최상급 + of all + 복수명사)

예

- The Nile River is longer than all the (other) rivers in the world.

  (= The Nile River is the longest of all the rivers in the world.)

(4) have never been + 비교급 : 더 ~한 적이 없다, 지금 가장 ~하다

예

- It has never been better. (= It couldn't be better. / It's the best.)
- She's never been happier in her whole life.

> 💡 **더 알아두기** 🔍
>
> **절대적 속성 표현(비교급과 최상급을 만들 수 없는 표현)**
> perfect, universal, round, dead, equal 등 절대적 속성을 지닌 형용사, 부사 표현들은 비교급과 최상급을 사용하지 않는다. 하지만 의미를 강조하기 위해 사용될 수 있다.
>
> 예
> - *deader, *deadest
> - *more perfect, *most perfect
> - a more perfect reunion

제 **7** 편 실전예상문제

01 다음 중 밑줄 친 부분에 들어갈 표현은 무엇인가?

> Saving money _____ making money.

① more important as
② as important as
③ is as important as
④ that is as important as

02 다음 중 밑줄 친 부분에 들어갈 표현은 무엇인가?

> • He is 15. She is 50. He is _____ old as she.
> • Difference in age is _____ important as clear communication across ages.

① almost as
② nearly as
③ not quite as
④ not nearly as

해설 & 정답   checkpoint

01 해설
as + 원급 + as (~만큼 ~한) 비교

해석
돈을 모으는 것은 돈을 버는 <u>것만큼 중요하다.</u>

02 해설
큰 차이를 나타내는 부정 표현(~만큼 -하지 않은)은 'not nearly as 원급 as'를 쓰는 반면에, 근소한 차이는 'not quite as 원급 as'로 표현한다. 'almost/nearly as 원급 as' 긍정 표현(거의~와 같은)이다.

해석
• 그는 15살이다. 그녀는 50세이다. 그는 그녀만큼 나이가 <u>많지 않다.</u>
• 연령의 차이는 세대를 넘어선 명확한 의사소통만큼 중요하지 <u>않다.</u>

정답 01 ③ 02 ④

안심Touch

checkpoint   해설 & 정답

03 해설
원급비교구문에 대한 문제이다.
① as(so) long as~ : (조건) ~하는 한
② as ~ as possible : 가능한 한 ~한/하게
③ as ~ as any + 명사 : 더없이 ~하여(최상급 의미, 무엇에도 못지않게 ~하여)
④ such a(n) 형용사 명사 as~ : ~만큼 ~한

해석
① 내가 마음과 건강을 유지하는 한, 나이는 숫자에 불과하다.
② 사람들은 가능한 한 패스트푸드를 먹지 않도록 노력해야 한다.
③ 이번 영화는 그가 지금까지 감독한 어떤 영화보다도 좋다.
④ 그녀는 고흐처럼 아름다운 그림을 본 적이 없다.

03 다음 중 어법상 잘못된 표현은 무엇인가?

① As long as I have my mind and health, age is just a number.
② People should try to avoid eating fast food as much as possible.
③ This is as good as any movie he has ever directed.
④ She has never seen so a beautiful painting as Gogh.

04 해설
far의 비교급은 두 형태가 있는데 물리적 거리(distance) '더 멀리'를 표현하는 경우 farther, further 모두 가능한 반면에 정도의 추가(additional) '더욱 더, 더 한층'을 의미하는 경우 further가 사용된다.

해석
• 더 궁금하신 점이 있으시면 언제든지 물어보세요.
• 그는 오래된 컴퓨터가 더 이상 쓸모가 없어서 동생에게 주었다.

정답 03 ④ 04 ③

04 다음 중 밑줄 친 부분에 공통으로 들어갈 표현은 무엇인가?

• If you have _____ questions, feel free to ask.
• He gave his old computer to his brother because he had no _____ use for it.

① far
② farther
③ further
④ more further

05 다음 중 밑줄 친 부분에 맞지 <u>않는</u> 표현은 무엇인가?

> • The GTX will travel _____ faster than traditional subway lines.
> • A person's personality is _____ more important than their appearance.

① much

② by far

③ a lot

④ very

05 해설

비교급을 강조하는 표현으로는 much, far, by far, a lot, even, rather 등이 쓰이는데 very는 비교급이 아니라 원급을 강조하는 표현이다.

해석
• GTX는 전통적인 지하철 노선보다 **훨씬 더** 빠르게 이동할 것이다.
• 사람의 성격은 외모보다 **훨씬 더** 중요하다.

06 다음 중 밑줄 친 부분에 들어갈 표현은 무엇인가?

> • The more he practiced, _____ he played.
> • The more she talks, _____ he listens.

① the good – the little

② the better – the less

③ better – less

④ the best – the least

06 해설

the + 비교급 (+ 주어 + 동사) ~, the + 비교급 (+ 주어 + 동사) ~ : '~하면 할수록 더 ~하다'의 표현, 첫 번째는 good의 비교급 the better, 두 번째는 little의 비교급 the less.

해석
• 그는 연습을 **하면 할수록** 더 잘했다.
• 그녀가 말을 많이 **할수록**, 그는 듣지 **않는다.**

정답 05 ④ 06 ②

안심Touch

07 해설

not less than : at least(적어도, 최소한)

① no more than : only(불과 ~에 지나지 않다)

② not more than : at most(많아야)

③ no less than : as many/much as(~만큼)

해석

- 하루에 <u>최소한</u> 8잔의 물을 마시도록 하세요.
- 편집자는 초고를 <u>최소한</u> 50개 수정했다.

08 해설

최상급 표현에 대한 문제이다.

one of the + 최상급 복수 명사, → cities

① 최상급 표현 + in + 명사(장소, 단체 단수명사)

② 동일인, 동일물의 성질, 상태를 서술하는 경우에는 the 생략 가능

④ 최상급 강조 much, far, by far, far and away, quite, even, the very 표현

해석

① Jamestown은 미국에서 첫 번째이며 가장 오래된 마을이다.

② 그녀는 주변에 책이 많으면 마음이 편하다.

③ 서울은 세계에서 가장 큰 도시 중 하나이다.

④ 동물 실험은 화장품이 사용하기에 안전한지를 평가하는 가장 정확한 방법이다.

정답 07 ④ 08 ③

07 다음 중 밑줄 친 부분과 같은 표현은 무엇인가?

> - Try to drink <u>at least</u> eight glasses of water a day.
> - The editor made <u>at least</u> 50 corrections to the first draft.

① no more than

② not more than

③ no less than

④ not less than

08 다음 중 어법상 <u>잘못된</u> 표현은 무엇인가?

① Jamestown is the first and the oldest town in the United States of America.

② She feels easiest with lots of books around her.

③ Seoul is one of the most largest city in the world.

④ Animal testing is by far the most accurate way of assessing whether cosmetic products are safe to use.

09 다음 중 어법상 <u>잘못된</u> 표현은 무엇인가?

① He is my the best friend.

② This is a most beautiful lake.

③ Those who climb highest can see farthest.

④ My father seems to be happiest when he is with my sister.

09 해설

the를 붙이지 않는 최상급 표현에 대한 문제이다.
명사 또는 소유격이 사용되는 경우
② most가 'very'의 의미로 사용되는 경우
③ 동사 수식 부사의 최상급 표현
④ 보어 역할을 하는 최상급 표현(다른 대상과의 비교가 아닌 경우)

해석
① 그는 나의 가장 친한 친구이다.
② 이곳은 가장 아름다운 호수이다.
③ 가장 높은 곳에 오르는 사람은 멀리 볼 수 있다.
④ 아버지는 여동생과 함께 있을 때가 가장 행복한 것 같다.

10 다음 중 밑줄 친 부분에 들어갈 표현은 무엇인가?

> _____ other river in the world is so long as the Nile River.

① All

② None

③ No

④ Any

10 해설

부정주어 ~ + as/so + 원급(형용사/부사) + as~ : '~만큼 -한 것은 없다'(= 최상급 + of all + 복수명사)의 표현

해석
세계의 어떤 강도 나일 강만큼 길지 않다.

정답 09 ① 10 ③

안심Touch

여기서 멈출 거예요? 끝까지 바로 눈앞에 있어요.
마지막 한 걸음까지 SD에듀가 함께할게요!

제 **8** 편

—

화법

단원 개요

화법(speech/narration)은 자신이나 타인의 말을 전달하는 방법이다. **직접화법**은 말을 있는 그대로 직접적으로 전달하는 방법이고, **간접화법**은 전달하는 사람의 입장에서 내용 중심으로 간접적으로 전달하는 방법이다. 직접화법을 간접화법으로 전환하는 경우 문장의 종류, 인용부호, 전달동사, 시간 및 장소 부사 표현, 주절과 종속절의 시제 등을 고려해야 한다.

출제 경향 및 수험 대책

1. 직접화법 → 간접화법 화법 전환 방법
   (1) 문장 형식(서술문, 의문문, 명령문, 감탄문, 기원문) 및 중, 복문 문장 전환 방법
   (2) 문장 종류에 따른 전달동사 용법
   (3) 지시 및 소유 대명사, 시간 및 장소 부사, 조동사 표현
   (4) 주절과 종속절의 시제 표현

잠깐!

자격증 · 공무원 · 금융/보험 · 면허증 · 언어/외국어 · 검정고시/독학사 · 기업체/취업

이 시대의 모든 합격! SD에듀에서 합격하세요!

www.youtube.com → SD에듀 → 구독

제 1 장 직접화법, 간접화법

제 1 절 직접화법(direct/quoted speech)

직접화법은 자신이나 타인의 말을 인용부호(" ", quotation mark), 즉 큰따옴표(double quotes, double quotation marks)를 이용해서 있는 그대로 전달하는 방법이다. 전달하는 문장은 독립된 문장이므로 대문자로 시작하고, 직접적으로 인용하기 때문에 인용부호로 표시한다.

예

- Josh said, "I'm hungry."
- Amy said, "I need my laptop."
- Jeff said, "I woke up feeling sick, so I didn't go to school."
- Cindy said, "I ate Korean barbecue yesterday."
- Choi said, "Dogs are fun to watch."

제 2 절 간접화법(indirect/reported speech)

간접화법은 말을 전달하는 사람의 입장과 시제에 맞게 말의 내용을 전달하는 방법이다. 전달하는 내용은 전체 문장의 일부이므로 대문자로 시작하지 않고 목적어절 역할을 한다. 간접적 인용 방법이기 때문에 인용부호를 사용하지 않고 comma로 분리하지 않으며 (전체) 문장, 즉 주절의 주어와 동사의 시제에 일치시킨다.

1 직접화법 → 간접화법 중요★

(1) 전달동사를 바꾼다.

(2) 인용부호를 없애고 접속사를 쓴다.

(3) 피전달문의 인칭 및 소유 대명사를 전달자의 입장에 맞게 바꾼다.

(4) 시간이나 장소의 부사(구)를 바꾼다.

(5) 주절과 종속절의 시제를 일치시킨다.

직접화법	간접화법
Josh said, "I'm hungry."	Josh said that he was hungry.
Amy said, "I need my laptop."	Amy said that she needed her laptop.
Jeff said, "I woke up feeling sick, so I didn't go to school."	Jeff said that he woke up feeling sick, so he didn't go to school.
Cindy said, "I ate Korean barbecue yesterday."	Cindy said that she ate Korean barbecue the day before.
Choi said, "Dogs are fun to watch."	Choi said that dogs were fun to watch.
Amy said, "My parents are fine."	Amy said that her parents were fine.
Jeff said, "I has quit my job."	Jeff said that he had quit his job.
Cindy said, "I'm going to learn to drive."	Cindy said that she was going to learn to drive.

2 전달동사

(1) say

say는 가장 일반적인 말하기 동사로서 간접화법의 경우 명사절(목적어절)이 오는 3형식 동사이다.

예
- Josh said, "I am hungry."
- Josh said that he was hungry.
  *Josh said me that he was hungry.
- Josh said to me that he was hungry.

(2) tell

tell은 간접화법에서 (대)명사 간접 목적어와 명사절(직접 목적어절)이 오는 4형식 동사이다.

예
- Josh told, "I am hungry."
  *Josh told that he was hungry.
- Josh told me that he was hungry.
- Josh told Amy that he was hungry.
  *Josh told to me that he was hungry.

(3) ask(want to know, wonder, inquire)

ask는 의문문의 간접화법에서 (대)명사 간접 목적어는 선택이고 명사절(직접 목적어절)이 오는 3·4형식 동사이다. 그 외 want to know, wonder, inquire 등의 동사가 사용된다.

[예]

- Josh asked, "Are you hungry?"

  Josh asked if I was hungry.

  Josh asked me if I was hungry.

  *Josh asked to me if I was hungry.

(4) answer, reply

대답을 표현하는 간접화법인 경우 동사 answer, reply 등이 사용된다.

[예]

- I said (to Josh), "I am hungry, too."
- I answered/replied that I was hungry, too.

(5) 그 외 동사

간접화법에 사용되는 동사로 announce, comment, complain, explain, remark, state 등의 동사가 있다.

[예]

- Jerold announced that he would retire soon.
- Donald commented that the idea would be the best.
- He complained that the price was too expensive.
- He explained that things were getting better.
- He remarked that online business changed the way people shop.
- He stated that the total fertility rate of Korea is less than 1.25.

3 지시·소유대명사, 시간·장소 부사, 조동사 종요★

직접화법	→	간접화법
I	→	she or he
we	→	they
our	→	their
this	→	that
these	→	those
here	→	there

now	→	then
ago	→	before
today	→	that day
tonight	→	that night
tomorrow	→	the next day/the following day
yesterday	→	the day before/the previous day
last night	→	the night before/the previous night
a week ago	→	a week earlier
next week	→	the next week
last year	→	the year before (the previous year)
next year	→	the next year (the following year)
will	→	would
can	→	could
may	→	might
must	→	had to

제 2 장 화법의 전환

제 1 절 **서술문(declarative sentence)**

1 직접화법 → 간접화법

(1) 쉼표와 인용부호 큰따옴표를 지운다.

(2) 전달동사 say/said는 그대로, say to/said to는 tell/told로 바꾼다.
say가 자동사일 경우 say to로, say가 타동사일 경우 4형식 동사 tell을 사용한다.

(3) 큰따옴표 대신에 명사절을 이끄는 that을 사용한다. (생략 가능)

(4) 명사절(종속절) that 내의 인칭, 시제, 부사(구)를 주절에 맞게 변화시킨다.

예

- He said, "I have a laptop in my bag."
  He said that he had a laptop in his bag.

- He said to her, "I will call on you tomorrow."
  He told her that he would call on her the next day.

2 인용문 안의 대명사

예

- He said, "I am a professor."
  He said that he was a professor.

- He said to me, "You are my close friend."
  He told me that I was his close friend.

3 주절과 종속절 시제 일치 및 전환 중요 ★

(1) 현재 → 과거

예

- He said, "I am a farmer."

  He said that he was a farmer.

- He said to me, "I will bear my responsibility."

  He told me that he would bear his responsibility.

(2) 현재진행 → 과거진행

예

- He said, "I am working on my homework."

  He said that he was working on his homework.

- He said to me, "I am cooking dinner."

  He said told me that he was cooking dinner.

(3) 현재완료 → 과거완료

예

- He said, "I has studied hard for my final exam."

  He said that he had studied hard for his final exam.

- He said to me, "I have made supper for all."

  He told me that he had made supper for all.

(4) 현재완료 진행 → 과거완료 진행

예

- He said, "I have been waiting for ages."

  He said that he had been waiting for ages.

- He said, "I have been living here for thirty years."

  He said that he had been living there for thirty years.

(5) 과거 → 과거완료

[예]
- He said, "I met the girl."
  He said that he had met the girl.

- He said to me, "I studied hard."
  He told me that he had studied hard.

4 주절과 종속절 시제 일치하지 않는 경우 종요 ★

(1) 인용문의 내용이 단순 과거사실이 아니라 현재도 계속되는 내용인 경우는 시제 일치와 상관없이 현재형 사용 가능

[예]
- He said, "The school starts at 9 am."
  He said that the school starts at 9 am.

(2) 인용문이 가정법인 경우 시제 일치와 상관없이 가정법 문장 그대로 사용 가능 (단, 인용문이 가정법 현재인 경우 시제일치에 따른다.)

[예]
- He said to me, "If I were rich, I could go to all European countries."
  He told me that if he were rich, he could go to all European countries.

(3) will, can, may, must의 조동사를 제외하면 인용문 내 would, could, should, might, must, ought to, had better, used to 등은 시제가 바뀌지 않음(단, must의 경우 had to 사용 가능)

[예]
- He said, "Taking a walk would be nice."
  He said that taking a walk would be nice.

- He said to me, "I must take my responsibility."
  He told me that he must(had to) take his responsibility.

제 2 절 의문문(interrogative sentence)

1 의문사가 있는 경우

(1) 쉼표와 인용부호 큰따옴표를 지운다.

(2) 전달동사는 ask나 wonder로 바꾼다.

(3) 큰따옴표 이하의 명사절 내 어순을 **평서문**(의문사 + 주어 + 동사) 어순으로 바꾼다.

(4) 명사절(종속절) that 내의 인칭, 시제, 부사(구)를 주절에 맞게 변화시킨다.

예
- He asked her, "Where are you going?"
  He asked her where he was going.

- He asked, "Who are you?"
  He asked me who I was.

2 의문사가 없는 경우

(1) 쉼표와 인용부호 큰따옴표를 지운다.

(2) 전달동사는 ask나 wonder로 바꾼다.

(3) 큰따옴표 자리에 if나 whether를 쓴다.

(4) 큰따옴표 이하의 명사절 내 어순을 **평서문**(if/whether + 주어 + 동사) 어순으로 바꾼다.

(5) 명사절(종속절) if/whether 내의 인칭, 시제, 부사(구)를 주절에 맞게 변화시킨다.

예
- He said to me, "Do you like this car?"
  He asked me if I liked that car.

- He said to me, "Have you ever seen this movie?
  He asked me whether I had ever seen that movie.

제 3 절 　명령문(imperative sentence)

1 　명령

(1) 쉼표와 인용부호 큰따옴표를 지운다.

(2) 전달동사는 tell이나 order로 바꾼다.

(3) 큰따옴표 자리에 to를 쓴다. 부정명령문의 경우 not to를 쓴다.

(4) 명사절(종속절) 내의 인칭, 시제, 부사(구)를 주절에 맞게 변화시킨다.

예

- He said to me, "Listen to me very carefully."
  He told/ordered me to listen to him very carefully.

2 　충고

(1) 쉼표와 인용부호 큰따옴표를 지운다.

(2) 전달동사는 advise로 바꾼다.

(3) 큰따옴표 자리에 to를 쓴다. 부정명령문의 경우 not to를 쓴다.

(4) 명사절(종속절) 내의 인칭, 시제, 부사(구)를 주절에 맞게 변화시킨다.

예

- The doctor said to my wife, "Don't make him stay up late."
  The doctor advised my wife not to make me stay up late.

3 요청

(1) 쉼표와 인용부호 큰따옴표를 지운다.

(2) 전달동사는 ask로 바꾼다.

(3) 큰따옴표 자리에 to를 쓴다. 부정명령문의 경우 not to를 쓴다.

(4) 명사절(종속절) 내의 인칭, 시제, 부사(구)를 주절에 맞게 변화시킨다.

예
- The flight attendant said to the passengers, "Please fasten your seat belts."
  The flight attendant asked the passengers to fasten our seat belts.

4 제안

(1) 쉼표와 인용부호 큰따옴표를 지운다.

(2) 전달동사는 suggest로 바꾼다.

(3) 큰따옴표 자리에 that을 쓰고 that절 내의 어순을 주어(+ should) + 동사로 바꾼다.

(4) 또는 큰따옴표 이하의 동사를 동명사로 바꾼다.

(5) 명사절(종속절) 내의 인칭, 시제, 부사(구)를 주절에 맞게 변화시킨다.

예
- He said to us, "Let's postpone our monthly conference."
- He suggested that we (should) postpone our monthly conference.
- He suggested us postponing our monthly conference.

제 **4** 절 　감탄문(exclamatory sentence)

(1) 쉼표와 인용부호 큰따옴표를 지운다.

(2) 전달동사는 exclaim, shout, cry out 등의 감탄표현 동사로 바꾼다.

(3) 큰따옴표 대신에 명사절을 이끄는 that을 사용한다. (생략 가능)

(4) 명사절(종속절) that 내의 인칭, 시제, 부사(구)를 주절에 맞게 변화시킨다.

　예

- He said, "What a beautiful this flower is!"
  He exclaimed that this flower is very beautiful.

- He said, "How foolish I am!"
  He cried out that he was very foolish.

제 **5** 절 　기타 구문 전환

1 　기원문(optative sentence)

(1) 쉼표와 인용부호 큰따옴표를 지운다.

(2) 전달동사는 pray, implore 동사로 바꾼다.

(3) 큰따옴표 대신에 명사절을 이끄는 that을 사용한다. (생략 가능)

(4) 명사절(종속절) that 내의 본동사 앞에 조동사 might를 쓰고, 인칭, 시제, 부사(구)를 주절에 맞게
변화시킨다.

　예

- He said, "God bless us."
  He prayed that God might bless us.

1 중문(compound sentence)

중문은 2개 이상의 단문(독립절)이 FANBOYS와 같은 등위접속사로 이루어진 문장이다.
등위접속사 and, but, or, so 등 다음에 that절을 반복적으로 사용하여 개별 목적절로 전환한다.

예

- He said, "I will go to the library and I will pick up some books."
  He said that he would go to the library and that he would pick up some book.

- He said, "I am leaving, but I will come back tomorrow."
  He said that he was leaving, but that he would come back the next day.

3 복문(complex sentence)

복문은 한 문장(독립절)은 주절이고 다른 문장은 종속접속사로 연결되어 있는 종속절로 이루어진 문장이다. 종속접속사를 그대로 사용하고 평서문과 동일한 방식으로 전환한다.

예

- He said to me, "You can go out when the rain stops."
  He told me that I could go out when the rain stopped.

- He said to me, "You can leave if you want."
  He told me that I could leave if I wanted.

제8편 실전예상문제

01 다음 중 밑줄 친 부분에 들어갈 표현은 무엇인가?

> He said, "I am hungry."
> ↕
> He said that ＿＿＿＿ hungry.

① I am
② he is
③ he was
④ I was

01 해설
직접화법을 간접화법으로 전환하는 경우 피전달문의 인칭대명사를 전달자의 입장에 맞게 바꾸고, 주절과 종속절의 시제를 일치시킨다.

해석
그는 "난 배고파."라고 말했다. → 그는 배고프다고 말했다.

02 다음 중 어법상 맞는 표현은 무엇인가?

① He said me that being a father is more important than being a movie star.
② He told that being a father is more important than being a movie star.
③ He told to me that being a father is more important than being a movie star.
④ He said to me that being a father is more important than being a movie star.

02 해설
전달동사 say는 3형식 동사로서 say that, say to someone that 형태가 적절한 반면에 전달동사 tell은 4형식 동사로서 tell someone that 의 형태가 적절하다.

해석
그는 나에게 아빠가 되는 것이 영화배우가 되는 것보다 더 중요하다고 말했다.

정답 01 ③ 02 ④

checkpoint 해설 & 정답

03 **해설**
- 전달동사 say는 3형식 동사로서 say that, say to someone that 형태가 적절
- 전달동사 tell은 4형식 동사로서 tell someone that 형태가 적절
- 전달동사 ask는 3, 4형식 동사로서 ask if/whether, ask someone if/whether 형태가 적절

해석
그는 나에게 행복하다고 말했다.

04 **해설**
직접화법 → 간접화법 전환 시 지시·소유대명사, 시간·장소 부사, 조동사는 간접화법에 맞게 전환하여야 한다. tomorrow → the next day 또는 the following day

해석
그는 "내가 내일 너희 집에 갈게."라고 말했다. → 그는 다음 날 우리 집에 온다고 말했다.

05 **해설**
직접화법 → 간접화법 전환 시 : 현재 → 과거, 현재진행 → 과거진행, 현재완료 → 과거완료, 현재완료 진행 → 과거완료 진행, 과거 → 과거완료로 전환한다.

해석
그는 "저는 30년 동안 영어를 가르쳐 왔어요."라고 말했다. → 그는 30년 동안 영어를 가르쳐 왔다고 말했다.

정답 03 ④ 04 ③ 05 ④

03 다음 중 어법상 <u>잘못된</u> 표현은 무엇인가?

① He said to me that he was happy.
② He told me that he was happy.
③ He asked if I was happy.
④ He asked to me if I was happy.

04 다음 중 밑줄 친 부분에 들어갈 표현은 무엇인가?

> He said, "I will go to your house tomorrow."
> ↕
> He said that he would come to my house _____.

① tomorrow
② that day
③ the next day
④ the day before

05 다음 중 밑줄 친 부분에 들어갈 표현은 무엇인가?

> He said, "I have been teaching English for thirty years."
> ↕
> He said that he _____ English for thirty years.

① has taught
② had taught
③ has been teaching
④ had been teaching

06 다음 중 밑줄 친 부분에 들어갈 표현은 무엇인가?

> He said, "I met her last year."
>
> ↕
>
> He said that he _____ her _____.

① met - the previous year

② met - the following year

③ had met - the year before

④ had met - the following year

06 해설
직접화법 → 간접화법 전환 시 : 과거 → 과거완료; 시간·장소 부사 표현, last year → the year before 또는 the previous year

해석
그는 "나는 그녀를 작년에 만났어요."라고 말했다. → 그는 작년에 그녀를 만났다고 말했다.

07 다음 중 밑줄 친 부분에 들어갈 표현은 무엇인가?

> He said to me, "Have you ever seen Bong's movie?"
>
> ↕
>
> He asked me _____ I had ever seen Bong's movie.

① which   ② whether

③ what   ④ that

07 해설
직접화법 → 간접화법 전환 시 의문사가 없는 경우는 명사절을 if 또는 whether로 전환한다.

해석
그는 나에게 "봉 감독의 영화를 본 적이 있니?"라고 말했다. → 그는 나에게 봉 감독의 영화를 본 적이 있느냐고 물었다.

08 다음 중 밑줄 친 부분에 들어갈 표현은 무엇인가?

> The doctor said to his wife, "Don't take vitamins too much."
>
> ↕
>
> The doctor said to his wife _____ vitamins too much.

① to taking

② not to taking

③ not to take

④ to take

08 해설
직접화법 → 간접화법 전환 시 부정명령문의 경우 not to부정사로 전환한다.

해석
의사는 아내에게 "비타민을 너무 많이 먹지 마세요."라고 말했다. → 의사는 아내에게 비타민을 너무 많이 먹지 말라고 했다.

정답 06 ③ 07 ② 08 ③

09 해설

직접화법 → 간접화법 전환 시 제안을 표현하는 명령문의 경우 전달동사 suggest를 사용하고 that절 내의 어순은 주어(+ should) + 동사 표현으로 전환한다.

해석

그는 우리에게 "월례회의를 연기하죠."라고 말했다. → 그는 우리에게 월례회의를 연기하자고 제안했다.

10 해설

직접화법 → 간접화법 전환 시 중문의 경우 등위접속사 and, but, or, so 등 다음에 that절을 반복적으로 사용하여 개별 목적절로 전환한다.

해석

그는 "나는 떠나지만, 내일 돌아올 거야."라고 말했다. → 그는 떠나지만 바로 다음 날 돌아온다고 말했다.

정답 09 ④ 10 ④

09 다음 중 밑줄 친 부분에 들어갈 표현은 무엇인가?

He said to us, "Let's postpone our monthly conference."
↕
He _____ that we should postpone our monthly conference.

① ordered
② advised
③ exclaimed
④ suggested

10 다음 중 밑줄 친 부분에 들어갈 표현은 무엇인가?

He said, "I am leaving, but I will come back tomorrow."
↕
He said that he was leaving, _____ he would come back the next day.

① that
② but
③ and that
④ but that

제 **9** 편

—

부정

www.sdedu.co.kr

단원 개요

영어의 부정(negation)은 문장의 전체 내용을 부정하는 **문장 부정**(sentential negation)과 단어에 접사를 붙여 부정을 표현하는 접사 부정(affixal negation)이 있다. 문장 부정은 be동사, 조동사, 대명사, 한정사, 부사, 접속사 등을 통해 표현하는 반면에 접사 부정은 단어에 접두사, 접미사의 접사를 붙여 표현한다.
영어 문장의 긍정, 부정과 관련하여 어휘 자체의 형태와 의미에 따라 긍정지향의 **단정형**(assertive), 부정 지향의 **비단정형**(non-assertive)으로 구분하는데 대표적인 표현으로 some vs. any가 있다.
또한 부정어 표현이 문장의 의미해석에 영향을 끼치는 범위에 따라 **전체부정, 부분부정, 이중부정**으로 구분하고 문장 내에서 함께 사용되는 부사구, 전치사구, 강세에 따라 그 영향권과 의미 해석이 달라진다.
문장의 부정 표현과 관련하여, 부가의문문, can, may, must 등과 같은 법조동사의 부정 표현도 포함한다.

출제 경향 및 수험 대책

1. 부정의 방법
   (1) 문장 부정 : be동사, 조동사, 일반동사 부정, 대명사, 한정사, 부사, 접속사 표현
   (2) 접사 부정 : 접사별 부정표현 의미, 반의어 및 동의어 관계 표현
2. 단정형과 비단정형
   (1) 단정형 some의 용법 및 의미
   (2) 비단정형 any의 용법 및 의미
   (3) 동일 문장 형식 내의 some vs any 용법 및 의미
3. need, dare의 본동사 vs 조동사 용법, 긍정 vs 부정 표현
4. 부가의문문
   (1) be동사, 조동사, 일반동사 부가의문문 형식
   (2) 지시사, 부정대명사, 중문·복문 부가의문문 형식
5. 부가어 전송 : 부가어 전송 가능 동사 표현 vs 불가능한 동사 표현
6. 전체부정, 부분부정, 이중부정 : 부정어 표현 형식 및 의미
7. 부정의 범위 : 부사구, 부정어, 전치사구, 강세, 부가의문문에 따른 부정 영향권 및 의미
8. 법조동사의 부정 : can, may, must의 부정 용법, 부정적 추측 정도

합격의 공식 SD에듀

잠깐!

자격증・공무원・금융/보험・면허증・언어/외국어・검정고시/독학사・기업체/취업
이 시대의 모든 합격! SD에듀에서 합격하세요!
www.youtube.com → SD에듀 → 구독

제 1 장 부정의 방법

영어의 문장 부정은 일반적으로 be동사, 조동사, 일반동사와 같은 (긍정문의) 동사에 not을 붙여 표현한다. 그 외에 대명사, 한정사, 부사, 접속사 등을 통해 문장을 부정할 수 있다.

1 be동사 : be동사 + not

be동사 다음에 not을 붙이면 부정문이 된다.

[예]

- I am a teacher. → I am not a teacher.
- You are a musician. → You are not a musician. (aren't)
- He is hungry. → He is not hungry. (isn't)
- She was born in Chicago. → She was not born in Chicago. (wasn't)
- We are interested in jazz. → We are not interested in jazz. (aren't)
- They were writing a book. → They were not writing a book. (weren't)

2 조동사 : 조동사 + not

'조동사 + 본동사'이면 조동사 다음에 not을 붙이면 부정문이 된다.

[예]

- He will give her another marshmallow. → He will not giver her another marshmallow. (won't)
- He can play the piano. → He cannot play the piano. (can't)
- We must go to the conference. → We must not go to the conference. (mustn't)
- This might be true. → This might not be true.
- He has been a teacher for ten years. → He has not been a teacher for ten years. (hasn't)

3 일반동사 : 조동사 + not + 일반동사(원형)

일반동사의 부정문은 일반동사 앞에 '조동사 do + not'으로 표현하면 부정문이 된다. 현재는 인칭에 따라 do not(don't), does not(doesn't), 과거는 인칭에 상관없이 did not(didn't)을 동사 앞에 표현하고 동사는 원형으로 쓰면 된다.

예

• I study Korean. → I do not study Korean. (don't)
• He has four sisters. → He does not have four sisters. (doesn't)
• They like baseball. → They do not like baseball. (don't)
• He ate the banana. → He did not eat the banana. (didn't)
• They went to Chicago. → They didn't go to Chicago. (didn't)

> **더 알아두기**
>
> **영어 (조동사) 부정의 축약형**
>
> | 동사 | 부정형 | |
> |---|---|---|
> | | 비축약형 | 축약형 |
> | be | am not | *amn't* |
> | | is not | isn't |
> | | are not | aren't |
> | | was not | wasn't |
> | | were not | weren't |
> | do | do not | don't |
> | | does not | doesn't |
> | | did not | didn't |
> | have | have not | haven't |
> | | has not | hasn't |
> | | had not | hadn't |
> | will | will not | won't |
> | would | would not | wouldn't |
> | can | can not | can't |
> | could | could not | couldn't |
> | shall | shall not | shan't |
> | should | should not | shouldn't |
> | must | must not | mustn't |
> | may | may not | mayn't |
> | might | might not | mightn't |

need	need not	needn't
dare	dare not	daren't

※ I am not에서 am과 not은 축약(*amn't)하지 않고, I'm not으로 축약한다.

4 그 외 문장 부정 표현 중요 ★

문장 부정은 동사 주위에 not을 표현하는 것 외에도 대명사, 한정사, 부사, 접속사 등을 통해 표현할 수 있다.

(1) 대명사

> no one, none, nobody, nothing, neither (of)

[예]

- No one knew the exact cause of this effect.
- None of them have ever lived in the wild before.
- Nobody could stop him.

(2) 한정사

> no, few, little

[예]

- No legacy is so rich as honesty. - William Shakespeare -
- Few people came to the conference.
- Little research has been done.

(3) 부사

> never, nowhere, hardly, scarcely, barely, rarely, seldom

[예]

- Computers will never replace teachers.
- He can hardly see it.
- He barely heard any noise in the house.

① 부가의문문

　　예 He is scarcely interested in jazz, is he/*isn't he?

② 도치 가능

　　예

- Never again has he seen her.
- Hardly do we go to a movie.
- Barely does he run.

(4) 접속사

> (neither) ～ nor

예

- Neither father nor mother is at home.
- Neither you nor I am wrong. (Neither I nor you are wrong.)
- The day was bright, nor were there clouds above.

제 2 절　접사 부정(affixal negation)

영어에는 문장 부정 외에 단어 내에서 접사(affix)를 통해 부정의 의미를 표현한다. 대표적인 부정 접사로 un-, in-, dis-, non-, a-, -free가 있다.

1　un-

접두사 un-은 형용사 어근에 붙어 부정을 표현하거나, 동사 어근에 붙어 다른 동사를 만들거나, 명사 어근에 붙어 다른 동사를 만든다.

(1) un- + 형용사 어근

unacceptable	unfamiliar	unskilled
unambiguous	unhappy	unskillful
unauthentic	unholy	unprepared
unbalanced	unimaginative	unpopular
undue	unintelligent	unready

uncanny	unjust	unreal
uncomfortable	unkind	unsafe
uncommon	unsafe	unwise
unfair	unscientific	unyielding

(2) un- + 동사 어근

unbend	undelete	unlearn
unbutton	undo	unlock
unchain	unfasten	unpack
uncork	undress	unveil
uncover	unfold	unzip

※ loose(n)-unloose(n), ravel-unravel은 반의어 관계가 아니라 동의어 관계

(3) un- + 명사 어근

unbosom	unhand	unhouse	unplug
unfrock	unhinge	unman	unsaddle

2 in-

접두사 in-은 어원상 라틴계 어휘의 부정을 표현하는 데 주로 사용된다. 다음에 오는 어근의 첫소리에 따라 im-, il-, ir-, in-의 이형태(allomorph)로 변한다.

환경	이형태	예시
(1) /b, p, m/ 앞에서	im-	imbalance, immature, immediate, immoral, immune, impossible, improper, imprudent, improvident
(2) /l/ 앞에서	il-	illegal, illegible, illiberal, illegitimate, illiterate, illogical
(3) /r/ 앞에서	ir-	irrational, irregular, irrelevant, irreligious, irresolute, irrespective, irresponsible, irrevocable
그 외	in-	inaccessible, inaccurate, inadequate, inapplicable, inapt, inattentive, inaudible, incapable, incessant, incoherent, incomplete, incorrect, indecent, indeciduous, indelible, independent, indefatigable, indifferent, inefficient, inept, insufficient

※ valuable-invaluable, flammable-inflammable은 반의어 관계가 아니라 동의어 관계

3 dis−

접두사 dis-는 동사, 형용사, 명사 어근에 붙어 반대의 동작을 표현한다.

어근		예시
+동사		disapprove, disband, disbar, disburden, discolor, discover, disestablish, disfranchise, dishonor, dishearten, dismantle, dismember, dislocate, dislodge, dispossess, disregard, disunite
+형용사	→ 형용사	disagreeable, discontent, discontiguous, disinterested, disqualified
	→ 동사	discontent, disable, disquiet
+명사		disaffection, disbelief, disbenefit, disorder, distrust, disunion

※ sever-dissever는 반의어 관계가 아니라 **동의어 관계**

※ dissect, dissolve, distort 등의 dis-는 부정과 관계 없음

4 non−

접두사 non-은 형용사, 명사 어근에 붙어 부정 표현을 만든다.

어근	예시
+형용사	nonabrasive, nonabstract, nonacademic, nonbelligerent, noncommercial, nonhuman, nonquantitative, nonracial, nonscientific
+명사	nonadmission, nonacceptance, nonanimal, nonanswer, nonbelief, nonbiologist, noncommunist, noneducation, nonfarmer, nongrowth, nonmainstream, noncommitment, nonconcurrence, nonreappointment, nonschool, nonscientist

> **⚠️ 더 알아두기** 🔍
>
> **접두사 non−**
> 부정 접두사 un-, in-, dis-는 화자의 주관적 판단에 따라 감정이나 평가가 개입된 부정 표현인 반면에 접두사 non-은 감정이 개입되지 않은 객관적인 표현으로 '없다', '아니다'라는 것을 단순히 기술하는 말이다.
> 예
> • His behavior is immoral. ([어휘] immoral : 도덕에 어긋나다, 부도덕한)
> • His behavior is nonmoral. ([어휘] nonmoral : 도덕적 판단의 대상이 아니다, 도덕과 무관한, ≒ amoral)
>
> | immoral | 사회적 윤리에 위배되는, 부도덕한, unethical |
> |---|---|
> | nonnormal | 일반적으로 도덕적 판단의 범위 밖에 있는 것 |
> | amoral | 일반적, 관습상 도덕적 판단에 따라 쓰이는 경향 |
> | unmoral | 자연력, 동물, 기계처럼 도덕과 관계없는, 초도덕적인 |
>
> 예
> • It is an irreligious gathering. ([어휘] irreligious : 종교에 반하는 행사)
> • It is a nonreligious gathering. ([어휘] nonreligious : 비종교적인 행사)

5 a-

접두사 a-는 not 또는 without의 의미로 부정표현을 나타내고 an-으로도 파생된다.

amoral	acellular	achromatic
acyclic	anarchy	anhydrous
anomy	asylum	asymmetrical
atheist	atonal	atypical

※ afoot, alive, asleep의 a-는 부정 접두사가 아니다.

6 -less

접미사 -less는 명사에 붙어 형용사 또는 부사로 '~이 없는', 동사에 붙어 형용사로 '~할 수 없는', '~하기 어려운'의 의미로 사용된다.

어근		예시
명사+	→ 형용사/부사	breathless, careless, childless, conscienceless, endless, fearless, flawless, groundless, harmless, helpless, homeless, limitless, meaningless, merciless, nameless, powerless, priceless, seamless, senseless, shapeless, speechless, timeless, treeless, useless, valueless, wireless, worthless
동사+	→ 형용사	blameless, ceaseless, changeless, cheerless, countless, doubtless, fadeless, fathomless, heedless, hopeless, loveless, moveless, reachless, reckless, regardless, relentless, resistless, searchless, sleepless, tasteless, tireless, thankless, utterless, wantless, watchless, worriless

※ priceless(= invaluable)은 '대단히 귀중한'이란 의미임(↔ valueless, worthless)

7 -free

접미사 -free는 명사에 붙어 '~이 없는', '~로부터 자유스러운', '~을 모면한'의 의미로 사용된다. 부정을 표현하는 대부분의 부정 접사와는 달리 '(부정적인 의미의) 명사' + -free로 사용되어 긍정적인 어감으로 표현된다.

accent-free	drug-free	stress-free
alcohol-free	duty-free	tariff-free
caffeine-free	emission-free	tax-free
car-free	meat-free	trouble-free
carbon-free	nuclear-free	tuition-free
cholesterol-free	pain-free	visa-free
fat-free	plastic-free	weapon-free
disease-free	sugar-free	worry-free
distortion-free	smoke-free	wrinkle-free

제 2 장 단정형과 비단정형

영어문장은 긍정(affirmative)과 부정(negative)로 구분하기도 하지만 단정형(assertive form)과 비단정형(non-assertive form)으로도 구분한다. 단정형은 긍정 지향(positive-oriented), 비단정형은 부정문, 의문문, 그 외 동사, 형용사, 전치사, 조건문(가정법), 비교문 등 부정의 의미를 포함하고 있는 부정지향(negative-oriented)을 의미한다.

단정형과 비단정형은 문장 구조 차이보다는 어휘 자체의 형태, 의미가 갖고 있는 극성(polarity) 때문에 발생하는데 긍정의 맥락에서만 사용하는 단정형 표현을 긍정극어(positive polarity item), 부정의 맥락에서만 사용하는 비단정형 표현을 부정극어(negative polarity item)라고도 한다.

제 1 절 some과 any의 용법 중요 ★★

1 단정형 some과 비단정형 any

영어의 단정형과 비단정형의 대표적인 표현은 각각 some과 any가 있고 그 외 극성표현들은 다음과 같다.

단정형 (assertive form)		비단정형 (non-assertive form)	부정형 (negative form)
긍정극어 (positive polarity item)		부정극어 (negative polarity item)	
SOME		ANY	-
(부정)형용사	some	any	no
(부정)대명사	some	any	none
someone		anyone	no one
somebody		anybody	nobody
something		anything	nothing
sometimes		ever	never
somehow		in any way(anyhow)	in no way(nohow)
somewhat		any	no
somewhere		anywhere	nowhere
someplace		anyplace	no place

그 외		
already	yet	-
always	anytime	-
still	any more	no more
too, as well	either	-
a great deal	much	-
a long way	far	-

단정형 표현인 긍정극어는 긍정문(긍정맥락)에서, 비단정형 표현인 부정극어는 부정문(부정 맥락)에서 사용되는데 관련 예문은 다음과 같다.

단정형 vs. 비단정형		예문	
		단정문	비단정문
형용사	some vs. any	He has some money.	He doesn't have any money.
대명사	some vs. any	He has some.	He doesn't have any.
someone vs. anyone		He met someone.	He didn't meet anyone.
somebody vs. anybody		He met somebody.	He didn't meet anybody.
something vs. anything		He gave her something.	He didn't give her anything.
sometimes vs. ever		He sometimes visits her.	He doesn't ever visit her.
somehow vs. anyhow		He will do it somehow.	He won't do it anyhow.
somewhat vs. any		He was somewhat surprised.	He wasn't any surprised.
somewhere vs. anywhere		He met her somewhere.	He didn't meet her anywhere.
someplace vs. anyplace		He met her someplace.	He didn't meet her anyplace.
already vs. yet		He has done it already.	He has not done it yet.
always vs. anytime		He always visits her.	He doesn't anytime visit her.
still vs. anymore		He still loves her.	He doesn't love her any more.
too vs. either		He saw her, too.	He didn't see her, either.
a great deal vs. much		He likes her a great deal.	He doesn't like her much.
a long way vs. far		He has been a long way.	He has not been far.

2 some

단정형인 some은 일반적으로 '수, 양, 특정한 수의 일부'의 의미로 긍정문에서 사용한다. 또한 상대방에게 긍정의 대답을 기대하거나 권유하는 의문문, 부정문, 조건절에서도 사용한다.

(1) 긍정문

① 수의 일부 : 가산명사

예

- Some children are barefoot.
- He wants some books.

② 양의 일부 : 불가산명사

예

- Some action is necessary.
- He wants some money.

③ 특정한 수·종류의 일부

예

- Some students study Korean and others study English.
- All metal is not hard, some metal is soft.
- There is still some time left.

(2) 의문문 : 긍정 대답 기대, 권유

예

- Are there some letter for me?
- Do you have some coins?
- Could you give me some idea of it?

- Will you have some coffee?
- Would you like something to drink?
- Would you care for some cake?

(3) 부정문

예

- Some students didn't do their homework. (일부 학생이 아직 안 했다는 의미)
- The building does not need some repairs. ([해석] 그 건물은 수리할 필요가 없는 것도 있다.)

(4) 조건절

예

- If he has some difficulty beating the deadline, please let her know. (마감시간을 맞추기 어려울 가능성이 있음)
- If you want some water, ask the server. (약간의 물을 원한다면)

3 any

비단정형 any는 일반적으로 some 긍정문과 상응하는 부정문, 의문문, 조건문에서 사용한다. 또한 any가 대상의 정체성이나 본질과 상관없다는 의미 내포하는 'no matter which', 'no matter what', 'no matter who'의 의미로 사용되는 경우 긍정문에도 쓰인다.

(1) 부정문 : '아무것도', '조금도', '아무도'

    ① 가산명사

        예 He doesn't have any questions about that.

    ② 불가산명사

        예 He doesn't have any money.

> **❗ 더 알아두기 Q**
>
> **부정문에서의 주어 any**
>
> any는 부정문에서 주어로 사용하지 않는다. (*Any ~ not; √Not (~) any)
> - *Any student did not solve it. → No student solved it.
>   *Anyone can not do it. → No one can do it.
>   *Any of them are not for sale. → None of them are for sale.
>
> - Not (just) anyone can do it. ([해석] 누구나 그 일을 할 수 있는 것은 아니다.)
>   Not (just) anyone can be a Beefeater. ([해석] 누구나 영국 왕실의 근위병이 될 수 있는 것은 아니다.)
> ※ √(v-check) 표시 : '문법적으로 맞다/괜찮다'의 의미

(2) 의문문 : '무슨', '어떤', '어느', '누군가'

    ① 가산명사

        예 Do you have any questions about that?

    ② 불가산명사

        예 Do you have any milk?

(3) 조건문 : '무슨', '어떤', '누군가', '약간'

    ① 가산명사

        예 If you have any questions, ask them.

    ② 불가산명사

        예 If you need any help, please let me know.

(4) 긍정문 : '어떤 ~이라도', '어느 ~이든', '누가 ~하든'

① '어떤 ~이라도'

[예]

- Any mystery books will do.
- Select any color you like.
- You may choose any chocolates you like.

② '어느 ~이든'

[예]

- Do anything you want.
- He is interested in anything uncommon.
- He is prepared to take any advice.

③ '누가 ~하든'

[예]

- Any boy can do it.
- Anyone knows that he is very kind.
- He can invite anybody to the party.

제 2 절 some/any 용법의 의미 중요★★

단정형 some은 기본적으로 '확실히 알고 있는 것' 단언의 의미를 내포하며 단정문에서 사용되는 반면에 비단정형 any는 '불확실한 것' 혹은 '모르는 것'의 비단언 의미를 내포하며 비단정문에서 사용된다.

1 긍정문

단정형인 some은 긍정문에서 '수(가산명사)', '양(불가산명사)', '특정한 수 및 종류의 일부'의 의미로 사용한다. 반면에 비단정형 any는 긍정문에서 사물 및 대상의 정체성이나 본질과는 상관없다는 '어떤 것이든(no matter which)', '어느 무엇이든(no matter what)', '누가 ~하든(no matter who)'의 의미를 내포한다.

(1) some

① **수의 일부** : 가산명사

[예]

- Some children are barefoot.
- He wants some books.

② **양의 일부 : 불가산명사**

예

- Some action is necessary.
- He wants some money.

③ **특정한 수, 종류의 일부**

예

- Some students study Korean and others study English.
- All metal is not hard, some metal is soft.
- There is still some time left.

(2) any

① '어떤 것이든'(= no matter which)

예

- Any mystery books will do.
- Select any color you like.
- You may choose any chocolates you like.

② '어느 무엇이든'(= no matter what)

예

- Do anything you want.
- He is interested in anything uncommon.
- He is prepared to take any advice.

③ '누가 ~하든'(= no matter who)

예

- Any boy can do it.
- Anyone knows that he is very kind.
- He can invite anybody to the party.

2 부정문

단정형 some이 부정어 not과 함께 사용될 경우 어느 정도 수와 양이 존재하는 것을 전제하는 반면에 부단정형 any는 확신이 없거나 모르는 상황을 의미한다.

예

- The building doesn't need some repairs. ([해석] 그 건물은 수리할 필요가 없는 것도 있다.)
- The building doesn't need any repairs. ([해석] 그 건물은 어떤 수리도 필요가 없다.)

- Some of the students couldn't answer the question. ([해석] 일부 학생은 대답할 수 없었을 것이다.)
- Any of the students couldn't answer the question. ([해석] 누구든지 대답할 수 없었을 것이다.)

- He <u>did not get</u> some(SOME) of the things he wanted most.
  (= There were some of the things he didn't get.)
  ([해석] 그가 가장 받고 싶었던 물건 중 받지 못한 몇 가지가 있다.)

- He <u>did not get any of the things he wanted most.</u>
  (= He wanted many things, but there were not any of the things that he got.)
  ([해석] 그가 가장 받고 싶었던 물건을 한 개도 못 받았다.)

3 의문문

단정형 some은 의문문에서 상대방에게 긍정적인 답변을 기대하거나 상대방에게 권유하는 의미의 의문문에 사용하는 반면에 비단정형 any는 어떠한 수와 양에 상관없거나, 확신이 없거나, 모르는 경우에 사용한다.

예

- Do you have some examples for that? (예시가 있을 거라고 기대)
- Do you have any examples for that? (예시가 없을 수도 있다고 생각)

- Didn't I give you some money? (돈을 주었다고 확신, 긍정적인 대답 기대)
- Didn't he give you any money? (돈을 준 것을 모름, 돈이 없을 수도 있다고 생각)

- Are there some bananas in the box? (바나나가 좀 있을 거라고 기대)
- Are there any bananas in the box? (바나나가 없을 수도 있다고 생각)

- Would you have some more coffee? (권유의 의문문)
- Do we have to buy any cookie? (수/양에 상관없이)

4 조건문

단정형 some은 조건문에서 긍정적인 가능성에 대해 언급하거나, 불특정하지만 일부를 의미하거나, 긍정의 문맥을 기대하는 경우에 사용하는 반면에 비단정형 any는 어떤 조건, 상태, 진술에 대해 불확실한 내용을 언급하거나, 수량에 상관없는 불특정다수를 의미하는 경우에 사용한다.

예

- If something happens, call me. (긍정적인 가능성에 대해 언급)
- If anything happens, call me. (어떠한 일이든지)

- If you have some difficulty beating the deadline, please let me know.
  (마감시간을 맞추기 어려울 가능성이 높음)

- If you have any difficulty beating the deadline, please let me know.
  (마감시간을 맞추는 일이 어려울 수도, 그렇지 않을 수도 있음)

- If you want some water, ask the server. (약간의 물을 원한다면)
  If you have any butter left, please give it to me. (남은 버터라도 있다면)

제 **3** 장 　 need, dare

need와 dare의 본동사는 평서문에서 일반동사로 사용되며 to부정사를 목적어로 취하고, 조동사는 부정문과 의문문에서 사용된다.

제 **1** 절 　 need 중요 ★

1 본동사 need

(1) 평서문 일반동사

① 긍정문

예

- We need your help.
- Burning needs oxygen.

② 부정문 : do not need(don't need)

예

- We don't need your help.
- He doesn't need any money now.

(2) need + to do

① 긍정문

예

- He needs to wax the car.
- This letter needs to be signed by the manager.

② 부정문

예

- You don't need to get used to it.
- He doesn't need to be told that.

(3) need + -ing

① 긍정문

예

- This chair needs fixing.
- Your room needs cleaning up.

② 부정문

예

- The car doesn't need washing.
- The plant doesn't need watering.

2 조동사 need

(1) 부정문 : need not(needn't)

예

- We need not do it.

  (→ 본동사 : We do not need to do it.)

- You need not tell her about the secret.

  (→ 본동사 : You do not need to tell her about the secret.)

(2) 의문문

예

- Need we do it?

  (→ 본동사 : Do we need to do it?)

- Need I tell them that we can help them?

  (→ 본동사 : Do I have to tell them that we can help them?)

※ need 다음에 원형부정사가 와서 조동사 역할을 할 수도 있다.

예

- You <u>need have</u> no fear.
- All you <u>need do</u> is ask a question.

제 2 절   dare 중요 ★

1 본동사 dare

(1) 긍정문 : dare + to부정사

예

- He dare to tell her the secret.
- He dared to jump across the brook.

(2) 부정문 : do not(don't) dare to

예

- He does not dare to challenge the society's rules.
- He did not dare to tell her how much it will cost.

2 조동사 dare

(1) 부정문 : dare not(daren't)

예

- He dares not tell you any more. ([해석] 그는 더 이상 너에게 말할 용기가 없다.)
- He dared not do something. ([해석] 그는 어떤 일을 할 용기가 없었다.)

(2) 의문문

예

- How dare you tell me such a thing?
- How dare you say such a word to her?

※ dare 다음에 원형부정사가 와서 조동사 역할을 할 수도 있다.

예

- You <u>dare tell</u> her lies!
- Don't you <u>dare tell</u> her lies.

제 **4** 장 부가의문문

제 1 절 부가의문문의 의미

부가의문문(tag question)은 서술문(평서문) 다음으로 상대방에게 기존의 사실을 확인하거나, 동의나 의견을 확인하는 경우에 사용한다. 본 문장의 서술문이 긍정이면 부정 부가의문문을, 본 문장의 서술 문이 부정이면 긍정 부가의문문을 사용하고 긍정 사실이면 yes, 부정 사실이면 no로 대답한다.

제 2 절 부가의문문의 종류

부가의문문은 be동사, 조동사, 일반동사에 따라 다르게 표현된다. 평서문이 긍정이면 부정의 부가의문 문을, 평서문이 부정이면 긍정의 부가의문문을 사용한다. 부가의문문의 대답은 부가의문문의 긍정·부 정 여부에 상관없이 사실 혹은 명제 자체가 사실이면 긍정 대답, 거짓이면 부정 대답을 한다.

1 be동사

서술문 + 부가의문문		대답
He is a smart professor, isn't he?*	긍정	Yes, he is.
He isn't a smart professor, is he?	부정	No, he is not(isn't).
He was sleeping, wasn't he?*	긍정	Yes, he was.
He wasn't sleeping, was he?	부정	No, he was not(wasn't).
They are students, aren't they?*	긍정	Yes, they are.
They are not students, are they?	부정	No, they are not(aren't).

※ 부가의문문이 부정이면 축약형을 사용한다.

2 조동사 중요 ★

	서술문 + 부가의문문		대답
(1) 일반조동사 (primary auxiliary verbs)	He has studied English, hasn't he? He hasn't studied English, has he?	긍정	Yes, he has.
		부정	No, he has not(hasn't).
(2) 양태조동사 (modal auxiliary verbs)	He can speak German, can't he?	긍정	Yes, he can.
	He cannot speak German, can he?	부정	No, he cannot(can't).
	He will clean the room, won't he?	긍정	Yes, he will.
	He will not clean the room, will he?	부정	No, he will not(won't).
	They should come back, shouldn't they?	긍정	Yes, they should.
	They shouldn't come back, should they?	부정	No, they should not(shouldn't).
	You ought to catch the first train, shouldn't you?	긍정	Yes, I should.
	You ought not to catch the first train, should you?	부정	No, I should not(shouldn't).
(3) 준조동사 (quasi auxiliary verbs)	You have to clean your room, don't you?	긍정	Yes, I do.
	You do not have to clean your room, do you?	부정	No, I do not(don't).
	You used to play baseball on Sundays, didn't you?	긍정	Yes, I did.
	*You did not used to play baseball on Sundays, did you?	부정	No, I did not(didn't)
	You had better wear your jacket, hadn't you?	긍정	Yes, I had.
	You had better not wear your jacket, had you?	부정	No, I had not(hadn't).

※ used to의 부정형은 didn't used to, didn't use to, used not to, usedn't to 모두 가능하다.

3 일반동사

서술문 + 부가의문문		대답
You love her, don't you?	긍정	Yes, I do.
You do not love her, do you?	부정	No, I do not(don't).
He loves her, doesn't he?*	긍정	Yes, he does.
He doesn't love her, does he?	부정	No, he does not(doesn't).
They have three children, don't they?*	긍정	Yes, they do.
They don't have three children, do they?	부정	No, they do not(don't).

4 this, that, these, those 표현

this, that	→	it
these, those	→	they

예

• This is your car, isn't it?
• Those are Josh's notebooks, aren't they?

5 everything, everyone, nothing, nobody 표현 중요★

everything, nothing, something	→	it
everyone, everybody, someone, somebody, no one, nobody	→	they

예

• Everything is perfect, isn't it?
• Everyone came to the meeting, didn't they?

• Nothing is wrong, is it?
• Nobody came to the meeting, did they?

• Something was strange, wasn't it?
• Somebody told you the correct answer, didn't they?

6 복문, 중문, 명사절 that절의 경우 중요★

(1) 복문 : 주절의 내용과 일치

예 He is the man who won the game, isn't he?

(2) 중문(FANBOYS 연결) : 뒷문장과 일치

예 He is a salesman and she is a teacher, isn't she?

(3) 명사절 that절

① 주절의 주어가 1인칭인 경우 종속절의 내용과 일치(think, suppose, bet 동사)

예

- I bet that <u>he</u> <u>is</u> handsome, isn't he?
- I think that <u>they</u> <u>are</u> <u>not</u> students, are they?

② 주절의 주어가 2, 3인칭인 경우 주절의 내용과 일치

예

- <u>You</u> <u>don't</u> think that he will come back, do you?
- <u>He</u> <u>thinks</u> that his brother is so kind, doesn't he?

7 am I not? / aren't I?

평서문 'I am~' 표현에 대한 부가의문문은 'am not I?'/ 'amn't I?'는 사용하지 않고, 격식 있는 표현은 'am I not?', 구어적인 표현은 'aren't I?'로 사용한다.

예

- I am late, am I not? / aren't I? (*amn't I?)
- I am right, am I not? / aren't I? (*amn't I?)
- I am going to get an email with the details, am I not? / aren't I? (*amn't I?)

제 3 절 명령문과 함께 쓰이는 부가의문문 종요★

1 일반 명령문

(1) 긍정문 : will you?

예

- Be quiet, will you?
- Open the door, will you?

(2) 부정문 : will you?

예

- Don't be late, will you?
- Don't be lazy, will you?

2 Let's 명령문

(1) 긍정문 : shall we?

예

- Let's go shopping, shall we?
- Let's play football, shall we?

(2) 부정문 : shall we?

예

- Let's not waste any more time, shall we?
- Let's not rush it, shall we?

제 5 장 부가어 전송

문장 부정 표현 not이 특정 (본)동사의 종속절에 오면 not의 의미 변화 없이 주절의 본동사 앞으로 전이 혹은 인상이 되는데 이런 현상을 부정 전이(transferred negation) 또는 부정 인상(Neg(ation)-raising)이라고 한다.

예

- This is not a good plan.
  - → I think + [this is not a good plan]
  - → I do not think this is a good plan.
- I think this is not a good plan.

제 1 절 부가어 전송 동사

영어에서는 주절의 술부에 생각, 의견, 지각, 가능성, 의도, 의지, 판단, 의무를 표현하는 동사가 오면 이런 부정 전이 현상이 일어난다.

1 부가어 전송 가능한 동사 표현

생각, 의견	think, believe, suppose, imagine, expect, reckon
지각	seem, appear, look like, sound like, feel like
가능성	be likely, be probable
의도, 의지	want, intend, plan, choose
판단, 의무	be supposed to, ought to, should, be desirable, advise, suggest

?	√
I think he is not going to the meeting.	I don't think he is going to the meeting.
I believe he is not going to the meeting.	I don't believe he is going to the meeting.
I suppose he is not going to the meeting.	I don't suppose he is going to the meeting.
I expect him not to go to the meeting.	I don't expect him to go to the meeting.
He seems not to like it.	He doesn't seem to like it.
I want him not go to the meeting.	I don't want him to go to the meeting.

※ ? 표시(unacceptable) : 어색한, √ 표시(acceptable) : 표현이 맞는, '문법적으로 맞다/괜찮다'의 의미

제 2 절 부가어 전송이 가능하지 않은 동사 표현 중요 ★

1 말하기 동사 표현

> say, tell, speak, mumble, retort

예

• He said that Josh does not love Amy.

([해석] Josh가 Amy를 사랑하지 않는다고 그가 말했다.)

≠

• He did not said that Josh loves Amy.

([해석] Josh가 Amy를 사랑한다고 그가 말하지 않았다.)

2 사실 동사 표현

> know, regret, forget, realize, note

예

• I know that he did not go to the meeting.

([해석] 나는 그가 회의에 가지 않았다는 사실을 알고 있다.)

≠

• I don't know that he went to the meeting.

([해석] 나는 그가 회의에 갔다는 사실을 알지못한다.)

3 놀람(surprise)을 나타내는 표현

예

• I thought you weren't going to the meeting!

• I thought you wouldn't get there on time!

4 동사 hope

예

• I hope he does not go to the meeting. (그가 회의에 가지 않기를 바랍니다.)

→ ? I do not hope he goes to the meeting.

※ 구어체

A : Did you fail the exam?

B : I hope not. (= I hope I didn't fail the exam.)

※ ? 표시(unacceptable) : 문법적으로 어색한

제 6 장 전체부정, 부분부정, 이중부정

제 1 절 전체부정(complete negation) 중요 ★★

문장에 전체부정어 및 부정 지향성 표현이 쓰여 '아무(것)도 (전혀, 결코) ~ 아니다'는 의미를 나타낸다.

1 전체부정어 표현

no, none, neither, nothing, nobody, never

[예]

- No student is lazy.
- He knows neither of the subjects.
- Nothing satisfied him.
- Nobody likes her.
- She will never forget his love as long as she lives.

2 부정 지향성 표현

not ~ any, not ~ either, not ~ anybody(anyone), not ~ anything, not ~ ever

[예]

- He doesn't eat any meat.
- He couldn't find any articles about linguistics.
- He haven't met either of the professors. (= neither, 전체부정)
  (vs He haven't met both of the professors. (= one, 부분부정))
- Not anybody like her.
- He doesn't ever get tired.

제 2 절   부분부정(partial negation) 중요 ★★

전체(모두)를 나타내는 표현과 부정표현 not이 만나 '모두가 (항상, 반드시) ~인 것은 아니다'는 의미의 부분 부정으로 사용된다.

not ~ +	all, both, every, everybody(everyone), always, entirely, everything, wholly, fully, completely, necessarily, absolutely

예

- He does not know all of them.
- The rich are not always happy.
- He agrees with most of what she said, but he doesn't agree with everything.
- Not everybody likes her.
- All that glitters is not gold. (Shakespeare's The Merchant of Venice)
  (= All is not gold that glitters.)

제 3 절   이중부정(double negation) 중요 ★

한 문장 안에 부정 표현을 두 개 사용하여 (강한) 긍정을 나타낸다.

> never ~ without, no ~ without, hardly ~ not

예

- He never sees the picture without thinking her.
  (= Whenever he sees the picture, he thinks of her.)
- There is no rule without some exceptions.
- There are no parents who don't love their children.
- He was so smart that there was hardly any reason why he couldn't solve the easy question.

제 7 장 부정의 범위

문장 내에서 부정어가 영향을 미치는 의미영역을 부정의 범위 또는 영향권(scope of negation)이라고 한다. 부정어가 문장 전체에 영향권을 갖게 되면 문장부정(sentence/clausal negation, 전체부정)이 되는 반면에 문장의 일부에만 영향권을 갖게 되면 부분부정(local negation)이 된다. 또한 부정어와 함께 사용되는 부사(구) 위치, 절의 위치, 전치사구에 따라 부정어의 영향권이 달라지고 의미도 다르게 해석된다.

제 1 절 부사구 (위치) 부정 중요 ★

부정어와 함께 사용되는 부사(구)는 그 위치에 따라 부정의 범위가 다르게 해석된다.

He deliberately <u>didn't answer the question</u>.
→ DELIBERATELY (not answer the question)
① 의도적으로 대답을 하지 않았다.
② 신중히 생각하고 대답하지 않았다.

He <u>didn't deliberately answer the question</u>.
(or He <u>didn't answer the question deliberately</u>.)
→ NOT (deliberately answer the question)
① 의도적으로 대답한 것은 아니었다.
② 신중하게 생각하고 대답한 것은 아니었다.

He intentionally <u>didn't ignore us</u>.
→ INTENTIONALLY (not ignore us)
(그가 우리를 무시하지 않은 것은 의도적이었다.)

He <u>didn't ignore us intentionally</u>.
(or He <u>didn't intentionally ignore us</u>.)
→ NOT (intentionally ignore us)
(그가 우리는 무시한 것은 고의가 아니었다.)

The students <u>didn't listen</u> all the time.
→ NOT (listen)
([해석] 학생들이 처음부터 끝까지 경청하지 않았다. 전체 부정)

The students <u>didn't</u> listen <u>all the time</u>.
→ NOT (all the time)
([해석] 학생들이 경청한 것은 처음부터 끝까지는 아니었다. 부분 부정)

※ 문미에 위치한 부사가 쉼표와 함께 사용되는 경우 부정어의 영향을 받지 않는다.

He <u>didn't avoid the accident</u>, unfortunately.
→ NOT (avoid the accident)
([해석] 그는 사고를 피하지는 못했다, 불행하게도)

He <u>didn't call her</u>, however.
→ NOT (call her)
([해석] 그는 그녀에게 연락을 안했다, 그렇지만)

제 2 절　절 부정 중요 ★

부정어와 함께 사용되는 (부사)절도 그 위치에 따라 부정의 범위가 다르게 해석된다.

She <u>didn't marry him because he was rich</u>.
→ NOT (marry him because he was rich)
([해석] 그녀는 그가 부자였기 때문에 그와 결혼했던 것은 아니다.)

Because he was rich, she <u>didn't marry him</u>.
→ NOT (marry him)
([해석] 그가 부자였기 때문에 그녀는 그와 결혼하지 않았다.)

He <u>didn't go to the meeting because she told him to</u>.
→ NOT (go to the meeting because she told him to)
([해석] 그는 그녀가 가지 말라고 말해서 회의에 간 것은 아니다.)

Because she told him to, he <u>didn't go to the meeting</u>.
→ NOT (go to the meeting)
([해석] 그는 그녀가 회의에 가지 말라고 말했기 때문에 회의에 가지 않았다.)

He <u>didn't know that he might need any help from her</u>.
→ NOT (know that he might need any help from her)
(종속절(that절)이 주절 본동사 부정어의 영향을 받고 있기 때문에 any로 표현한다.)

He <u>didn't mean to hurt anyone</u>.
→ NOT (mean to hurt anyone)
(부정사절(구)이 주절 본동사 부정어의 영향을 받고 있기 때문에 anyone으로 표현한다.)

제 3 절   전치사구 부정

부정어와 함께 사용되는 전치사구도 부정의 범위에 따라 다르게 해석된다.

She <u>didn't sleep</u> until midnight.
→ NOT (sleep)
([해석] 그녀는 자정까지는 잠들지 않았다.)

She <u>didn't sleep until midnight</u>.
→ NOT (sleep until midnight)
([해석] 그녀가 자정까지 잔 것은 아니다.)

→ It was not until midnight that she slept. [해석] 그녀는 자정이 되어서야 잠들었다.)

제 4 절   강세

부정어와 함께 사용되는 표현의 강세 유무에 따라 부정의 범위가 다르게 해석된다.

He didn't STUDY all day.
→ NOT(study all day)
([해석] 그는 하루 종일 공부하지 않았다. 조금도 공부하지 않았다.)

He didn't study ALL DAY.
→ NOT(study)
([해석] 그가 하루 종일 공부한 것은 아니다. 조금이라도 공부했다.)

제 5 절   부가의문문

부정어가 사용된 평서문 이후에 긍정 부가의문문 사용이 가능하면 전체 부정, 부정 부가의문문 사용이
가능하면 부분 부정으로 해석된다.

He doesn't lie, does he? (전체부정 → 긍정 부가의문문)
([해석] 그는 거짓말을 안 합니다, 합니까?)

He pleaded not guilty to the charges, didn't he? (부분부정 → 부정 부가의문문)
([해석] 그는 혐의에 대해 무죄를 주장했다. 그렇지 않나요?)

제 8 장 | 법조동사의 부정

제 1 절 can의 부정

1 능력의 결여

[예]

- Dogs can bark, but they cannot(can't) speak.
- He cannot(can't) speak English as well as Korean.

2 금지

[예]

- Although you finish the test, you cannot(can't) leave now.
- You cannot have some cookies before you finish your homework.

3 부정적 추측, 강한 의혹(99%) 중요 ★

[예]

- It cannot be true.
- He already ate two sandwiches. He cannot be hungry.

제 2 절 may의 부정

1 (can보다는 좀 더 formal한) 금지

[예]

- Soldiers may not wear earrings at drill.
- Although you finish the test, you may not leave now.

2 (can보다는 가능성이 낮은) 부정적 추측(50% 이하) 중요 ★

[예]

- It may not rain tomorrow.
- He is yawning after lunch. He may not be hungry.

제 3 절 must의 부정

1 (강한) 금지

[예]

- You must not(mustn't) open the window.
- You must not(mustn't) go now.

2 (강한) 부정적 추측(95%) 중요 ★

[예]

- He is not eating lunch. He must not be hungry.
- He is yawning after lunch. He must not be hungry.

※ (강한) 필요성 결여 → do not have to(don't have to, = don't need to)
[예]

- Tomorrow is Saturday. You do not have to go to class.
- Test are optional. You don't have to answer all the questions.

실전예상문제

checkpoint 해설 & 정답

01 해설

be동사 I am not의 축약형은 I amn't
가 아닌 I'm not으로 표현해야 함
① 부정형 were not의 축약형 weren't
② 조동사 부정형 has not의 축약형 hasn't
③ 일반동사 부정형 does not의 축약형 doesn't

해석
① 그들은 시카고에서 태어나지 않았다.
② 그는 10년 동안 정비공이 아니었다.
③ 그녀는 형제가 없다.
④ 나는 작사가 겸 작곡가가 아니다.

02 해설

준부정 표현 scarcely는 자체에 부정의 의미가 있기 때문에 부가의문문은 긍정으로 표현, is he?
① 준부정 표현 (a) few는 가산명사를 수식
② 준부정 표현 (a) little은 불가산명사를 수식
④ 준부정 표현 hardly의 도치 표현

해석
① 극소수의 사람들만이 그것을 소유하거나 사용할 수 있었다.
② 정보를 찾는 데는 약간의 노력만 필요하다.
③ 그는 예술에 거의 관심이 없죠, 그렇죠?
④ 아무도 그런 행운을 기대하지 않았다.

정답 01 ④ 02 ③

---

01 다음 중 어법상 <u>잘못된</u> 표현은 무엇인가?

① They weren't born in Chicago.
② He hasn't been a mechanic for ten years.
③ She doesn't have a brother.
④ I amn't a singer songwriter.

02 다음 중 어법상 <u>잘못된</u> 표현은 무엇인가?

① Very few people could own or use it.
② It only takes a little effort to search for information.
③ He is scarcely interested in art, isn't he?
④ Hardly did anyone expect such good fortune.

03 다음 중 어법상 맞는 표현은 무엇인가?

① He can hardly believe she passed the exam, can't he?

② Few students didn't answer that question.

③ Neither you nor she are wrong.

④ A : I will not go there again.

　B : Neither will I.

04 다음 중 두 단어의 관계가 <u>다른</u> 표현은 무엇인가?

① veil – unveil

② loose – unloose

③ valuable – invaluable

④ flammable – inflammable

해설 & 정답 — checkpoint

03 해설

부정 표현 I will not(won't) go there, either에서 not ~ either에 대한 표현 neither의 도치표현 Neither + 조동사 + 주어

① 준부정 표현 hardly는 자체에 부정의 의미가 있기 때문에 부가의문문은 긍정으로 표현, can he?

② 준부정 표현 few는 자체에 부정의 의미가 있기 때문에 not을 사용하지 않아도 된다.

③ 부정 상관접속사 neither A nor B표현에서 동사와의 수일치는 B와 한다, Neither you nor she is wrong.

해석

① 그는 그녀가 시험에 합격했다는 것을 믿기 어렵다. 그렇죠?

② 그 질문에 답하는 학생은 거의 없었다.

③ 너도 그녀도 틀리지 않았어.

④ A : 나는 거기에 두 번 다시 가지 않을 거야.
　B : 나도 안 갈 거야.

04 해설

부정 접두사 un-이 있는 반의어 관계

②·③·④ 반의어 관계가 아닌 동의어 관계

해석

① 가리다, 감추다 – 밝히다, 공표하다

② 느슨해지다, 풀다 – 풀다, 풀어주다

③ 가치 있는, 귀중한 – 가치 있는, 귀중한

④ 가연성의, 인화성의 – 가연성의, 인화성의

정답　03 ④　04 ①

안심Touch

05 해설

valueless는 부정 접미사 -less가 붙은 반의어

①·②·④ valuable, invaluable, priceless 모두 '귀중한, 가치 있는' 표현

해석

대통령 기록관은 왕조 시대의 기록물처럼 귀중한 역사적 문서이다.

06 해설

④ 단정형 표현 too ↔ 비단정형 표현 not either

① 단정형 표현 already ↔ 비단정형 표현 yet

② 단정형 표현 some ↔ 비단정형 표현 not any

③ 단정형 표현 sometimes ↔ 비단정형 표현 not ever

해석

① 그는 이미 그것을 했다. ↔ 그는 아직 그것을 하지 않았다.

② 그는 돈이 좀 있다. ↔ 그는 돈이 한 푼도 없다.

③ 그는 가끔 그녀에게 자신을 드러내기도 한다. ↔ 그는 절대로 그녀에게 자신을 드러내지 않는다.

④ 그 역시 500야드를 수영할 수 있다. ↔ 그 역시 500야드도 헤엄치지 못한다. (500야드 : 약 45.72미터)

정답 05 ③ 06 ④

---

05 다음 중 밑줄 친 부분에 들어갈 수 없는 표현은 무엇인가?

> Presidential archives are _____ historical documents like the archives of dynasty eras.

① valuable

② invaluable

③ valueless

④ priceless

06 다음 중 단정문 – 비단정문의 관계가 잘못된 표현은 무엇인가?

① He had done it already. ↔ He hasn't done it yet.

② He has some money. ↔ He doesn't have any money.

③ He sometimes discloses himself to her. ↔ He doesn't ever disclose himself to her.

④ He can swim 50 yards, too. ↔ He can't swim 50 yards, too.

07 다음 중 밑줄 친 부분과 의미가 같은 표현은 무엇인가?

> <u>Anyone</u> deserves a second chance for the application.

① no matter which
② no matter what
③ no matter who
④ no matter how

08 다음 문장을 바르게 해석한 표현은 무엇인가?

> He didn't get any of the things he wanted most.

① There were a few things he wanted to get, and he got something.
② There were not any of the things he got although he wanted many things.
③ There were some of the things he did get.
④ There were few thing he wanted to get, but he got just one.

해설 & 정답   checkpoint

07 **해설**
any(anything, anyone)의 의미는 no matter which(어떤 것이든), no matter what(무엇이든), no matter who(누구든)의 의미가 있는데 이 문장에서는 no matter who의 의미다.

해석
누구나 두 번째 지원 기회를 얻을 자격이 있다.

08 **해설**
부정문에서 any의 의미 및 부정의 영향권 : He <u>did not get any of the things he wanted most</u>. (그가 가장 받고 싶었던 물건을 한 개도 못 받았다.)

해석
그는 그가 가장 원하는 것을 하나도 얻지 못했다.
① 그가 얻고 싶었던 몇 가지가 있었고, 그는 무언가를 얻었다.
② 그는 많은 것을 원했지만 얻은 것은 하나도 없었다.
③ 그가 얻은 것 중 몇 가지가 있었다.
④ 그가 갖고 싶은 게 몇 개 없었는데 딱 한 개만 얻었다.

정답 07 ③ 08 ②

09 해설

동사 need와 dare의 본동사, 조동사 쓰임에 대한 문제이다.

본동사로 사용된 dare의 부정문 표현으로 조동사 did not이 쓰임

① 조동사 need의 부정문

② 조동사 need의 의문문

④ 조동사 dare 다음에 원형부정사가 와서 조동사 역할을 함

해석

① 그들은 할 필요가 없다.

② 제가 도울 수 있다고 말해야 하나요?

③ 그는 감히 그 차가 얼마인지 그녀에게 말하지 못했다.

④ 감히 거짓말하지 마.

10 해설

④ 주절의 주어가 1인칭인 경우 종속절의 내용과 부가의문문을 일치시킨다.

① 지시사 these, those가 포함된 문장의 부가의문문은 they를 사용한다.

② 부정대명사 everyone, nobody, somebody 표현에 대한 부가의문문은 they를 사용한다.

③ 일반 명령문의 긍정, 부정문에 대한 부가의문문은 will you?로 사용한다.

해석

① 이 책들은 그의 것이 아니군요, 그렇죠?

② 국제회의에 아무도 오지 않았지요, 그렇죠?

③ 늦지 마, 알았지?

④ 제 생각에 그들은 학생이 아닌 것 같아요, 그렇죠?

09 다음 중 밑줄 친 부분의 쓰임이 <u>다른</u> 표현은 무엇인가?

① They <u>need</u> not do it.

② <u>Need</u> I tell her that I can help her?

③ He did not <u>dare</u> to tell her how much the car costs.

④ Don't you <u>dare</u> tell her lies.

10 다음 중 어법상 맞는 표현은 무엇인가?

① These are not his books, are these?

② Nobody came to the international meeting, did he?

③ Don't be late, won't you?

④ I think that they are not students, are they?

11 다음 중 어법상 잘못된 표현은 무엇인가?

① He doesn't seem to like it.

② I suppose he is not going to the meeting.

③ He said that he did not love his ex-wife.

④ She knows that he did not go to the meeting.

12 다음 중 부정 표현의 쓰임이 다른 것은?

① She haven't met either of the provosts.

② She doesn't' know all of them.

③ The poor are not always unhappy.

④ All that glitters is not gold.

---

11 해설

부가어 전송 동사 표현에 대한 문제이다.

① 의 지각 동사 seem과 ②의 생각, 의견 동사 suppose는 부가어 전송, 즉 주절로 부정 전이 현상이 가능하다. → I don't suppose he is going to the meeting. ③의 말하기 동사 표현 say와 ④의 사실성 동사 표현 know는 부가어 전송, 즉 주절로 부정 전이 현상이 가능하지 않은 동사 표현으로 that절 내에 부정 표현 사용 가능

해석

① 그는 그것을 좋아하지 않는 것 같다.

② 그 사람은 회의에 안 갈 것 같아요.

③ 그는 전 부인을 사랑하지 않는다고 말했다.

④ 그녀는 그가 회의에 가지 않았다는 것을 알고 있다.

12 해설

부분 부정 표현에 대한 문제로 '모두가 (항상, 반드시) ~인 것은 아니다'의 표현이다.

① not ~ either = neither 표현으로 전체부정의 의미

② not ~ all 부분 부정

③ not ~ always 부분 부정

④ all ~ not 부분 부정(= All is not gold that glitters.)

해석

① 그녀는 두 처장을 만난 적이 없다.

② 그녀는 그들 모두를 아는 것은 아니다.

③ 가난한 사람들이 항상 불행한 것은 아니다.

④ 반짝이는 것이 모두 금은 아니다.

정답 11 ② 12 ①

13 해설

이중부정에 관한 문제로 한 문장 안에 부정 표현을 두 개 사용하여 (강한) 긍정을 나타낸다(never ~ without, no ~ without, hardly ~ not).

해석

그는 할머니를 생각하지 않고 그 사진을 본 적이 없다.

① 그는 그 사진을 보지 않고 할머니 생각은 한다.

② 그는 할머니를 생각할 때 그 사진을 본 적이 없다.

③ 그는 할머니를 생각할 때만 그 사진을 본다.

④ 그는 그 사진을 볼 때마다 할머니를 생각한다.

13 다음 문장과 의미가 같은 표현은 무엇인가?

> He never sees the picture without thinking his grandmother.

① He thinks of his grandmother without seeing the picture.

② When he thinks of his grandmother, he never sees the picture.

③ Only when he thinks of his grandmother, he sees the picture.

④ Whenever he sees the picture, he thinks of his grandmother.

14 해설

부정표현 not과 부사구 deliberately의 위치에 따른 부정표현의 영향권, 범위에 대한 문제로 NOT(deliberately answer the question), '신중하게 생각하고 대답한 것은 아니었다.'

해석

그는 신중하게 생각하고 그 질문에 대답한 것은 아니었다.

① 그는 그 질문에 대답하지 않았지만, 신중하게 생각하지는 않았다.

② 그는 그 질문에 대답을 했지만, 신중하게 생각하지는 않았다.

③ 그는 그 질문에 대답을 했지만, 신중하게 생각했다.

④ 그는 그 질문에 대답하지 않았지만, 신중하게 생각했다.

14 다음 문장과 의미가 같은 표현은 무엇인가?

> He didn't deliberately answer the question.

① He didn't answer the question, but he didn't think of it deliberately.

② He answered the question, but he didn't think of it deliberately.

③ He answered the question, but he thought of it deliberately.

④ He didn't answer the question, but he thought of it deliberately.

정답 13 ④ 14 ②

15 다음 중 부정 표현 강도 및 가능성이 가장 높은 표현은 무엇인가?

① He might not have been sick.

② He can't have been sick.

③ He must not have been sick.

④ He may not have been sick.

해설 & 정답   checkpoint

15 [해설]

법조동사의 부정 표현(부정적 추측, 강한 의혹)

(is/was/were, 100%, 〉) cannot (/couldn't, 99%) 〉 must not (95%) 〉 may not (/might not, less than 50%)

[해석]

① 그는 아프지 않았을지도 모른다.

② 그는 아팠을 리가 없다.

③ 그는 아프지 않았음에 틀림없다.

④ 그는 아프지 않았을지도 모른다.

정답 15 ②

여기서 멈출 거예요? 끝이가 바로 눈앞에 있어요.
마지막 한 걸음까지 SD에듀가 함께할게요!

제 **10** 편

강조와 도치

단원 개요

강조(emphasis)란 문장을 쓰거나 말하는 사람이 전하고자 하는 문장의 의미에서 자신의 의견, 감정, 태도 등을 표현하고자 특정부분을 두드러지게 하려는 강세, 억양, 어순 변화, 삽입, 반복, 강조어 표현을 말한다.

도치(inversion)란 문장을 쓰거나 말하는 사람이 전하고자 하는 문장의 의미에서 자신의 의견, 감정, 태도 등을 특정부분에 표현하고자 영어의 '주어 + 동사' 기본 어순에 변화를 주는 것을 말한다. 일반적으로 주어와 본동사 위치를 바꾸는 방법과 주어와 조동사의 위치를 바꾸는 방법이 있고, 주어 이외의 부정 표현이나 부사(구) 등 다른 요소를 문두에 위치시킨다.

출제 경향 및 수험 대책

1. 강조
    (1) 분열문, 유사분열문 용법
    (2) 어순의 변경 : 전치 vs 후치 용법
    (3) 강의어의 사용 : 긍정문, 부정문, 의문문
2. 도치
    (1) be동사, 조동사, 일반동사 부정 전치 표현
    (2) 형용사, 분사, so, 부사, 목적어 전치 용법
    (3) than, as, the+비교급 전치 용법
    (4) there 존재문, 관계사절 도치 용법

자격증 · 공무원 · 금융/보험 · 면허증 · 언어/외국어 · 검정고시/독학사 · 기업체/취업
이 시대의 모든 합격! SD에듀에서 합격하세요!
www.youtube.com → SD에듀 → 구독

제 **1** 장 **강조**

제 1 절 분열문, 유사분열문

영어에서 강조를 표현하는 대표적인 표현으로 'it + be 동사 ~ that' 분열문과 'what + 주어 + 동사 ~' 유사분열문이 있다.

1 분열문(cleft sentence) 중요 ★★

> it + be동사 ~ that

분열문은 문장 내에서 강조하고자 하는 표현을 'it + be동사'와 'that절' 사이에 위치시키는 문장 형식이고 강조 표현이 강세를 받는다(단, 분열문에서 문장의 (본)동사는 강조하지 못한다).

- Josh loved Amy.
  → It was **Josh** that loved Amy.

- Josh loved Amy.
  → It was **Amy** that Josh loved.

- Josh broke the vase.
  → It was **Josh** that broke the vase.

- Josh broke the vase.
  → It was **the vase** that Josh broke.

예

- Josh met Lori in the library yesterday.
  → It was **Josh** that met Lori in the library yesterday.

- Josh met Lori in the library yesterday.
  → It was **Lori** that Josh met in the library yesterday.

- Josh met Lori in the library yesterday.
  → It was **in the library** that Josh met Lori yesterday.

- Josh met Lori in the library yesterday.
  - → It was **yesterday** that Josh met Lori in the library.

- Josh sent the bill to the secretary yesterday.
  - → It was **Josh** that sent the bill to the secretary yesterday.

- Josh sent the bill to the secretary yesterday.
  - → It was **the bill** that Josh sent to the secretary yesterday.

- Josh sent the bill to the secretary yesterday.
  - → It was **to the secretary** that Josh sent the bill yesterday.

- Josh sent the bill to the secretary yesterday.
  - → It was **yesterday** that Josh sent the bill to the secretary.

- They got married in 1998.
  - → It was **in 1998** that they got married.

- Josh likes green best.
  - → It is **green** that Josh likes best.

❗ 더 알아두기 🔍

분열문 강조 불가 표현 중요 ★★
동사, 형용사 보어, 양태부사, 문장부사는 'it + be동사 ~ that 구문'에서 강조하지 못한다.

(1) 동사(→ 조동사 do)
   예
   - Jeff met Laurel in the library yesterday.
     - → *It was met that Jeff Laurel in the library yesterday.
     - → Jeff did meet Laurel in the library yesterday.

(2) 형용사 보어(→ very)
   예
   - She is beautiful.
     - → *It is beautiful that she is.
     - → She is **very** beautiful.

(3) 양태 부사 및 문장 부사(→ '전치사 + 명사' 표현은 자연스러움)
   예
   - She read the guideline carefully.
     - → *It was carefully that she read the guideline.
     - → It was **with care** that she read the guideline.

- He regretfully declined the invitation.
  → *It was regretfully that he declined the invitation.
  → It was **with regret** that he declined the invitation.

2 유사분열문(pseudo-cleft sentence) : what + 주어 + 동사 중요 ★★

유사분열문은 'what + 주어 + 동사'로 시작하고 강조하고자 하는 표현을 본동사인 'be동사' 다음에 위치시키는 문장 형식이다.

(1) 보어

예

- Josh wants to be a scholar.
  → What Josh wants to be is **a scholar**.

(2) 목적어

예

- Josh wanted to write a grammar book.
  → What Josh wanted to write was **a grammar book**.

- Josh sent a letter of congratulation to Nathan by email.
  → What Josh sent to Nathan by email was **a letter of congratulation**.

(3) 동사(구)

① to부정사

예 Josh has created a whole new thing.
  → What Josh has done is **to create a whole new thing**.

② 원형부정사

예 Josh has created a whole new thing.
  → What Josh has done is **create a whole new thing**.

③ 시제를 갖는 동사

예

- Josh has created a whole new thing.
  → What Josh has done is **created a whole new thing**.

안심Touch

- He cried.
  → What he did was (to) **cry**.

- He writes a grammar book.
  → What he does is (to) **write** a grammar book.

(4) 문장 전체

예 The vase broke down.
  → What happened was (that) **the vase broke down**.

🔅 더 알아두기 🔍

기타 (유사)분열문 강조 표현 중요 ★

장소, 시간, 이유, 동사(구)를 강조하는 (유사)분열문도 있다.

1. where
   예
   - They had a barbecue in the backyard.
     → The place where they had a barbecue was **the backyard**.
     → **The backyard** was the place where they had a barbecue.

2. when
   예
   - They had a barbecue on Saturday.
     → The day when they had a barbecue was **Saturday**.
     → **Saturday** was the day when they had a barbecue.

3. why
   예
   - They had a barbecue to see family members together.
     → The reason why they had a barbecue was **to see family members together**.
     → **To see family members together** was the reason why they had a barbecue.

4. all (+that) 분열문 / thing 분열문
   예
   - All you need is **love**.
   - All (that) he wanted was **a new car**.

   - The first thing he has to do was to **take a deep breath**.
   - The only thing he remembers is **the happiest moment with her**.

제 2 절 강세

강세(stress)는 일반적인 강조 방법으로 강조하고자 하는 특정 표현을 강하게 읽어서 의미를 전달한다.

1 평서문

예

- JOSH gave Amy a call yesterday. (다른 누가 아니라 Josh가 전화했음)
- Josh GAVE Amy A CALL yesterday. (다른 방법이 아니라 전화를 걸었음)
- Josh gave AMY a call yesterday. (다른 사람이 아니라 Amy에게 전화했음)
- Josh gave Amy a call YESTERDAY. (Josh가 Amy에게 전화한 것은 오늘이 아니라 어제임)

2 의문문

예

- What are you DOING? (일반적인 의문문은 문미에 강세가 옴, '너는 무엇을 하고 있니?')
- What ARE you doing? (화남이나 질책을 표현, '도대체 뭘 하고 있는 거니?')
- What are YOU doing? ('(다른 사람이 아닌 바로) 너는 무엇을 하고 있는 거니?')

제 3 절 어순의 변경

강조하고자 특정 표현을 문장 내 원래 기본 위치가 아닌 문두 또는 문미에 위치시킬 수 있다.

1 전치(preposing)

문장 내 목적어나 보어를 문두에 위치시켜 강조한다.

(1) 목적어

예

- Josh loves Amy.
  - → **Amy** Josh loves.

- He has kept the secret for her.
  - → **The secret** he has kept for her.

(2) 보어

예

- His full name is Joshua Jensen.
  - → **Joshua Jensen** his full name is.

- You can call it Korean manners.
  - → **Korean manners** you can call it.

2 후치(postposing) 중요 ★★★

문장 내 주어나 목적어가 긴 경우 그 자리에 각각 가주어 it 혹은 가목적어 it으로 대용하고 문미로 보내 강조하는데 이러한 현상을 문미 비중의 원리(end-weight principle)라고 한다. 또한 문미로 보내진 표현은 문미 초점을 받게 되어 의미가 더 강해지는데 이러한 현상을 정보 구조(information structure)와 관련하여 문미 초점의 원리(end-focus principle)라고 한다.

(1) 주어

① to부정사

예

- To make a reservation early is important.
  - → It is important **to make a reservation early**.

② 동명사

예

- Starting a new semester in April is very unusual.
  - → It is very unusual **starting a new semester in April**.

③ 접속사 that : ~하는 것/한 것

예

- That he is generous is certain.
  - → It is certain **that he is generous**.

- That he fail the bar exam is surprising.
  - → It is surprising **that he failed the bar exam**.

- That he will come to the international conference tomorrow is likely.

  → It is likely **that he will come to the international conference tomorrow**.

④ 접속사 whether : ~인지 아닌지

　예

- Whether you win the gold medal or not is not important.

  → It is not important **whether you win the gold medal or not**.

⑤ 의문대명사 who(m), which, what : ~하는(한) 누구/것

　예

- Who the woman was is all he wanted to know.

  → All he wanted to know is **who the woman was**.

- What he created was phenomenal.

  → It was phenomenal **what he created**.

⑥ 의문부사 when, where, how, why

　예

- When you restart is not important.

  → It is not important **when you restart**.

⑦ 복합관계대명사 whoever, whichever, whatever

　예

- Whoever loves her doesn't matter.

  → It doesn't matter **whoever loves her**.

(2) 목적어 중요 ★★★

　예

- *He is always finding [to study English] difficult.
  → He is always finding it difficult **to study English**.

- *He confirmed [that he would come again next year] very clear.
  → He confirmed it very clear **that he would come again next year**.

- He can find [working with her] enjoyable.
  → He can find it enjoyable **working with her**.

- He makes [to go walking for at least 30 minutes after he has a meal] a rule.
  → He makes it a rule **to go walking for at least 30 minutes after he has a meal**.

3 간접목적어 후치

수여동사의 목적어 중 간접목적어를 to전치사구로 후치시키면 강조의 의미를 더한다.

예

- Josh gave Amy a gold ring.
  → Josh gave a gold ring **to Amy**.

※ 질문 – 답변

예

- Q : **What** did Josh give Amy?
  A : Josh gave Amy **a gold ring**.

- Q : **Who(m)** did Josh give a gold ring **to**?
  A : Josh gave a gold ring **to Amy**.

---

4 재귀대명사 후치

주어를 강조하기 위해 주어 바로 옆에 사용한 재귀대명사를 문미에 위치시키면 강조의 의미가 더 강해진다.

예

- Josh himself won the grand prize.
  → Josh won the grand prize **himself**.
  (It was Josh, and no one else, who won the grand prize.)

- The musicians themselves wanted to have a face-to-face concert.
  → The musicians wanted to have a face-to-face concert **themselves**.
  (It was the musicians, and on one else, who wanted to have a face-to-face concert.)

제 4 절 강의어의 사용

단어 자체에 강조의 의미가 있는 표현을 강의어 또는 강조어(intensifier)라고 하는데 긍정문, 부정문, 의문문에 사용되는 표현들이 있다.

1 긍정문

긍정문에 사용되는 강조표현은 다음과 같다.

> indeed, just, really, clearly, definitely, absolutely, obviously, certainly, simply, surely, plainly, honestly, for sure, for certain, so, such, the very + 명사('바로~')

예

- Thank you **so** much.
- It was **such** a wonderful party.
- He **really** enjoyed the food.
- He **just** wanted to know what she wanted.
- That film is **absolutely** hilarious.
- He appreciated her help **indeed**.
- It is going to be a perfect day **for sure**.
- He is **the very** man that she met in the bank yesterday.
- This is **the very** book that he has read for three weeks.

2 부정문

부정문에 사용되는 강조표현은 '전혀, 조금도 ~하지 않다'의 의미로 사용된다.

> at all, a bit, by any means, whatever, whatsoever, in the least

예

- He didn't touch anything **at all**.
- He wouldn't care **a bit**.
- It is not balanced **by any means**, not even close.
- He has no excuse **whatever**.
- There was no difference **whatsoever**.
- Nothing **in the least** suspicious here.

3 의문문

의문문에 사용되는 강조표현은 '도대체'의 의미로 사용된다.

> ever, on earth, in the world, the hell

예

- Why **ever** didn't you say so?
- How **ever** did you get here?
- Who **on earth** are you?
- Why **on earth** didn't he come to the conference?
- What **in the world** are you talking about?
- What **in the world** did you do last night?

제 5 절 반복

문장 내에서 특정 표현을 반복하면 강조하는 의미를 전달한다.

예

- It is **still**, **still** too expensive.
- She is **very**, **very** beautiful.
- You are such a **kind**, **kind** man.
- He agrees with **every word** she has said – **every** single **word**.
- He looks **much**, **much** older than he used to.

제 6 절 do의 사용

강조를 표현하는 조동사 do는 본동사 바로 앞에 위치하고 주어와 수 일치하고 시제도 표현한다. 또한 명령문을 강조하는 경우도 사용된다.

예

- I want a new car. → I **do** want a new car.
- He loves his wife. → He **does** love his wife.
- We love to go skiing. → We **do** love to go skiing.
- They went to the meeting. → They **did** go to the meeting.
- She sang a jazz song well when young. → She **did** sing a jazz song well when young.
- Be quiet in the library. → **Do** be quite in the library.
- Come if you are available. → **Do** come if you are available.

제 2 장 도치

부정어는 다음과 같은 부정 표현이 문두에 위치하고 주어와 동사가 도치된다.

> no, never, not, hardly, seldom, scarcely, rarely, few, little, not only,
> not until, no sooner

1 be동사/조동사

> 부정 표현 + be동사/조동사 + 주어 + 동사 ~

예

- The professor is seldom here on time.
  → **Seldom** is the professor here on time.

- They have never known such uncertainties.
  → **Never** have they known such uncertainties.

- He had never made such a tasty pasta before he really learned how to cook.
  → **Never** had he made such a tasty pasta before he really learned how to cook.

- He not only has been to Germany, but he has also been to France.
  → **Not only** has he been to Germany, but he has also been to France.

2 일반동사

> 부정 표현＋do동사(do, does, did)＋주어＋동사 ～

예

- He never saw her again.
  - → **Never** did he see her again.

- He never thought she would betray him.
  - → **Never** did he think she would betray him.

- He didn't read a book during the winter break.
  - → **Not** a book did he read during the winter break.

- He didn't say a single word.
  - → **Not** a single word did he say.

- He rarely praised the students.
  - → **Rarely** did he praise the students.

- He little dreamed that he won the lottery.
  - → **Little** did he dream that he won the lottery.

3 not A until B(B하고 나서야 비로소 A하다) 중요 ★★★

> → not until B(주어+동사)＋조동사＋A(주어＋동사) ～

예

- She will not(won't) forgive him until he apologizes to her.
  - → **Not until** he apologizes to her **will** she forgive him.

- He didn't feel better until he took medicine.
  - → **Not until** he took medicine **did** he feel better.

- We didn't find her until hours later.
  - → **Not until** hours later **did** we find her.

4 no sooner A than B(A하자마자 B하다) 중요 ★★★

> → no sooner + had + 주어 + -en(p.p.) ～ than + 주어 + 과거시제 동사
> = Hardly(/Scarcely) + had + 주어 + -en(p.p.) ～ before(/when) + 주어 + 과거시제 동사
> = As soon as + 주어 + 과거시제동사 ～, 주어 + 과거시제 동사
> = Upon(/On) 동사-ing ～, 주어 + 과거시제 동사

예

• He had no sooner left the office than it began to rain.
  → **No sooner** had he left the office **than** it began to rain.
    = **Hardly** had he left the office **before** it began to rain.
    = **As soon as** he left the office, it began to rain.
    = **Upon** leaving the office, it began to rain.

• He had no sooner said it than he left the room.
  → **No sooner** had he said it **than** he left the room.

• He had no sooner closed his eyes than he fell asleep.
  → **No sooner** had he closed his eyes **than** he fell asleep.

5 도치를 하지 않는 경우

부정 표현이 문장 전체를 부정하는 것이 아니라 바로 다음에 오는 표현만 부정하는 경우에는 도치되지 않는다.

예

[**No doubt**] he will come.
[**No wonder**] he loves her.
[**Not many years ago**], real-time online class was impossible.

제 2 절 형용사의 전치 중요★★

형용사가 문장의 보어로 사용되는 경우, (이유, 양보) 부사절을 as절로 표현하는 경우에 전치된다.

1 보어

보어 역할을 하는 형용사가 문두에 위치하고 주어와 동사가 도치된다.

[예]

- His pleasure is great when he heard the news.
  → **Great** is his pleasure when he heard the news.

- Those who have friends in need are happy.
  → **Happy** are those who have friends in need.

2 부사 + 형용사 보어

형용사 보어를 수식하는 부사가 있는 경우 부사도 함께 도치된다.

[예]
- This case is particularly interesting.
  → *Interesting is this case particularly.
  → **Particularly interesting** is this case.

3 형용사 + as 구문

(1) 이유구문

[예]
- Because he is young, he has little experience.
  → **Young as** he is, he has little experience.

(2) 양보구문

[예]
- Though the rose is pretty, it has too many thorns.
  → **Pretty as** the rose is, it has too many thorns.

- Though he is young, he is brave.
  → **Young as** he is, he is brave.

4 형용사 + 절 구문

예

- Even though he was poor, he would never ask for any help.
  → **Poor that** he was, he would never ask for any help.

5 도치가 안 되는 경우

주어가 대명사인 경우는 주어와 동사가 도치되지 않는다.

예

- You are right.
  → **Right** you are.

- It was great.
  → **Great** it was.

제 3 절 분사의 전치 중요 ★★

현재분사와 과거분사가 문장의 보어로 사용되는 경우, (이유, 양보) 부사절을 as절로 표현하는 경우에 전치된다.

1 현재분사

(1) 보어

예

- The chance of the accidents is more frightening.
  → **More frightening** is the chance of the accidents.

- The decline of the school-age population is more surprising.
  → **More surprising** is the decline of the school-age population.

(2) (이유) 부사절 : as + 주어 + 동사

> -ing + as + 대명사주어 + do

[예]
- As he lives in the country, he is good at planting.
  → **Living as** he does in the country, he is good at planting.

2 과거분사

(1) 보어

[예]
- The order form that was issued on Thursday, January 20 is attached.
  → **Attached** is the order form that was issued on Thursday, January 20.

- The official documents that will be sent to the dean tomorrow are attached.
  → **Attached** are the official documents that will be sent to the dean tomorrow.

- Booklets for your company are enclosed.
  → **Enclosed** are booklets for your company.

- Please find a postal money order for $100 enclosed.
  → **Enclosed** please find a postal money order for $100.

(2) 부사절 : as + 주어 + be + 과거분사(-en, p.p.)

> 과거분사(-en, p.p.) + as + (대명사) 주어 + be동사

① 이유

[예]
- As it is written in academic English, the book is famous for college students.
  → **Written as** it is in academic English, the book is famous for college students.

② 양보

[예] **"Interested as** I am in the physical universe, it is in man, in his loves and hatreds, his noble achievements and absurd failures, that I am more interested." - Albert Einstein -

([해석] "비록 내가 물리적인 세계(우주)에 관심이 있지만, 내가 더 관심을 갖는 것은 바로 인간, 인간의 사랑과 증오, 인간의 고귀한 업적과 터무니없는 실패이다" - 알베르트 아인슈타인 -)

제 4 절 so의 전치

긍정문에서 so가 문두에 위치하고 주어와 (조)동사가 전치된다.

1 일반동사 대용 do(do, does, did)

[예]
- He loves her and **so does she**.
- He went there and **so did she**.

2 be동사, 조동사

[예]
- He is very generous and **so is she**.
- He would like to succeed and **so would she**.
- He can achieve his goal and **so can she**.

3 도치가 일어나지 않는 경우

(1) may(might), ought to 다음

[예]
- ? He may come and so may she.
  → He may come and she may, too.

• ? He ought to study hard and so ought she.

　→ He ought to study hard and he ought to, too.

※? 표시(unacceptable) : 문법적으로 어색한

(2) 주어가 아니라 동사를 강조하는 경우

예

• She told him to shut up and so he DID.

• He asked her to come to the party and so she DID.

4 neither/nor 전치

부정문에서 neither/nor가 문두에 위치하고 주어와 조동사가 도치된다.

예

• He does not like to tell a lie, neither(nor) does his sister.

• He did not do something wrong, neither(nor) did she.

• He is not wrong, neither(nor) is she.

• He cannot swim, neither(nor) can she.

제 5 절 부사어의 전치

장소를 나타내는 부사(구)가 문두에 위치하고 주어와 동사가 도치된다.

1 주어(일반명사) + 자동사 → 부사(구) + 동사 + 주어 ~

자동사는 be, go, come, stand, sit, lie, walk, hand, roll, jump 등의 동사이다.

예

• A vase of beautiful tulips is on the table.

　→ **On the table** is a vase of beautiful tulips.

- A furniture van was outside the house.
  → **Outside the house** was a furniture van.

- An oak tree stands in the backyard.
  → **In the backyard** stands an oak tree.

- A tall man sat on the beach.
  → **On the beach** sat a tall man.

- A newspaper lay on the sofa.
  → **On the sofa** lay a newspaper. (vi. lie - lay - lain)

2 주어 + 타동사 → 부사(구) + do동사(do, does, did) + 주어 + 동사 + 목적어

예

- He remembers the scene of the accident very exactly.
  → **Very exactly** does he remember the scene of the accident.

- People appreciate her great voice as a jazz singer only after her death.
  → **Only after her death** do people appreciate her great voice as a jazz singer.

- She sometimes warned him not to do so.
  → **Sometimes** did she warn him not to do so.

- He finally found his wallet under the desk.
  → **Under the desk** did he finally find his wallet.

- He carried out his duties with great ability.
  → **With great ability** did he carry out his duties.

3 도치가 되지 않는 경우 중요 ★

(1) 부사어는 위치, 동작을 나타내는 동사(go, come, sit, stand, lie 등) 다음에 있는 경우 도치된다. 다른 동사에서는 도치가 일어나지 않는다.

예

- Two men were <u>talking</u> outside the house.
  → *__Outside the house__ were talking two men.

(2) 주어가 (인칭)대명사이면 부사구가 문두로 전치되어도 주어와 동사는 도치되지 않는다.

예

- He stood at the bus stop.
  → *At the bus stop stood he.
  → At the bus stop he stood.

- *There goes he. → There he goes.
- *There are you. → There you are.
- *Here go you. → Here you go.
- *Here are we. → Here we are.

제 6 절 목적어의 전치

목적어는 앞 문장과 대조, 연결, 내용 강조를 위해 주어 앞으로 전치된다. 하지만 주어 + 동사의 어순은 그대로다.

예

- Q : Does she prefer dogs or cats?
  A : __Dogs__ she loves, but __cats__ she likes.

- He would never eat lime, but he eats lemons.
  → __Limes__ he would never eat, but __lemons__ he eats.

- He will remember visiting Giant's Causeway forever.
  → __Visiting Giant's Causeway__ he will remember forever.

- We will remember that day for years.
  → __That day__ we will remember for years.

- He bought something special for her.
  → __Something special for her__ he bought.

※ 부정어를 포함하면 주어와 동사를 도치한다(동편 제2장 도치 – 제1절 부정어의 전치, 368쪽 참조).

예

• The quintet didn't sing a jazz song at the concert.

  → **Not** a jazz song **did** the quintet sing at the concert.

※ 목적어가 대명사인 경우 목적어는 문두로 도치되지 않는다.

예

• We will remember him forever.

  → *****Him** we will remember forever.

제 **7** 절 │ than, as, the + 비교급 중요 ★★

비교급은 동사가 도치되는 것이 아니라 조동사나 do 동사가 도치된다.

1 than 비교급

(1) 조동사 도치

예

  • Electricity costs less than petroleum would cost.

    → Electricity costs less than **would petroleum**.

예

  • He is more interested in AI than she is (interested).

    → He is more interested in AI than **is she**.

  • He has bought far more stocks than his sister has (bought).

    → He has bought far more stocks than **has his sister**.

(2) do 동사 도치

예

  • She plays more the piano than her friends play the piano.

    → She plays more the piano than **do her friends**.

- Most professors study more than their students study.
  → Most professors study more than **do their students**.

※ than 비교급 구문에서 주어가 대명사인 경우는 주어와 동사를 도치시키지 않는다.

[예]
- He plays more video games than his friends play the video games.
  → He plays more video games than ***do they** / ***does they** / **they do**.

- He spends more time working now than **he did** several months ago.
  → *He spends more time working now than ***did he** several months ago.

※ *표시(unacceptable) : 문법적으로 어색한

2 as 비교급

as ~ as 비교급에서는 주어가 대명사인 경우도 도치가 가능하다.

[예]
- He often goes to the movies as she does.
  → He often goes to the movies **as does** she.

- He climbed to the top of Mt. Halla, as most of his friends did.
  → He climbed to the top of Mt. Halla, **as did** most of his friends.

- Many people enjoyed a lovely autumn day, as the last weekend was.
  → Many people enjoyed a lovely autumn day, **as was** the last weekend.

- He hasn't bought as many stocks as his sister has. (bought)
  → He hasn't bought as many stocks **as has** his sister.

3 the + 비교급

[예]
- A man is more learned. He is more modest.
  → More learned a man is, more modest he is.
  → **The more learned** a man is, **the more modest** he is.

- You study more. You learn more.
  - → More you study, more you learn.
  - → **The more** you study, **the more** you learn.

- The weather is warmer. she likes it better.
  - → Warmer the weather is, better she likes it.
  - → **The warmer** the weather is, **the better** she likes it.

제8절 직접화법에서의 도치

예

- Josh said, "I have just heard that news."
  - → "I have just heard that news," **said Josh**.

- Amy said, "My sister is a famous novelist."
  - → "My sister is a famous novelist," **said Amy**.

- His father said, "You can do that for yourself."
  - → "You can do that for yourself," **said his father**.

※ 주어가 (인칭)대명사이면 도치되지 않는다.

예

- *"My sister is a famous novelist," said she.
  - → "My sister is a famous novelist," **she said**.

제 9 절　존재문, 관계사절

1　존재문

(1) there 구문

존재를 나타내는 there 구문에서 there 표현은 be동사, 상태동사(live, remain, stand, lie 등), 기동동사(rise, arise, emerge, spring up, result, ensue 등), 동작동사(go, come, arise, enter, pass 등)와 함께 사용되는 경우에 도치된다.

예

• A police officer is at the door.
  → **There** is a police officer at the door.

• Two dogs are under the table.
  → **There** are two dogs under the table.

• A famous novelist lived in that village.
  → **There** lived a famous novelist in that village.

There comes the subway.	Here is your laptop.
There comes a taxi!	Here comes a taxi!
There goes all our money!	Here comes the spring.

(2) 도치되지 않는 경우 중요 ★

① 주어가 대명사인 경우

예

• *There comes he. → There he comes.
• *Here go we. → Here we go.

② 주어에 정관사(the) 표현이 있는 경우

예

• *There is the cat under the mat.
• *There are the singers in the live concert.

③ 존재와 관련 없는 동사인 경우

예

• *There sang jazz singer a new song.
• *There left early three participants.

2 관계사절

(1) 전치구문

① whom

관계대명사 whom은 전치사 at의 목적어인데 관계대명사가 관계사절(형용사절)을 유도하기 위해 절 앞으로 도치된다.

〔예〕

- The gentleman you are looking **at whom** now is my English professor.
  → The gentleman **whom** you are looking **at** ∅ now is my English professor.

② whose

소유격 관계대명사 whose의 경우 명사가 함께 도치된다.

> 〔예〕
> - Dr. Lee will give a special lecture at the international conference.
>
>   +
> - You will **find his presentation** very helpful.
>   → Dr. Lee will give a special lecture at the international conference **whose presentation** you will **find** ∅ very helpful.

(2) 후치구문

주어나 목적어로 사용된 명사의 관계사절(형용사절)이 긴 경우 관계사절을 술어 이후로 후치할 수 있다.

〔예〕

- A man who spoke only Gaelic was visiting us.
  → A man was visiting us **who spoke only Gaelic**.

- He gave everyone who wanted one a dried plum(prune).
  → He gave everyone a dried plum(prune) **who wanted one**.

(3) 관계사절 내 도치

〔예〕

- She handed him an envelope in which a hundred-dollar bill was tucked.
  → She handed him an envelope in which **was** tucked **a hundred-dollar bill**.

- The movie will be premiered on Thursday, January 20 in a historic film theater, on which actors appear.
  → The movie will be premiered on Thursday, January 20 in a historic film theater, on which **appear actors**.

- The police chief will look into the fundamental principle by which a citizen did what she had to do bravely.

 → The police chief will look into the fundamental principle by which **what she had to do a citizen did** bravely.

제10편 실전예상문제

checkpoint 해설 & 정답

01 해설

it ~ that 강조구문에서 문장의 주어, 목적어, 부사를 강조할 수 있는데 본동사는 강조하지 못한다. 동사 강조는 다음과 같이 표현한다. 'Joey <u>did meet</u> Laurel in the library yesterday.'

해석

Joey는 어제 도서관에서 Laurel을 보았다.
① 어제 도서관에서 Laurel을 만난 사람은 Joey였다.
② Joey가 어제 Laurel을 만난 곳은 도서관이었다.
③ Joey가 어제 도서관에서 만난 사람은 Laurel이었다.
④ Joey가 어제 도서관에서 Luarel은 만났다.

02 해설

형용사 보어는 it ~ that 강조구문에서 강조하지 못한다. (→ He is very generous.)
② 양태부사는 it ~ that 강조구문에서 강조하지 못하는데 '전치사 + 명사' 형태가 자연스럽다.
③·④ 유사분열구문에서 동사(구)는 to부정사, 원형부정사, 시제를 갖는 동사 모두 가능하다.

해석

① 그는 매우 너그럽다.
② 그는 매우 조심스럽게 창문을 닦았다.
③ 그가 어제 한 일은 영어 공부였다.
④ 그가 한 일은 완전히 새로운 이야기를 만들어 낸 것이다.

정답 01 ④ 02 ①

---

01 다음 문장을 강조한 표현이 <u>잘못된</u> 것은?

> Joey met Laurel in the library yesterday.

① It was Joey that met Laurel in the library yesterday.
② It was in the library that Joey met Laurel yesterday.
③ It was Laurel that Joey met in the library yesterday.
④ It was did meet that Joey met Laurel in the library yesterday.

02 다음 중 강조와 관련하여 어법상 <u>잘못된</u> 표현은 무엇인가?

① It is generous that he is.
② It was with caution that he wiped the window.
③ What he did yesterday was to study English.
④ What he has done is created a whole new story.

03 다음 중 강조와 관련하여 어법상 <u>잘못된</u> 표현은 무엇인가?

① The place where they had a picnic was the city park.

② What she has done is give her consent.

③ All she wanted was to visiting her sister.

④ The consumer lifestyle you can call it.

04 다음 중 어법상 <u>잘못된</u> 표현은 무엇인가?

① The secret he has kept for her.

② All he wanted to know is who the woman was.

③ Josh won the grand prize himself.

④ It was so a wonderful party.

---

03 해설

all (+ that) 분열문, 동사(구)는 to부정사, 원형부정사, 시제를 갖는 동사 가능하다. 'All she wanted was to visit her sister.'

① 장소, 시간, 이유, 동사(구)를 강조하는 (유사)분열문이다.

② 유사분열구문에서 동사(구)는 to부정사, 원형부정사, 시제를 갖는 동사 모두 가능하다.

④ 전치를 통한 강조 표현으로 문장 내 목적어, 보어 가능하다. → it, 목적어; the consumer lifestyle, 목적격보어

해석

① 그들이 소풍을 간 곳은 도시 공원이었다.

② 그녀가 한 일은 그녀의 동의를 얻은 것이다.

③ 그녀는 단지 언니를 방문하기를 원했다.

④ 그것을 소비자 라이프스타일이라고 부를 수 있다.

04 해설

긍정문에 사용되는 강조표현 so는 형용사, 부사를 강조한다. a wonderful party는 명사이므로 such로 강조한다.

① 목적어 the secret 전치 표현이다.

② 의문대명사 who(m), which, what : ~하는(한) 누구/것

③ 주어를 강조하기 위해 주어 바로 옆에 사용한 재귀대명사를 문미에 위치시키면 강조의 의미가 더 강해진다.

해석

① 그가 그녀를 위해 비밀을 지켜왔다.

② 그가 알고 싶었던 건 그 여성이 누구냐는 거였다.

③ Josh 자신이 대상을 받았다.

④ 정말 멋진 파티였다.

정답 03 ③   04 ④

안심Touch

checkpoint 해설 & 정답

05 해설

후치 표현에 대한 문제이다.
to부정사의 후치 표현, 가목적어로 사용하고 to부정사절은 후치 → She is finding it difficult to find any answers.
② 동명사 표현의 후치이다.
③ 의문부사 when절의 후치이다.
④ 수여 동사 표현 중 간접 목적어의 후치이다. (4형식→3형식)

해석

① 그녀는 그 어떤 해답도 찾는 것을 어려워하고 있다.
② 5월에 봄 학기를 시작하는 것은 매우 놀라운 일이었다.
③ 네가 다시 시작할 때가 중요할 거야.
④ 그는 그녀에게 해바라기를 주었다.

06 해설

강의어 사용애 관한 문제이다.
긍정문에서 명사 last hole을 강조하는 부사표현 very는 the와 함께 쓰인다, 'the very last hole, 우승은 바로 그 마지막 홀에서 결정되었다.'
① 부정문 강조표현 by any means (결코, 아무래도)이다.
② 의문사 강조표현 in the world (도대체)이다.
④ 명령문을 강조하는 경우 조동사 do를 사용한다.

해석

① 그것은 어떤 식으로든 균형이 맞지 않고, 심지어 비슷하지도 않다.
② 당신은 어제 도대체 무엇을 했나요?
③ 우승은 마지막 홀에서 결정되었다.
④ 도서관에서는 조용히 합시다.

정답 05 ① 06 ③

---

05 다음 중 어법상 잘못된 표현은 무엇인가?

① She is finding to find any answers difficult.
② It was very surprising starting a Spring semester in May.
③ It will be important when you start again.
④ He gave a sunflower to her.

06 다음 중 강조와 관련하여 어법상 잘못된 표현은 무엇인가?

① It is not balanced by any means, not even close.
② What in the world did you do yesterday?
③ The win came down to very last hole.
④ Do be quite in the library.

07 다음 중 밑줄 친 부분에 들어갈 표현은 무엇인가?

> _____ he been to Spain, but he has also been to Portugal.

① Never has
② Not only has
③ Not until has
④ No sooner has

07 해설

부정어의 전치 표현에 대한 문제로 부정 표현 + 조동사 + 주어 + 동사 ～ 여기서는 not only A but also B(A 뿐만 아니라 B 역시); not A until B (B하고 나서야 비로소 A하다); no sooner A than B(A하자마자 B하다)가 들어가야 한다.

해석

그는 스페인에 간 적이 있을 뿐만 아니라 포르투갈에도 간 적이 있다.

08 다음 중 밑줄 친 부분에 들어갈 표현은 무엇인가?

> _____ he apologizes to her will she forgive him.

① Never
② Not only
③ Not until
④ No sooner

08 해설

not A until B : 'B하고 나서야 비로소 A하다'의 의미이다.
She will not forgive him until he apologizes to her. → not until B(S + V) + 조동사 + A(S + V) ～ (Not until he apologizes to her will she forgive him.)

해석

그가 그녀에게 사과를 하고 나서야 그녀는 그를 용서할 것이다.

정답 07② 08③

안심Touch

09 해설

no sooner + had + 주어 + –en(p.p.)
~ than + 주어 + 과거시제 동사
① 조동사 부정 표현 도치 : 부정 표현 + 조동사 + 주어 + 동사 ~
② 일반동사 부정 표현 도치 : 부정 표현 + do 동사(do/does/did) + 주어 + 동사 ~
④ not A until B (B하고 나서야 비로소 A하다) → not until B(주어 + 동사) + 조동사 + A(주어 + 동사) ~ : 'Not until he took medicine did he feel better.'

해석
① 그 교수는 거의 제시간에 오지 않는다.
② 그는 겨울 방학 동안 책을 읽지 않았다.
③ 그는 그것을 말하자마자 방을 나갔다.
④ 그는 약을 먹기 전까지 나아지지 않았다. (그는 약을 먹고 나서야 괜찮아졌다.)

10 해설

no sooner A than B = hardly (/scarcely) A before B = As soon as A, B = Upon A–ing, B : A하자마자 B하다

해석
그녀의 눈을 감자마자 그녀는 잠이 들었다.

09 다음 중 문장의 부정 표현이 잘못 도치된 것은?

① The professor is seldom here on time.
　→ Seldom is the professor here on time.
② He didn't read a book during the winter break.
　→ Not a book did he read during the winter break.
③ He had no sooner said it than he left the room.
　→ No sooner had he said it than he left the room.
④ He didn't feel better until he took medicine.
　→ Not until he felt better did he take medicine.

10 다음 중 밑줄 친 부분에 들어갈 표현은 무엇인가?

> _____ had she closed her eyes than she fell asleep.
> = _____ had she closed her eyes before she fell asleep.

① Upon – Hardly
② Not until – Scarcely
③ No sooner – As soon as
④ No sooner – Hardly

11 다음 중 도치와 관련하여 어법상 맞는 표현은 무엇인가?

① At the bus stop stood he.

② He would like to succeed and so she would.

③ Interesting is the case particularly.

④ Pretty as the rose is, it has too many thorns.

12 다음 문장 중에서 도치가 잘된 표현은 무엇인가?

① Two men were talking outside the house.

　→ Outside the house were talking two men.

② The police officer is at the door.

　→ There is the police officer at the door.

③ He plays more video games than his friends play the video games.

　→ He plays more video games than they do.

④ People will remember him forever.

　→ Him people will remember forever.

11 해설

형용사＋as 구문 양보구문에서 형용사 도치 표현한다.

① 주어가 (인칭)대명사이면 부사구가 문두로 전치되어도 주어와 동사는 도치되지 않는다. → At the bus stop he stood.

② 긍정문에서 so가 문두에 위치하고 주어와 (조)동사가 전치된다. → so would she

③ 형용사 보어를 수식하는 부사가 있는 경우 부사도 함께 도치된다. → Particularly interesting is this case.

해석

① 그는 버스 정류장에 서 있었다.

② 그는 성공하고 싶어하고 그녀도 그러할 것이다.

③ 이 사건은 특히 흥미롭다.

④ 장미꽃은 예쁘지만 가시가 너무 많다.

12 해설

than 비교급 구문에서 주어가 대명사인 경우는 주어와 동사를 도치시키지 않는다.

① 부사어는 위치, 동작을 나타내는 동사(go, come, sit, stand, lie 등) 다음에 있는 경우 도치되지만 다른 동사에서는 도치가 일어나지 않는다.

② 주어에 정관사(the) 표현이 있는 경우 도치되지 않는다.

④ 목적어가 대명사인 경우 목적어는 문두로 도치되지 않는다.

해석

① 두 남자가 집 밖에서 이야기하고 있었다.

② 경찰관이 문 앞에 있다.

③ 그는 그의 친구들이 비디오 게임을 하는 것보다 더 많은 비디오 게임을 한다.

④ 사람들은 그를 영원히 기억할 것이다.

정답 11 ④　12 ③

13 해설

주어가 대명사인 경우는 주어와 동사가 도치되지 않는다. → Right you are.
① 부정 표현이 문장 전체를 부정하는 것이 아니라 바로 다음에 오는 표현만 부정하는 경우에는 도치되지 않는다.
② 보어 역할을 하는 형용사가 문두에 위치하고 주어와 동사가 도치된다.
③ 형용사＋절 구문 전치 표현

해석

① 틀림없이 그는 올 것이다.
② 그 소식을 들었을 때 그는 매우 기뻤다.
③ 그는 가난했지만 도움을 요청하지 않았다.
④ 네 말이 맞아!

14 해설

may(might), ought to 다음에는 도치가 일어나지 않는다. → He may come and she may, too.
① 현재분사 보어 전치 표현이다.
② 과거분사 보어 전치 표현이다.
③ 부정문에서 neither/nor가 문두에 위치하고 주어와 조동사가 도치된다.

해석

① 사고가 날 가능성은 더 무시무시하다.
② 첨부된 파일은 1월 20일 목요일에 발행된 주문서이다.
③ 그는 잘못한 것이 없고, 그녀도 잘못한 것이 없다.
④ 그가 올 수도 있고 그녀도 올 수 있다.

정답 13 ④ 14 ④

13 다음 중 도치와 관련하여 어법상 잘못된 표현은 무엇인가?

① No doubt he will come.
② Great is his pleasure when he heard the news.
③ Poor that he was, he would never ask for any help.
④ Right are you.

14 다음 중 도치와 관련하여 어법상 잘못된 표현은 무엇인가?

① More frightening is the chance of the accidents.
② Attached is the order form that was issued on Thursday, January 20.
③ He did not do something wrong, neither did she.
④ He may come and so may she.

15　다음 중 도치와 관련하여 어법상 <u>잘못된</u> 표현은 무엇인가?

① Limes he would never eat, but lemons he eats.

② Not a jazz song did the quintet sing at the concert.

③ Electricity costs less than would petroleum.

④ He often goes to the movies as she does.

15　**해설**

④ as ～ as 비교급에서는 주어가 대명사인 경우도 도치가 가능하다. → He often goes to the movies as does she.

① 목적어의 전치 표현이다.

② 부정어를 포함하면 주어와 동사를 도치한다.

③ 비교급은 동사가 도치되는 것이 아니라 조동사나 do 동사가 도치된다.

해석

① 그는 라임은 절대 안 먹지만 레몬은 먹는다.

② 그 5인조 밴드는 콘서트에서 재즈 노래를 부르지 않았다.

③ 전기는 석유보다 비용이 적게 든다.

④ 그는 종종 그녀처럼 영화를 보러 간다.

정답　15 ④

여기서 멈출 거예요? 끝이가 바로 눈앞에 있어요.
마지막 한 걸음까지 SD에듀가 함께할게요!

추록

2025년 시험부터 추가되는 내용

※ **학습참고** 본문 291~308쪽의 내용(제8편 화법)은 2025년부터 평가영역에서 제외되었으므로, 학습 시 참고하시기 바랍니다.

훌륭한 가정만한 학교가 없고, 덕이 있는 부모만한 스승은 없다.

– 마하트마 간디 –

합격의 공식 ▶

SD에듀

자격증 · 공무원 · 금융/보험 · 면허증 · 언어/외국어 · 검정고시/독학사 · 기업체/취업

이 시대의 모든 합격! SD에듀에서 합격하세요!

www.youtube.com → SD에듀 → 구독

추록 I | 제1편 문장

※ 도서 17쪽에 추가되는 내용입니다.

제2장 문장 5형식

제6절 기타 문형

1 제6문형

6형식 문형은 자동사와 부사어(Adverb)가 함께 쓰여 뜻이 완성되는 '주어, 동사, 부사어'로 이루어진 문형이고, 동사는 부사어가 필요한 자동사가 사용된다.

> 주어(S) + 동사(V) + 부사어(A) [부사어가 필요한 자동사]

> agree with, agree to, rely on, depend on, major in, specialize in, succeed in, look at, listen to, speak to, refer to, respond to, deal with, deal in, differ from, apply for, apply to, arrive at, arrive in, live at, live in, consist of

[예]

- Josh headed to the airport.

  [[주어 Josh] [동사 headed] [부사어 to the airport]].

  (Josh는 공항으로 향했다.)

- The system computerization remains at a rudimentary stage.

  [[주어 The system computerization] [동사 remains] [부사어 at a rudimentary stage]].

  (그 시스템 전산화는 기초 단계이다.) (computerization : 전산화 / rudimentary : 기본의, 초보의, 미발달의)

2 제7문형

7형식 문형은 타동사와 부사어가 함께 쓰여 뜻이 완성되는 '주어, 동사, 목적어, 부사어'로 이루어진 문형이고, 동사는 부사어가 필요한 타동사가 사용된다.

> 주어(S) + 동사(V) + 목적어(O) + 부사어(A) [부사어가 필요한 타동사]

> consider as, appoint as

[예]

- Josh sent a reference letter to the university.

  [[주어 Josh] [동사 sent] [목적어 a reference letter] [부사어 to the university]].

  (Josh는 추천서를 그 대학으로 보냈다.) (reference letter : 추천서)

- Josh brought the gift to the office.

  [[주어 Josh] [동사 brought] [목적어 the gift] [부사어 to the office]].

  (Josh는 사무실에 선물을 갖고 왔다.)

제1편 추가 실전예상문제

01 다음 중 문장의 형식이 <u>다른</u> 것은?

① The palatial residence stands on the hill.

② Josh stayed in Korea for a week.

③ People rely on technology.

④ Josh put the books on the desk.

> **해설**
> ①·②·③은 '주어 + 자동사 + 부사어' 형식의 6문형 문장이고, ④는 '주어 + 타동사 + 목적어 + 부사어' 형식의 7문형 문장이다.
> **해석**
> ① 그 대저택은 언덕 위에 있다.
> ② Josh는 1주일 동안 한국에 머물렀다.
> ③ 사람들은 과학기술에 의존한다.
> ④ Josh는 책을 책상 위에 올려놓았다.
> **정답** ④

추록 II | 제2편 품사(의미, 구조, 형태상 특성)

※ 도서 51쪽에 추가되는 내용입니다.

제2장 관사

제4절 관사와 한정사

영어의 한정사(determiner)에는 관사(article) 외에도 소유형용사(possessive), 지시형용사(demonstrative), 수량형용사(quantifier), 수사(numeral) 등이 있다.

1 소유형용사

예

- Her best friend is a pet.
- She broke her leg.
- It was his own idea.
- The dog quivered its tail. (quiver : 꼬리 등을 흔들다)

2 지시형용사

예

- This picture is drawn by a famous artist.
- Josh bought these flowers for Amy.
- That book is worth more than $3 million.
- Josh wants to see those movies.

3 수량형용사

예

- Josh took all the books.
- Josh always puts some carrots in son's soup.

- (A) few students came to the academic conference. [a few : (긍정) 조금 있는 / few : (부정) 거의 없는]
- Josh has (a) little money. [a little : (긍정) 약간 있는 / little : (부정) 거의 없는]

4 수사

예
- There is one person in the room.
- There are nine people in the room.

더 알아두기

1. 배수사
(1) 가산명사, 불가산명사 앞 위치
(2) '배수사 + (정관사, 소유격, 지시한정사) + 명사' 형태
예
- twice my age, twice his height
- three times its current size

2. 분수
(1) 가산명사, 불가산명사 앞 위치
(2) 분자의 수가 2 이상인 경우 분모를 복수로 표현
(3) '분수 + (정관사, 소유격, 지시한정사) + 명사' 형태
(4) '분수 + of + (정관사, 소유격, 지시한정사) + 명사' 형태
예
- one fourth(a quarter)
- two quarters, three quarters
- one third of the students

3. 'of 형태' 수량형용사
(1) '명사 + of' 형태
(2) 복수가산명사 앞 : a good/great/large number of, numbers of, many of
(3) 불가산명사 앞 : a (good/great) deal/amount/quantity of
(4) 복수가산명사/불가산명사 모두 사용 : a lot of, lots of, plenty of, the rest of

---

5 한정사 간 위치

한정사는 위치에 따라 전치·중간·후치한정사로 나눈다. 한정사가 한 번에 여러 개 사용되는 경우 그 위치에 따른 순서가 정해지며, 중간한정사는 중복 사용이 안 된다.

구분	전치한정사	중간한정사	후치한정사	명사
종류	• 수량한정사(all, both) • 배수사(double) • 분수(half, two thirds) • such • what	• 관사(a, an, the) • 소유격(her, his) • 수량한정사(some, any, every) • 지시한정사(this, that)	• 수량한정사(many, much, more, most, few, little, less, least) • 기수사(one, two) • 서수사(first, second) • 수량표시어(a cup of, a glass of, a bottle of, a loaf of)	-
예	all	the	more	reasons
	all	the	-	students
	-	her	two/little	daughters

※ 전치-중간-후치 순서대로 한정사를 중복해서 표현하지 않는 경우, of 표현을 사용하여 순서를 바꿔 쓸 수 있다.

예

• many of the students
• two of the students

제2편 추가 실전예상문제

01 다음 중 어법상 가장 적절하지 <u>않은</u> 표현은?

① Many students are taught by their peers.

② Amy spent a good deal of her time to get the work done.

③ Josh has few money left.

④ Children should eat a lot of vegetables.

해설

수량형용사 few는 가산명사 앞에 쓰인다. 따라서 불가산명사 앞에 올 수 있는 수량형용사 little이 들어가야 적절하다 (③ few → little).

① 수량형용사 many + 가산명사

② 수량형용사 a good deal of + 불가산명사

④ 수량형용사 a lot of + 복수가산명사/불가산명사

해석

① 많은 학생들이 그들의 또래들에게 배운다.

② Amy는 그 일을 끝내는 데 많은 시간을 들였다.

③ Josh는 남아 있는 돈이 거의 없다.

④ 아이들은 채소를 많이 먹어야 한다.

정답 ③

02 다음 중 어법상 가장 적절한 표현은?

① All more the reasons were economic.

② It can kill animals its four times size.

③ Two third of the people use smartphones.

④ Some of the university students sold food.

해설

전치-중간-후치 순서대로 한정사를 중복해서 표현하지 않는 경우, of 표현을 사용하여 순서를 바꿔 쓸 수 있다. ④는 '중간한정사 + of + 중간한정사 + 명사'로 쓰인 경우이다.

① '전치(all)-중간(the)-후치(more)' 순에 따라, 'all the more reasons'로 들어가야 적절하다.

② '배수사(four times) + 소유격(its) + 명사(size)' 순으로 쓰여야 하므로, 'four times its size'로 들어가야 적절하다.

③ 분자의 수가 2 이상인 경우 분모를 복수로 표현하므로, 'two thirds of'로 들어가야 적절하다.

해석

① 모든 이유들은 경제적인 것이었다.

② 그 동물은 자신보다 몸집이 네 배 큰 동물도 죽일 수 있다.

③ 사람들의 3분의 2가 스마트폰을 사용한다.

④ 일부 대학생들이 음식을 팔았다.

정답 ④

추록 III | 제4편 구와 절

※ 도서 206쪽에 추가되는 내용입니다.

제5장   비정형동사 사이의 관계

제1절   부정사와 동명사

1 to부정사를 목적어로 취하는 동사

(1) 동사 + to부정사

★표시 동사는 to부정사뿐만 아니라 동명사도 목적어로 취한다.

동사	예문
afford	He can't afford to buy a new car.
agree	He agreed to help them.
appear	He appears to be tired.
arrange	He arranged to meet her at the radio station.
ask	He asked to help them.
★can't bear	He can't bear to wait in long lines.
beg	He begged to help them.
★begin	It began to snow.
care	He doesn't care to watch the opera.
claim	He claimed to have found more evidence.
consent	He consented to help them.
★continue	He continued to talk to her.
decide	He decided to leave early today.
demand	He demanded to help the underprivileged.
deserve	He deserves to be paid well.
expect	He expects to return to graduate school next year.
fail	He didn't fail to return the books to the city library on time.
★forget	He forgot to lock the front door.
★hate	He hates to tell a white lie.
hesitate	Please don't hesitate to contact us.
hope	He hopes to arrive on time.
intend	He intends to be a novelist.
learn	He learned to play the guitar.

★like	He likes to watch sports games.
★love	He loves to watch baseball games.
manage	He managed to complete his task early.
mean	He didn't mean to underestimate the situation.
need	He needs to have her opinion about the issue.
offer	He offered to help them.
plan	He is planning to study abroad next year.
★prefer	He prefers to drink coffee in the morning.
prepare	He prepared to study abroad.
pretend	He pretended to understand everything she said.
promise	He promised to come early.
refuse	He refused to leak confidential information.
★regret	He regretted to tell her that he didn't pass the exam.
★remember	He remembered to lock the front door.
seem	New comers seemed to be friendly.
★can't stand	He can't stand to wait in long lines.
★start	It started to snow.
struggle	He struggled to survive.
swear	He swore to tell the truth.
tend	He tends to use slang.
threaten	He threatened to quit the support.
★try	He is trying to learn a foreign language.
volunteer	He volunteered to help them.
wait	He waited to see you.
want	He wanted to participate in the conference.
wish	He wishes to visit Korea next year.

(2) 동사 + (대)명사 + to부정사

★표시 동사는 to부정사뿐만 아니라 동명사도 목적어로 취한다.

동사	예문
★advise	He advised her to start early today.
allow	He allowed me to use his laptop.
ask	He asked her to help them.
beg	He begged us to help them.
cause	His carelessness caused him to break the vase.
challenge	He challenged her to break the world record.
convince	He convinced her to accept their offer.

dare	He dared her to swim across the river.
encourage	He encourages the students to take part in the workshop.
expect	He expected her to find a good job.
forbid	He forbids her to install other programs in his laptop.
force	He forced her to help them.
hire	He hired a native English speaker to teach students.
instruct	He instructed the students to study English.
invite	He invited her to participate in the movie preview.
need	He needed her to work with them.
order	He ordered them to reconsider the plan.
permit	He permitted the students to look the word up in the dictionary.
persuade	He persuaded her to go to the conference.
remind	He reminded her to write her sister.
require	He required the students to finish the test on time.
teach	He taught her to drive a car.
tell	He told her to go to the party.
urge	He urged the students to prepare for the final exams.
want	He wanted her to participate in the international conference.
warn	He warned her to drive safely.

2 동명사를 목적어로 취하는 동사

★표시 동사는 동명사뿐만 아니라 to부정사도 목적어로 취한다.

동사	예문
admit	He admitted using an unreasonable source.
★advise	He advised starting early today.
anticipate	He anticipates having a good time during the winter break.
appreciate	He appreciated coming in on Christmas Eve.
avoid	He avoided answering her question in a direct way.
★can't bear	He can't bear waiting in long lines.
★begin	It began snowing.
complete	He finally completed writing his final paper.
consider	He will consider visiting two national parks.
★continue	He continued talking to her.
delay	He delayed leaving for Korea.

deny	He denied holding the world record.
discuss	They discussed entering into a new business.
dislike	He dislikes eating alone.
enjoy	He enjoyed watching movies.
finish	He finished studying at 11 p.m.
★forget	He never forgot visiting Giant's Causeway.
★hate	He hates telling a white lie.
can't help	He can't help smiling at her.
keep	He keeps hoping she will come.
★like	He likes watching sports games.
★love	He loves watching baseball games.
mention	He mentioned going on a picnic.
mind	Would you mind opening the window?
miss	He missed being with his family.
postpone	He postponed leaving Korea until next month.
practice	He practiced kicking balls.
★prefer	He prefers drinking coffee to drinking tea in the morning.
quit	He quit drinking last year.
recall	He doesn't recall meeting her last year.
recollect	He doesn't recollect meeting her last year.
recommend	He recommended using the new product.
★regret	He regretted telling her his secret.
★remember	He remembered meeting her last year.
resent	He resented having been misled.
resist	He couldn't resist smiling at her.
risk	He risked losing all his money.
★can't stand	He can't stand waiting in long lines.
★start	It started snowing.
stop	He stopped drinking last year.
suggest	He suggested going to the opera.
tolerate	He doesn't tolerate making a mistake.
★try	He tried closing the window, but he couldn't budge the window.
understand	He didn't understand her leaving graduate school.

3 to부정사와 동명사를 모두 목적어로 취하는 동사

(1) 의미 차이가 (거의) 없는 경우

> begin, like, hate, start, love, continue, prefer, can't stand, can't bear

예

- It began to rain.

  = It began raining.

- He likes to fish.

  = He likes fishing.

- He can't bear to tell a white lie.

  = He can't bear telling a white lie.

※ 동사의 시제가 진행형인 경우 동명사보다는 to부정사를 사용한다.

예 It was beginning to rain.

(2) 의미 차이가 있는 경우

① remember

  ㉠ remember + to부정사 : 책임, 의무, 업무 수행을 기억하는 경우

  ㉡ remember + 동명사 : 과거에 있었던 일을 기억하는 경우

  예

  - He always remembers to lock the front door.
  - He remembers seeing the Giant's Causeway. That was impressive.

② forget

  ㉠ forget + to부정사 : 책임, 의무, 업무 수행을 잊은 경우

  ㉡ forget + 동명사 : 과거에 있었던 일을 잊은 경우

  예

  - He often forgets to lock the front door.
  - He forgot seeing the Giant's Causeway last year.

③ regret

  ㉠ regret + to부정사 : 좋지 않은 소식을 알리게 되어 유감인 경우

  ㉡ regret + 동명사 : 과거의 일에 대해 후회하는 경우

  예

  - He regrets to tell her that she failed the exam.
  - He regrets leaving the USA early.

④ try

　㉠ try + to부정사 : 노력하다

　㉡ try + 동명사 : 시험 삼아 해 보다

　예

　• He tried to climb Mount Everest last year.

　• We tried closing the window, but we couldn't budge the window. (budge : 움직이다)

⑤ stop

　㉠ stop + to부정사 : ~하기 위해 멈추다(목적 = in order to)

　㉡ stop + 동명사 : ~하는 것을 멈추다(동사 stop의 목적어)

　예

　• He stopped (in order) to talk to her.

　• He stopped talking to her.

제2절　동명사와 현재분사

1　강세

동명사는 목적, 용도의 '~하기 위한'의 의미로 사용되어 명사 역할을 한다. 반면, 현재분사는 상태, 동작의 '~하고 있는'의 의미로 사용되어 형용사 역할을 한다. 동명사는 동명사에, 현재분사는 명사에 강세가 온다.

2　명사와의 결합

(1) **복합 명사** : 동명사 + 명사

(2) **현재분사의 명사 수식** : 현재분사 + **명사**

동명사	현재분사
a **sléeping** car : 침대차	a sleeping **chíld** : 자고 있는 아이
a **dáncing** room : 무용실	a dancing **gírl** : 춤추고 있는 소녀
bóxing gloves : 권투 장갑	a boxing **mán** : 권투하는 사람
a **búrning** glass : 화경(태양열/집광 렌즈)	a burning **mountáin** : 불타는 산
a **wáiting** room : 대기실	a waiting **lády** : 기다리고 있는 부인
a **knítting** needle : 뜨개바늘	a knitting **móther** : 뜨개질하시는 어머니

3 동명사의 명사적 역할

동명사는 문장 내에서 주어, 목적어(동사, 전치사), 보어의 명사적 역할을 한다.

(1) 주어

예

- [Seeing] is believing.
- [Running] is one of the easiest ways to lose weight.

(2) 목적어

① 동사

예

- He enjoyed [studying] in the graduate school.
- He likes [fishing] and [hunting].

② 전치사

예

- He is very fond [of studying] in the library.
- He is very good [at singing].

(3) 보어

예

- Seeing is [believing].
- His dream is [studying] abroad.

4 현재분사의 형용사적 역할

현재분사의 형용사적 기능에는 명사를 수식하는 한정적 용법과 명사의 동작과 상태를 설명하는 서술적 용법이 있다.

(1) 한정적 용법 : 명사 전치 수식과 후치 수식

① 전치 수식

예

- A rolling stone gathers no moss.
- Melting chocolate can be an excellent dessert.

② **후치 수식**

[예]

- The birds singing on a tree are magpies. (magpie : 까치)
- The sun rising from the East gives hope.

(2) 서술적 용법 : 주격 보어와 목적격 보어의 능동 관계

① **주격 보어**

[예]

- He sat reading the novel.

  = He sat and was reading the novel.
- He kept waiting in the lobby.

② **목적격 보어 : 지각동사**

[예]

- He saw her listen/listening to music.
- He heard her play/playing the cello.

제4편   추가 실전예상문제

01 다음 중 괄호 안의 단어를 알맞은 형태로 바꾸어 쓴 것은?

> He remembers (<u>see</u>) the Giant's Causeway in Northern Ireland. That was impressive.

① see

② to see

③ seeing

④ to be seen

해설

'remember + to부정사'는 책임, 의무, 업무 수행을 기억하는 경우에 쓰인다. 한편, 'remember + 동명사'는 과거에 있었던 일을 기억하는 경우에 쓰인다. 여기서는 문맥상 후자로 보는 것이 적절하다.

해석

그는 Northern Ireland에 있는 Giant's Causeway를 본 기억이 있다. 그것은 아주 인상적이었다.

정답 ③

02 다음 중 괄호 안의 단어를 알맞은 형태로 바꾸어 쓴 것은?

> We tried (<u>close</u>) the window, but we couldn't budge the window.

① close

② to close

③ closing

④ to be closing

해설

'try + to부정사'는 '노력하다'를, 'try + 동명사'는 '시험 삼아 해 보다'를 의미한다. 여기서는 문맥상 후자로 보는 것이 적절하다.

해석

우리는 창문을 닫으려고 (여러 번 시도) 했지만, 창문은 꼼짝도 안했다.

정답 ③

03 다음 중 밑줄 친 부분의 용법이 다른 표현은?

① Are there <u>sleeping</u> cars to the train?

② The patient sits in the clinic <u>waiting</u> room.

③ Instead of <u>knitting</u> needles, a crochet hook was used.

④ <u>Burning</u> mountain was finally brought under control.

해설

burning mountain(불타는 산)에서 burning은 현재분사이다.

① sleeping car(침대차)에서 sleeping은 동명사이다.

② waiting room(대기실)에서 waiting은 동명사이다.

③ knitting needle(뜨개바늘)에서 knitting은 동명사이다.

해석

① 그 열차에 침대차가 있나요?

② 그 환자는 진료 대기실에 앉아 있다.

③ 뜨개바늘 대신에 코바늘이 사용되었다. (crochet hook : 코바늘)

④ 불타는 산이 마침내 진화되었다. (under control : 통제되는, 지배되는, 진화되는)

정답 ④

추록Ⅳ | 제11편 일치(Agreement)

단원 개요

일치(agreement)는 문장에서 주어와 동사의 인칭(person)과 수(number)의 일치를 나타낸다. 또한 주어 및 목적어가 각각의 주격 보어, 목적격 보어와도 수 일치를 이루고, 명사 표현에서 성(gender) 및 집합명사도 수 일치를 이루고, 주절과 종속절의 시제 표현도 수 일치를 이룬다.

출제 경향 및 수험 대책

1. 주어와 동사의 일치 : '인칭'과 '수'의 개념
2. 주요 수 일치 표현 : 상관접속사, 부정대명사, 부분 표현, 상시 복수, 단일 개념, 동격, 형용사절 동사, It ~ that 강조 구문
3. 주어/목적어와 보어의 일치
4. 여성형 · 남성형 명사의 성(gender)의 일치, 집합명사
5. 시제의 일치 및 예외 표현

제1장 주어와 동사의 일치

영어 문장에서 주어와 동사의 일치(subject-verb agreement) 현상은 동사의 형태를 주어의 인칭(person)과 수(number)에 맞게 일치시키는 것을 말한다.

제1절 인칭

1 1인칭(1st person)

예

- I teach English. (단수)
- We teach English. (복수)

2 2인칭(2nd person)

예 You learn English. (단수 · 복수)

3 3인칭(3rd person)

예

- She/He teaches Linguistics. (단수)
- They teach Linguistics. (복수)

제2절 수

1 단수(singular)

예

- I teach English. (1인칭)
- You learn English. (2인칭)
- She/He teaches Linguistics. (3인칭)

2 복수(plural)

예

- We teach English. (1인칭)
- You learn English. (2인칭)
- They teach Linguistics. (3인칭)

제3절 주요 수 일치 표현

1 상관접속사 수 일치

상관접속사	의미	주어 및 수 일치
both <u>A</u> and <u>B</u> (A and B)	A와 B 둘다	A, B
either A or <u>B</u>	A 또는 B	B
neither A nor <u>B</u>	A도 B도 아닌	B
whether A or <u>B</u>	A든 B든	B
not A but <u>B</u>	A 아니고 B	B
not only A but (also) <u>B</u> not merely/simply A but (also) <u>B</u>	A뿐만 아니라 B도	B
<u>B</u> as well as A	A뿐만 아니라 B도	B

예

- Both <u>humans</u> and <u>animals</u> <u>are</u> living creature. (인간과 동물 모두 살아있는 생명체이다.)
- Either you or <u>she</u> <u>is</u> to go. (너나 그녀 둘 중 한 사람이 가야 한다.)
- Neither hair dryers nor <u>dyeing</u> <u>is</u> recommended. (헤어드라이어와 염색은 (모두) 권장되지 않는다.)
- Whether it rains or <u>it snows</u> <u>is</u> not certain. (비가 오는지 눈이 오는지 확실하지 않다.)
- Not you but <u>he</u> <u>is</u> right. (네가 아니라 그가 옳다.)
- Not only you but also <u>he</u> <u>is</u> right. (너뿐만 아니라 그도 옳다.)
- <u>He</u> as well as you <u>is</u> right. (너뿐만 아니라 그도 옳다.)
- <u>I</u> as well as you <u>am</u> interested in nature. (너뿐만 아니라 나도 자연에 관심이 있다.)

2 부정대명사 표현

(1) every, each, no one, another, either, neither

every, each, no one, another, either, neither가 주어가 되거나 주어를 수식하는 경우 단수 취급한다.

예

- <u>Every</u> pupil <u>respects</u> her/his teacher. (모든 학생들은 선생님을 존경한다.)
- <u>Each</u> child <u>likes</u> to play. (아이들은 저마다 놀기를 좋아한다.)
- <u>No</u> students <u>fails</u> the exam. (시험에 실패한 학생은 아무도 없다.)
- <u>Neither</u> father nor mother <u>is</u> at home. (아버지도 어머니도 집에 안 계십니다.)

※ every, each, no 뒤에 두 개의 명사가 와도 단수 취급한다.

예

- Every boy and girl knows the answer. (모든 소년과 소녀는 그 답을 안다.)
- Each woman and man has her/his own room. (여자와 남자 각각 자신의 방이 있다.)
- No female and male student fails the exam. (시험에 실패한 여학생과 남학생은 아무도 없다.)

(2) −one, −body, −thing

-one, -body, -thing이 주어가 되거나 주어를 수식하는 경우 단수 취급한다.

예

- Everyone makes mistakes. (모든 사람들은 실수를 한다.)
- Everybody has her/his own ideas. (누구나 자기 생각이 있다.)
- Everything in the store is on sale. (가게에 있는 것은 모두 팔 물건입니다.)

(3) some, any, no

① some, any, no + 단수명사 → 단수 취급
② some, any, no + 복수명사 → 복수 취급

예

- Some action is necessary. (어떤 조치가 필요하다.)
- Some children are barefoot. (몇몇 아이들은 맨발이다.)
- Any hypothesis is a leap into the unknown. (모든 가설은 갑자기 미지의 상태에 이르는 것이다.) (leap : 뛰기, 도약, 변화)
- Any special requests are cordially declined. (특별한 요청은 정중히 거절합니다.) (cordially : 진심으로, 성심껏 / decline : 거절하다)
- No one is exactly sure what he looked like. (아무도 그가 어떻게 생겼는지 정확하게 확신하지 못한다.)
- No carrots were left in the refrigerator. (냉장고에 당근이 하나도 남지 않았다.)

(4) all, enough

① all, enough 사물 지시 → 단수 취급
② all, enough 사람 지시 → 복수 취급

예

- All that ends well is well. (= All is well that ends well.) (속담 : 끝이 좋으면 만사가 좋다.)
- All that took part in the meeting were satisfied. (그 회의에 참석한 모든 사람이 만족했다.)
- Enough has been said about the issue. (그 문제에 대해서는 이미 충분히 말했다.)
- Enough are here to make a quorum. (정족수를 이루기에 충분하다) (make a quorum : 정족수를 이루다)

3 부분 표현

부분을 나타내는 표현이 주어인 경우 of 뒤에 나오는 명사에 수 일치한다.

(1) 주요 부분 표현

부분 표현	of 표현
all most the majority a lot, lots plenty the bulk(대부분) half some a large part part the rest percent none percentage(%) 분수	of + 단수명사 + 단수동사 of + 복수명사 + 복수동사

(2) 분수 표현

① 분자-기수, 분모-서수

② **분자가 단수인 경우** : 분자-기수, 분모-서수

1/2 = a half, 1/3 = one third, 1/4 = one fourth(a quarter)

③ **분자가 복수인 경우** : 분자-기수, 분모-서수s

2/3 = two thirds, 3/5 = three fifths

④ **대분수 표현**

1과 1/3 = one and one third, 1과 1/2 = one and a half

예

- All of the action is informed by the real 911 recorded calls to the police. (모든 동작은 실제 경찰에 한 신고 전화 녹음본에 기반해 만들어졌다.)
- All of the major car makers are upgrading their product line. (모든 주요 자동차 제조사들은 생산 라인을 업그레이드하고 있다.)
- Most of Norway is covered with mountains. (노르웨이의 대부분은 산으로 덮여 있다.)
- Most of the baseball stadiums are open-air stadium. (대부분의 야구장들은 야외 구장이다.)

- Some of the book is quite good. (그 책의 일부는 꽤 좋다.)
- Some of the books are quite good. (그 책들 중 몇 권은 꽤 좋다.)
- 30 percent of the company's revenue is allocated to taxes. (회사 수입의 30%는 조세로 납부되고 있다.) (revenue : (총)수입)
- 30 percent of students read one or two books each month. (학생 중 30%는 매달 한 권이나 두 권의 책을 읽는다.)
- Two thirds of the money is saved. (그 돈의 3분의 2는 저축되어 있다.)
- Two thirds of the students are Asian. (학생의 3분의 2는 아시아계 학생이다.)

4 단수 취급하는 'A and B' 표현

상관접속사 '(both) A and B'는 기본적으로 복수 취급하지만, 다음의 경우 단수 취급한다.

(1) 개념상 하나의 개념을 의미하는 경우

예

- Slow and steady wins the race. (속담 : 느려도 착실히 하면 이긴다.)
- I admit that it is obvious that trial and error works. (나는 시행착오가 효과가 있다는 것이 명백하다는 것을 인정한다.) (trial and error : 시행착오)

(2) 불가분의 관계에 있는 명사 표현

예

- Needle and thread was found in the drawer. (바늘과 실이 서랍에서 발견되었다.) (drawer : 서랍)
- Bread and butter is his favorite breakfast. (버터를 바른 빵이 그가 가장 좋아하는 아침식사이다.)

(3) 관사(정관사 the, 부정관사 a/an)나 소유격('s)이 한 번만 사용되는 표현

예

- An actor and director was in the movie preview. (배우 겸 감독이 영화 시사회에 있었다.)
- A black and white dog is following him. (바둑이가 그를 따라오고 있다.)

※ '관사 + A and 관사 + B'는 복수 취급한다.

예

- An actor and a director were in the movie preview. (배우와 감독이 영화 시사회에 있었다.)
- A black and a white dog are following him. (검은 개 한 마리와 하얀 개 한 마리가 그를 따라오고 있다.)

(4) 부정대명사 every, each, no의 수식을 받는 표현

예

- Every boy and girl knows the answer. (모든 소년과 소녀는 그 답을 안다.)
- Each woman and man has her/his own room. (여자와 남자 각각 자신의 방이 있다.)
- No female and male student fails the exam. (시험에 실패한 여학생과 남학생은 아무도 없다.)

5 'Many a + 단수명사'와 'Many + 복수명사'

(1) 'Many a + 단수명사' → 단수 취급

예 Many a pickle makes a mickle. (속담 : 티끌 모아 태산) (mickle : 많음, 다량)

(2) 'Many + 복수명사' → 복수 취급

예 Many people are suffering from the flu. (많은 사람들이 독감을 앓고 있다.)

6 'the number of + 복수명사'와 'a number of(= many) + 복수명사'

(1) 'the number of + 복수명사' → 단수 취급

예 The number of drivers using the service is expected to increase. (그 서비스를 이용하는 운전자들의 수는 늘어날 것으로 전망된다.)

(2) 'a number of(= many) + 복수명사' → 복수 취급

예 A number of drivers are using the service. (많은 운전자들이 그 서비스를 이용하고 있다.)

※ 'a total of, a series of, a sample of, one and a half of + 복수명사'는 단수 취급한다. 단, 'a total of + 복수명사'는 일반적으로 단수 취급하나, 일상체 영어에서는 복수 취급하기도 한다.

예

- A total of 22 students is playing soccer in the playground. (총 22명의 학생들이 운동장에서 축구를 하고 있다.)
- A total of 20 tracks are listed on the new album. (새 앨범에는 모두 20곡이 수록되어 있다.)

7 상시 복수

상시 복수, 즉 절대 복수(plurale tantum)는 단수형은 없고 복수형만 있는 명사를 말하는데 그 쓰임에 따라 단수·복수 취급이 달라진다.

(1) 순수 상시 복수는 일반적으로 복수 취급하나 aerobics, news는 단수 취급

> thanks(감사), odds(확률), valuables(귀중품), belongings(소유물), eaves(처마), aerobics(에어로빅), news(뉴스)

예

- Statistically, the odds are low. (통계적으로 그럴 확률은 거의 없다.)
- The eaves are dripping. (처마에서 물이 뚝뚝 떨어지고 있다.)
- Aerobics is typically practiced to music. (에어로빅은 보통 음악에 맞춰 연습한다.)
- No news is good news. (무소식이 희소식)

(2) 쌍(pair)으로 이루어진 상시 복수는 복수 취급

> glasses(안경), goggles(고글), binoculars(쌍안경), trousers(바지), pants(바지), pajamas(파자마), scissors(가위), shears(큰 가위), shorts(반바지), socks(양말), tweezers(핀셋)

예

- Glasses are not expensive. (안경은 비싸지 않다.)
- These trousers are baggy at the knees. (이 바지는 무릎이 헐렁하다.)
- These scissors are not sharp. (이 가위는 날카롭지 않다.)

※ 단, 'a pair of, pairs of' 표현과 함께 쓰이면 pair에 수 일치한다.

예

- A pair of glasses is on sale. (안경이 판매 중이다.)
- Two pairs of trousers are on the shelf. (바지 두 벌이 진열대에 있다.)

(3) 학과명, 학문명은 복수 형태이지만 단수 취급

> linguistics(언어학), mathematics(수학), politics(정치학), economics(경제학), physics(물리학), statistics(통계학), ethics(윤리학), electronics(전자공학), mechanics(역학), optics(광학)

[예]

- Linguistics is fundamental to the human expression of thought and ideas. (언어학은 인간의 사고와 사상 표현의 기본이 되는 학문이다.)
- Statistics is taught in all universities. (통계학은 모든 대학에서 가르친다.)

※ 단, statistics가 '통계학'이 아니라 '통계수치'를 의미하는 경우 복수 취급한다.

[예]

- These statistics are troubling, but also misleading. (이러한 통계수치는 우려스럽지만 또한 판단을 오도할 수 있다.)
- Our state health statistics are doing better. (우리 주의 건강 지표들은 훨씬 더 나아졌다.)

(4) 복수 형태의 국가명은 단수 취급

> the United States, the United Nations, the Netherlands, the Philippines

[예]

- The United States is responsible for one-quarter of the world's greenhouse gases. (미국은 세계 온실가스의 4분의 1의 책임이 있다.)
- The Netherlands is a peaceful country. (네덜란드는 평화로운 나라이다.)

(5) 게임은 복수 형태이지만 단수 취급

> rock-paper-scissors(가위바위보), darts, dominoes, crickets, checkers, billiards(당구)

[예]

- Dominoes is played with 28 flat, oblong pieces of bone or wood. (도미노 놀이는 뼈나 나무로 만든 28장의 납작한 장방형의 패를 가지고 노는 것이다.) (oblong : 직사각형의, 타원형의)
- Checkers is played on a chess board. (체커는 체스 판에서 이루어진다.)

(6) 질병 이름은 복수 형태이지만 단수 취급

> diabetes(당뇨병), measles(홍역), blues(우울증), rabies(광견병), smallpox(천연두)

예

- Diabetes is treatable, but there is no cure you have it. (당뇨병은 치료가 가능하지만 일단 발병하면 완전한 치료법은 없다.)
- Measles was killing a couple of million a year. (홍역으로 몇 백만 명이 죽어갔다.)
- Blues has explored in the industrial world in the last generation. (우울증은 지난 세대의 산업화된 사회에서 폭발적으로 증가했다.)

8 단일 개념의 시간, 거리, 가격, 중량은 단수 취급

예

- In Europe 100 miles is a long way; in America 100 years is a long time. (유럽에서 100마일은 먼길이고, 미국에서 100년은 긴 시간이다.)
- Four hours of sleep is not enough. (4시간의 잠은 충분하지 않다.)
- 1,000 dollars is too much to pay. (1,000달러는 지불하기에는 너무 많다.)
- 1,000 miles is not a short distance to travel. (1,000마일이 여행하기에 짧은 거리는 아니다.)
- Two and three is five. (2 더하기 3은 5이다.)
- Three times five is fifteen. (3 곱하기 5는 15이다.)

9 'there is 단수명사'와 'there are 복수명사'

예

- There is a special museum in that city. (그 도시에는 특별한 박물관이 있다.)
- There is an area of taking pictures. (사진을 찍기 위한 장소가 있다.)
- Nowadays, there are many kinds of milk, whole, low-fat, or non-fat milk. (요즘에는 전유, 저지방, 무지방 등 우유에도 여러 종류가 있다.)
- There are various international competitions held. (많은 국제적인 경기가 열린다.)

10 동격 구문 A, B에서는 A에 수 일치

[예]

- <u>My friend</u>, the current president's son, <u>is</u> to win the election. (현 대통령의 아들인 내 친구가 선거에서 이길 것이다.)
- <u>You</u>, my friend's daughter, <u>are</u> now my daughter-in-law. (내 친구의 딸인 네가 이제 내 며느리구나.)

11 형용사절 주격 관계대명사 다음에 나오는 동사는 주절의 선행사에 수 일치

[예]

- She knows <u>the man</u> who <u>is</u> studying next her. (그녀는 옆에서 공부하고 있는 남자를 알고 있다.)
- The <u>pens</u> which <u>are</u> on the desk are hers. (책상 위에 있는 펜들은 그녀의 것이다.)

12 'It ~ that 강조 구문'에서 주어가 강조되는 경우 강조된 주어와 동사 수 일치

[예]

- It is <u>his mother</u> who <u>leads</u> him to success. (그를 성공으로 이끄는 것은 바로 그의 어머니이다.)
- It is <u>he</u> who <u>wants</u> to study abroad in the States. (미국에 유학가기를 원하는 사람은 바로 그다.)

제2장   주어/목적어와 보어의 일치

문장에서 명사구가 보어(complement)일 경우 주격 보어는 주어와, 목적격 보어는 (직접)목적어와 수 일치한다.

제1절   주어 – 주격 보어

1 주어(단수) – 동사 – 주격 보어(단수)

[예] <u>My daughter</u> is <u>an angel</u>.

2 주어(복수) – 동사 – 주격 보어(복수)

예 <u>My daughters</u> are <u>angels</u>.

제2절   목적어 – 목적격 보어

1 주어 – 동사 – 목적어(단수) – 목적격 보어(단수)

예 I believe <u>my daughter</u> <u>an angel</u>.

2 주어 – 동사 – 목적어(복수) – 목적격 보어(복수)

예 I believe <u>my daughters</u> <u>angels</u>.

제3장   성(Gender)의 일치

제1절   baby, infant, child

여성(feminine)과 남성(masculine) 양쪽 성에 공통으로 사용하는 명사를 통성명사 또는 보통명사
(commons, common noun)라고 하는데 'baby, infant, child, parent, spouse, cousin, monarch, doctor,
teacher, friend, animal, bird' 등이 있다.

(1) 일반적으로 관계대명사 who/which, 인칭대명사 she/he/it을 사용한다.

(2) 성별이 불분명하거나, 중요 관심사가 아닌 경우, 중립성 및 객관성을 강조하는 내용에서 관계대명사
which, 인칭대명사 it을 사용한다.
    예
    • The baby favors <u>its</u> mother. (아기는 어머니를 닮았습니다.)
    • This baby is a human body; <u>it</u> evolved. (이 아기는 진화를 한 인간입니다.)

(3) 가족관계, 친근한 관계, 성별을 알고 있는 경우 she/he로 지시한다.

예

- While still an infant, <u>she</u> is betrothed to the also-young Prince Phillip. (아직 아기였을 때, 그녀는 역시 어린 필립 왕자와 약혼했다.) (betroth to : 약혼시키다)
- Even as a child <u>she</u> had displayed an unusually quick mind. (그녀는 어렸을 때도 비범한 총명함을 보였다.)

제2절　애완동물, 나라, 배

1 (애완)동물

동물은 일반적으로 성을 고려하지 않는 it을 사용하는데, 특정 동물은 여성은 she로, 남성은 he로 지시한다.

(1) it 또는 남성 he로 지시하는 경우

> dog, bull(황소), boar(수퇘지), cock(수탉) 등

예 Every dog has <u>its/his</u> day. (속담 : 쥐구멍에도 볕 들 날이 있다.)

(2) it 또는 여성 she로 지시하는 경우

> cat, cow(암소), sow(암퇘지), hen(암탉) 등

예 The cat stalked <u>her</u> prey. (그 고양이는 먹이에 살그머니 다가갔다.) (stalk : 사냥감 등에 몰래 다가가다, 접근하다 / prey : 먹이)

2 나라(국가명)

국가명은 지리적인 측면을 지시하는 경우 it으로, 이 외에 정치 · 경제 · 사회 · 문화적 내용에 대한 지시이면 여성형 she로 표현한다.

(1) 지리적 정보 지시 it

　예 Korea is a peninsula in East Asia. Its western border is formed by the Yellow Sea, while its eastern border is defined by the East Sea. (한국은 동아시아에 있는 반도 국가이다. 서쪽으로는 황해(서해), 동쪽으로는 동해와 접한다.)

(2) 정치 · 경제 · 사회 · 문화적 정보 지시 she

　예 Korea is currently proud of her great cultural power. (한국은 현재 엄청난 문화적 힘을 자랑스러워하고 있습니다.)

3 배(boat, ship)

사물을 의인화(personification)하는 경우 boat, ship과 같은 배는 남성(형) 이름을 갖고 있더라도 여성형(she)으로 표현한다.

예 On October 4, 2010 Queen Elizabeth was formally handed over to Cunard. She sailed on her maiden voyage from Southampton on October 12, 2010. (2010년 10월 4일, Queen Elizabeth호는 쿠나드에게 공식적으로 넘겨졌다. 그 배는(Queen Elizabeth호)는 2010년 10월 12일 사우샘프턴에서 첫 항해를 떠났다.)

제3절　집합명사

1 집합명사 용법

집합명사(collective nouns)는 동질의 종류를 하나의 '집합' 또는 '집단'으로 다루는 명사를 말한다. 그 집단이 단일체를 지시하면 단수형 대명사로, 개별 구성원의 합, 즉 군집을 지시하면 복수형 대명사로 표현한다.

(1) 단일체를 지시하는 경우(a single impersonal unit)

일반적으로 단수 형태로 사용되어 부정관사(a/an)와 단수동사가 사용되지만, 복수 형태도 가능하여 복수동사가 사용되기도 한다.

[예]

- Her family is large. It is composed of seven members. (그녀의 가족은 대가족이다. 7명으로 구성되어 있다.)
- Today, seven families live on the island. (현재 일곱 가족이 그 섬에 거주한다.)
- The committee consists of scientists and engineers. (그 위원회는 과학자들과 기술자들로 구성되어 있다.)
- In practice, the four committees work in parallel. (실제로 네 위원회는 병행해서 활동한다.)

(2) 개별 구성원의 합, 즉 군집을 지시하는 경우(a collection of various individuals)

단수 형태이지만 복수 취급하여 복수동사가 사용된다. 이러한 명사를 군집명사 또는 중다명사(noun of multitude)라고 한다.

[예]

- Her family are (all) supportive. They are always ready to help her. (그녀의 가족은 (모두) 그녀를 지지한다. 항상 그녀를 도울 준비가 되어 있다.)
- The committee were all satisfied by the decision. (그 위원회는 모두 결정에 만족했다.)

2 집합명사 종류

집합명사에는 정관사 the와 함께 사용되어 계층 또는 계급의 의미로 복수 취급하는 'POLICE 유형', the를 사용하지 않고 단수 형태이지만 집단의 의미로 복수 취급하는 'CATTLE 유형', 단수·복수 취급이 모두 가능한 'FAMILY, PUBLIC, FRUIT, GOVERNMENT 유형', 물질명사를 지시하는 'FURNITURE 유형'이 있다.

유형	종류	단수/복수 취급
POLICE	(the +) the police, the clergy(목회자), the gentry(신사), the aristocracy(귀족), the nobility(귀족), the peasantry(농민), the press(언론), the elite, the management(경영진), the intelligentsia(지식인), the prosecution(검찰측), the defense(피고측)	복수 (군집명사)
CATTLE	cattle(소떼), people(사람), livestock(가축), fish(물고기), vermin(해충), poultry(가금류)	복수 (군집명사)

FAMILY	family, committee, audience, nation, army, team, class, staff, group, jury(배심원), people(민족), party(정당)	단수, 복수(군집명사)
PUBLIC	public, enemy	단수, 복수
FRUIT	fruit, vegetable	단수, 복수
GOVERNMENT	government	단수, 복수 [미국영어(AmE) : 단수, 영국영어(BrE) : 복수]
FURNITURE	(a piece of, an article of, much, some, little 등 양으로 표시) furniture, clothing(의류), machinery(기계장치), produce(농산물, 수확물), game(사냥감), baggage(수하물), merchandise(상품, 물품)	단수 (a/an 사용 X)

예

- The police were able to capture the robber and free the hostages. (경찰은 도둑을 체포하고, 인질들을 풀어줄 수 있었다.)
- Cattle are grazing in the pasture. (소(떼)가 목장에서 풀을 뜯고 있다.)
- The public is harshly affected during economic downturns. (경기 불황 때 대중은 상당한 타격을 받는 다.) [downturn : (단수형) (경기) 하강, 침체, (물가) 하락 ↔ upturn : 상승(세)]
- The public are entitled to know what happened. (대중들은 무슨 일이 일어났는지 알 권리가 있다.)
- The furniture is in suit with the room. (그 가구는 방에 잘 어울린다.) (in suit with : 일치하는, 조화되 는 ↔ out of suit with : 일치하지 않는)

3 집단을 집합으로 표현하기

사람, 동물, 사물을 집단(group)으로 표현하는 경우 '단위'를 사용하여 복수 취급한다.

사람	• a crowd of people(한 무리의 사람들) • a group of tourists(한 무리의 관광객들) • a choir of singers(성가대) • a class of the English department(영문학과 한 반) • a team of admin officials(행정부서 한 팀) • a band of musicians(음악가 한 팀) • a company of choreographers(안무가 한 팀) • a panel of legal consultants(법률 자문단 한 팀) • an army of soldiers(한 부대 군인들) • a crew of sailors(한 무리의 선원들) • a gang of thieves(한 패의 도둑들)

동물	• a pack of dogs(한 무리의 개들) • a litter of puppies(한 배의 강아지들) • a brood of chickens(한 배의 병아리들) • a flock of birds(한 떼의 새들) • a school of fish(한 떼의 물고기들) • a catch of fish(한 번에 잡은 물고기들) • a swarm of bees(한 떼의 벌들) • a drove of sheep(한 무리의 양들) • a pride of lions(한 무리의 사자들) • a herd of cattle(한 무리의 소들) • a troop of monkeys(한 무리의 원숭이들) • a pod of dolphins(한 무리의 돌고래들) • a gaggle of geese(한 무리의 거위들)
사물	• a series of books/articles(한 시리즈의 책들/기사들) • a set of tools(한 벌의 도구들) • a bouquet of flowers(한 다발의 꽃) • a bunch of flowers/bananas/keys(한 묶음의 꽃/바나나/열쇠들) • a cluster of grapes(한 송이의 포도) • a deck of cards(한 벌의 카드) • a fleet of vehicles/ships(한 무리의 차량들/배들) • a suite of furniture/rooms(한 벌의 가구/스위트룸) • a pile of dishes(한 더미의 접시들) • a heap of toys(한 무더기의 장난감들) • a stack of boxes(한 더미의 상자들)

제4절 탈 것

사물을 의인화하는 경우 car, train, airplane, locomotive 등과 같은 탈 것은 여성형(she)으로 표현한다.
예 Whose car is that? <u>She</u> is a beauty. (저건 누구 차예요? 멋지군요.)

제4장	시제의 일치

주절(matrix clause, main clause, independent clause)과 종속절(subordinate clause, dependent clause)로 이루어진 복문(complex sentence)에서 주절의 시제와 종속절의 시제를 일치시키는 것을 '시제의 일치'라고 한다.

제1절	시제의 일치

주절	종속절
현재, 현재완료, 미래	모든 시제 가능
과거, 과거완료	현재 → 과거 현재완료, 과거 → 과거완료

(1) 주절 동사의 시제가 현재, 현재완료, 미래이면 종속절 동사의 시제에 대한 제약은 없다.

예

• She tells me that he is/was/has been/will be generous.

• She will tell me that he is/was/has been/will be generous.

(2) 주절 동사의 시제가 과거 또는 과거완료이면 종속절 동사의 시제의 경우 현재는 과거로, 현재완료 또는 과거는 과거완료로 쓴다.

예

• She told me that she was a detective.

• She told me that she had been a detective.

• She had told me that nothing fazed her before. (faze : 당황하게 하다)

• She had told me that nothing had fazed her before.

제2절 시제 일치의 예외

1 현재의 사실, 습관 : 현재시제

[예]

- He told me that he always commutes on foot.
- He told me that his lecture begins at 9 a.m. all the year around.

2 속담, 격언 : 현재시제

[예]

- He told me that time is money.
- He told me that the early bird catches the worm.

3 불변의 진리, 보편적인 사실 : 현재시제

[예]

- He told me that the sun rises in the east and sets in the west.
- It was reported that folic acid is good for one's health. (folic acid : 엽산)

4 역사적 사실 : 과거시제

[예]

- He told me that Sejong the Great was born in 1397.
- He told me that the Civil War broke out in 1861. (the Civil War : 미국 남북전쟁)

5 미래시제를 대신하는 현재시제(시간, 조건의 부사절)

[예]

- Dinner will be ready by the time you get home.
- As long as the earth remains, day and night will never cease.

6 **가정법 구문(종속절의 가정법 형식은 주절의 시제와 무관)**

예

- He wishes/wished he were a mathematical genius.
- He says/said that he would be happy if he were rich.

7 **시간 비교 구문**

예

- The Arctic is less cold today than it was 100 years ago. (the Arctic : 북극)
- He is not as young as he was 30 years ago. (그는 30년 전만큼 젊지 않다.)

8 **과거의 일이 현재 또는 미래에까지 지속되는 경우**

예

- He told me that the new bridge in this river is still under construction. (under construction, in the course of construction : 공사 중)
- He told me that his case is still under investigation. (under investigation, in the course of investigation : 조사 중)

9 **조동사 must(추측), need, need not, ought to, had better, would rather 등은 종속절에 그대로 사용**

예

- He told me that she must go home at once.
- He told me that she must be tired.

제11편 실전예상문제

01 다음 중 빈칸에 들어갈 가장 알맞은 표현은?

> Not only I but also she ＿＿＿ very fast.

① be

② is

③ am

④ are

해설
'not only A but (also) B'는 B에 수 일치하므로 is가 들어가는 것이 가장 적절하다.

해석
나뿐만 아니라 그녀도 매우 빠르다.

정답 ②

02 다음 중 빈칸에 들어갈 가장 알맞은 표현은?

> I as well as you ＿＿＿ interested in nature.

① be

② is

③ am

④ are

해설
'B as well as A'는 B에 수 일치하므로 am이 들어가는 것이 가장 적절하다.

해석
너뿐만 아니라 나도 자연에 관심이 있다.

정답 ③

03 다음 중 빈칸에 들어갈 가장 알맞은 표현은?

> Neither hair dryers nor dyeing _____ recommended.

① be

② is

③ are

④ were

해설

'neither A nor B'는 B에 수 일치하므로 is가 들어가는 것이 가장 적절하다.

해석

헤어드라이어와 염색은 (모두) 권장되지 않는다.

정답 ②

04 다음 중 어법상 잘못된 표현은?

① A pair of glasses is on sale.

② Aerobics is typically practiced to music.

③ Our state health statistics are doing better.

④ The Netherlands are a peaceful country.

해설

복수 형태의 국가명은 단수 취급한다(④ are → is).

① 'a pair of, pairs of' 표현과 함께 쓰이면 pair에 수 일치한다.

② 순수 상시 복수는 일반적으로 복수 취급하나 'aerobics, news'는 단수 취급한다.

③ statistics가 '통계학'이 아닌 '통계수치/지표'를 표현하는 경우 복수 취급한다.

해석

① 안경이 판매 중이다.

② 에어로빅은 보통 음악에 맞춰 연습한다.

③ 우리 주의 건강 지표들은 훨씬 더 나아졌다.

④ 네덜란드는 평화로운 나라이다.

정답 ④

05 다음 중 어법상 잘못된 표현은?

① Three times five is fifteen.

② Four hours of sleep is not enough.

③ 1,000 dollars is too much to pay.

④ In Europe 100 miles are a long way; in America 100 years are a long time.

해설
단일 개념의 시간, 거리, 가격, 중량은 단수 취급한다(④ are → is).

해석
① 3 곱하기 5는 15이다.
② 4시간의 잠은 충분하지 않다.
③ 1,000달러는 지불하기에는 너무 많다.
④ 유럽에서 100마일은 먼 길이고, 미국에서 100년은 긴 시간이다.

정답 ④

06 다음 중 빈칸에 들어갈 가장 알맞은 표현은?

> Every student _____ what matters and what is required to be successful.

① know

② knows

③ have known

④ is knowing

해설
'every, each, no one, another, either, neither'가 주어가 되거나 주어를 수식하는 경우 단수 취급한다.

해석
모든 학생들은 무엇이 중요한지, 성공하기 위해서 무엇이 필요한지 알고 있다.

정답 ②

07 다음 중 빈칸에 들어갈 가장 알맞은 표현은?

> Each of those explanations _____ a likely bit and an unlikely bit.

① have

② has

③ have had

④ is having

해설

'each (of) 표현'은 단수 취급하므로 has가 들어가는 것이 가장 적절하다

해석

각각의 설명에는 가능성이 있는 부분과 그렇지 않은 부분들이 있다.

정답 ②

08 다음 중 빈칸에 들어갈 가장 알맞은 표현은?

> Each girl and boy in the tenth-grade class _____ to do a math project.

① have

② has

③ have had

④ are having

해설

'each A and B'는 단수 취급한다.

해석

10학년 반의 각각의 여학생과 남학생은 수학 프로젝트를 수행해야 한다.

정답 ②

09 다음 중 어법상 잘못된 표현은?

① No female and male student fails the exam.

② Everything in the store is on sale.

③ All that ends well is well.

④ Enough is here to make a quorum.

해설

'all, enough 사람 지시'는 복수 취급한다(④ is → are).

① 'every, each, no' 뒤에 두 개의 명사가 와도 단수 취급한다.

② '-one, -body, -thing'이 주어가 되거나 주어를 수식하는 경우 단수 취급한다.

③ 'all, enough 사물 지시'는 단수 취급한다. (= All is well that ends well.)

해석

① 시험에 실패한 여학생과 남학생은 아무도 없다.

② 가게에 있는 것은 모두 팔 물건입니다.

③ 끝이 좋으면 만사가 좋다.

④ 정족수를 이루기에 충분하다.

정답 ④

10 다음 중 빈칸에 들어갈 가장 알맞은 표현은?

> Josh is now working as ＿＿＿ on Broadway.
> (Josh는 현재 브로드웨이에서 극작가 겸 감독으로 일하고 있다.)

① playwright and director

② a playwright and a director

③ a playwright and director

④ playwrights and directors

해설

관사가 한 번만 사용되는 경우 '동일인'을 표현하므로 단수 취급한다.

정답 ③

11 다음 중 빈칸에 들어갈 가장 알맞은 표현은?

> Two thirds of Americans _____ 5 to 25 online sites per day.

① view

② views

③ has viewed

④ is viewing

해설
분수 표현과 같이 부분을 나타내는 표현이 주어인 경우 of 뒤에 나오는 명사에 수 일치한다.

해석
미국인의 3분의 2는 하루에 5~25개의 온라인 사이트를 본다.

정답 ①

12 다음 중 어법상 <u>잘못된</u> 표현은?

① Some of the books are quite good.

② 30 percent of the company's revenue is allocated to taxes.

③ Most of Norway is covered with mountains.

④ All of the major car makers is upgrading their product line.

해설
부분을 나타내는 표현이 주어인 경우 of 뒤에 나오는 명사에 수 일치한다(④ is → are).

해석
① 그 책들 중 몇 권은 꽤 좋다.
② 회사 수입의 30%는 조세로 납부되고 있다.
③ 노르웨이의 대부분은 산으로 덮여 있다.
④ 모든 주요 자동차 제조사들은 생산 라인을 업그레이드하고 있다.

정답 ④

13 다음 중 어법상 <u>잘못된</u> 표현은?

① Many a pickle makes a mickle.

② A black and a white dog are following him.

③ He admits that it is obvious that trial and error work.

④ The number of drivers using the service is expected to increase.

> **해설**
> 개념상 하나의 개념을 의미하는 경우 단수 취급한다(③ work → works).
> ① 'Many a + 단수명사'는 단수 취급한다.
> ② '관사 + A and 관사 + B'는 복수 취급한다.
> ④ 'the number of + 복수명사'는 단수 취급한다.

> **해석**
> ① 티끌 모아 태산
> ② 검은 개 한 마리와 하얀 개 한 마리가 그를 따라오고 있다.
> ③ 그는 시행착오가 효과가 있다는 것이 명백하다는 것을 인정한다.
> ④ 그 서비스를 이용하는 운전자들의 수는 늘어날 것으로 전망된다.

> **정답** ③

14 다음 중 어법상 <u>잘못된</u> 표현은?

① Hound dog bays its quarry.

② The jet-black cat and her two kittens are in a basket.

③ Korea is a peninsula in East Asia. Its western border is formed by the Yellow Sea.

④ Korea is currently proud of its great cultural power.

> **해설**
> ①·② 동물은 일반적으로 성을 고려하지 않는 it을 사용하는데, 특정 동물은 여성은 she로, 남성은 he로 지시한다.
> ③·④ 국가명은 지리적인 측면을 지시하는 경우 it으로, 이 외에 정치·경제·사회·문화적 내용에 대한 지시이면 여성형 she로 표현한다(④ its → her).

> **해석**
> ① 사냥개가 짐승을 몰아세운다.
> ② 새까만 고양이와 그 고양이의 새끼 고양이가 두 마리가 바구니에 있다.
> ③ 한국은 동아시아에 있는 반도 국가이다. 서쪽으로는 황해(서해)와 접한다.
> ④ 한국은 현재 엄청난 문화적 힘을 자랑스러워하고 있다.

> **정답** ④

15 다음 중 어법상 가장 적절하지 <u>않은</u> 것은?

① Her family is large. It is composed of seven members.

② The furniture is in suit with the room.

③ The police were able to capture the robber and free the hostages.

④ Cattle is grazing in the pasture.

해설

집합명사(군집명사) cattle은 복수 취급한다(④ is → are).

① 단일체를 지시하는 경우 단수 취급한다.

② FURNITURE 유형의 집합명사는 단수 취급한다.

③ 집합명사(군집명사) the police는 복수 취급한다.

해석

① 그녀의 가족은 대가족이다. 7명으로 구성되어 있다.

② 그 가구는 방에 잘 어울린다.

③ 경찰은 도둑을 체포하고, 인질들을 풀어줄 수 있었다.

④ 소(떼)가 목장에서 풀을 뜯고 있다.

정답 ④

추록 V | 제12편 태(Voice)

| 단원 개요 |

영어에서 태(voice)란 문장에서 누가, 무엇이 주어 역할을 하느냐와 관련이 있는 문법적 특성이다. 구문적으로는 동사가 주어의 동작을 나타내면서 주어–동사–목적어로 표현되면 능동태(active voice)이다. 한편, 능동태의 목적어가 주어로, 동사는 'be + V-ed/V-en(p.p.)' 형태로, 능동태의 주어가 'by + 명사구'로 표현되면 수동태(passive voice)이다. 의미적으로는 동사가 표현하는 주어와 목적어의 관계에 있어서 문장의 주어 위치에 동사의 동작을 수행하는 행동주(agent) 또는 행위자(doer)가 오면 능동태이고, 주어의 자리에 피동주(patient) 또는 경험자(experiencer or undergoer)가 오고 동작의 주체인 행동주나 행위자가 by 전치사구에 오면 수동태이다.

| 출제 경향 및 수험 대책 |

1. 수동태로의 전환
   (1) 단순, 진행, 완료시제의 be + V-ed
   (2) get + V-ed 특성
   (3) 동사구, 목적어, 의문문/명령문의 수동태 처리
2. 주의해야 할 수동태 구문
   (1) 상태 수동태 종류
   (2) 수동태 전환이 불가능한 경우
   (3) 형용사적 과거분사 유형
   (4) 능동 수동태(중간태)

제1장 수동태로의 전환

제1절 be + V-ed

1 능동태/수동태 전환 방법

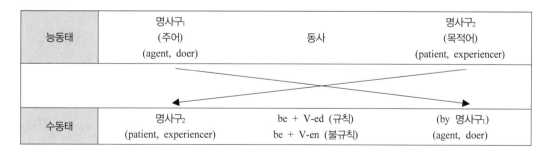

능동태	명사구₁ (주어) (agent, doer)	동사	명사구₂ (목적어) (patient, experiencer)
수동태	명사구₂ (patient, experiencer)	be + V-ed (규칙) be + V-en (불규칙)	(by 명사구₁) (agent, doer)

2 단순(simple)시제 수동태

시간	능동태			수동태			
현재	Josh	helps	Amy.	Amy	is	helped	by Josh.
과거	Josh	helped	Amy.	Amy	was	helped	by Josh.
미래	Josh	will help	Amy.	Amy	will be	helped	by Josh.

3 진행형(progressive)시제 수동태

시간	능동태			수동태			
현재	Josh	is helping	Amy.	Amy	is being	helped	by Josh.
과거	Josh	was helping	Amy.	Amy	was being	helped	by Josh.
미래	Josh	will be helping	Amy.	Amy	will be being	helped	by Josh.

4 완료형(perfect)시제 수동태

시간	능동태			수동태			
현재	Josh	has helped	Amy.	Amy	has been	helped	by Josh.
과거	Josh	had helped	Amy.	Amy	had been	helped	by Josh.
미래	Josh	will have helped	Amy.	Amy	will have been	helped	by Josh.

※ 현재, 과거, 미래 완료 진행형(perfect progressive)시제의 수동태 사용은 매우 드물다.

5 조동사 수동태

시간	능동태			수동태			
현재	Josh	will help	Amy.	Amy	will be	helped	by Josh.
	Josh	is going to help	Amy.	Amy	is going to be	helped	by Josh.
	Josh	can help	Amy.	Amy	can be	helped	by Josh.
과거	Josh	should have helped	Amy.	Amy	should have been	helped	by Josh.
	Josh	could have helped	Amy.	Amy	could have been	helped	by Josh.
	Josh	must have helped	Amy.	Amy	must have been	helped	by Josh.

제2절 get + V-ed

일반적인 수동태 구문의 'be + V-ed(p.p.)' 형태 외에 'get + V-ed(p.p.)' 형태가 있다.

1 동작이나 상태의 변화(idea of change)

'get + V-ed(p.p.) 수동태 구문'은 비격식체 영어에서 (순간적, 우연한) 동작이나 상태의 변화(the idea of becoming)를 의미하고, 과거분사는 형용사 역할을 하는데 주로 다음 표현들이 사용된다.

• get accepted (for/into)	• get dressed (in)	• get invited (to)
• get accustomed to	• get drunk (on)	• get involved (in/with)
• get acquainted (with)	• get elected (to)	• get killed (by/with)
• get arrested (for)	• get engaged (to)	• get lost (in)
• get bored (with)	• get excited (about)	• get married (to)
• get confused (about)	• get finished (with)	• get prepared (for)
• get crowded (with)	• get fixed (by)	• get scared (of)
• get divorced (from)	• get hurt (by)	• get sunburned
• get done (with)	• get interested (in)	• get worried (about)

예
- He got accustomed to living in a big city. (그는 대도시에 사는 것에 익숙해졌다.)
- She got elected to the National Assembly Speaker. (그녀는 국회의장에 선출되었다.)

2 능동적인 의미

'be + V-ed'의 수동태보다는 상대적으로 주어의 행동(action onto itself)에 능동적인 의미를 지닌다. 행동이 동반되어 완전한 상태동사와는 사용할 수 없다.

예
- She was invited to the party.
- She got herself invited to the party.
- *He got loved.
- *He got known.

제3절   동사구의 처리

1 동사 + 전치사

'동사 + 전치사' 형태의 구동사(phrasal verb)구는 수동태 구문에서 하나의 구성단위 타동사로 사용된다.
예
- He was brought up to a career for an entrepreneur. (그는 사업가가 되기 위한 교육을 받았다.)
- The outdoor games were called off due to the weather. (실외 경기는 날씨 때문에 취소되었다.)

2 동사 + 명사 + 전치사구(전치사 + 명사)

'동사 + 명사 + 전치사구(전치사 + 명사)' 형태의 수동태 구문에서 주어는 ⅰ) 명사가 주어 역할(격식체)을 하거나, ⅱ) 전치사구의 명사가 주어 역할(비격식체)을 한다.
예 He caught sight of something on the floor at his feet.
 ⅰ) Sight of something on the floor at his feet was caught by him.
 ⅱ) Something on the floor at his feet was caught sight of by him.
 (catch sight of : ~을 발견하다, 힐끔 쳐다보다)

3 원형부정사 수반 동사 : 지각동사, 사역동사

지각동사, 사역동사에 수반되는 원형부정사는 수동태 구문에서 'to + 부정사' 구문으로 표현된다.
예
- The phone call was heard to ring. (전화벨이 울리는 소리가 들렸다.)
- She was seen to go out of her office. (그녀가 사무실 밖으로 나가는 것이 보였다.)

제4절   목적어의 처리

1 4형식 수동태

간접목적어와 직접목적어가 있는 4형식 이중타동사(ditransitive verb) 또는 수여동사(dative verb)의 수동태 구문은 다음과 같다.

(1) 능동태(4형식)

주어 + 수여동사 + 간접목적어 + 직접목적어

(2) 수동태(3형식)

ⅰ) '간접목적어 + be V-ed/V-en + 직접목적어 + by 전치사구' 또는 ⅱ) '직접목적어 + be V-ed/V-en + <u>to/for/of</u> + 간접목적어 + by 전치사구'로 표현된다.

예

- They gave him a $400 certificate.
  ⅰ) He was given a $400 certificate by them.
  ⅱ) A $400 certificate was given to him by them.
- The professor recommended him the online dictionary.
  ⅰ) He was recommended the online dictionary by the professor.
  ⅱ) The online dictionary was recommended to him by the professor.

2 목적어가 that절

that절, if절, whether절이 목적어로 표현되면 절 전체가 수동태의 주어가 되지 못하므로 ⅰ) 가주어 it을 사용하거나 ⅱ) 'say, think, believe, expect, consider, assume, understand, suppose, know, feel, report, declare, see' 등의 동사는 'to + 부정사구'로 전환한 후 의미상의 주어만 문두로 이동시킨다.

ⅰ)의 경우
예 He says that it was his first major role on screen.
  → It is said that it was his first major role on screen.

ⅱ)의 경우
예 They expect that he will pass the bar exam. (bar exam : 변호사 시험)
  → It is expected that he will pass the bar exam.
  → He is expected to pass the bar exam.

제5절   의문문/명령문의 처리

1 의문문

(1) 의문사가 주어인 경우

　　예 능동태 : Who ate the cake?

　　　→ 수동태 : By whom was the cake eaten?

(2) 의문사가 목적어인 경우

　　예 능동태 : What did he eat last night?

　　　→ 수동태 : What was eaten last night by him?

2 명령문

(1) 긍정형 수동태

　　Let + 목적어 + be V-ed/V-en

　　예 능동태 : Complete it right now!

　　　→ 수동태 : Let it be completed right now!

(2) 부정형 수동태

　　ⅰ) 'Don't let + 목적어 + be V-ed/V-en' 또는 ⅱ) 'Let + 목적어 + not + be V-ed/V-en'으로 표현된다.

　　예 능동태 : Don't touch it!

　　　→ 수동태

　　　　ⅰ) Don't let it be touched!

　　　　ⅱ) Let it not be touched!

제2장   수동태의 유의사항

제1절   동작 수동태와 상태 수동태

1 동작 수동태

동작을 표현하는 의미가 서로 상응하는 능동태 구문과 수동태 구문에 나타나고, 수동태 구문에서는 동작의 행동주 또는 행위자가 전치사구인 'by + N(명사구)' 형태로 표현된다.

능동태	They paint their house every three years. (그들은 집을 3년마다 칠한다.)
↕	
수동태	Their house is painted every three years by them. (그들의 집은 3년마다 칠해진다.)

2 상태 수동태(비진행형 수동태)

상황(situation)이나 상태(state)를 표현하는 수동태 구문을 '상태 수동태' 또는 동작을 표현하는 진행형으로 표현되지 않아 '비진행형 수동태'(non-progressive passive)라고 한다. 일반적으로 상응하는 능동태 구문이 있지 않은 경우가 많고, 수동태 구문에서 행동주 또는 행위자를 표현하는 전치사구인 'by + N(명사구)'에서 전치사 by가 아닌 다른 전치사를 사용하는데, 이때 과거분사는 형용사 역할을 한다.

be concerned be excited be worried	+ about	be accustomed be addicted be committed	
be discriminated	+ against	be connected be dedicated be devoted(헌신하는, 열심인) be engaged(약혼한)	+ to
be known be prepared be qualified be remembered be well known	+ for	be exposed be limited be married be opposed be related	

be divorced be exhausted be gone be protected	+ from	be acquainted be associated be cluttered(어질러진) be crowded be done be equipped(갖추어진) be filled be finished be pleased be provided be satisfied	+ with
be dressed be interested be located	+ in		
be disappointed be involved	+ in/with		
be composed be made be tired	+ of	be annoyed be bored be covered	+ with/by
be frightened be scared be terrified	+ of/by		

예

- He was concerned about the intensity of the training. (그는 훈련의 강도에 대해 걱정했다.)
- He is qualified for teaching English. (그는 영어를 가르칠 자격이 있다.)

제2절 수동태 전환이 불가능한 경우

1 자동사

수동태 구문의 주어는 능동태 구문의 목적어와 상응하기 때문에 자동사는 수동태가 불가능하다.

예

- She disappeared.
  - → *She was disappeared.
- Something happened.
  - → *Something was happened.

※ 단, 자동사가 전치사와 함께 쓰이는 구동사 형태는 '자동사 + 전치사'가 함께 수동태 구문에 사용된다.

예

- The man was laughed at by his colleagues.
- Flowers are looked at by people.
- The game was put off by the plate umpire. (plate umpire : 야구의 주심 / base umpire : 누심)

2 상태동사(능동의 의미가 약한 동사)

수동태 구문의 주어는 행동주 또는 행위자에 의해 동작의 행위를 받는 피동주 또는 경험자이기 때문에 동사의 행위가 행위자에 의해 가해져야 한다. 따라서 동사의 행위가 주어의 의지와 상관없이 가해지는 '인식, 소유, 감정, 지각, 상태' 등을 표현하는 상태동사들의 경우 수동태 구문이 불가능하다.

(1) 상태

> be, seem, appear, resemble, consist, exist 등

예

- *He was appeared to hesitate by us.
- *She was resembled by her daughter.

(2) 지각

> feel, see, hear, smell, taste, sound, notice, observe 등

예

- *The cake was tasted delicious by me.
- *The news was heard by us.

(3) 감정

> like, love, hate, need, want, desire, envy, forgive 등

예

- *This book is liked by me.
- *That sports car was wanted by him.

(4) 소유

> have, belong, own, possess 등

예

- *The house is had by her.
- *This building was belonged by them.

(5) 인식

> think, believe, know, understand, recognize, forget 등

〔예〕
- *The police are known by us.
- *The committee were recognized by them.

(6) 그 외

> cost, fit, meet, suffice, lack, suit(잘 맞다), become(어울리다) 등

〔예〕
- *That dress was cost $3,000 by them.
- *Your sister was become by that dress.

3 수동태의 주어가 되지 못하는 목적어

(1) 부정사와 동명사

〔예〕
- I hope to go to Brisbane this winter.
  → *To go to Brisbane this winter is hoped by me.
- They enjoy living in Seoul.
  → *Living in Seoul is enjoyed by them.

(2) 재귀대명사

〔예〕 She described herself as the biggest fan of BTS in the whole world.
  → *Herself was described as the biggest fan of BTS in the whole world by her.

(3) 상호대명사

〔예〕 They liked each other.
  → *Each other was liked by them.

(4) 주어 (자신의) 신체 일부

예 All employees wash their hands thoroughly before preparing for food. (모든 직원은 음식을 준비하기 전에 손을 철저히 씻는다.)

→ *Their hands are washed thoroughly by all employees before preparing for food.

※ 단, 주어 자신의 신체가 아닌 경우에는 수동태 전환이 가능하다.

예 She seized his arm.

→ His arm was seized by her.

제3절 형용사적 과거분사

기쁨, 놀람, 실망, 관심 등 감정의 변화가 수동태 구문으로 표현되는 경우 과거분사는 형용사적 성격을 갖는데, 이때 과거분사는 부사의 수식을 받거나 다른 형용사와 접속사로 연결이 가능하다.

1 부사 수식

형용사 역할을 하는 과거분사는 very, quite, rather 등의 부사의 수식을 받는다.

예
• The president was very interested in your idea.
• He was quite surprised at the dramatic result.

2 형용사와 접속사

예
• He was amused and mildly flattered. (그는 즐거워했고 약간 우쭐해했다.)
• He was annoyed and irritated. (그는 짜증나고 화가 났다.)

제4절 **능동 수동태 또는 중간태 동사**

주어의 의미는 수동태 구문의 피동주 또는 경험자, 동사의 형태는 능동태 구문의 형태를 하는 것을 영어에서 '능동 수동태' 또는 '중간태'(middle voice)라고 한다. 능동태와 수동태가 동작(action)을 강조하는 반면, 중간태는 사건의 발생(happening)을 강조한다. 이러한 중간태 동사에는 중간동사(middle verb)와 능동격 동사(ergative verb)가 있고, 능동격 동사는 타동사와 자동사의 쌍이 있는 경우(paired)와 자동사만 가능한 경우(unpaired)가 있다.

능동태 (active voice)	명사구₁ (주어) (agent, doer)	동사	명사구₂ (목적어) (patient, experiencer)
예	His high voice	broke	the glass.
수동태 (passive voice)	명사구₂ (patient, experiencer)	be + V-ed (규칙) be + V-en (불규칙)	(by 명사구₁) (agent, doer)
예	The glass	was broken	by his high voice.
중간태 (middle voice)	명사구₂ (patient, experiencer)	능동태 형태 동사	주어 의미 : 수동태 구문 동사 형태 : 능동태 구문
예	The glass	broke.	-

1 중간동사(middle verb)

중간동사는 주어의 특정한(specific) 사건이 아닌 일반적/총칭적인(generic) 특성 또는 고유의 속성을 표현한다. 전치사구인 'by + N(행위자)'과 함께 사용되지 않고, 일반적으로 현재시제가 사용되나 과거시제나 진행형으로 표현되기도 하며, 'easily, well, quickly, smoothly'와 같은 양태부사와 함께 쓰인다.

종류	예문
총칭적 중간동사	That book reads well.
비총칭적 중간동사(과거)	That book sold well.
비총칭적 중간동사(진행형)	That book is selling well.

예

- The linen wrinkles easily. (wrinkle : 주름이 지다, 구겨지다)
- Sports cars sell quickly.

2 능동격 동사(ergative verb, unaccusative verb, change of state verb)

상태의 변화(change of state) 또는 사건을 나타내는 중간태 동사가 능동격 동사이고, 반드시 그렇진 않지만 일반적으로 능동과 수동의 쌍이 있다. (paired ergative의 경우) 전치사구 'by + N(행위자)'과 함께 사용되지만, 부사와 함께 쓰이지 않는다.

(1) 자동사-타동사 쌍을 이루는 능동격 동사(paired ergative)

타동사와 자동사 모두 사용될 수 있는 동사로, 타동사로 사용되는 경우 수동태 구문이 가능하다.

예

- 능동태 (타)동사 : The chef broke the glass.
  → 수동태 : The glass was broken by the chef.
- 능동격 (자)동사 : The glass broke.
  → 능동격 수동태 : *The glass broke by someone. ('by + 행동주'를 허용하지 않음)

① 요리(cooking)

> cook, bake, boil, fry, roast, defrost(해동시키다) 등

예 The chef baked the bread.
  → The bread was baked by the chef.
  → The bread baked.

② 움직임(movement)

> move, spin, turn, rock, shake, swing 등

예 He turned the window.
  → The window was turned by him.
  → The window turned.

③ 탈 것(vehicle)

> drive, park, run, fly, reverse, sail 등

예 He parked the car.
  → The car was parked by him.
  → The car parked.

(2) 자동사-타동사 쌍을 이루지 않는 능동격 동사(unpaired ergative)

자동사로만 사용 가능한 동사로, 수동태 구문은 불가능하다.

① 발생(occurrence)

> happen, occur, take place 등

예
- The two incidents happened in the separate trains. (두 사건은 각각 다른 열차에서 일어났다.)
- The supernova explosion occurred 25 times closer than usual. (초신성 폭발은 보통 때보다 25배나 더 가까이에서 일어났다.)

② 방향성 운동(directed motion)

> arrive, fall, rise, emerge, go 등

예
- New forms of wealth emerged. (새로운 형태의 부가 등장했다.)
- The dough rose too quickly. (밀가루 반죽이 매우 빠르게 부풀었다.)

③ 묘사, 서술(description)

> appear, disappear, vanish 등

예
- Hair gel as consumer goods appeared in the 20th century. (소비재로서의 헤어젤은 20세기에 등장했다.)
- Half of all pine tree forests disappeared. (소나무 숲의 절반이 사라졌다.)

④ 그 외

예
- The game consists of three rounds.
  → *The game is consisted of three rounds.
- After the hard work, he fainted.
- More chloroplasts resulted in a sweeter tomato. (엽록체가 많으면 더 달콤한 토마토가 되었다.)
  (chloroplast : 엽록체)

제12편 실전예상문제

01 다음 중 수동태 구문이 <u>잘못</u> 표현된 것은?

① He helps her. → She is helped by him.

② He is helping her. → She is being helped by him.

③ He has helped her. → She has been helped by him.

④ He will have helped her. → She will be helped by him.

> **해설**
> ④ 미래완료형시제 수동태(→ She will have been helped by him.)
> ① 단순시제 수동태
> ② 진행형시제 수동태
> ③ 현재완료형시제 수동태
> **해석**
> ① 그는 그녀를 돕는다.
> ② 그는 그녀를 돕고 있다.
> ③ 그는 그녀를 도왔다.
> ④ 그는 그녀를 도울 것이다.
> **정답** ④

02 다음 중 빈칸에 공통으로 들어갈 가장 알맞은 표현은?

> • Josh _____ married to Amy last month.
> • Josh _____ accustomed to living in a big city.

① is being

② get

③ got

④ was gotten

> **해설**
> 'get + V-ed(p.p.) 수동태 구문'은 비격식체 영어에서 (순간적, 우연한) 동작이나 상태의 변화를 의미하고, 과거분사는 형용사 역할을 하는데 'by 전치사구'가 아닌 주로 다른 전치사들이 사용된다.
> **해석**
> •Josh는 지난달에 Amy와 결혼했다.
> •Josh는 대도시에 사는 것에 익숙해졌다.
> **정답** ③

03 다음 중 빈칸에 들어갈 가장 알맞은 표현은?

> The outdoor games were called ____ due to the weather.

① up

② on

③ by

④ off

해설

'동사 + 전치사' 형태의 구동사(phrasal verb)구는 수동태 구문에서 하나의 구성단위 타동사로 사용된다.

• call off : 취소하다

• call on : 방문하다, 부탁하다, 요구하다

해석

실외 경기는 날씨 때문에 취소되었다.

정답 ④

04 다음 중 빈칸에 공통으로 들어갈 가장 알맞은 표현은?

> • Josh was heard ____ criticize the plan.
> • Josh was seen ____ go out of his office.

① being

② by

③ to

④ with

해설

지각동사, 사역동사에 수반되는 원형부정사는 수동태 구문에서 'to + 부정사' 구문으로 표현된다.

해석

• Josh는 그 계획을 비판하는 것이 들렸다.

• Josh가 사무실 밖으로 나가는 것이 보였다.

정답 ③

05 다음 중 어법상 가장 적절하지 <u>않은</u> 표현은?

① It is said that it was his first major role on screen.

② It was asked if there were any job openings.

③ It is expected that Josh will pass the bar exam.

④ That he is hilarious is said.

해설

that절, if절, whether절이 목적어로 표현되면 절 전체가 수동태의 주어가 되지 못하므로 ⅰ) 가주어 it을 사용하거나 ⅱ) 'say, think, believe, expect, consider, assume, understand, suppose, know, feel, report, declare, see' 등의 동사는 'to + 부정사구'로 전환한 후 의미상의 주어만 문두로 이동시킨다. 이때 that절이나 'to + 부정사구' 전체가 이동하여 수동태의 주어가 될 수는 없다. 따라서 ④는 'It is said that he is hilarious.' 또는 'He is said to be hilarious.' 로 표현되어야 적절하다.

해석

① 그것은 그가 스크린에서 맡은 첫 주연이었다고 한다.

② 일자리가 있느냐는 질문을 받았다.

③ Josh는 변호사 시험에 합격할 것으로 예상된다.

④ 그는 유쾌하다고 한다.

정답 ④

06 다음 중 어법상 가장 적절하지 <u>않은</u> 표현은?

① He was concerned about the intensity of the training.

② He is well acquainted about the affairs of Korea.

③ He is qualified for teaching English.

④ The Seoul Plaza is covered with green lawns.

해설

상황이나 상태를 표현하는 비진행형 수동태 구문 속 행동주 또는 행위자 표현은 'by + N(명사구)'에서 전치사 by가 아닌 다른 전치사를 사용하고, 과거분사는 형용사 역할을 한다. ②의 경우 be acquainted with를 이용하여 표현한다.

해석

① 그는 훈련의 강도에 대해 걱정했다.

② 그는 한국 사정에 밝다.

③ 그는 영어를 가르칠 자격이 있다.

④ 서울 광장은 푸른 잔디로 덮여 있다.

정답 ②

07 다음 중 어법상 가장 적절한 표현은?

① He was appeared to hesitate by us.

② This building was belonged by them.

③ The watch was cost $30,000 by them.

④ The fortunate event happened.

해설
④의 happen은 자동사여서 수동태가 불가능하므로 적절한 표현이다.
①·②·③ '인식, 소유, 감정, 지각, 상태' 등을 표현하는 상태동사들의 경우 수동태 구문이 불가능하다.

해석
① 우리는 그가 주저하는 것처럼 보였다.
② 그 건물은 그들이 소유하고 있다.
③ 그 시계는 그들에 의해 3만 달러가 들었다.
④ 운이 좋은 일이 일어났다.

정답 ④

08 다음 중 어법상 가장 적절한 표현은?

① To go to Brisbane this winter is hoped by me.

② Living in Seoul is enjoyed by them.

③ His arm was seized by her.

④ Each other was liked by them.

해설
수동태의 주어가 되지 못하는 목적어로는 '부정사, 동명사, 재귀대명사, 상호대명사, 주어의 신체 일부' 등이 있다.
단, 주어 자신의 신체가 아닌 경우에는 수동태 전환이 가능하다.

해석
① 나는 이번 겨울에 브리즈번에 가는 것을 희망한다.
② 그들은 서울에 사는 것을 즐긴다.
③ 그의 팔이 그녀에게 잡혔다.
④ 그들은 서로를 좋아했다.

정답 ③

09 다음 중 수동태 구문에 쓰인 과거분사의 용법이 <u>다른</u> 것은?

① The president was very interested in your idea.

② Josh was quite surprised at the dramatic result.

③ He was amused and mildly flattered.

④ These films were made by the same director.

해설

④의 수동태 구문 속 과거분사는 동작(의 전환)을 의미하는 일반적인 수동태 구문에서 표현된 과거분사이다.
①·②·③의 수동태 구문 속 과거분사는 형용사 역할을 한다. ①과 ②는 형용사처럼 very, quite와 같은 부사의 수식을 받고, ③은 접속사 and로 연결되어 있다.

해석

① 사장님은 당신의 아이디어에 매우 관심이 많으셨다.
② Josh는 극적인 결과에 상당히 놀랐다.
③ 그는 즐거워했고 약간 우쭐해했다.
④ 이 영화들은 같은 감독에 의해 만들어졌다.

정답 ④

10 다음 중 어법상 <u>잘못된</u> 표현은?

① The student broke the window.

② The window was broken by the student.

③ The window broke by the student.

④ The window broke.

해설

중간태 동사인 능동격 동사는 일반적으로 타동사와 자동사 모두 사용 가능한 동사이지만, 타동사로 사용되는 경우에만 수동태 구문이 가능하고, 능동격 자동사의 수동태 구문인 'by + 행동주'를 허용하지 않는다.

해석

① 학생이 창문을 깼다.
② 창문이 학생에 의해 깨졌다.
③ 창문이 학생에 의해 깨졌다.
④ 창문이 깨졌다.

정답 ③

11 다음 중 어법상 <u>잘못된</u> 표현은?

① The two incidents happened in the separate trains.

② New forms of wealth emerged.

③ Half of all pine tree forests disappeared.

④ The game is consisted of three rounds.

해설

능동격 동사 중 unpaired ergative는 자동사로만 사용 가능하고, 수동형은 불가능한 동사이다. 그중 ④의 consist of는 '~로 구성되다'라는 뜻으로, 수동형으로 사용되지 않는다. 따라서 'The game consists of three rounds.'(= The game is composed of three rounds.)로 쓰여야 적절하다.

① '발생'(occurrence)을 나타내는 동사로, 'happen, occur, take place' 등이 있다.

② '방향성 운동'(directed motion)을 나타내는 동사로, 'arrive, fall, rise, emerge, go' 등이 있다.

③ '묘사, 서술'(description)을 나타내는 동사로, 'appear, disappear, vanish' 등이 있다.

해석

① 두 사건은 각각 다른 열차에서 일어났다.

② 새로운 형태의 부가 등장했다.

③ 소나무 숲의 절반이 사라졌다.

④ 경기는 3라운드로 구성되어 있다.

정답 ④

12 다음 중 괄호 안의 단어를 알맞은 형태로 바꾸어 쓴 것은?

> He caught sight of something on the floor at his feet.
> → Sight of something on the floor at his feet (<u>catch</u>   ) by him.

① caught

② was caught

③ has been caught

④ was being caught

해설

'동사 + 명사 + 전치사구(전치사 + 명사)' 형태의 수동태 구문에서 주어는 ⅰ) 명사가 주어 역할(격식체)을 하거나, ⅱ) 전치사구의 명사가 주어 역할(비격식체)을 한다.

ⅰ) Sight of something on the floor at his feet was caught by him.

ⅱ) Something on the floor at his feet was caught sight of by him.

해석

그는 자신의 발밑 바닥에 무언가가 있는 것을 보았다.

정답 ②

13 다음 중 괄호 안의 단어를 알맞은 형태로 바꾸어 쓴 것은?

> We took good care of pending business issues.
> → Pending business issues (take) good care of by us.

① taken

② was taken

③ were taken

④ were being taken

해설

'동사 + 명사 + 전치사구(전치사 + 명사)' 형태의 수동태 구문에서 주어는 ⅰ) 명사가 주어 역할(격식체)을 하거나, ⅱ) 전치사구의 명사가 주어 역할(비격식체)을 한다.

ⅰ) Good care was taken of pending business issues by us.

ⅱ) Pending business issues were taken good care of by us.

해석

우리는 사업 현안을 잘 처리했다. (take good care of : 잘 돌보다, 관리하다 / pending issue : 현안)

정답 ③

14 다음 문장의 수동태 구문으로 가장 적절한 것은?

> My mother made me a sweater.

① My mother was made me a sweater.

② My mother was made a sweater by me.

③ I was made a sweater by my mother.

④ A sweater was made for me by my mother.

해설

4형식(주어 + 수여동사 + 간접목적어 + 직접목적어) 수여동사의 수동태 구문은 ⅰ) '간접목적어 + be V-ed/V-en + 직접목적어 + by 전치사구' 또는 ⅱ) '직접목적어 + be V-ed/V-en + to/for/of + 간접목적어 + by 전치사구' 형태의 3형식 문장으로 표현된다. 단, 'make, pass, write, sing, send, sell' 등의 동사는 수동태가 ⅱ)의 경우뿐이다. 따라서 ③의 'I was made a sweater by my mother.'는 비문이 된다.

해석

어머니께서 내게 스웨터를 만들어 주셨다.

정답 ④

15 다음 문장의 수동태 구문으로 가장 적절한 것은?

> Josh sent Amy a gift.

① Josh was sent Amy a gift.

② Josh was sent a gift to Amy.

③ A gift was sent to Amy by Josh.

④ Amy was sent a gift by Josh.

해설

4형식(주어 + 수여동사 + 간접목적어 + 직접목적어) 수여동사의 수동태 구문은 ⅰ) '간접목적어 + be V-ed/V-en + 직접목적어 + by 전치사구' 또는 ⅱ) '직접목적어 + be V-ed/V-en + to/for/of + 간접목적어 + by 전치사구' 형태의 3형식 문장으로 표현된다. 단, 'make, pass, write, sing, send, sell' 등의 동사는 수동태가 ⅱ)의 경우뿐이다. 따라서 ④의 'Amy was sent a gift by Josh.'는 비문이 된다.

해석

Josh가 Amy에게 선물을 보냈다.

정답 ③

부록

최종모의고사

교육은 우리 자신의 무지를 점차 발견해 가는 과정이다.

– 윌 듀란트 –

합격의 공식 ▶
SD에듀

자격증 · 공무원 · 금융/보험 · 면허증 · 언어/외국어 · 검정고시/독학사 · 기업체/취업
이 시대의 모든 합격! SD에듀에서 합격하세요!
www.youtube.com ➜ SD에듀 ➜ 구독

제한시간: 50분 | 시작 ___시 ___분 − 종료 ___시 ___분

⊡ 정답 및 해설 488p

01 다음 중 밑줄 친 부분이 문장의 주요소가 <u>아닌</u> 것은?

① He came <u>to school</u> on time.

② He went <u>hungry</u>.

③ He loves <u>reading books</u>.

④ He gave <u>her</u> a gift.

02 다음 중 밑줄 친 부분의 성격이 <u>다른</u> 것은?

① Mr. Biden, <u>the president of the United States</u>, will visit Korea.

② She knows the fact <u>that Josh had cookies</u>.

③ The professor, <u>I think</u>, is a living dictionary.

④ The news <u>that she had left</u> was surprising.

03 다음 중 문장의 형식이 <u>다른</u> 것은?

① She saw him crossing the street.

② He had his radio repaired.

③ He asked the students to join the workshop.

④ She requested him an apology.

04 다음 중 어법상 <u>잘못된</u> 표현은?

① He passed the prize to her.

② He made a spaghetti for her.

③ She played a joke on him.

④ She announced us her wedding date.

05 다음 중 어법상 맞는 표현은?

① Statistics is his favorite subject.

② All the cattle is in the prairie.

③ His family are large.

④ We can't live without an air and a water.

06 다음 중 빈칸에 공통으로 들어갈 표현은?

• Seoul is _____ capital of Korea.

• She patted him on _____ shoulder.

• _____ young have ambition.

• They came from _____ same city.

① a   ② the

③ any   ④ some

07 다음 중 어법상 맞는 표현은?

① Almost every of the students like the professor.

② Most of all of the students like the professor.

③ All the students like the professor.

④ All them like the professor.

08 다음 중 밑줄 친 표현의 생략이 가능한 것은?

① He knows the lady <u>whose</u> book was published lately.

② She thanked the gentleman <u>who</u> helped her.

③ The music to <u>which</u> she listened last night was beautiful.

④ The celebrity <u>whom</u> people loved donated to several charities.

09 다음 중 밑줄 친 that의 쓰임이 다른 것은?

① He believes <u>that</u> you are generous.

② There is no doubt <u>that</u> he did something wrong.

③ It is the house <u>that</u> they used to live.

④ <u>That</u> he passed the test was true.

10 다음 중 어법상 잘못된 표현은?

① The money will be used by the charity.

② He is getting used to living in the country.

③ He used to keep a diary when he was a child.

④ The steam engine was used to pumping water.

11 다음 중 어법상 잘못된 표현은?

① She is pleasant to be with.

② He is very difficult to please.

③ It is dangerous for him to swim in the river.

④ He is impossible to master English in a few years.

12 다음 중 어법상 <u>잘못된</u> 표현은?

① His argument was highly problematic.

② The new rule of this game is pretty simple.

③ He studied English very hardly.

④ Nearly 70 percent of students bought that watch.

13 다음 중 빈칸에 들어갈 표현으로 알맞지 <u>않은</u> 것은?

> The battery charges _____ faster and lasts longer than before.

① far

② very

③ much

④ a lot

14 다음 중 빈칸에 들어갈 알맞은 표현은?

> The summer climate of the Sahara Desert is much hotter than that of Antarctica.
> = The summer climate of Antarctica is _____ that of the Sahara Desert.

① almost as hot as

② as hot as

③ not quite as hot as

④ not nearly as hot as

15 다음 중 빈칸에 들어갈 표현이 순서대로 짝지어진 것은?

> • The airport was closed ___㉠___ account of the fog.
> • Owing ___㉡___ his lack of study, he failed the examination.
> • ___㉢___ spite of the genre difference, they make the best duet every time on stage.

	㉠	㉡	㉢
①	for	to	in
②	on	to	in
③	from	of	by
④	on	to	with

16 다음 중 빈칸에 들어갈 표현이 순서대로 짝지어진 것은?

> • ___㉠___ necessary, I can cook dinner for you tonight.
> • We can't do something better ___㉡___ we have change.
> • She wrote down his email address ___㉢___ she forgets it.

	㉠	㉡	㉢
①	as	if	in case
②	as	unless	if
③	if	unless	in case
④	if	in case	as long as

17 다음 중 어법상 잘못된 표현은?

① His plane departs at 8 a.m. tomorrow.

② He waters the yard every day.

③ He is leaving the USA next week.

④ He will give her the gift when she will arrive.

18 다음 중 어법상 <u>잘못된</u> 표현은?

① He was born in 2002.

② When have you met him?

③ The World War I ended in 1918.

④ The bridge was built about ten years ago.

19 다음 중 빈칸에 공통으로 들어갈 표현은?

> • _____ he was 7, the musician had written five symphonies.
> • _____ he finishes writing this book, he will have written over 300 pages.
> • _____ we see that climate change is really bad, your ability to fix it is extremely limited. The carbon gets up there, but the heating effect is delayed.
> • You can't just ask customers what they want and then try to give that to them. _____ you get it built, they'll want something new.

① while

② by the time

③ as soon as

④ since

20 다음 중 빈칸에 들어갈 알맞은 표현은?

> _____ the president in my country, I would change the way schools are run.

① If I am

② If were I

③ Had Been I

④ Were I

21 다음 중 밑줄 친 부분을 가장 잘 표현한 것은?

> <u>But for</u> her timely advice, he could not have passed the bar exam.

① If had not been for
② If were not for
③ Had it not been for
④ Were it not for

22 다음 중 빈칸에 들어갈 알맞은 표현은?

> A : I understood the differential and integral after the math exam.
> B : I wish you _____ earlier than the exam.

① studied it
② could study it
③ had studied it
④ had not studied it

23 다음 중 밑줄 친 부분의 사용이 <u>다른</u> 것은?

① It is very interesting <u>to study</u> a foreign country's history and culture.
② We have got to be in the highest place <u>to recognize</u> how small we are.
③ It is also useful when you want <u>to give</u> a nice gift to the person you love.
④ It helps employees <u>to understand</u> why they are learning certain things.

24 다음 중 어법상 <u>잘못된</u> 표현은?

① The committee consists of scientists and designers.

② Family is a huge influence on younger kids.

③ The audience was all impressed by his performance.

④ The audience was a huge one in the concert.

25 다음 중 '엎지른 우유는 주워 담지 못한다.'라는 표현으로 가장 적절하지 <u>않은</u> 것은?

① There is no point crying over spilt milk.

② It is useless to cry over spilt milk.

③ It is no use crying over spilt milk.

④ It is of no use crying over spilt milk.

26 다음 중 어법상 <u>잘못된</u> 표현은?

① His recklessness came near to causing a disaster.

② People object to building a new factory in their neighborhood.

③ The city government is committed to stabilize property prices.

④ What would be your idea worth spreading for this country?

27 다음 중 어법상 문장을 <u>잘못</u> 옮긴 것은?

① If we speak strictly, tomatoes are vegetables in culinary terms.

→ Strictly speaking, tomatoes are vegetables in culinary terms.

② As it had rained all night, the road was wet.

→ It having rained all night, the road was wet.

③ When he called her, she was eating dinner.

→ He calling her, she was eating dinner.

④ As he was angry at her words, he made no reply.

→ Angry at her words, he made no reply.

28 다음 중 빈칸에 공통으로 들어갈 표현은?

- The gentleman _____ you met is a professor of linguistics.
- The man had a beautiful wife, _____ he loved greatly.

① whose
② whom
③ which
④ of which

29 다음 중 어법상 맞는 표현은?

① The professor, that teaches English 101, is a famous playwright.

② Josh has a cat color is black and white.

③ What he needed most were computers.

④ Air is to man what water is to fish.

30 다음 중 빈칸에 공통으로 들어갈 표현은?

> • This is the same food _____ he had for dinner yesterday.
> • He is absent today, _____ is often the case with him.

① as
② but
③ than
④ what

31 다음 중 빈칸에 들어갈 알맞은 표현은?

> They just quite happily show their masterpiece to _____ wants to look at it.

① whoever
② whomever
③ whatever
④ whichever

32 다음 중 빈칸에 공통으로 들어갈 표현은?

> • Some of these planets are very similar to Earth, so there is a good chance _____ they also contain life.
> • We have also got to be aware _____ experts also make mistakes.

① if
② whether
③ what
④ that

33 다음 중 어법상 맞는 표현은?

① If it's rainy or it's sunny was not important to the climbers.

② Careful determination is required about if human rights were violated or not.

③ People should always be considerate of others, regardless of if they are successful or not.

④ The executive team is considering if to change the name of the company.

34 다음 중 어법상 <u>잘못된</u> 표현은?

① That he won the lottery was apparent.

② The cake was so delicious that they had all at once.

③ Oil leaks can be a serious environmental problem that can threaten marine ecology.

④ Parents have more experience and wisdom, so they know that is best for their children.

35 다음 중 빈칸에 공통으로 들어갈 표현은?

• Crow brains are balanced, in the same proportion _____ chimpanzee brains are.

• According _____ the demand increases, prices go up.

• _____ she grew older, she looks more like her mother.

---

① fear

② lest

③ as

④ as long as

36 다음 중 어법상 <u>잘못된</u> 표현은?

① Nothing is so important as love.

② He is as good a man as ever trod shoe leather.

③ The height of the left tower is twice as tall as that of the right one.

④ The public interest is not always same as the national interest.

37 다음 중 빈칸에 공통으로 들어갈 표현은?

> • One of major contributing factors is _____ higher education level.
> • She likes him all _____ better because of his frankness.
> • A : Who is taller, Jeff or Joey?
>   B : Jeff is _____ taller of the two.

① better

② worse

③ the

④ much

38 다음 중 밑줄 친 부분과 같은 표현은?

> • The A380 will carry <u>as many as</u> 800 passengers on two decks.
> • Some fans paid <u>as much as</u> $400 for a single ticket.

① no more than

② not more than

③ no less than

④ not less than

39 다음 중 빈칸에 공통으로 들어갈 표현은?

> • If you do it enough times, your brain may become accustomed _____ the activity.
> • The EU has committed _____ cutting carbon emissions by 20% by 2030.

① about

② with

③ by

④ to

40 다음 중 어법상 맞는 표현은?

① Any student can not solve this math question.

② Any of them are not for sale.

③ Not just anyone can be a Beefeater.

④ He didn't have some questions about climate change.

제한시간: 50분 | 시작 _____시 _____분 – 종료 _____시 _____분

⏎ 정답 및 해설 497p

01 다음 중 어법상 잘못된 표현은?

① He made his laptop repaired.

② He provided her with a new desk and chair.

③ She reminded him his grandmother.

④ She asked him a favor.

02 다음 중 have의 쓰임이 다른 것은?

① She had her watch stolen in the street.

② He had his homework all done.

③ Everyone has the right to vote.

④ She had him come here at five.

03 다음 중 어법상 잘못된 표현은?

① She resembles her father.

② He is reaching Seoul, Korea.

③ The professor mentioned the power of Korean culture.

④ He entered into the classroom with his mask on.

04 다음 중 빈칸에 공통으로 들어갈 표현은?

> • Please forgive me _____ keeping you waiting.
> • She bought a new car _____ him.

① to

② for

③ of

④ with

05 다음 중 어법상 맞는 표현은?

① She bought new iron.

② He will be a Shakespeare in the future.

③ A milk is made into butter and cheese.

④ Big fire broke out in downtown last night.

06 다음 중 어법상 맞는 표현은?

① England is proud of its playwright Shakespeare.

② He likes his father's car.

③ She is all the beauty.

④ He gathered ears of corn.

07 다음 중 어법상 잘못된 표현은?

① Each of them has own's car.

② Everyone have chances in their life.

③ Neither of the two plans is excellent.

④ Both Laurel and Jeff are all professors.

08 다음 중 빈칸에 공통으로 들어갈 표현은?

> • Knowing is one thing and experience is _____.
> • Would you give me _____ cup of coffee?
> • I don't like this one; give me _____.
> • He has three trees in his garden. One is pine, _____ persimmon tree, and the other white birch.

① other
② the other
③ another
④ others

09 다음 중 빈칸에 공통으로 들어갈 표현은?

> • Health is above wealth; this cannot give us so much happiness as _____.
> • To be, or not to be: _____ is the question.
> • The climate of California is milder than _____ of Minnesota in winter.

① this
② that
③ these
④ those

10 다음 중 어법상 <u>잘못된</u> 표현은?

① Few people prefer to walk around barefoot.
② Much more information was given to him.
③ He corrected quite a few mistakes.
④ Many a pickle make a mickle.

11 다음 중 어법상 <u>잘못된</u> 표현은?

① Unicorns are imaginary animals.

② Electric lights are economic, clean, and give more light than gas.

③ Most people have their own respective goals as New Year's resolutions.

④ Lincoln delivered a historic speech in Gettysburg in 1863.

12 다음 문장을 가장 잘 설명한 표현은?

> It is not so much a hobby as a job.

① It is a hobby as well as a job.

② It is not only a job but also a hobby.

③ It is either a hobby or a job.

④ It is more a job than a hobby.

13 다음 중 어법상 <u>잘못된</u> 표현은?

① He is friendlier than any other students at his school.

② She has never been happier than in her whole life.

③ Jeju Island is more beautiful than all the other islands in the world.

④ No other river in the world is as long as the Nile River.

14 다음 중 빈칸에 들어갈 표현이 순서대로 짝지어진 것은?

> He was born ____㉠____ 32nd Street ____㉡____ New York ____㉢____ 8 p.m. ____㉣____ Tuesday, June 4, 2002.

	㉠	㉡	㉢	㉣
①	on	at	in	at
②	on	in	in	on
③	at	in	at	on
④	in	at	at	in

15 다음 중 어법상 <u>잘못된</u> 표현은?

① Not only you but also she is a close friend of mine.

② Both Laurel and Joey are all wonderful professors.

③ The students as well as the professor is looking for the summer vacation.

④ Such professors as Cindy are rare.

16 다음 중 밑줄 친 as와 의미가 같은 것은?

> <u>As</u> he had no money, he wasn't able to buy a new car.

① He told me the story <u>as</u> we went along.

② <u>As</u> she often lies, he doesn't like her.

③ He became more silent <u>as</u> he grew older.

④ Child <u>as</u> he was, he was very courageous.

17 다음 중 어법상 <u>잘못된</u> 표현은?

① Have you ever been to Africa before?

② He has been knowing her for thirty years.

③ He studied linguistics at Yale for five years.

④ It has been raining a lot for five days.

18 다음 표현을 가장 잘 설명한 것은?

> He was standing under a tree when it began to rain.

① He has been standing since it began to rain.

② He was standing under a tree while it was raining.

③ He stood under a tree before it rained.

④ He stood under a tree after it rained.

19 다음 중 빈칸에 공통으로 들어갈 표현은?

- The resort was full, so I was glad that we _____ made a reservation in advance.
- He couldn't make a burger because he _____ forgotten to buy a beef patty.
- Thousands of runner _____ been stopped before they even finished the race.

① have

② has

③ had

④ would have

20 다음 중 빈칸에 들어갈 알맞은 표현은?

_____ harder, she could have become a medical doctor.

① Had she

② If had she studied

③ Had she studied

④ If she studied

21 다음 중 빈칸에 들어갈 알맞은 표현은?

If he had accepted their offer last year, he _____ working at this university now.

① be

② were to

③ would be

④ would have been

22 다음 중 빈칸에 들어갈 표현이 순서대로 짝지어진 것은?

> • He talked to her intimately as if he ___㉠___ her for a long time.
> • The doctor was very attentive to her patient. she kindly asked, observed, and listened to him as if she ___㉡___ his medical records before.

	㉠	㉡
①	knew	never saw
②	knew	had never seen
③	had known	had never seen
④	had known	never saw

23 다음 중 밑줄 친 부분의 쓰임이 다른 것은?

① He was very pleased <u>to hear</u> her success.

② He lived <u>to be</u> a hundred years old.

③ He awoke <u>to find</u> himself famous one day.

④ He studied very hard for the test <u>only to fail</u>.

24 다음 중 어법상 잘못된 표현은?

① She was too sick to go on the field trip and made her stay at home.

② He is ready enough to accept her invitation.

③ You have to get up at 5 a.m. so early as to catch the first subway.

④ He was so well known as to need no introduction to students.

25 다음 중 어법상 잘못된 표현은?

① Children are looking forward to seeing their uncle in August.

② Audiences should see to buying the tickets for the entrance.

③ Many foreign students have difficulty learning Korean.

④ The government will make it a point to creating an extensive new network of gurus.

26 다음 중 밑줄 친 부분을 잘못 표현한 것은?

① <u>Being invited to the party</u>, she didn't come.

　　→ Since she was invited to the party, she didn't come.

② <u>Walking down the street</u>, she met her old friend.

　　→ While she was walking down the street, she met her old friend.

③ <u>Overcome with surprise</u>, he was completely numb.

　　→ Because he was overcome with surprise, he was completely numb.

④ <u>Turning to the right</u>, you can find the city hall.

　　→ If you turn to the right, you can find the city hall.

27 다음 중 빈칸에 공통으로 들어갈 표현은?

> • She ran into the house _____ tears running down her cheeks.
> • The manager sat on the table _____ his arms folded.
> • He was climbing the mountain _____ a stick in his hand.

① before

② while

③ with

④ by

28 다음 중 빈칸에 공통으로 들어갈 표현은?

> • Books _____ sell well are not necessarily excellent ones.
> • This is the pen with _____ he wrote the poem.
> • Poems of _____ the poets are famous sell readily.

① who

② that

③ which

④ whose

29 다음 중 어법상 문장을 <u>잘못</u> 옮긴 것은?

① This is the sports car which was made in Korea.

　　→ This is the sports car made in Korea.

② He knows a jazz singer who is a professor of music.

　　→ He knows a jazz singer a professor of music.

③ She has done all well that there is to be done.

　　→ She has done all well there is to be done.

④ It was he that met the professor yesterday.

　　→ It was he met the professor yesterday.

30 다음 중 빈칸에 공통으로 들어갈 표현은?

> • The president accepted ＿＿＿＿ the company offered.
> • ＿＿＿＿ with the heat and humidity, they could not sleep well last night.
> • Words are to language ＿＿＿＿ notes are to music.

① by

② that

③ what

④ as

31 다음 중 빈칸에 들어갈 알맞은 표현은?

> ＿＿＿＿ cold it is, my father always goes swimming in winter.

① Whenever

② Wherever

③ However

④ Whichever

32 다음 중 빈칸에 공통으로 들어갈 표현은?

> • He wants to know what may happen to the glaciers in the future, _____ he is making computer-simulated models.
> • Please check carefully _____ that you won't miss any mistakes.

① therefore

② however

③ so

④ and

33 다음 중 빈칸에 공통으로 들어갈 표현은?

> • Sometimes fashion reflects _____ the times desire.
> • The manager can decide _____ color the product will be.

① whom

② whose

③ what

④ which

34 다음 중 빈칸에 들어갈 표현이 순서대로 짝지어진 것은?

> • Her achievements are all the more remarkable ___㉠___ that she is only 21 years of age.
> • Many young Korean students don't have to go abroad to learn English ___㉡___ that we have Experience English Village in each city.

	㉠	㉡
①	now	now
②	now	given
③	given	now
④	given	given

35 다음 중 빈칸에 들어갈 표현이 순서대로 짝지어진 것은?

> • Make haste ___㉠___ you should be late.
> • The doctor forbade family members for ___㉡___ that patient's condition might change for the worse.

	㉠	㉡
①	so	lest
②	lest	fear
③	fear	so that
④	in case	order

36 다음 중 빈칸에 공통으로 들어갈 표현은?

> • Josh is 10. Laurel is 50. Josh _____ old as Laurel.
> • Money is slightly important. But it _____ important as happiness and love.

① is almost as

② is nearly as

③ is not quite as

④ is not nearly as

37 다음 중 빈칸에 들어갈 알맞은 표현은?

> Mr. Jensen is not so much smart as intelligent.
> = Mr. Jensen is _____ smart than intelligent.

① no more

② more

③ less

④ no less

38 다음 중 어법상 <u>잘못된</u> 표현은?

① The Nile River is the longest of all the rivers in the world.

② No other river in the world is longer than the Nile River.

③ The Nile River is longer than any other rivers in the world.

④ The Nile River is longer than all the rivers in the world.

39 다음 중 빈칸에 들어갈 가장 알맞은 표현은?

> ROKS Sejong the Great (DDG-991) is the lead ship of guided missile destroyer built for the Republic of Korea Navy. _____ was the first Aegis-built destroyer of the service and was named after the fourth king of the Joseon Dynasty of Korea, Sejong the Great.

① It

② She

③ He

④ They

40 다음 중 어법상 적절한 표현은?

① The first outbreak was occurred in November last year.

② When turkey is defrosted, it should be cooked the same day.

③ Last month, customer prices were risen sharply in four month.

④ The scientists argued that all parasites will be disappeared in 2070 due to climate change.

01	02	03	04	05	06	07	08	09	10
①	③	④	④	①	②	③	④	③	④
11	12	13	14	15	16	17	18	19	20
④	③	②	④	②	③	④	②	②	④
21	22	23	24	25	26	27	28	29	30
③	③	②	③	④	③	③	②	④	①
31	32	33	34	35	36	37	38	39	40
①	④	③	④	③	④	③	③	④	③

01 정답 ①

해설

문장의 주요소는 주어, 동사, 목적어, 보어이다. ②는 2형식 문장 보어, ③은 3형식 문장 목적어, ④는 4형식 문장 (간접)목적어이다. 반면, ①은 1형식 문장 부사구로서 종요소이다.

해석

① 그는 제시간에 학교에 왔다.
② 그는 배가 고팠다.
③ 그는 책 읽는 것을 좋아한다.
④ 그는 그녀에게 선물을 주었다.

02 정답 ③

해설

③은 삽입어구이고, ①·②·④는 동격어구이다. ①은 명사구 동격, ②·④는 that절 동격이다.

해석

① 미국 대통령, 존 바이든이 한국을 방문할 것이다.
② 그녀는 Josh가 쿠키를 먹었다는 사실을 알고 있다.
③ 교수님은, 내 생각에, 살아 있는 사전 같다.
④ 그녀가 떠났다는 소식은 놀라웠다.

03 정답 ④

해설

①(지각동사), ②(사역동사), ③(목적보어 to부정사)은 모두 5형식 문형이다. 반면, ④는 간접목적어(him)와 직접목적어(an apology)가 있는 4형식 문형이다.

해석

① 그녀는 그가 길을 건너는 것을 보았다.
② 그는 라디오를 수리했다.
③ 그는 학생들에게 워크숍에 참여하라고 부탁했다.
④ 그녀는 그에게 사과를 요청했다.

04 정답 ④

해설

4형식 문장을 3형식 문장으로 만드는 유형으로서 ①의 pass는 전치사 to, ②의 make는 전치사 for, ③의 play는 전치사 on을 사용한다. 반면에 ④의 announce는 3형식 동사이기 때문에 4형식처럼 사용하지 못하고 'She announced her wedding date to us'로 표현해야 한다.

해석

① 그는 그녀에게 상을 수여했다.
② 그는 그녀를 위해 스파게티를 만들었다.
③ 그녀는 그에게 장난을 쳤다.
④ 그녀는 우리에게 결혼 날짜를 알렸다.

05 정답 ①

해설

① 학문명 statistics는 단수 취급한다.

② the cattle은 단수 형태이지만 복수 취급한다.

③ family는 집합 전체(단일체)를 의미하는 경우 단수 취급한다.

④ 물질명사 air와 water는 관사를 사용하지 않는다.

해석

① 통계학은 그가 가장 좋아하는 과목이다.

② 모든 소들이 대초원에 있다.

③ 그의 가족은 대가족이다.

④ 우리는 공기와 물 없이는 살 수 없다.

06 정답 ②

해설

• 첫 번째 : 수식받는 명사 표현 앞에 정관사 the 사용

• 두 번째 : 신체의 일부를 표현하는 경우 정관사 the 사용

• 세 번째 : 'the + 형용사 = 복수 보통명사' 표현

• 네 번째 : same이 명사를 수식하는 경우 정관사 the 사용

해석

• 서울은 대한민국의 수도이다.

• 그녀가 그의 어깨를 토닥거렸다.

• 젊은이들은 야망이 있다.

• 그들은 같은 도시 출신이다.

07 정답 ③

해설

③ all (of) (the) 명사

① almost every 명사

② most of the (형용사) 명사

④ 복수 인칭대명사 앞에서는 of 생략 불가, all of them

해석

① 거의 모든 학생들이 그 교수를 좋아한다.

② 대부분의 학생들이 그 교수를 좋아한다.

③ 모든 학생들이 그 교수를 좋아한다.

④ 모두 그 교수를 좋아한다.

08 정답 ④

해설

④ 목적격 관계대명사 who(m)는 생략 가능하다.

① 소유격 관계대명사는 생략할 수 없다.

② 주격 관계대명사는 생략할 수 없다.

③ 목적격 관계대명사는 생략 가능하나 '전치사 + 관계대명사'는 생략할 수 없고, 'The music ∅ she listened to last night was beautiful.'은 가능하다.

해석

① 그는 최근에 책을 출판한 그 여성을 알고 있다.

② 그녀는 자신을 도와준 신사분에게 감사했다.

③ 그녀가 어젯밤에 들었던 음악은 아름다웠다.

④ 사람들이 사랑했던 그 연예인은 여러 자선단체에 기부했다.

09 정답 ③

해설

③의 that은 선행사 the house를 수식하는 관계대명사이고, 나머지는 명사절을 이끄는 접속사 that이다.

해석

① 그는 당신이 마음이 넓다고 믿는다.

② 그가 뭔가 잘못했다는 것에는 의심의 여지가 없다.

③ 그 집은 그들이 살던 집이다.

④ 그가 시험에 합격했다는 것은 사실이었다.

10 정답 ④

해설

④ 타동사 use의 수동태 구문으로 to부정사(in order to)이므로 동사의 기본형 pump를 사용해야 한다.

① 타동사 use의 수동태 구문이다.

② 'be(get) used to (동)명사'(~에 익숙해지다) 표현이다.

③ used to는 과거의 습관을 표현한다(~하곤 했다).

해석

① 그 돈은 자선단체에 의해 사용될 것이다.

② 그는 전원생활에 점점 익숙해지고 있다.

③ 그는 어렸을 때 일기를 쓰곤 했다.

④ 증기 기관은 물을 퍼 올리는 데 사용되었다.

11 정답 ④

해설

형용사 easy, difficult, (un)important, (un)necessary, (im)possible, (in)convenient, proper, natural, strange, pleasant, comfortable, dangerous 등과 같이 난이도, 중요도, 당위성 등을 의미하는 경우 'It is + 형용사 (+ for 목적격) + to부정사' 구문으로 표현한다. 이러한 표현은 사람을 주어로 하지 않고, to부정사 구문의 타동사 목적어나 전치사의 목적어가 문두에 위치한다.

해석

① 그녀와 함께 있으면 즐겁다.

② 그의 기분을 맞추는 게 매우 어렵다.

③ 그가 강에서 수영하는 것은 위험하다.

④ 그가 몇 년 안에 영어를 마스터하는 것은 불가능하다.

12 정답 ③

해설

③ '열심히'를 의미하는 부사는 hard가 적절하고, hardly는 '거의 ~ 않다'라는 부정 표현이다.

① high는 형용사(높은)와 부사(높게)가 같은 형태이지만, 여기서는 '매우'라는 의미의 highly가 적절하다.

② pretty는 형용사와 부사가 같은 형태로서, 여기서는 '매우, 상당히'라는 의미의 부사 표현이다.

④ '거의'를 의마하는 부사는 nearly가 적절하고, near는 '가까이'라는 의미이다.

해석

① 그의 주장은 매우 문제가 많았다.

② 이 게임의 새로운 규칙은 꽤 간단하다.

③ 그는 영어를 매우 열심히 공부했다.

④ 거의 70%의 학생들이 그 시계를 샀다.

13 정답 ②

해설

비교급을 강조하는 경우 much, (by) far, a lot, a little, even, still 등을 사용한다. very는 원급의 형용사, 부사를 강조한다.

해석

배터리는 이전보다 훨씬 더 빨리 충전되고 더 오래 지속된다.

14 정답 ④

해설

부정 표현의 'not as 원급 as'(~만큼 -하지 않은)에서 큰 차이가 나는 경우 'not nearly as 원급 as' 표현을 사용한다. 근소한 차이는 'not quite as 원급 as'를 사용한다.

해석

사하라 사막의 여름 기후는 남극의 여름 기후보다 훨씬 더 덥다.

= 남극의 여름 기후는 사하라 사막의 여름 기후만큼 덥지 않다.

15 정답 ②

해설

이유(~ 때문에)를 나타내는 전치사 표현 on account of, owing to와 양보(~에도 불구하고)를 나타내는 전치사 표현 in spite of가 사용되었다.

해석

- 공항은 안개 때문에 폐쇄되었다.
- 그는 공부 부족으로 시험에 떨어졌다.
- 장르적 차이에도 불구하고, 그들은 무대 위에서 매번 최고의 듀엣을 만든다.

16 정답 ③

해설

조건을 나타내는 종속접속사 if, unless, in case의 사용이다. 첫 번째 예문에서는 if (it is) necessary, 두 번째 예문에서는 unless we have change(= if we don't have change), 세 번째 예문에서는 in case she forgets it으로 조건 종속절을 이끈다.

해석

- 필요하다면, 오늘 저녁은 제가 해 드릴게요.
- 변화가 없으면 더 좋은 일을 할 수 없다.
- 그녀는 잊어버릴까 봐 그의 이메일 주소를 적었다.

17 정답 ④

해설

① 정해진 시간표나 일정에 대한 미래, ② 습관, ③ 가까운 미래, ④ 시간의 부사절에서는 미래시제 대신 현재시제를 사용한다.

해석

① 그가 탈 비행기는 내일 오전 8시에 출발한다.
② 그는 매일 마당에 물을 준다.
③ 그는 다음 주에 미국을 떠난다.
④ 그는 그녀가 도착하면 선물을 줄 것이다.

18 정답 ②

해설

① 과거 연도, 월, 일, ② 의문사 when, what time, ③ 역사적 사실, ④ last, ago 표현은 과거시제를 사용한다.

해석

① 그는 2002년에 태어났다.
② 너는 그를 언제 만났니?
③ 1차 세계대전은 1918년에 끝났다.
④ 그 다리는 약 10년 전에 지어졌다.

19 정답 ②

해설

의미상 '~할 때까지', '~할 즈음'의 시간 부사절을 이끄는 접속사가 가장 적절하다. 'by the time + 과거, 주절 과거완료', 'by the time + 현재, 주절 미래완료'뿐만 아니라 주절에는 과거, 현재, 현재완료, 미래시제 등이 올 수 있다.

해석

- 그 음악가가 7살이 되었을 때, 5개의 교향곡을 작곡했다.
- 그가 이 책을 다 썼을 때, 그는 300페이지 이상을 썼을 것이다.
- 기후 변화가 정말 심각하다는 것을 알게 될 때쯤, 그것을 개선할 수 있는 여러분의 능력은 극도로 제한되어 있다. 탄소는 위로 올라가지만, 난방효과는 지연된다.
- 고객한테 뭘 원하는지 물어보고 나서 그것을 만들어 주려고 하면 안 된다. 당신이 그것을 만들 때쯤이면, 고객들은 새로운 것을 원할 것이다.

20 정답 ④

해설

주절이 'would + 동사원형'의 형태인 것으로 보아 가정법 과거이고, if절의 be동사의 형태는 were를 쓰는데, 여기서는 if가 생략된 후 be동사가 도치된 형태이다.

해석

내가 우리나라 대통령이라면 학교 운영 방식을 바꿀 거야.

21 정답 ③

해설

but for 가정법이다. 주절 'could not + have + p.p.'의 형태로 보아 가정법 과거완료(if it had not been for, 만일 ~이 없었더라면)를 나타내는데, 이 문장에서는 if가 생략된 후 조동사 had가 도치된 형태이다.

해석

그녀의 시의적절한 조언이 없었더라면, 그는 사법시험에 합격하지 못했을 것이다.

22 정답 ③

해설

I wish 가정법이다. A에서 동사 understood로 보아 과거 사실에 대한 소망이나 유감을 나타내므로 B의 대답은 I wish 가정법 과거완료가 적절하다.

해석

A : 저는 수학시험을 보고 나서야 미분과 적분을 이해했어요.
B : 시험 전에 미리 공부했으면 좋았을 텐데.

23 정답 ②

해설

② to부정사의 부사적 용법(in order to recognize)
① to부정사의 명사적 용법(주어)
③ to부정사의 명사적 용법(목적어)
④ to부정사의 명사적 용법(목적격 보어)

해석

① 외국의 역사와 문화를 공부하는 것은 매우 흥미롭다.
② 우리는 우리가 얼마나 작은 존재인지 인식하기 위해 가장 높은 곳에 있어 봐야 한다.
③ 이것은 당신이 사랑하는 사람에게 좋은 선물을 주고 싶을 때도 유용하다.
④ 그것은 직원들이 왜 특정한 것들을 배우는지 이해할 수 있도록 도와준다.

24 정답 ③

해설

집합명사는 동질의 종류를 하나의 '집합' 또는 '집단'으로 다루는 명사를 말한다. 그 집단이 단일체를 지시하는 경우 단수 형태와 복수 형태가 가능하고, 각각 단수동사, 복수동사가 사용된다. 반면에 개별 구성원의 합, 즉 군집을 지시하는 경우 단수 형태이지만 복수 취급하여 복수동사가 사용된다.
③ 군집 지시 - 단수 형태 - 복수동사, audience가 개별 구성원의 합을 표현하는 군집명사로 사용되는 경우, 단수 형태이지만 복수 취급한다(was → were).
① · ② · ④ 단일체 지시 - 단수 형태 - 단수동사

해석

① 그 위원회는 과학자들과 디자이너들로 구성되어 있다.
② 가족은 어린아이에게 막대한 영향을 준다.
③ 관람객들은 그의 연주에 감명 받았다.
④ 콘서트장에 관람객이 많았다.

25 정답 ④

해설

'It is of no use to + 동사원형'이므로, 'It is of no use to cry over spilt milk.'로 써야 적절하다.

해석

이미 엎질러진 우유를 보고 울어도 소용없다. → 속담 : 이미 엎질러진 물이다.

26 정답 ③

해설

동명사 관용 표현

③ be committed to 동명사 : ~에 전념하다 → stabilizing

① come near to 동명사 : 하마터면 ~할 뻔하다

② object to 동명사 : ~하는 것을 반대하다

④ be worth 동명사 : ~할 가치가 있다

해석

① 그의 무모함은 하마터면 재앙을 초래할 뻔했다.

② 사람들은 자기 동네에 새로운 공장을 짓는 것을 반대한다.

③ 시 정부는 부동산 가격을 안정시키는 일에 전념하고 있다.

④ 이 나라를 위해 퍼뜨릴 가치가 있는 당신의 생각은 무엇입니까?

27 정답 ③

해설

③ 부사절과 주절의 주어가 일치하지 않을 때 부사절 주어가 인칭대명사인 경우 분사구문으로 바꿀 수 없다.

① 비인칭 독립분사구문으로, 불특정 다수 we로 표현되는 경우 부사절과 주절의 주어가 일치하지 않아도 분사구문에서 주어 생략이 가능하다.

② 이유를 나타내는 독립분사구문으로, 부사절과 주절의 주어가 일치하지 않을 때 분사구문에서 주어를 생략하지 않아도 된다.

④ Being angry at her words 분사구문에서 being은 형용사 앞에서 생략 가능하다.

해석

① 엄밀히 말하면, 토마토는 요리 용어로는 채소이다.

② 밤새 비가 와서 길이 젖어 있었다.

③ 그가 그녀에게 전화했을 때, 그녀는 저녁을 먹고 있었다.

④ 그는 그녀의 말에 화가 나서 아무 대답도 하지 않았다.

28 정답 ②

해설

관계사절 동사의 목적어인 목적격 관계대명사이고 선행사가 사람인 경우 who(m)를 사용한다. 첫 번째는 제한적(한정적) 용법, 두 번째는 비제한적(계속적) 용법이다.

해석

• 당신이 만난 그 신사분은 언어학 교수이다.

• 그 남자는 아름다운 아내가 있었는데, 그는 그녀를 매우 사랑했다.

29 정답 ④

해설

④ A is to B what C is to D : A와 B에 대한 관계는 C와 D에 대한 관계와 같다

① 비제한적(계속적) 용법에서 관계대명사 that은 사용 불가능 → who

② 선행사 cat과 관계사절 명사 color는 소유격 관계이고 생략 불가능 → a cat whose color

③ 주어 역할의 what절이 주격 보어를 취하는 경우 보어가 복수형이어도 be동사는 단수형 → was

해석

① 영어 101을 가르치는 그 교수는 유명한 극작가이다.
② Josh는 색깔이 흑백인 고양이가 있다.
③ 그가 가장 필요로 한 것은 컴퓨터였다.
④ 공기와 사람에 대한 관계는 물과 물고기에 대한 관계와 같다.

30 정답 ①

해설

유사관계대명사 as 용법
• 첫 번째 : 선행사에 as, so, such, the same 등의 표현이 있는 경우
• 두 번째 : 선행 또는 후속하는 주절이 있는 경우

해석
• 이것은 어제 그가 저녁으로 먹었던 것과 같은 음식이다.
• 그에게는 흔히 있는 일이지만, 그는 오늘 결석했다.

31 정답 ①

해설

복합관계대명사(관계대명사+ever) 형태 명사절(anyone who, 누구든지)로, 전치사 to의 목적어 형태 whomever가 아니라, 동사 want의 주어에 해당하는 whoever가 필요하다. 복합관계대명사의 격(case)은 관계사절 내에서 결정된다.

해석
그들은 그들의 걸작을 보고 싶어 하는 누구에게나 아주 기쁘게 보여준다.

32 정답 ④

해설
• 첫 번째 : chance that, 동격 명사절을 취하는 명사 표현(~할 가능성이 있다)
• 두 번째 : be aware that, 명사절을 취하는 형용사 표현(~을 알고 있다)
두 문장 모두 that절 내 '주어 + 동사'가 있는 완전한 문장을 취한다.

해석
• 이 행성들 중 일부는 지구와 매우 비슷해서, 생명체를 포함하고 있을 가능성이 크다.
• 우리는 또한 전문가들도 실수를 한다는 것을 알아야 한다.

33 정답 ③

해설
③ or not이 바로 이어지는 명사절은 if가 아니라 whether로 표현하지만, or not이 문미에 오는 경우는 if를 쓸 수 있다.
① 주어 역할을 하는 명사절은 if가 아니라 whether를 쓴다.
② about 전치사와 함께 쓰이는 명사절은 if가 아니라 whether를 쓴다.
④ to부정사로 이어지는 명사절의 경우 if가 아니라 whether를 쓴다.

해석
① 비가 오는지 날씨가 맑은지는 등산객들에게 중요하지 않았다.
② 인권침해 여부에 대한 신중한 판단이 요구된다.
③ 사람들은 성공하든 실패하든 상관없이 항상 타인을 배려해야 한다.
④ 경영진은 회사명을 교체할지 말지 고민하고 있다.

34 정답 ④

해설

④ 타동사 know의 목적어 명사절 that 다음에
완전한 절이 와야 하는데, 여기서는 불완전
한 절이 오기 때문에 what이 적절하다. →
what is best for their children
① 주어 역할을 하는 명사절이 쓰였다.
② 'so + 형용사/부사 + that' 표현이다.
③ 선행사 problem을 수식하는 형용사 역할을
하는 관계대명사 that 다음에 불완전한 절이
온다.

해석

① 그가 복권에 당첨된 것은 분명했다.
② 케이크가 너무 맛있어서 한꺼번에 다 먹었다.
③ 기름 유출은 해양 생태계를 위협할 수 있는
심각한 환경 문제가 될 수 있다.
④ 부모들은 더 많은 경험과 지혜가 있기 때문
에 아이들에게 무엇이 최선인지 안다.

35 정답 ③

해설

비례를 나타내는 부사절 표현
• 첫 번째 : in proportion as(~에 비례하여)
• 두 번째 : according as(~에 준하여, ~에 따라)
• 세 번째 : as(~에 따라)

해석

• 까마귀의 뇌는 침팬지의 뇌와 같은 비율로 균
형 잡혀 있다.
• 수요가 증가함에 따라, 가격은 상승한다.
• 그녀는 나이가 들면서, 엄마를 더 닮아 보인다.

36 정답 ④

해설

원급비교구문
④ the same (+ 명사) as 표현 : ~와 같은 →
same은 정관사 the와 함께 쓰인다.
① 부정주어 ~ + as(so) + 원급 + as ~ : ~만큼 -
한 것은 없다(최상급 의미)
② as ~ as ever + 과거동사 : 더없이 ~하여(최
상급 의미, 누구 못지않은 성실한 사람)
③ 배수사 + as ~ as - : -만큼 ~한

해석

① 사랑만큼 중요한 것은 없다.
② 그는 누구 못지않은 성실한 사람이다.
③ 왼쪽 타워의 높이는 오른쪽 타워의 높이의
두 배이다.
④ 공익이 항상 국익과 같은 것은 아니다.

37 정답 ③

해설

• 첫 번째 : the higher education 절대비교 표현
• 두 번째 : 원인, 이유의 부사구나 부사절이 있
는 비교급 구문에서 'all the + 비교급 +
because of'(-하기 때문에 더욱 ~하다)
• 세 번째 : of A and B 또는 of the two(둘
중에 더 ~하다) 구문에서 'the + 비교급'

해석

• 주요 기여 요인 중 하나는 높은 교육 수준이다.
• 그녀는 그의 솔직함 때문에 그를 더욱 좋아
한다.
• A : Jeff랑 Joey 중에 누가 키가 더 크니?
  B : Jeff가 둘 중에 키가 더 크다.

38 정답 ③

해설

③ no less than = as many/much as(~만큼)

① no more than = only(불과 ~에 지나지 않다)

② not more than = at most(많아야)

④ not less than = at least(적어도, 최소한)

해석

• A380기종 항공기는 2개의 갑판에 800명의 승객을 태운다.

• 어떤 팬들은 표 한 장에 400달러나 지불했다.

39 정답 ④

해설

상황이나 상태를 표현하는 비진행형 수동태 구문 속 행동주 또는 행위자 표현은 'by + N(명사구)'에서 전치사 by가 아닌 다른 전치사를 사용하고, 과거분사는 형용사 역할을 한다. 첫 번째 문장의 경우 accustomed to(익숙하다)를, 두 번째 문장의 경우 committed to(약속하다, 전념하다)를 이용하여 표현한다.

해석

• 이것을 충분히 하면, 당신의 뇌는 이 활동에 익숙해질 수 있다.

• 유럽연합은 2030년까지 탄소 배출량을 20% 줄일 것을 약속했다.

40 정답 ③

해설

비단정형 표현 any는 부정문에서 주어로 사용하지 않는데(*any ~ not), 부정 표현이 선행하는 경우 가능하다(not ~ any). 일반적으로 의문문과 부정문에서는 비단정형 표현 any를 사용한다.

해석

① 어떤 학생도 이 수학 문제를 풀 수 없다.

② 하나도 안 팔아요.

③ 누구나 영국 왕실의 근위병이 될 수 있는 것은 아니다. (Beefeater : 영국 왕실의 근위병)

④ 그는 기후변화에 대해 질문이 없었다.

01	02	03	04	05	06	07	08	09	10
③	③	④	②	②	④	②	③	②	④
11	12	13	14	15	16	17	18	19	20
②	④	①	③	③	②	②	③	③	③
21	22	23	24	25	26	27	28	29	30
③	③	①	③	④	①	③	③	②	③
31	32	33	34	35	36	37	38	39	40
③	③	③	③	②	④	③	③	②	②

01 정답 ③

해설

③ remind는 '타동사 + 목적어 + of 전치사구' 구문의 3형식 완전타동사이므로 of가 들어가야 한다.

① make는 목적어(his laptop)와 과거분사 목적보어(repaired)를 사용한 5형식 불완전타동사이다.

② provide는 '타동사 + 목적어 + with 전치사구' 구문의 3형식 완전타동사이다.

④ ask는 간접목적어(him)와 직접목적어(a favor)가 필요한 4형식 이중타동사이다.

해석

① 그는 노트북을 수리했다. (수리하게 했다.)

② 그는 그녀에게 새 책상과 의자를 마련해 주었다.

③ 그녀는 그에게 그의 할머니를 상기시켰다.

④ 그녀가 그에게 부탁했다.

02 정답 ③

해설

③은 본동사로 사용된 have(갖다)이다. 반면, ① · ② · ④는 사역동사로 사용된 have 표현이다.

해석

① 그녀는 길에서 시계를 도둑맞았다.

② 그는 숙제를 다 했다.

③ 모든 사람은 투표할 권리가 있다.

④ 그녀는 그를 5시에 여기로 오게 했다.

03 정답 ④

해설

④ 동사 enter는 '들어가다'의 의미로 사용되는 3형식 완전타동사이므로 전치사 into가 없이 목적어를 취한다. 'enter into'(시작하다)는 'enter into conversation with a person'(대화를 시작하다) 등의 다른 의미로 사용된다.

① resemble, ② reach, ③ mention은 모두 목적어를 취하는 3형식 완전타동사이다.

해석

① 그녀는 아버지를 닮았다.

② 그가 한국 서울에 도착하고 있다.

③ 그 교수는 한국 문화의 힘을 언급했다.

④ 그는 마스크를 쓰고 교실로 들어갔다.

04 정답 ②

해설

첫 번째 문장은 3형식 문장으로, '타동사 + 목적어 + 전치사구' 구문에서 동사 forgive는 for를 취한다. 두 번째 문장의 경우, 4형식을 3형식으로 전환할 때 동사 buy는 전치사 for를 취한다.

해석

• 당신을 기다리게 한 점을 용서해 주세요.
• 그녀는 그에게 새 차를 사주었다.

05 정답 ②

해설

② Shakespeare는 고유명사이지만 '~와 같은 사람'을 의미하는 경우 부정관사 a를 사용한다.
① iron은 물질명사 '철'의 의미가 아닌 가산명사 '다리미'로 사용되어 a new iron으로 표현해야 한다.
③ milk는 물질명사이므로 milk로 표현해야 한다.
④ fire는 물질명사이지만 여기서 개별 사건으로 취급하기 때문에 a big fire로 표현해야 한다.

해석

① 그녀는 새 다리미를 샀다.
② 그는 미래에 셰익스피어와 같은 작가가 될 것이다.
③ 우유는 버터와 치즈로 만들어진다.
④ 어젯밤 시내에 큰 불이 났다.

06 정답 ④

해설

④ 물질명사 corn의 (복)수는 '수사 + 단위명사 + of'로 표현한다.
① 국가명이 경제, 사회, 문화를 의미하는 경우 여성형 대명사 her를 사용한다.
② 이중 소유격의 경우 the car of his father's로 표현한다.

③ 'all + 추상명사'의 경우 정관사 the를 사용하지 않는다.

해석

① 영국은 극작가 셰익스피어를 자랑스러워한다.
② 그는 아버지 차를 좋아한다.
③ 그녀는 정말 미인이다.
④ 그는 옥수수 이삭을 주웠다. (ear : 보리, 옥수수 등의 이삭, 열매)

07 정답 ②

해설

② every 표현은 단수명사를 쓰고, 단수 취급한다.
① each 표현은 단수 취급한다.
③ either, neither 표현은 단수 취급한다.
④ both 표현은 복수 취급한다.

해석

① 그들은 각자 자기 차가 있다.
② 누구에게나 기회는 있다.
③ 두 계획 중 어느 것도 좋지 않다.
④ Laurel과 Jeff 둘 다 교수다.

08 정답 ③

해설

• 첫 번째 : A is one thing and B is another(A와 B는 별개다)
• 두 번째 : one more(하나 더)의 의미
• 세 번째 : different(다른)의 의미
• 네 번째 : 셋 중에서 순서 없이 열거할 경우 두 번째 another 표현

해석

• 아는 것과 경험은 별개다.
• 커피 한 잔 더 주시겠어요?
• 저는 이것은 마음에 들지 않으니 다른 것을 주세요.
• 그의 정원에는 세 그루의 나무가 있다. 하나는 소나무, 다른 하나는 감나무, 그리고 나머지 하나는 흰 자작나무이다.

09 정답 ②

해설
- 첫 번째 : this(후자, the latter) = wealth, that(전자, the former) = health
- 두 번째 : 선행 문장을 대용하는 that
- 세 번째 : 명사 반복을 대용하는 that

해석
- 건강이 부보다 우선이다. 부는 우리에게 건강만큼 많은 행복을 주지 못한다.
- 사느냐, 죽느냐: 그것이 문제다. (이대로냐, 아니냐: 그것이 문제다.)
- 캘리포니아의 기후는 미네소타의 겨울 기후보다 온화하다.

10 정답 ④

해설
④ many a/an 표현은 단수명사를 수식하고 단수 취급한다.
① 가산명사 people을 수식하는 many, (a) few, most 등의 수량 표현이 있다.
② 불가산명사 information을 수식하는 much, (a) little, less 등의 수량 표현이 있다.
③ 가산명사 mistakes를 수식하는 not a few, a good many, many 등의 수량 표현이 있다.

해석
① 맨발로 다니는 것을 선호하는 사람은 거의 없다.
② 훨씬 더 많은 정보가 그에게 전해졌다.
③ 그는 꽤 많은 실수를 바로잡았다.
④ 티끌 모아 태산(pickle : 소량 / mickle : 다량)

11 정답 ②

해설
② '경제적인', '절약하는'의 의미로 사용되는 형용사 표현은 economical이다. economic은 '경제(상)의'의 의미이다.

① imaginary는 '상상의', '공상의'의 의미로 사용되는 형용사 표현이다.
③ respective는 '각자의'의 의미로 사용되는 형용사 표현이다.
④ historic은 '역사적인', '역사상 중요한'의 의미로 사용되는 형용사 표현이다.

해석
① 유니콘은 상상의 동물이다.
② 전등은 경제적이고, 깨끗하고, 가스보다 더 많은 빛을 낸다.
③ 대부분의 사람들은 새해 결심으로 각자의 목표를 갖는다.
④ 링컨은 1863년 게티즈버그에서 역사적인 연설을 했다.

12 정답 ④

해설
④ 'not so much A as B'는 'A라기보다는 차라리 B인'의 의미이기 때문에 이 표현에서는 '취미라기보다는 직업이다.'의 의미이다. (not so much A as B = not A so much as B = less A than B = B rather than A = more B than A)
① 'B as well as A'는 'A뿐만 아니라 B도'의 의미이다(동사는 B에 일치).
② 'not only A but also B'는 'A뿐만 아니라 B도'의 의미이다(동사는 B에 일치).
③ 'either A or B'는 'A 또는 B'의 의미이다 (동사는 B에 일치).

해석
그것은 취미라기보다는 직업이다.
①·② 그것은 직업일 뿐만 아니라 취미이기도 하다.
③ 그것은 취미이거나 직업이다.
④ 그것은 취미라기보다는 직업이다.

13 정답 ①

해설
① '주어 + 비교급 + than any other + 단수명사'의 최상급 표현으로, any other student가 되어야 한다.
② 'have never been + 비교급'의 최상급 표현이다.
③ '주어 + 비교급 + than all the (other) + 복수명사'의 최상급 표현이다.
④ '부정어 ~ + as 원급 as'(~만큼 ~한 것은 없다)의 최상급 표현이다.

해석
① 그는 학교에서 어떤 다른 학생들보다 더 친절하다.
② 그녀는 평생 이렇게 행복한 적이 없었다.
③ 제주도는 세계의 다른 어떤 섬들보다 아름답다.
④ 세계의 어떤 강도 나일강만큼 길지 않다.

14 정답 ③

해설
장소 '번지'는 전치사 at, 장소 '도시'는 전치사 in, 시간 '시각'은 전치사 at, 시간 '특정일'은 전치사 on을 사용한다.

해석
그는 2002년 6월 4일 화요일 오후 8시에 뉴욕 32번가에서 태어났다.

15 정답 ③

해설
③ 상관접속사 'B as well as A'에서 동사의 수 일치는 B에 한다.
① 상관접속사 'not only A but also B'에서 동사의 수 일치는 B에 한다.
② 상관접속사 'both A and B'는 복수동사를 사용한다.
④ 상관접속사 'such A as B'에서 동사의 수 일치는 A에 한다.

해석
① 너뿐만 아니라 그녀도 나와 친한 친구 사이이다.
② Laurel과 Joey 둘 다 훌륭한 교수이다.
③ 교수뿐만 아니라 학생들도 여름방학을 기다리고(원하고) 있다.
④ Cindy 같은 교수는 드물다.

16 정답 ②

해설
제시된 예문의 종속접속사 as는 '원인', '이유'를 의미한다.
① as는 '시간(~때)', ② as는 '원인', '이유', ③ as는 '비례(~에 따라)', ④ as는 '양보(~이지만, ~함에도 불구하고)'를 나타내는 종속접속사이다.

해석
그는 돈이 없었기 때문에 새 차를 살 수 없었다.
① 우리가 같이 걸을 때 그는 나에게 그 이야기를 들려주었다.
② 그녀가 거짓말을 자주 해서 그는 그녀를 좋아하지 않는다.
③ 그는 나이가 들면서 더 조용해졌다.
④ 그는 어렸지만 매우 용감했다.

17 정답 ②

해설

② 상태동사 know는 진행형을 사용하지 못하기 때문에 has known으로 써야 한다.
① 현재완료 경험이다.
③ 과거의 일정기간(전체)을 표현하는 경우 과거시제를 쓴다(현재와는 관계 없음).
④ 5일 동안 계속 비가 내리고 있는 현재완료진행형 표현이다(현재와 관계 있음).

해석

① 당신은 전에 아프리카에 가본 적 있나요?
② 그는 그녀를 30년 동안 알고 지내고 있다.
③ 그는 예일 대학교에서 5년 동안 언어학을 전공했다.
④ 5일 동안 비가 많이 왔다.

18 정답 ③

해설

주절 과거진행형시제와 시간의 부사절 (단순)과거시제로 표현하는 경우, 과거진행형시제 표현의 사건이 단순과거시제 표현의 사건보다 선행하는 사건이다.

해석

비가 내리기 시작했을 때 그는 나무 아래에 서 있었다.
① 그는 비가 오기 시작한 이후로 계속 서 있었다.
② 그는 비가 오는 동안 나무 아래에 서 있었다.
③ 그는 비가 오기 전에 나무 아래에 서 있었다.
④ 그는 비가 온 후 나무 아래에 서 있었다.

19 정답 ③

해설

빈칸이 포함된 문장들은 모두 비교되는 동사의 사건보다 한 시제 선행하는 사건들이다. 따라서 과거완료(had + p.p.)로 표현된다.

해석

• 그 리조트는 예약이 다 찼는데 미리 예약을 해놔서 기뻤다.
• 그는 소고기 패티를 사는 것을 잊어버려서 햄버거를 만들 수 없었다.
• 수천 명의 주자들이 경주를 마치기도 전에 제지당했다.

20 정답 ③

해설

주절이 'could + have + become'의 형태인 것으로 보아 가정법 과거완료이고, if절이 'if she had studied harder'인데, 이 문장에서는 if가 생략된 후 조동사 had가 도치된 형태이다.

해석

그녀가 더 열심히 공부했더라면, 그녀는 의사가 될 수 있었을 것이다.

21 정답 ③

해설

if절은 'last year' 표현으로 보아 과거사실과 반대되는 가정법 과거완료, 주절은 'now' 표현으로 보아 현재사실과 반대되는 가정법 과거이다. 즉, 혼합가정법 구문이다. 따라서 주절에는 'would + 동사원형(be동사)' 형태가 온다.

해석

만약 그가 작년에 그들의 제안을 받아들였다면, 그는 지금 이 대학에서 일하고 있을 것이다.

22 정답 ③

해설

as if 가정법 과거완료이다. 두 문장 모두 문맥상 as if절이 주절의 과거시제보다 앞선 시제를 의미하므로 'as if + 과거완료'가 적절하다.

해석

· 그는 그녀를 오래 전부터 알고 지낸 것처럼 친근하게 말을 걸었다.

· 그 의사는 자신의 환자에게 매우 세심했다. 그녀는 마치 전에 환자의 의료 기록을 본 적이 없다는 듯이 친절하게 묻고, 관찰하고, 경청했다.

23 정답 ①

해설

① to부정사의 부사적 용법 중 be sorry to, be glad to, be pleased to, be surprised to와 같이 쓰이는 원인 표현이다.

②·③·④ to부정사의 부사적 용법 중 주로 live, grow up, wake up, awake 등과 같은 무의지 동사와 함께 쓰이는 결과적 용법이다.

해석

① 그는 그녀의 성공 소식을 듣고 매우 기뻤다.

② 그는 백 살까지 살았다.

③ 그는 어느 날 자신이 유명하다는 것을 알게 되었다.

④ 그는 열심히 공부했지만 시험에 떨어졌다.

24 정답 ③

해설

③ so as to + 동사원형(in order to + 동사원형) : ~를 위해 ~하다

① too + 형용사/부사 + to부정사 : 너무 ~해서 ~할 수 없다

② 형용사/부사 + enough + to부정사 : ~할 정도로 충분히 ~하다

④ so ~ as to + 동사원형 : ~할 만큼 ~하여

해석

① 그녀는 현장 학습을 가기에는 너무 아파서 집에 머물게 했다.

② 그는 그녀의 초대에 응할 준비가 되어 있다.

③ 지하철 첫차를 타려면 새벽 5시에 일어나야 한다.

④ 그는 학생들에게 소개가 필요 없을 정도로 정평이 나 있었다.

25 정답 ④

해설

④ 'make it a point to + 동사원형', 'make a point of + 동명사' 표현 : ~하는 것을 원칙으로 삼다 → create

① 'look forward to + 동명사(또는 명사)' 표현 : 기대하다

② 'see to + 동명사' 표현 : 반드시 ~하다

③ 'have difficulty (in) + 동명사' 표현 : 어려움을 겪다

해석

① 아이들은 8월에 삼촌을 보기를 고대하고 있다.

② 관객들은 반드시 입장권을 구매해야 한다.

③ 많은 외국인 학생들이 한국어를 배우는 데 어려움을 겪는다.

④ 정부는 전문가들의 광범위하고 새로운 네트워크를 만드는 것을 핵심으로 할 것이다. (guru : (비격식) 전문가, 권위자)

26 정답 ①

해설

분사구문과 부사절 간의 관계를 나타낸다.

① 양보 분사구문으로 since가 아니라 although, though가 적절하다.

②는 시간, ③은 이유, ④는 조건을 나타내는 분사구문이다.

해석
① 그녀는 파티에 초대받았지만 오지 않았다.
② 그녀는 길을 걷다가 옛 친구를 만났다.
③ 그는 너무 놀라서 정신이 몽롱했다.
④ 오른쪽으로 돌면 시청이 있어요.

27 정답 ③

해설

'with + 목적어 + 목적보어' 부대상황 분사구문이다. 목적보어로 현재분사, 과거분사, 형용사, 부사(구), 전치사구가 가능하다.

해석
• 그녀는 눈물이 뺨에 흘러내리는 채 집으로 뛰어 들어갔다.
• 관리자는 팔짱을 끼고 테이블에 앉았다.
• 그는 손에 등산폴대를 들고 산을 오르고 있었다.

28 정답 ③

해설
• 첫 번째 : 선행사 사물에 대한 주격 관계대명사 which
• 두 번째 : 전치사의 목적격 관계대명사 with which
• 세 번째 : 소유격 관계대명사 of which
관계대명사 that은 전치사와 함께 쓰이지 못한다.

해석
• 베스트셀러 책이 반드시 훌륭한 책은 아니다.
• 이것은 그가 그 시를 썼던 펜이다.
• 유명한 시인들의 시집은 판매가 잘 된다.

29 정답 ②

해설
② '주격 관계대명사 + be동사 + 명사' 표현에서 주격 관계대명사는 생략이 불가능하다.

주격 관계대명사가 생략이 가능한 경우
① (주격 관계대명사 + be동사) + 전치사구/형용사/현재분사/과거분사
③ 관계대명사절이 there is/are로 시작하는 경우
④ 분열구문 it is ~ that 강조구문

해석
① 이 차는 한국에서 제조된 스포츠카이다.
② 그는 음악 교수인 재즈 가수를 안다.
③ 그녀는 해야 할 일을 모두 잘 해냈다.
④ 어제 그 교수를 만난 사람은 그였다.

30 정답 ③

해설
• 첫 번째 : 선행사를 포함하는 관계대명사는 what을 사용, 선행사가 the proposal이었다면 'The president accepted the proposal which/that the company offered.'
• 두 번째 : what with A and (what with) B(어느 정도는 A 때문에, 어느 정도는 B 때문에)
• 세 번째 : A is to B what C is to D(A와 B에 대한 관계는 C와 D에 대한 관계와 같다)

해석
• 사장은 그 회사가 제안한 것을 받아들였다.
• 덥고 습해서, 그들은 어젯밤에 잠을 잘 못 잤다.
• 단어와 언어의 관계는 음표와 음악의 관계와 같다.

31 정답 ③

해설
복합관계부사(관계부사 + ever) 양보절(no matter how, 아무리 ~해도)로, 'however + 형용사/부사 + 주어 + 동사' 형태이다.

해석
아무리 추워도 아버지는 항상 겨울에 수영하러 가신다.

32 정답 ③

해설

- 첫 번째 : 접속사 so의 결과 표현(그래서, 그 결과, therefore)
- 두 번째 : 접속사 so that의 목적 표현(~하기 위하여, in order that)

해석

- 그는 미래에 빙하에 무슨 일이 일어날지 알고 싶어서 컴퓨터 시뮬레이션 모델을 만들고 있다.
- 실수하지 않도록 주의 깊게 확인해 주세요.

33 정답 ③

해설

- 첫 번째 : 의문대명사 what은 의문사절 내에서 동사 desire의 목적어 역할을 하고, 의문사절은 주절 동사 reflect의 목적어 명사절 역할을 한다.
- 두 번째 : 의문형용사 what은 명사 color와 함께 의문사절 내에서 보어 역할을 하고, 의문사절은 주절 동사 decide의 목적어 명사절 역할을 한다.

두 표현 모두 문장 내에서 그 자체가 주어, 목적어, 보어 역할을 하고 있기 때문에 불완전한 문장이 온다. which도 동일 조건에서 사용되나, 여기서는 한정된 것 중에서 선택을 하는 의미가 아니므로 what이 적절하다(what은 한정되지 않은 불특정한 것 또는 부정수 중에서 선택하는 '무슨, 무엇'의 의미인 반면, which는 한정된 특정한 것 또는 일정 수 중에서 선택하는 '어느 것/쪽'의 의미).

해석

- 때때로 패션은 시대가 원하는 것을 반영한다.
- 경영자는 제품의 색상을 결정할 수 있다.

34 정답 ③

해설

- 첫 번째 : given that(~을 감안하면)
- 두 번째 : now that(~때문에)

해석

- 21살밖에 되지 않은 점을 감안하면 그녀의 성과는 놀랍다.
- 각 도시에 영어체험마을이 생겼기 때문에 많은 젊은 한국 학생들이 영어를 배우기 위해 해외로 갈 필요가 없다.

35 정답 ②

해설

lest, for fear that : ~하지 않도록(so that ~ should not), 목적을 나타내는 부사절 표현

해석

- 늦지 않게 서둘러라.
- 의사는 환자의 상태가 나빠질까봐 가족 면회를 금했다.

36 정답 ④

해설

큰 차이를 나타내는 부정 표현(~만큼 -하지 않은)은 'not nearly as 원급 as'를 쓰는 반면, 근소한 차이는 'not quite as 원급 as'로 표현한다. 'almost/nearly as 원급 as'는 긍정 표현(거의 ~와 같은)이다.

해석

- Josh는 10살이다. Laurel은 50살이다. Josh는 Laurel만큼 나이가 많지 않다.
- 돈은 어느 정도 중요하다. 그러나 행복과 사랑만큼 중요하지 않다.

37 정답 ③

해설

not so much A as B : 'A라기보다는 B'(= less A than B, more B than A)

① no more A than B : 'B와 같은 수/양/액수의 A밖에 없다'

④ no less ~ than -(= just as ~ as) : '~만큼, 같은 정도로, ~에 못지않게 ~하여'

해석

Jensen씨는 영리하기보다는 지적이다.

38 정답 ③

해설

최상급을 포함하는 비교 구문

① 최상급 + of all + 복수명사

② 부정주어 + 비교급 + than

③ 주어 + 비교급 + than any other + 단수명사

④ 주어 + 비교급 + than all the (other) + 복수명사

해석

나일강은 세계에서 가장 긴 강이다.

39 정답 ②

해설

사물을 의인화하는 경우 boat, ship과 같은 배는 남성(형) 이름을 갖고 있더라도 여성형(she)으로 대용한다.

해석

DDG-991 세종대왕은 대한민국 해군을 위해 건조된 유도탄 구축함의 선두함이다. 이 배는 대한민국 해군 최초의 세종대왕급 이지스 구축함으로, 조선시대 제4대 임금인 세종대왕을 기념하여 명명되었다. (destroyer, DD : 구축함 / guided missile, G : 유도 미사일)

40 정답 ②

해설

②는 능동격 동사 중 paired ergative로, 타동사와 자동사 모두 사용될 수 있는 동사이다. ① · ③ · ④는 능동격 동사 중 unpaired ergative로, 자동사로만 사용 가능하고 수동형은 불가능한 동사이다.

① '발생'(occurrence)을 나타내는 동사로, 'happen, occur, take place' 등이 있다(was occurred → occurred).

③ '방향성 운동'(directed motion)을 나타내는 동사로, 'arrive, fall, rise, emerge, go' 등이 있다(were risen → rose).

④ '묘사, 서술'(description)을 나타내는 동사로, 'appear, disappear, vanish' 등이 있다 (will be disappeared → will disappear).

해석

① 첫 번째 발병은 작년 11월에 발생했다. (outbreak : (유행병의) 출현, 발병)

② 칠면조는 해동되면, 같은 날 요리해야 한다. (defrost : 해동하다)

③ 지난달에 소비자 물가는 4개월 만에 큰 폭으로 올랐다.

④ 과학자들은 2070년에 기후변화로 인해 모든 기생충이 사라질 것이라고 주장했다.

독학학위제 2단계 전공기초과정인정시험 답안지(객관식)

컴퓨터용 사인펜만 사용

★ 수험생은 수험번호와 응시과목 코드번호를 표기(마킹)한 후 일치여부를 반드시 확인할 것.

전공분야

성명

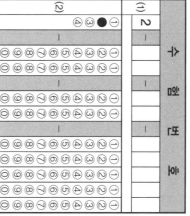

(1)	2			

수험번호

(2)	①						

교시코드
① ② ③ ④

※ 감독관 확인란

(연번)
관 리 번 호
(응시자수)

답안지 작성시 유의사항

1. 답안지는 반드시 컴퓨터용 사인펜을 사용하여 다음 [보기]와 같이 표기할 것.
   [보기] 잘 된 표기: ●
   잘못된 표기: ⊗ ⊕ ◐ ○ ◑ ◓ ◒

2. 수험번호 (1)에는 아라비아 숫자로 쓰고, (2)에는 ● "와 같이 표기할 것.

3. 과목코드는 뒷면 "과목코드번호"를 보고 해당과목의 코드번호를 찾아 표기하고,
   응시과목란에는 응시과목명을 한글로 기재할 것.

4. 교시코드는 문제지 전면 의 교시를 해당란에 ● "와 같이 표기할 것.

5. 한번 표기한 답은 긁거나 수정액 및 스티커 등 어떠한 방법으로도 고쳐서는
   아니되고, 고친 문항은 "0"점 처리함.

과목코드

응시과목					응시과목				
1	① ② ③ ④	21	① ② ③ ④
2	① ② ③ ④	22	① ② ③ ④
3	① ② ③ ④	23	① ② ③ ④
4	① ② ③ ④	24	① ② ③ ④
5	① ② ③ ④	25	① ② ③ ④
6	① ② ③ ④	26	① ② ③ ④
7	① ② ③ ④	27	① ② ③ ④
8	① ② ③ ④	28	① ② ③ ④
9	① ② ③ ④	29	① ② ③ ④
10	① ② ③ ④	30	① ② ③ ④
11	① ② ③ ④	31	① ② ③ ④
12	① ② ③ ④	32	① ② ③ ④
13	① ② ③ ④	33	① ② ③ ④
14	① ② ③ ④	34	① ② ③ ④
15	① ② ③ ④	35	① ② ③ ④
16	① ② ③ ④	36	① ② ③ ④
17	① ② ③ ④	37	① ② ③ ④
18	① ② ③ ④	38	① ② ③ ④
19	① ② ③ ④	39	① ② ③ ④
20	① ② ③ ④	40	① ② ③ ④

교시코드
① ② ③ ④

절취선

독학학위제 2단계 전공기초과정인정시험 답안지(객관식)

★ 수험생은 수험번호와 응시과목 코드번호를 표기(마킹)한 후 일치여부를 반드시 확인할 것.

컴퓨터용 사인펜만 사용

전공분야	
성 명	

수 험 번 호					
(1)	2	-			
(2)	①②③④⑤⑥⑦⑧⑨⓪	①②③④⑤⑥⑦⑧⑨⓪	①②③④⑤⑥⑦⑧⑨⓪	①②③④⑤⑥⑦⑧⑨⓪	①②③④⑤⑥⑦⑧⑨⓪
	①●③④		-		

※ 감독관 확인란

(인)

관 리 번 호	(연번)	(응시자수)

과목코드	응시과목
①②③④⑤⑥⑦⑧⑨⓪	1 ①②③④ 21 ①②③④
①②③④⑤⑥⑦⑧⑨⓪	2 ①②③④ 22 ①②③④
①②③④⑤⑥⑦⑧⑨⓪	3 ①②③④ 23 ①②③④
①②③④⑤⑥⑦⑧⑨⓪	4 ①②③④ 24 ①②③④
①②③④⑤⑥⑦⑧⑨⓪	5 ①②③④ 25 ①②③④
	6 ①②③④ 26 ①②③④
교시코드	7 ①②③④ 27 ①②③④
①②③④	8 ①②③④ 28 ①②③④
	9 ①②③④ 29 ①②③④
	10 ①②③④ 30 ①②③④
	11 ①②③④ 31 ①②③④
	12 ①②③④ 32 ①②③④
	13 ①②③④ 33 ①②③④
	14 ①②③④ 34 ①②③④
	15 ①②③④ 35 ①②③④
	16 ①②③④ 36 ①②③④
	17 ①②③④ 37 ①②③④
	18 ①②③④ 38 ①②③④
	19 ①②③④ 39 ①②③④
	20 ①②③④ 40 ①②③④

과목코드	응시과목
①②③④⑤⑥⑦⑧⑨⓪	1 ①②③④ 21 ①②③④
①②③④⑤⑥⑦⑧⑨⓪	2 ①②③④ 22 ①②③④
①②③④⑤⑥⑦⑧⑨⓪	3 ①②③④ 23 ①②③④
①②③④⑤⑥⑦⑧⑨⓪	4 ①②③④ 24 ①②③④
①②③④⑤⑥⑦⑧⑨⓪	5 ①②③④ 25 ①②③④
	6 ①②③④ 26 ①②③④
교시코드	7 ①②③④ 27 ①②③④
①②③	8 ①②③④ 28 ①②③④
	9 ①②③④ 29 ①②③④
	10 ①②③④ 30 ①②③④
	11 ①②③④ 31 ①②③④
	12 ①②③④ 32 ①②③④
	13 ①②③④ 33 ①②③④
	14 ①②③④ 34 ①②③④
	15 ①②③④ 35 ①②③④
	16 ①②③④ 36 ①②③④
	17 ①②③④ 37 ①②③④
	18 ①②③④ 38 ①②③④
	19 ①②③④ 39 ①②③④
	20 ①②③④ 40 ①②③④

답안지 작성시 유의사항

1. 답안지는 반드시 컴퓨터용 사인펜을 사용하여 다음 보기와 같이 표기할 것.
   보기 잘 된 표기: ● 잘못된 표기: ⊗ ⊘ ⊙ ◑ ◐ ○

2. 수험번호 (1)에는 아라비아 숫자로 쓰고, (2)에는 "●"와 같이 표기할 것.

3. 과목코드는 뒷면 "과목코드번호"를 보고 해당과목의 코드번호를 찾아 표기하고, 응시과목란에는 응시과목명을 한글로 기재할 것.

4. 교시코드는 문제지 전면 의 교시를 해당란에 "●"와 같이 표기할 것.

5. 한번 표기한 답은 긁거나 수정액 및 스티커 등 어떠한 방법으로도 고쳐서는 아니되고, 고친 문항은 "0"점 처리함.

[이 답안지는 마킹연습용 모의답안지입니다.]

참고문헌

- 이동국·이성범, 『영문법』, 한국방송통신대학교출판부, 2006.

- 이동국·이성범, 『영문법의 활용』, 한국방송통신대학교출판문화원, 2020.

- Azar, Betty S. and Stacy A. Hagen. 2011. Fundamentals of English grammar, 4th ed. Hoboken, NJ: Pearson Education.

- Azar, Betty S. and Stacy A. Hagen. 2017. Understanding and using English grammar, 5th ed. Hoboken, NJ: Pearson Education.

〈Web page & Blog〉

- British Council, Learn English Online(https://learnenglish.britishcouncil.org)

- DAUM dictionary(https://dic.daum.net/index.do?dic=eng)

- English Cube(https://www.englishcube.net)

합격의 공식
SD에듀
S D E D U

시대에듀 독학사 영어영문학과 2단계 영문법

개정1판1쇄 발행	2024년 07월 10일(인쇄 2024년 05월 29일)
초 판 발 행	2022년 06월 08일(인쇄 2022년 04월 21일)
발 행 인	박영일
책 임 편 집	이해욱
편 저	김석훈
편 집 진 행	송영진 · 양희정
표지디자인	박종우
편집디자인	차성미 · 채현주
발 행 처	(주)시대고시기획
출 판 등 록	제10-1521호
주 소	서울시 마포구 큰우물로 75 [도화동 538 성지 B/D] 9F
전 화	1600-3600
팩 스	02-701-8823
홈 페 이 지	www.sdedu.co.kr
I S B N	979-11-383-7161-2 (13740)
정 가	25,000원

※ 이 책은 저작권법의 보호를 받는 저작물이므로 동영상 제작 및 무단전재와 배포를 금합니다.
※ 잘못된 책은 구입하신 서점에서 바꾸어 드립니다.